Models of Learning, Memory, and Choice

Centennial Psychology Series
Charles D. Spielberger, *General Editor*

Models of Learning, Memory, and Choice

Selected Papers

William K. Estes

PRAEGER

PRAEGER SPECIAL STUDIES • PRAEGER SCIENTIFIC

Library of Congress Cataloging in Publication Data

Estes, William Kay.
 Models of learning, memory, and choice.

 (Centennial psychology series)
 Bibliography: p.
 Includes indexes.
  1. Learning, Psychology of—Addresses, essays,
lectures. 2. Memory—Addresses, essays, lectures.
3. Choice (Psychology)—Addresses, essays, lectures.
4. Psychology—Mathematical models—Addresses, essays,
lectures. I. Title. II. Series.
BF318.E87 1982   153   82–9823
ISBN 0–03–059266–6   AACR2

BF
318
.E87
1982

Published in 1982 by Praeger Publishers
CBS Educational and Professional Publishing
a Division of CBS, Inc.
521 Fifth Avenue, New York, New York 10175, U.S.A.

© 1982 by Praeger Publishers

23456789 052 987654321

Printed in the United States of America

For Kay

Contents

Editor's Introduction

The founding of Wilhelm Wundt's laboratory at Leipzig in 1879 is widely acclaimed as the landmark event that provided the initial impetus for the development of psychology as an experimental science. To commemorate scientific psychology's one-hundredth anniversary, Praeger Publishers commissioned the Centennial Psychology Series. The general goals of the Series are to present, in both historical and contemporary perspective, the most important papers of distinguished contributors to psychological theory and research.

As psychology begins its second century, the Centennial Series proposes to examine the foundation on which scientific psychology is built. Each volume provides a unique opportunity for the reader to witness the emerging theoretical insights of eminent psychologists whose seminal work has served to define and shape their respective fields, and to share with them the excitement associated with the discovery of new scientific knowledge.

The selection of the Series authors was an extremely difficult task. Indexes of scientific citations and rosters of the recipients of prestigious awards for research contributions were examined. Nominations were invited from leading authorities in various fields of psychology. The opinions of experienced teachers of psychology and recent graduates of doctoral programs were solicited. There was, in addition, a self-selection factor: a few of the distinguished senior psychologists invited to participate in the Series were not able to do so, most often because of demanding commitments or ill health.

Each Series author was invited to develop a volume comprising five major parts: (1) an original introductory chapter; (2) previously published articles and original papers selected by the author; (3) a concluding chapter; (4) a brief autobiography; and (5) a complete bibliography of the author's publications. The main content of each volume consists of articles and papers especially selected for this Series by the author. These papers trace the historical development of the author's work over a period of forty to fifty years. Each volume also provides a cogent presentation of the author's current research and theoretical viewpoints.

In their introductory chapters, Series authors were asked to describe the intellectual climate that prevailed at the beginning of their scientific careers, and to examine the evolution of the ideas that led them from one study to another. They were also invited to comment on significant factors—both scientific and personal—that stimulated and motivated them to embark on their research programs and to consider special opportunities or constraints that influenced their work, including experimental failures and blind alleys only rarely reported in the literature.

In order to preserve the historical record, most of the articles reprinted in the Series volumes have been reproduced exactly as they appeared when they were first published. In some cases, however, the authors have abridged their original papers (but not altered the content), so that redundant materials could be eliminated and more papers could be included.

In the concluding chapters, the Series authors were asked to comment on their selected papers, to describe representative studies on which they are currently working, and to evaluate the status of their research. They were also asked to discuss major methodological issues encountered in their respective fields of interest and to identify contemporary trends that are considered most promising for future scientific investigation.

The biographical sketch that is included in each Series volume supplements the autobiographical information contained in the original and concluding chapters. Perhaps the most difficult task faced by the Series authors was selecting a limited number of papers that they considered most representative from the complete bibliography of the author's life work that appears at the end of each volume.

The Centennial Psychology Series is especially designed for courses on the history of psychology. Individual volumes are also well-suited for use as supplementary texts in those areas to which the authors have been major contributors. Students of psychology and related disciplines, as well as authorities in specialized fields, will find that each Series volume provides penetrating insight into the work of a significant contributor to the behavioral sciences. The Series also affords a unique perspective on psychological research as a living process.

Estes's Contributions

Although general guidelines were suggested for each Series volume, the authors were encouraged to adapt the Series format to meet their individual needs. For this volume, Professor Estes has selected fourteen papers that trace the emergence of his penetrating theoretical insights into the nature of learning, reinforcement, and memory over a period of more than forty years of productive scientific work.

The subject matter of this volume spans a broad range of phenomena, from simple animal conditioning experiments to the complex interplay of perceptual and memory structures and processes that are involved in reading. In the comprehensive introductory chapter, Professor Estes discusses his research strategy and his use of formal models for guiding empirical work and as a framework for interpreting research findings. He also identifies two major underlying themes that serve to integrate the diverse phenomena he has investigated: the relation between learning and behavior, and representation of stimuli and learning experiences in the memory system.

The introductory chapter, the introductions to the chapters on learning theory and memory, and the author's comments in Chapter 5 on critical issues in theory and research methodology are original essays prepared especially for this volume. Professor Estes offers a penetrating analysis of the evolution of learning theory into cognitive psychology, which could only be written by someone who has been intimately involved with this process and has strongly influenced it.

The selected readings are organized into three chapters. Chapter 2 consists of six papers that trace the development of Estes's conceptions about learning theory. His early work on learning and reinforcement theory was guided by a strong behavioral viewpoint; his more recent work on probability learning reflects his current cognitive orientation. The five papers in Chapter 3 begin with a review and reinterpretation of the fundamental ideas of statistical learning theory and examine the transition of Estes's earlier conceptions as they have been modified by experimental findings and elaborated and augmented by concepts of stimulus coding and memory structures and processes. Chapter 4 consists of three papers that deal specifically with the contributions of mathematical models to learning theory and cognitive psychology.

The autobiography that appears as Chapter 6 is especially illuminating. It provides the reader with a clear understanding of how personal factors and the prevailing *zeitgeist* contributed to the development of the author's theoretical conceptions and his research program. Indeed, a profitable appraoch to examining the contents of this book would be to begin with the autobiography and then read the general introductions to the chapters on learning theory and memory. With the historical perspective and theoretical frame of reference provided by these original materials, the reader can then more fully comprehend and appreciate the unique combination of creative theoretical insights and rigorous systematic research that characterize the selected papers.

Acknowledgments

The interest and enthusiasm of all with whom we have consulted concerning the establishment of the Series have been most gratifying, but I am especially grateful to Professors Anne Anastasi, Hans J. Eysenck, and Irving L. Janis for their many helpful comments and suggestions and for their early agreement to contribute to the Series. For his invaluable advice and consultation in the conception and planning of the Series, and for his dedicated and effective work in making it a reality, I am deeply indebted to Dr. George Zimmar, psychology editor for Praeger Publishers.

The Series was initiated while I was a Fellow-In-Residence at the Netherlands Institute for Advanced Study, and I would like to express my appreciation to the director and staff of the Institute and to my NIAS colleagues for their stimulation, encouragement, and strong support of this endeavor.

Charles D. Spielberger

Models of Learning, Memory, and Choice

1

Introduction

The overriding motivation directing the forty-odd years of research sampled in this volume has been to build a conceptual picture of what happens in the mind and brain during learning. Presumably, explanations of learning and cognition will ultimately be found at the level of the physics and chemistry of biochemical reactions and electrical properties of cell membranes. One must suppose, however, that many layers of theoretical structure and process will be found to intervene between those physical or chemical events and observable phenomena of learning, just as has proved to be the case for atomic events relative to the properties of materials and for chemical transfers in cells relative to the physiology of organs. As a student of science, I have been much influenced by the successful use of mathematical, geometrical, and logical methods to construct models of the internal workings of gases, electrical conductors, and living cells—long before more direct observations were possible—and by the importance of those models in directing and interpreting empirical investigations. My long-term scientific objective has been to work toward doing the same for the psychology of learning, memory, and choice.

OVERVIEW OF THE VOLUME

In response to the question, "What is this book about?" a scan of the table of contents might suggest a variegated offering—conditioning theory, human learning, short- and long-term memory, visual information processing, and miscellaneous aspects of mathematical psychology. Still, all the topics presented represent research of a single individual. What else do they have in common?

1

The most conspicuous theme, I would say, is the use of formal models in close conjunction with experimental research. This motif is shared with many other investigators, but not many in psychology have followed it so persistently or along so many empirical paths.

To my mind, at least, the work extending over several decades exhibits also some common conceptual threads. Two of these seem especially clear in hindsight—one having to do with the relation between learning and behavior, the other with the form in which reactions to stimuli and the results of learning experiences are represented in the memory system.

Learning and Behavior

The question of whether one should recognize a basic distinction between learning and performance was one of the foremost issues in learning and behavior theory during my student days, revolving especially around the differences among the views of Tolman (1932), Hull (1937), and Skinner (1938). For Skinner, under whom I received my early training, there was no distinction; learning was simply the modification of behavior as a consequence of reinforcement. In Hull's theory, a distinction between learning and performance was important, but still learning resulted simply in modifications of stimulus-response connections, the strength or activation level of which was modified by motivation so that performance was a multiplicative function of drive and habit. For Tolman, the distinction was basic; learning led to the formation of mental states or representations (expectancies or sign-gestalts), which were only indirectly related to behavior.

Despite my indoctrination at one end of this continuum, I believed intuitively that the consequences of learning were much more general and abstract than simple modifications of response tendencies. My early work on punishment (Estes, 1944), which did not seem to fit into a simple law-of-effect paradigm, reinforced these intuitions, and pursuit of a satisfactory interpretation of the learning-behavior relationship led immediately to research on learning from stimulus-stimulus contingencies, and then, successively, to a concern with the learning of probabilistic relationships, the information-versus-effect issue in human learning, and, most recently, to extended efforts toward interpreting human choice behavior as a function of memory structures and retrieval and decision processes. Only a sampling of my rather lengthy sequence of researches on this theme is represented in this book, but I think one can trace through these papers the emergence of my present viewpoint, which would generally be characterized as cognitive, from a much earlier one, which was certainly characterized as behavioristic. This shift in orientation seems to have been a consequence of the joint influence of the continual confrontation of ideas with observations in the laboratory, on the one hand, and the changing zeitgeist, or general theoretical outlook of psychologists in the broad area of cognition and learning, on the other.

Representation

By the end of my first ten years as an experimental psychologist, I had come to the basic idea that both the process of reacting to stimuli and the learning that results should be interpreted in terms of the activation and categorization of elementary units. In my immediate scientific environment in the 1940s, such words as *perception* and *memory* were inadmissible for any serious purpose, and therefore, in my earliest theoretical papers, the elementary units that had to be assumed to be activated by stimulus inputs were simply termed *stimulus elements,* although with properties continuous with the later conception of features. A learning experience was assumed to map these units onto representations of actions and their consequences, the result being retained in some kind of storage. Learning, relearning, discrimination, and concept formation were all interpreted in terms of categorizations and recategorizations of these basic units. In essentials, this view of representation has been unchanged over the years, although the manner of speaking about the assumed units has shifted from expression in terms of learning and the results of learning to expression in terms of perceptual processing and memory structures.

Similarly, essential constituents of what I came to speak of as memory search or scanning in the 1960s were present in my earlier models, which were developed in the behavioral tradition. Within statistical learning theory, it was clear from the start that one needed to develop explicit theoretical models for the relations between states of memory and performance. Although, so far as I can recall, I did not explicitly use the term *memory scanning* until my early papers on visual processes (Estes & Taylor, 1964; Estes, 1965), all the essential ideas had been developed and incorporated in earlier stimulus-sampling models, the specific form of these developments having been strongly influenced by my interactions with Gordon Bower and David LaBerge.[1]

These principal, common themes in my work are directly reflected in this book. Chapter 2 samples research related to learning theory, including my original conception of statistical learning theory, and the evolution of current ideas on reinforcement as a combination of memory and feedback processes in the control of behavior. Within this chapter, the transition from the earlier, strongly behavioral viewpoint to the later, more cognitive one will be apparent. Chapter 3 samples research on memory, starting with models that emerged simply as a reinterpretation of some of the basic ideas of statistical learning theory and continuing with later models, progressively augmented and elaborated by concepts having to do with levels of stimulus coding, organization, and such cognitive operations as memory scanning. Although the role of models and mathematical thinking will be apparent throughout the book, this theme has been so strongly characteristic of my work that it seemed suitable to include in the book a brief section, Chapter 4, in which the papers presented reflect more specifically my ideas about the role of mathematical models as a specialty within experimental and cognitive psychology.

What does one hope to accomplish by bringing together accounts of research and scientific thinking previously reported in a variety of contexts over a long period? A major purpose, I think, is to bring out the way in which the investigator's philosophy regarding methods and objectives of research and theory construction have evolved in interaction with the research and, in turn, are influencing its continuing directions. Thus, before turning to the introduction of the first substantive part of the book, I shall try my hand at a retrospective account of the development of my viewpoint and orienting attitudes on methodology.

DEVELOPMENT OF A WORKING PHILOSOPHY

During the 1940s, my orientation was characteristic of the psychology of learning and motivation of the period in some respects but not in others. After a long period of rather austere empiricism under the aegis of behaviorism and functionalism, great interest had arisen during the 1930s in the more self-conscious development of theories of learning. This development took place, however, under several contrasting sets of attitudes and constraints. Skinner (1938), who influenced me most directly, was concerned simply with the refinement of experimental laws of behavior, reflecting the philosophy of Bridgman and Heisenberg. To my view, Guthrie (1935) differed only in particulars. In their objectives, Tolman (1932) and Hull (1937, 1943) were much closer to my own aspirations toward more general and more powerful theories, but they differed in preferred routes toward the common goal. Tolman wished to enrich the behavioral approach by expressing laws or principles in terms not only of relations between observable stimuli and responses but of relations between these and carefully defined "intervening variables." However, the intervening variables always proved to be internalizations of familiar psychological categories or states, such as expectancy or purpose, and did not seem to open the way to the employment of more powerful symbolic or mathematical methods. Hull, for whose motivations and general philosophy I had great respect, hoped for the same quantification of behavioral laws that had been achieved in other sciences, but again accepted rather severe constraints on the form of his theorizing, which was limited to quantification of stimulus-response relationships expressed in terms of habits, and excitatory and inhibitory tendencies.

Like many other young investigators of that period, I found these theoretical developments most exciting but at the same time had difficulty in relating them to the tasks I myself most wished to accomplish. Skinner and Guthrie had strong appeal for their insistence on tying theory closely to detailed observations of behavior and the situations in which it occurs, but at the same time they were entirely unsympathetic to what I considered the more constructive aspects of theoretical development. I found Tolman and Hull more positive in this regard, but their approaches did not seem to offer enough play for the theorist's imagination or to encourage exploration of the variety of formal methods that seemed surely to be needed.

It did not seem unreasonable to me to begin the task of theorizing about learning by formalizing everyday life concepts or stimulus-response relationships. Pursued with the militancy characteristic of many learning theorists of that era, however, the approach seemed unnecessarily limited. In other sciences spectacular advances occasionally have come from activities of theorists who have explored various formalisms (for example, geometries) at a very abstract level and then have found useful ways to interpret them in terms of empirical problems. Why should we not hope for the same kind of developments in psychology, or at least claim the privilege of trying our hands at this exciting enterprise?

I could see that whether the hope would prove realistic might depend critically on how the task of implementing it was approached. In particular, I found myself concerned with the apparent failure of the various preceding efforts to yield much cumulative development toward a common body of theory regarding learning and behavior that could direct research as do the theories of physics, chemistry, and biology. One reason for this failure seemed to have to do with the tendency of psychological theorists to indulge in much postulation but to do little with the postulates. In the systems of Hull and Tolman, for example, the way of explaining new findings seemed to be mainly by postulating new processes or constructs rather than by exploiting in any depth the implications of assumptions already made on other grounds. Thus, though not as a result of any single self-conscious decision, I found myself increasingly drawn to the task of trying to abstract from the extant theories the concepts that seemed most securely founded and most pervasive, with a guiding idea of adopting new theoretical assumptions grudgingly and, once they were bought, exploring their implications exhaustively. It seemed worth almost any effort to find out whether, as in physical science, we could arrive at a small number of concepts and principles that, applied in varying combinations, could help illuminate a wide variety of psychological phenomena.

Following is a brief résumé of the specific strategies that guided my own ensuing and long-continuing efforts toward theory construction, first in learning, later in the broader range of cognitive psychology and information processing. These strategies were not all set down in advance, of course, but most of them seem, in hindsight, to have been implicit in my approach from the beginning. They gradually became explicit as I began to write about the work and to try to put across to students and colleagues not only *what* I was doing but *why*.

Continuity

In keeping with the hope of working toward more cumulative development of theory, I have consistently worked within the constraint that the best-established concepts of an earlier theory should enter into its successors either as axioms or as special cases of more elaborate conceptions. Thus, in my initial work on learning, influenced by the writings of both the more traditional associationists (such as Robinson, 1932) and the learning theorists who followed them (especially Guthrie, 1935), I took the concept of association to be a basic ingredient of a learning theory. The essence of learning is that objects, events, or actions previously unrelated for an organism come to be related in ways that are significant for the organism's interaction with the environment. A stimulus comes to signify the impending occurrence of another, to instigate recall of circumstances in which it previously occurred, or to activate a tendency to repeat or avoid a previous response. In my early theoretical efforts, association had to be a link between stimulus and response, or representations of them, since these entities correspond directly to the observables entering into the prediction of behavior. In the long run, however, this restriction did not prove viable.

When I began to take an active interest in human probability learning some years later, it became apparent that what is learned can be better described in terms of relations between events, rather than between stimuli and responses. Why not, then, depart entirely from associative concepts and seek to interpret probability learning in terms of some new analogy? Just this course was taken by some investigators, such as Hake and Hyman (1953), who spoke of subjects perceiving the statistical structure of a sequence of events. That proposal, and others that similarly involved a sharp break with learning theory, might have proved fruitful but in fact never led to a substantial new body of theory or entered in a major way into the direction and interpretation of continuing research. The approach I favored—starting with associative concepts already established for simpler forms of learning and progressively modifying and elaborating them as successive approximations to an adequate theory are confronted by new facts—has led over several decades to models very different in form from the early one based on an analogy to conditioning.[2] However, the continuity in the approach has kept the evolving theory in contact with other developments in the study of learning and memory, so that support for current models (for example, Estes, 1972, 1976) comes from many related lines of research and theory on learning and cognition. Further, the complex and multifaceted process of probability learning we see in the adult can be better understood by virtue of an ability to trace the connection between the concepts of models for adult learning and those entering into the interpretation of children's probability learning (as in the work of Bogartz, 1969; Brainerd, 1981).

In other lines of research on learning, running more or less parallel to that on probability learning, I found repeatedly that stimulus-response associations alone provided an insufficient basis for the theories needed to interpret new findings. Again, however, my preferred strategy was not to discard the original concept but rather to extend it to a broader conception of association among representations of events, and in such a way that stimulus-response connections would be simply a special case of the more general concept, perhaps clearly exemplified only in some forms of conditioning for human beings and in learning of lower organisms (Estes, 1969).

   This one modification of the association concept was not sufficient to take account of accumulating evidence that discriminative
or signal stimuli and contextual or background cues enter in a
nonadditive way into the determination of responses, even in conditioning (Estes, 1973), but still more conspicuously in human
learning and memory. The approach to this problem, in the strategy
based on continuity, was to elaborate the concept of association
further, introducing the idea of multiple associations mediated by
control elements in a network (see second reprint in Chapter 3),
rather than breaking with the past and adopting entirely new terminology (as is the preference, for example, of Johnson, 1978).

   In a similar vein, as my attention has turned in more recent
years to problems having to do with choice and preference, short-
term memory, and visual information processing, I have continued
to attempt to build new models directly on earlier ones rather than
leapfrogging ahead to postulate new kinds or levels of conceptual
entities. I know that, at times, this strategy seems conservative or
even reactionary to some; nonetheless, it appears to be an important
condition for cumulative theoretical progress in this as in other
fields.

Breadth of Conceptual Basis

Before undergoing fine tuning to adjust to particular experimental
facts, theories should be formulated so as to incorporate general
principles and knowledge drawn from broad experience beyond the
particular domain of the theory. In the case of behavior theory, one
of the foremost broad generalizations has to do with the almost
incredible robustness of the results of learning. At the time I first
contemplated entering into theorizing on learning, it was already
well known that the effects of particular learning experiences are
extremely resistant to disruption by the effects of wide variations in
body temperature in lower organisms and by gross extirpations of
brain tissue even in animals close in the phylogenetic scale to man
(Lashley, 1929). Thus, it was apparent that adequate models for
learning should represent the storage of memory for a learning
experience in a form distributed somehow over a variety of elementary structures or processes in such a way that destruction or inacti-
vation of many of these can still leave memories essentially intact.
Further, it was apparent, both from records of electrical activity of
the brain and from observations and recordings of behavior of
organisms by animal psychologists, that the levels of excitability or
activity of neural and behavioral units at all levels of organization

must be presumed to fluctuate constantly, the smooth course of overall physiological and behavioral activities being the result of averaging over the fluctuating contributions of many individual units. The need to embody these two pervasive qualities of robustness and variability in the foundations of the model led very directly to the representation assumptions of my statistical theory of learning and behavior (Estes, 1950).

Similarly, in my much more recent work on visual processing, I have followed the strategy of drawing both on information about basic properties of the visual system and on results of research at more cognitive levels in working toward models of perceptual processes underlying character recognition and reading.

Generalization and Categorization

In pursuit of the generally accepted goal of generality, it seems a sound strategy to attempt to find instances in which the same process recurs at different levels of behavioral organization and to attempt continually to derive relationships among superficially different forms or instances of learning or behavior rather than assuming basically different types. Several issues very germane to this motif were in the forefront of attention in the 1940s, particularly the recurring question of learning as a growth process versus an all-or-none process, the question of contiguity versus reinforcement as the basic principle of learning, and the distinction between learning and motivation (or, rather, the question of whether motivation influences learning or only performance).

With regard to the first of these issues, one of my original hopes was to formulate a model that would allow for both gradual or all-or-none learning, depending on whether one looks at changes in individuals or in grouped data and depending on particular boundary conditions. With regard to the second issue, it seemed that the concept of reinforcement was relatively complex and should be derivable from more elementary or primitive ideas rather than being assumed as a basic condition of learning. Again, this strategic idea entered directly into the original formulation of statistical learning theory. With regard to the third issue, motivation and drive (the term preferred by learning theorists) seemed such ill-defined concepts as to demand some kind of analysis into simpler ones. My own initial strategy was to seek to account for the observed properties of variations of drive in animal learning situations in terms of demonstrable stimulus properties of the bodily states set up by drive-inducing operations (Estes, 1958). I now think that the idea of reducing drive and motivation to stimulus variables is going too far on the side of parsimony, as will become apparent in later chapters. I also think (as does Bower, 1975) that much of what is known about motivation at the human level requires interpretation within the framework of more general concepts of cognitive psychology.

Although the methodological preference for avoiding typologies, as just expressed, represents well enough my views as of 1950, I now see the issues involved as rather more complex. Rather than following either a categorizing or a generalizing strategy uniformly, I think that in theoretically oriented research we tend to follow a repeating cycle of categorizing phenomena or empirical principles, finding relationships or commonalities that cut across the categorical boundaries, then constructing new and presumably more significant categorizations. Thus, for example, I think the resolution of the incremental versus all-or-none learning issue achieved in statistical learning theory was a step forward, and that it holds up very well over the kinds of learning ordinarily studied in the laboratory. However, I have been increasingly impressed with the utility of the distinction made by Hebb (1949) between the fast and generally all-or-none learning characteristic of the normal adult, which constitutes the object of most experimental studies, and the slow, incremental learning that goes on during perceptual development (Estes, in press).

In work on memory, I again began with a strong presumption in favor of a monistic association theory. When confronted with the flood of new results on short-term memory around 1960, I came to accept the need for a clear distinction between short- and long-term memory. That phase was transient, however, and an important segment of my recent work has been addressed to showing that the distinction, though useful, is superficial and represents only differing relative weights of processes that are implicated throughout the range of short- to long-term retention.

The moral, it seems, is that we must continually seek better ways of categorizing phenomena but that, once achieved, categorizations should be not a source of satisfaction but rather a source of instigation to the deeper analyses that inevitably undermine them and lead to new ones.

NOTES

1. LaBerge (1959) was responsible for introducing the idea of a central attentional process whereby stimulus elements activated on a trial are, in effect,

examined sequentially until one is encountered that falls in a target category. Bower (1959) showed that Tolman's concept of "vicarious trial and error" could be implemented in a stimulus-sampling model in terms of a process whereby stimuli available at a choice point are successively sampled by the organism until a "random walk" over the available alternatives eventuates in a choice. Both ideas entered importantly into my first paper that was explicitly directed to the relation between memory and choice (Estes, 1960).

2. Among the major contributors who should be mentioned are LaBerge (1959), Millward and Reber (1968), Myers (1970), Restle (1957, 1961), Siegel (1961), Suppes and Atkinson (1960), and Yellott (1969).

REFERENCES

Bogartz, R. S. Short-term memory in binary prediction by children: Some stochastic information processing models. In G. H. Bower & J. T. Spence (Eds.), *Psychology of learning and motivation: Advances in research and theory*. Vol. 3, pp. 299–391. New York: Academic Press, 1969.

Bower, G. H. Choice-point behavior. In R. R. Bush & W. K. Estes (Eds.), *Studies in mathematical learning theory*, pp. 109–124. Stanford, Calif.: Stanford University Press, 1959.

Bower, G. H. Cognitive psychology: An introduction. In W. K. Estes (Ed.), *Handbook of learning and cognitive processes*. Vol. 1, pp. 25–80. Hillsdale, N.J.: Lawrence Erlbaum Associates, 1975.

Brainerd, C. J. Working memory and the developmental analysis of probability judgment. *Psychological Review*, 1981, *88*, 463–502.

Estes, W. K. An experimental study of punishment. *Psychological Monographs*, 1944, *57* (3, Whole No. 263).

Estes, W. K. Toward a statistical theory of learning. *Psychological Review*, 1950, *57*, 94–107.

Estes, W. K. Stimulus-response theory of drive. In M. R. Jones (Ed.), *Nebraska symposium on motivation*, pp. 35–68. Lincoln: Nebraska University Press, 1958.

Estes, W. K. A random-walk model for choice behavior. In K. J. Arrow, S. Karlin, and P. Suppes (Eds.), *Mathematical methods in the social sciences*, pp. 265–276. Stanford, Calif.: Stanford University Press, 1960.

Estes, W. K. A technique for assessing variability of perceptual span. *Proceedings of the National Academy of Sciences*, 1965, *54*, No. 2, 403–407.

Estes, W. K. New perspectives on some old issues in association theory. In N. S. Mackintosh & W. K. Honig (Eds.), *Fundamental issues in associative learning*, pp. 162–189. Halifax: Dalhousie University Press, 1969.

Estes, W. K. Research and theory on the learning of probabilities. *Journal of the American Statistical Association*, 1972, *67*, 81–102.

Estes, W. K. Memory and conditioning. In F. J. McGuigan and D. B. Lumsden (Eds.), *Contemporary approaches to conditioning and learning*, pp. 265–286. Washington, D.C.: V. H. Winston, 1973.

Estes, W. K. The cognitive side of probability learning. *Psychological Review*, 1976, *83*, 37-64.

Estes, W. K. Learning, memory, and intelligence. In R. J. Sternberg (Ed.), *Handbook of human intelligence*. New York: Cambridge University Press, in press.

Estes, W. K., & Taylor, H. A. A detection method and probabilistic models for assessing information processing from brief visual displays. *Proceedings of the National Academy of Sciences*, 1964, *52*, 446-454.

Guthrie, E. R. *The psychology of learning*. New York: Harper, 1935.

Hake, H. W., & Hyman, R. Perception of the statistical structure of a random series of binary symbols. *Journal of Experimental Psychology*, 1953, *45*, 64-74.

Hebb, D. O. *The organization of behavior*. New York: Wiley, 1949.

Hull, C. L. Mind, mechanism, and adaptive behavior. *Psychological Review*, 1937, *44*, 1-32.

Hull, C. L. *Principles of behavior*. New York: Appleton-Century-Crofts, 1943.

Johnson, N. F. Coding processes in memory. In W. K. Estes (Ed.), *Handbook of learning and cognitive processes*. Vol. 6, pp. 87-129. Hillsdale, N.J.: Lawrence Erlbaum Associates, 1978.

LaBerge, D. L. A model with neutral elements. In R. R. Bush & W. K. Estes (Eds.), *Studies in mathematical learning theory*, pp. 53-64. Stanford, Calif.: Stanford University Press, 1959.

Lashley, K. S. Learning: I. Nervous mechanisms in learning. In C. Murchison (Ed.), *The foundations of experimental psychology*, pp. 524-563. Worcester, Mass.: Clark University Press, 1929.

Millward, R. B., & Reber, A. S. Event-recall in probability learning. *Journal of Verbal Learning and Verbal Behavior*, 1968, *7*, 980-989.

Myers, J. L. Sequential choice behavior. In G. H. Bower (Ed.), *The psychology of learning and motivation: Advances in research and theory*, Vol. 4, pp. 109-170. New York: Academic Press, 1970.

Restle, F. Theory of selective learning with probable reinforcements. *Psychological Review*, 1957, *64*, 182-191.

Restle, F. *Psychology of judgment and choice: A theoretical essay*. New York: Wiley, 1961.

Robinson, E. S. *Association theory today*. New York: Century, 1932.

Siegel, S. Decision making and learning under varying conditions of reinforcement. *Annals of the New York Academy of Science*, 1961, *89*, 766-782.

Skinner, B. F. *The behavior of organisms: An experimental analysis*. New York: Appleton-Century-Crofts, 1938.

Suppes, P., & Atkinson, R. C. *Markov learning models for multiperson interactions*. Stanford, Calif.: Stanford University Press, 1960.

Tolman, E. C. *Purposive behavior in animals and men*. New York: Appleton-Century, 1932.

Yellott, J. I., Jr. Probability learning with noncontingent success. *Journal of Mathematical Psychology*, 1969, *6*, 541-575.

2
Learning Theory

This chapter, dealing with work on learning and general behavior theory, represents my first major research effort in psychology, which began in the 1940s and continues to the present, though with increasing competition from other themes. Looked at in retrospect, at least, the contributions to learning theory arising from this work fall in two main categories: (1) what is learned and (2) what causes learning. The first of these issues has perhaps been closer to my heart, leading first to my efforts toward a mathematical theory of learning, represented in the first two papers reprinted in this chapter, and shading later into the varied approaches to memory, as sampled in the last two papers in this chapter and all of Chapter 3. The second issue instigated my equally persisting interest in the nature of reinforcement, expressed first by studies at the level of conditioning, later by much more extensive efforts to differentiate and interpret the contributions of informational and motivational variables to reinforcement and decision making in human behavior.

Because this preview is too compressed to convey the spirit of the enterprise, I shall proceed to expand it in some respects, especially to bring out the ideas that have provided continuity and direction.

GETTING INTO THEORY

A perennial problem for apprentice investigators is that it is not easy to benefit from the teaching of one's generally wise mentors and at the same time throw off the inhibiting influences of their views regarding what is and what is not proper strategy for research and theory construction. The influence of the learning theorists of the 1940s on my intellectual development as a theorist was pervasive and lasting. It proved possible to depart only gradually, and a small step at a time, from the path set by their ideas. My first departure from the existing theoretical framework seemed a small one at the time but proved to have persisting and widening ramifications. What I wished to do was to formulate a model that might capture the important aspects of Hull's conception of learning as a growth process but at the same time represent the effects of learning on a conceptual level distinct from that of response tendencies. I might thus allow for the more cognitive properties of learning emphasized by Tolman without lapsing into the sin, as it appeared to me at the time, of attributing mental processes to animals.

Hints regarding how one might proceed were to be found in the writings of Thurstone (1930) and Guthrie (1935), both of whom had noted that learning often seems to resemble some kind of sampling process. Even on repeated encounters with the same situation, an animal or person does not always appear to attend to the same stimuli or to utilize the same constituent actions in carrying out a task. The source of the variability might lie in the environment, as Guthrie evidently assumed. Alternatively, it might lie in the varying states of activity or availability of units or elementary processes in the memory system. This conception of inherent variability was exemplified in my first theoretical paper, in which the basic tenets of a statistical theory of learning were put forward (Estes, 1950). In specifics, however, the orientation of that paper is somewhat dated, and it seemed better to include here, as the first paper on learning, the substance of a lecture given at the University of London, ten years later, on my conception of the elements of association theory. The paper gives a résumé of the basic ideas of the statistical approach as well as answers to various questions about its philosophy that had come up during the intervening decade.

It is interesting to note how often in science new theories or models achieve visibility primarily as a consequence of association with a popular experimental paradigm (witness operant conditioning and the Skinner box, selective attention and dichotic listening, memory search and the Sternberg experiment). About 1950, a flow of experiments on learning in probabilistic situations began to appear, and, as noted in the first paper reproduced in this chapter, the structure of the statistical model provided a natural interpretation of such learning. This coincidence led to a substantial research effort in which the model was tested and elaborated in conjunction with numerous variants of probability learning. An early example of this research constitutes the second paper in this chapter.

THEORY OF REINFORCEMENT

In the literature of the reinforcement-versus-contiguity period (and in some instances down to the present), two aspects of reinforcement have been inextricably mixed. On the one hand, the term reinforcement refers to the operation presumed responsible for learning of the response that occurs in a given situation; on the other, it refers to an operation that controls the probability, rate, or speed of already learned behaviors. Because the empirical procedures (giving food, terminating shock, or the like) are often the same, these operationally distinct procedures tend to be lumped into one concept. However, the two aspects of reinforcement can be and have been separated experimentally, perhaps most notably in the rather extensive literature on latent learning (see, for example, Bower & Hilgard, 1981; MacCorquodale & Meehl, 1954). Another example is work on magnitude of reward in animal learning, in which it has been shown that magnitudes of reward too small to produce learning may nonetheless maintain an already learned habit (Guttman, 1953); yet another is the literature on avoidance learning, in which, under some circumstances, omission of a shock cannot produce learning initially but nonetheless maintains a learned avoidance response over long periods.

Because of these considerations, the central theoretical issue of the 1940s— the explanation of the effect of reinforcement on learning in terms of drive reduction or other concepts—seemed to me to beg the question. Rather than presuming that reinforcement is necessary for learning and then trying to explain it, I thought a better strategy would be first to seek to identify the critical conditions for learning and then, only with that done, to ask how the conditions depend on reinforcing operations:

> The fact that a wide variety of superficially diverse operations turn out to have quantitatively equivalent effects on learning demands some explana-tion, and almost every learning theorist has tried his hand at answering this call. In the case of me and my associates, the drive for explanation has taken the form of continuing attempts to derive the independently estab-lished quantitative laws of reinforcement from more primitive assumptions concerning contiguity, interference, and stimulus sampling. (Estes, 1959, p. 404)

At the time the foregoing passage was written, my ideas about the role of contiguity had begun to change, but not to the point that I was ready to articu-late the changes clearly. In my early work bearing on the interpretation of learning, conducted entirely with animals, I had unquestioningly followed the lead of traditional association theory and its more recent embodiment in Guth-rie's (1935) view of conditioning by taking temporal contiguity of events to be associated (whether these were ideas, stimulus and response, or whatever) as a basic condition for learning that did not in itself call for any explanation. Gradu-ally and over a long period, however, I began to come to the alternative view— that contiguous occurrence is only one way of conveying information to a learner about conjunctions of events that may recur. Contiguity may be an almost essential condition of learning for animals, except under special circumstances (for example, the Garcia effect), but may be only one among many sources of equivalent information for human learners. Once this idea had come to threshold, it led to a lengthy series of researches, running from the mid-1960s down to the present, designed to tease out the ways in which reinforcing pro-cedures supply the information that constitutes the basis of what is learned in situations ranging from simple trial-and-error to human multiple-choice learning and problem solving.

In my own work, I have been less concerned with the other aspect of rein-forcement—that is, as a basis for the control of behavior. If, as must normally be the case, the stimuli sampled by a learner in a situation lead to the recall of more than one possible response, what determines the selection of the action actually to be carried out? In any situation, some memory units must carry more weight than others in the process of response selection, and the differential weights must somehow reflect the learner's current state of drive or motivation.

In early theoretical formulations, I assumed that all behaviors were directly evoked by stimuli; reinforcement simply ensured that responses leading to reward would become associated with drive, which would give them a competitive advantage over responses not so associated. That idea now seems insufficient, as it does not account, for example, for the flexibility of higher organisms in selecting adaptively among alternative responses that are all associated with the same drives but lead to different reinforcing events. Clearly, drives and needs not only produce internal stimuli but also, and perhaps more importantly, potentiate or modulate the signal value of external signal stimuli as cues for action. Reinforcement in the sense of a controller of behavior, then, constitutes operations that arrange an organism's environment so that this selective potentiation of some stimulus-response relations over others occurs in a feedback relation to performance.

The ideas needed to indicate how selective potentiations may be accomplished were suggested by exciting findings on electrical stimulation of the brain, which showed that centers or mechanisms in the midbrain associated with appetitive and nociceptive drives activate neural pathways that can selectively amplify or inhibit the tendencies of stimuli to evoke their normally associated responses (Olds & Olds, 1964; Stein, 1964).

If these drive mechanisms could become associated with signals through learning and could then be reactivated upon recurrence of the signals, we would have just the basis needed for feedback control of performance. Actually, the learning process that would have to be assumed had been all but directly demonstrated in some of my earliest experiments on learning. Characteristically, my animals were well isolated from the outside world, usually in Skinner boxes or the equivalent, and the data reported came solely from the records of responses taken down as objectively as one might hope for by recording instruments. At the same time, however, I spent many hours observing the animals, one result being a strengthening conviction that, even in a learning experience as apparently simple as a rewarded or punished lever press by a rat, the animal learned more about what to expect than was manifest in the response records. This feeling was kept well disciplined but did lead, first, to a study with Skinner (Estes & Skinner, 1941), which showed that a previously neutral stimulus that preceded a shock acquired a capacity to suppress ongoing behavior when it later recurred (the conditioned emotional response). Second, this conviction led to a set of studies showing that a stimulus that preceded the ingestion of food acquired a capacity to selectively facilitate responses previously associated with food in the same context (Estes, 1943, 1948). These results initially were interpreted in terms of the concept of an animal's state of anticipation of a stimulus, a notion put forward with some lip service to its being potentially definable in terms of specific stimulus-response relations, though with some recognition at the same time of the plain fact that such definitions had not been accomplished and perhaps could not be.

In any event, the distinct sets of findings from the physiological and behavioral levels came together conceptually in a new proposal for the interpretation of reinforcement (Estes, 1969a). In substance, the new account begins with the supposition that a learner in any trial-and-error situation stores in memory information concerning relations between cues in the situation, actions taken in response to the cues, and outcomes of the actions. Then, later, when the learner scans the stimulus situation, the cues that have entered into learned associations lead to recall of the actions taken on previous occasions and their outcomes. An important component of the recalled outcomes is the reactivation of the drive mechanisms that had been active during the original learning experience and that now exert facilitating or inhibiting influences on tendencies to carry out the recalled actions.

It was a strain on my regard for parsimony to make the leap from animal to human behavior and suppose that human motives enter into associations and control positive and negative feedback in similar fashion, but the idea was irresistibly attractive. A lengthy program of experimentation on reinforcement in human learning, carried out during the 1960s, lent the idea considerable support (Estes, 1966, 1969b, 1971). The resulting picture of the way information about rewards and punishments enters into human learning seems, at least in outline, to be standing the test of time and continuing research inputs.

These different strands of thought on reinforcement are brought together and illustrated in the third paper included in this chapter. The newer view of reinforcement, developed further in the fourth paper, can only be fully understood, however, in relation to a much broader shift in theoretical framework, which was accelerating from about 1960 in my thinking and in the field at large.

BEHAVIOR AND COGNITION

The shift from a stimulus-response to an informational frame of reference may sound simple and straightforward in hindsight, but it was very difficult to achieve in the climate of the learning theories of the 1940s. Behavior was the proper study of psychology; the mind was simply a subjective and fictitious entity, drawing its strength from everyday language habits and not fitting into a properly constructed chain of constructs leading from observable stimuli to observable actions. Learning theory and behavior theory were essentially synonymous; both were aimed at accounting for the way an organism's behavior is modified by effects of experience, generally in the direction of becoming more adaptive. For Guthrie, Hull, and Skinner, especially, the focus on behavior was unwavering, and the effects of learning were interpreted in one way or another as modifications of associative linkages between situations and behaviors. In the same context, achieving the capability to predict and control behavior was taken to be an end in itself, if not the major purpose of psychology. I was not comfortable with that view but was not yet ready to see the main function of predicting behavior as a means of testing theories.

In human learning, similarly, the dominant paradigm, deriving from functionalism and association theory, viewed learning in terms of the improvement of performance rather than the accrual of information or the formation of memory structures (McGeoch, 1942). The term *memory* appeared not infrequently in the literature on human learning, but generally only in the sense of retention of learned associations or of the effects of practice on skills.

During my own training as an investigator, I absorbed the prevailing frame of reference thoroughly, and, in my first theoretical paper (Estes, 1950), I subscribed wholeheartedly to the idea that laws or principles of learning could be expected to take their simplest form when expressed in terms of stimulus-response relationships (even while I myself was deviating from the paradigm by introducing abstract theoretical concepts not strictly definable in terms of observable stimulus or response variables). It was only many years later that I began to see the possibility that expressing laws of learning in terms of relations between behavior and observable determining conditions might not, in any significant sense, be the simplest or most parsimonious approach. Rather, the laws might take on simpler forms when expressed in terms of concepts of information or memory (Estes, 1975, 1978).

Even in my first papers on statistical learning theory, which appeared about ten years after the first studies of anticipation, I remained rather closely bound to the stimulus-response framework conceptually. In the model, it was assumed that repeated experiences with a stimulus situation generate a distribution of elementary sensory or perceptual reactions in the organism. These reactions are categorized, in effect, relative to significant events such as signals or rewards, these categorical relations being the abstract representations of stimulus-response associations. The state of availability of these elementary associations was assumed to vary randomly from time to time, so that when a test occurs at the end of a retention interval following a learning experience, there is generally only some probability that the effects of the learning will be available to direct test behavior. It was only much later that I began to see clearly that the identification of the elementary processes or relations with elementary reactions to stimuli or stimulus-response associations was gratuitous. One could as well conceive of the elements undergoing sampling and fluctuation as abstract representations of aspects or constituents of memory traces, not rigidly coupled to either particular observable stimuli or particular observable responses (Bower, 1967; Estes, 1976, and the first paper reprinted in Chapter 3 of this book).

This conception was not particularly novel and in fact reflected in some respects ideas being expressed by Konorski (1967) and Miller, Galanter, and Pribram (1960), among others. It seemed, however, to be a necessary step toward freeing the main line of development of learning theory from the excessively constricting framework of the stimulus-response-reinforcement theories that had dominated research of the previous 20 to 30 years and toward opening the way to the much richer conception of associative memory that came to the fore in the following decade (and is well represented in Chapter 3 of this volume).

COGNITION AND PROBABILITY LEARNING

As others have noted (for example, Myers, 1976), I entered into my early work on probability learning not only because of its intrinsically interesting aspects but also because it proved a nice vehicle for the interpretation and extension of a statistical model for learning, originally formulated only in connection with simple forms of conditioning. Indeed, history did not relax its grasp easily, and as late as the mid-1960s I continued to describe probability learning in terms of the change of the probability of predictive responses as a consequence of reinforcement, in close analogy to classical conditioning (Estes, 1964). Once again, events in the laboratory ultimately began to overcome the effects of preconceptions, though sometimes in a raggedly uneven manner. Although on some days in the 1960s I continued to write of probability learning as a form of "verbal conditioning," on others I was formulating a model in which a learner in an uncertain-choice situation is presumed to build up representations of event probabilities in memory and then operate on these to generate expectations of events, whose attributes (such as utilities) are mentally scanned in order to arrive at decisions leading to observed choice responses (Estes, 1960, 1962).

One consequence of revising a general theoretical framework is that it may lead to the discovery of new veins in what had seemed to be worked-out territory. The point is nicely illustrated in relation to research on the problem of how people learn to anticipate uncertain events. During the 1950s, appreciable progress toward understanding how such learning proceeds had been made by the numerous studies motivated and shaped by statistical models for learning. These researches produced some fairly striking results but then seemed to taper off into a period of diminishing returns.

Looking at the same problem from a new perspective some years later, with processes of memory and decision more distinctly separated, led to new questions and hence to new results. A sample of these is given in the fifth paper reprinted in this chapter. The broadened theoretical outlook also made it more natural to begin looking at the implications that developments in learning theory might have for psychological problems not customarily thought to be within the tradition of research on learning. An example is interpretations of intelligence, a motif illustrated in the concluding paper of this chapter. As will be apparent in subsequent chapters of this book, memory, rather than learning, was the central concept in my research and theoretical efforts from about 1960 down to the present.

REFERENCES

Bower, G. H. A multicomponent theory of the memory trace. In K. W. Spence & J. T. Spence (Eds.), *The psychology of learning and motivation: Advances in research and theory,* Vol. 1, pp. 229–325. New York: Academic Press, 1967.

Bower, G. H., & Hilgard, E. R. *Theories of learning* (5th ed.). Englewood Cliffs, N.J.: Prentice-Hall, 1981.

Estes, W. K. Discriminative conditioning. I. A discriminative property of conditioned anticipation. *Journal of Experimental Psychology*, 1943, *32*, 150–155.

Estes, W. K. Discriminative conditioning. II. Effects of a Pavlovian conditioned stimulus upon a subsequently established operant response. *Journal of Experimental Psychology*, 1948, *38*, 173–177.

Estes, W. K. Toward a statistical theory of learning. *Psychological Review,* 1950, *57*, 94–107.

Estes, W. K. The statistical approach to learning theory. In S. Koch (Ed.), *Psychology: A study of science.* Vol. 2, pp. 380–491. New York: McGraw-Hill, 1959.

Estes, W. K. A random-walk model for choice behavior. In K. J. Arrow, S. Karlin, & P. Suppes (Eds.), *Mathematical methods in the social sciences,* 1959 pp. 265–276. Stanford, Calif.: Stanford University Press, 1960.

Estes, W. K. Theoretical treatments of differential reward in multiple-choice learning and two-person interactions. In J. H. Criswell, H. Solomon, and P. Suppes (Eds.), *Mathematical methods in small group processes,* pp. 133–149. Stanford, Calif.: Stanford University Press, 1962.

Estes, W. K. Probability learning. In A. W. Melton (Ed.), *Categories of human learning,* pp. 89–128. New York: Academic Press, 1964.

Estes, W. K. Transfer of verbal discriminations based on differential reward magnitudes. *Journal of Experimental Psychology*, 1966, *72*, 276–283.

Estes, W. K. Outline of a theory of punishment. In B. A. Campbell and R. M. Church (Eds.), *Punishment and aversive behavior,* pp. 57–82. New York: Appleton-Century-Crofts, 1969. (a)

Estes, W. K. Reinforcement in human learning. In J. Tapp (Ed.), *Reinforcement and behavior,* pp. 63–94. New York: Academic Press, 1969. (b)

Estes, W. K. Reward in human learning. Theoretical issues and strategic choice points. In R. Glaser (Ed.), *The nature of reinforcement,* pp. 16–36. New York: Academic Press, 1971.

Estes, W. K. The state of the field: General problems and issues of theory and metatheory. In W. K. Estes (Ed.), *Handbook of learning and cognitive processes,* Vol. 1, pp. 1–24. Hillsdale, N.J.: Lawrence Erlbaum Associates, 1975.

Estes, W. K. The cognitive side of probability learning. *Psychological Review,* 1976, *83*, 37–64.

Estes, W. K. On the organization and core concepts of learning theory and cognitive psychology. In W. K. Estes (Ed.), *Handbook of learning and cognitive processes,* Vol. 6, pp. 235–292. Hillsdale, N.J.: Lawrence Erlbaum Associates, 1978.

Estes, W. K., & Skinner, B. F. Some quantitative properties of anxiety. *Journal of Experimental Psychology,* 1941, *29,* 390–400.

Guthrie, E. R. *The psychology of learning.* New York: Harper, 1935.

Guttman, N. Operant conditioning, extinction, and periodic reinforcement in relation to concentration of sucrose used as reinforcing agent. *Journal of Experimental Psychology,* 1953, *46,* 213–224.

Konorski, J. *Integrative activity of the brain.* Chicago: University of Chicago Press, 1967.

MacCorquodale, K., & Meehl, P. E. Edward C. Tolman. In W. K. Estes, S. Koch, K. MacCorquodale, P. E. Meehl, C. G. Mueller, Jr., W. N. Schoenfeld, & W.

S. Verplanck. *Modern learning theory*, pp. 177–266. New York: Appleton-Century-Crofts, 1954.

McGeoch, J. A. *The psychology of human learning.* New York: Longmans, Green, 1942.

Miller, G. A., Galanter, E., & Pribram, K. H. *Plans and the structure of behavior.* New York: Holt, Rinehart & Winston, 1960.

Myers, J. L. Probability learning and sequence learning. In W. K. Estes (Ed.), *Handbook of learning and cognitive processes*, Vol. 3, pp. 171–205. Hillsdale, N.J.: Lawrence Erlbaum Associates, 1976.

Olds, J., & Olds, M. E. The mechanisms of voluntary behavior. In R. G. Heath (Ed.), *The role of pleasure in behavior*, pp. 23–53. New York: Harper & Row, 1964.

Stein, L. Reciprocal action of reward and punishment mechanisms. In R. G. Heath (Ed.), *The role of pleasure in behavior*, pp. 113–139. New York: Harper & Row, 1964.

Thurstone, L. L. The learning function. *Journal of General Psychology*, 1930, *3*, 469–493.

New Approaches to the Elements of Association Theory

It is hard to see any possible reason why the mathematical treatment of learning should not be one of the oldest branches of psychological theory. Among what we now consider to be psychological phenomena, human learning and memory were early candidates for extensive theoretical analysis. Indeed, theories of association had approached the limits of formal organization and elaboration that can be attained in purely verbal systems long before the first psychologist in the modern sense, whether laboratory experimentalist, Piagetian theorist, or rotator of test factors, had appeared on the scene. Further, mathematics and psychology have seemed to be natural collaborators from the earliest emergence of the latter as a scientific discipline. Fechner's psychophysics was quantitative in its very conception, and the early development of mental testing led almost precipitously into the development of mathematical models for the organization of mental abilities (Spearman, 1927; Thurstone, 1935).

But regardless of what might, or even should, have been, as late as the 1930s, essays in mathematical learning theory were appearing in the literature at the rate of no more than one or two per year, and these were almost totally without influence on the rapidly expanding experimental investigations of learning. A perceptible increase in this rate was first manifest in the early 1950s; and, as often is the case with autocatalytic processes, this upturn was followed by an almost explosive acceleration. At the end of the decade, a review of the last three years' research on learning theory included references to more than 75 contributions of clearly mathematical character, not to speak of the even more numerous related experimental contributions (Estes, 1962).

In retrospect it is most difficult to specify the combination of ingredients that was an essential prerequisite for the present flourishing of research in this area. As has always been the case when men have sought interpretations of complex phenomena, little progress could be made in theory until footholds had been provided by the

This paper was given as a Special University Lecture at University College, London, in December 1961.

abstracting of some manageable simple facts from the overwhelming morass of raw observations. Standing in contrast to the kaleidoscopic changes in performance identified with learning in non-laboratory situations, the scores generated by experimental subjects while learning mazes, lists of nonsense syllables, or the like have generally impressed the nonspecialist as simplified to the point of sterility. Perhaps this impression has itself been an obstacle to progress. For in truth, the measures on which investigators of learning relied almost exclusively until very recently, e.g., the criterion of learning or curves representing time or errors per trial, are far too coarse for any but the crudest preliminary phases of theory construction. Just as models for biological growth have found it almost trivially easy to account for the form of the curve representing, say, changes in a child's weight as a function of time, early learning theories found no real challenge in deriving the typical form of the learning curve. Only during the last few years has the laboratory analysis of learning reached the stage of providing measures capable of differentiating sharply between alternative theoretical conceptions.

THE SEARCH FOR ELEMENTARY PROCESSES

The initiation of useful quantitative theories in any field seems nearly always to have to wait on the discovery of suitable elementary processes. Despite all the fashionable objections to atomism, we have rarely been able to get far in the interpretation of complex phenomena except by reducing them to elementary events or processes whose behavior is described by simple laws. This approach characterized the British associationists of the 18th Century—but only up to a point. The associationists postulated elements of association, and they intended to postulate laws also, but in fact they did not. The so-called laws of association, familiar to every student of elementary psychology, were simply statements identifying presumably necessary or sufficient conditions for association, not predictive laws specifying how strength of association changes with experience. And elements without laws are like an engine without fuel; they provide a theory in form but not in function. It is probably no mere happenstance that the recent acceleration of research in mathematical learning theory began with the discovery that certain extremely simple mathematical assumptions provide a combination of elements and laws from which one can derive genuine predictions about details of the learning process.

Both the motivation leading to persisting efforts toward a mathematical theory of learning and some of the problems attending these efforts may be better understood by considering the analogy to the now further developed science of genetics. The raw data for the student of human genetics are the extraordinarily complex and variable patterns of resemblances and differences among successive generations of a family line with respect to structural and behavioral characteristics. In seeking to understand genetic phenomena, the investigator has at least two broad objectives, which seem, super-ficially at least, quite distinct. One of these is to discover rules or laws that will make hereditary relationships more predictable; the other is to find structural or physiological mechanisms underlying these relationships, with the objective, however remote, of ultimately explaining genetic phenomena in terms of the presumably more fundamental theories of chemistry and physics.

My purpose in bringing up this analogy is not to intimidate the psychologist by contrasting our meager knowledge of the mechanisms underlying learning with the impressive recent advances toward specifying the molecular bases of genetic mechanisms, but rather to emphasize the circuitous route by which these advances have been achieved. Without denying that much useful information has been gained by the study of human family histories, we cannot but be struck by the fact that this direct approach to the subject matter of immediate interest has had little to do with advances in our under-standing of heredity. When, for example, one wishes to predict the effect of some new circumstance, e.g., radiation fallout, upon human heredity, one turns to theories based on elementary mechanisms revealed by the quantitative analysis of inheritance in fruit flies and garden plants. Further, we may note that there is little reason to think the present grasp of genetic mechanisms could have been achieved if cytological and biochemical investigations had not been guided by the originally purely functional Mendelian model. How, for example, would evidence for crossing-over in chromosomes have been utilized if investigators had not been in a position to interpret their observations in the light of the theory of the gene?

Similarly in the study of learning, our purposes are to gain understanding of learning phenomena by determining rules or laws of operation of the learner that will permit us to predict the effects of new combinations of conditions, and, at the same time, to un-cover the structural—and ultimately the physico-chemical—changes underlying learning. But, considering the analogy to genetics, we must be prepared for the possibility that the factual basis for explan-atory theories may come primarily, not from observations of learning under natural circumstances, but from highly analytical studies conducted under simplified and artificial laboratory conditions.

Further, we may well keep in mind the possibility that attempts to uncover events or processes in the brain that underlie learning phenomena will grope endlessly in the dark but for the concurrent development of concepts and laws comparable to those of mathematical genetics in their ability to guide and facilitate the interpretation of neurophysiological observations.

The search for elementary learning processes is by no means a new one. Within both psychological theories, notably those of Hull (1943) and Hebb (1949), and neurophysiological theories, e.g., those of Rashevsky (1937) and Eccles (1953), postulates have been formulated specifying the loci and modes of operation of events in the brain corresponding to elementary learning processes. These approaches have aroused much interest, and I wish by no means to depreciate the contributions they may have to offer. There are, however, substantial reasons to think that our theoretical strategies should not be limited to these types of approaches. With all the advances in electrophysiology and brain biochemistry, our knowledge concerning events occurring in the living brain is so meager that postulates about detailed brain mechanisms must necessarily be highly speculative. The difficulty posed by the almost unlimited room for postulates is formidable in any event, and perhaps insurmountable in the absence of theoretical machinery for bringing experimental data cogently to bear on the problem of differentially testing the postulated mechanisms.

ELEMENTS OF ASSOCIATION

The line of theoretical research in which I and a number of associates have been engaged for upwards of a dozen years has as a principal aim the conceptualization of elementary processes. Both the broad strategy and the specific methodology differ in important respects from other approaches, including those I have mentioned above; and the purpose of my introductory remarks has been to make clearer than I have in previous discussions some of the reasons for these differences. Psychologists have found it puzzling that I should continually speak of "elements" without ever specifying just where I conceive these elements to be located or what I believe them to be made of. Unfortunately, I cannot do very much for the moment to dispel their puzzlement.

My elements are not hypothetical neural processes; but on the other hand, neither are they simply calculational devices, as in the urn model of Audley and Jonckheere (1956). They have for the present a status somewhat similar to that of unknowns in algebraic equations. In dealing with purely mathematical problems, one frequently has to deal with a number without knowing what the number is, or even, in some cases, whether it exists. Now, the best practice in such cases is neither to dismiss the unknown number as a mere fiction nor to postulate a value for it and then defend our postulate against any critics who may have different ideas about it. Rather, we assign an otherwise meaningless symbol, say x, to represent the number, in case it should exist; then we look for relationships that would have to hold between x and other numbers about which we do know something. Proceeding in this way to imbed the unknown in a matrix of relationships, we may begin to narrow down the limits on its possible values, and sometimes we succeed ultimately in determining the unknown quantity precisely. Similarly in learning theory, it has been my strategy to begin simply by entertaining the possibility that there exist elementary learning processes that follow simple quantitative laws. Introducing notation to represent these elements, should they indeed exist, I have then attempted to determine their properties by the cyclical interactions of hypothesis, calculation, and experiment.

So long as the experiments are all conducted at the level of the behavior of the intact organism, there are limitations on the possible output of this procedure. If we should find that a sufficiently large body of facts about learning can be accounted for in detail on the assumption of certain elementary processes with specified properties, we might be convinced that these elements must have structural counterparts in the organism and yet be unable to say precisely where these structures must be: The situation would be akin to that existing in genetics at a time when more was known about the function of genes than about their loci. Perhaps the situations would prove to be similar also in the respect that the behavioral theory would function as a useful tool in facilitating the search for the structural changes associated with learning.

Now, having, I hope, given you some feeling for the general strategy of my own attempts to locate the elements of association, I should like to give you an idea as to how the strategy is working out in practice.

TOWARD A MODEL FOR ELEMENTARY LEARNING

Let us sketch some of the considerations that have entered into the formulation of a general structure for representing the effects of learning in memory. A central problem for the interpretation of learning is that the set of actions open to an organism, human or animal, is much smaller than the set of situations that may be encountered and call for action. A learning mechanism that just recorded the action taken in each situation and its outcome would be inadequate because situations do not recur exactly. An animal learns which turn at a fork in a path leads to water, or a child learns what to say to a parent in order to obtain a desired object; but on the next return to the same general situation, in each case, many features of the situation will be different. Sometimes the differences will signify the need for different actions but sometimes they will be immaterial. Thus it is necessary to learn what to do in classes of situations (an idea developed fully by Skinner, 1938).

This aspect of learning is the basis for the idea that an organism learns a relation between a behavior and a situation as perceived and coded in memory rather than between behavior and the stimulus situation as it would be recorded by a camera (see, for example, Lawrence, 1963). What the camera or an external observer categorizes as a recurring situation (and in particular nearly any experimental situation used for the laboratory study of learning) presents varying aspects to the organism who encounters it repeatedly; only those aspects perceived on a given occasion enter into learning. In order, then, to represent the learning that occurs on an organism's repeated encounters with, say, the choice point of a T-maze or the lever in a Skinner box, it has been found a useful tactic to define for each situation a population of stimulus components or aspects, termed *elements*. On any one trial of an experiment this population is sampled and the learning that occurs is represented by a classification of the sampled elements relative to some significant event (an unconditioned stimulus, reward, or, in general, *reinforcement*).

The typical course of events in an elementary learning situation progresses, according to this idea, as illustrated in Figure 2.1. The column of cells or boxes at the top left of the diagram represents the state of the organism's memory about the situation at the beginning of learning, the emptiness of the cells corresponding to the absence of any knowledge concerning relations between actions and outcomes in the given situation. On the first trial of an experiment, some of these elements are sampled, this event being represented by the subset of the boxes shown in the second column. The learning that occurs when an outcome A is observed is represented in the next column, where the sampled members of the population of elements are now labelled A, indicating that in the learner's memory recurrence of these on a later trial would signify that the likely outcome again would be event A. On the next trial a new sample is drawn, perhaps including some of the same elements sampled on

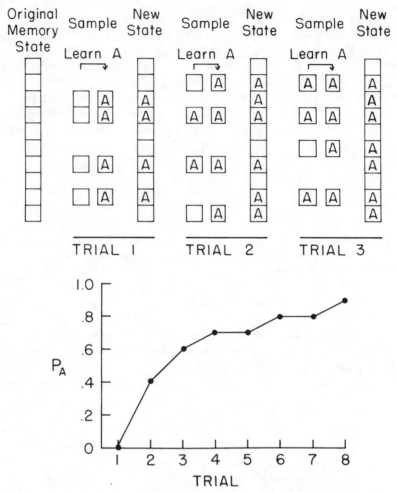

Figure 2.1 Schematization of a simple learning process in terms of a statistical model. In the upper panel, cells represent elements in a memory system, those active (sampled) on a trial becoming associated with the outcome (e.g., unconditioned stimulus or reward). The lower panel shows the course of learning in terms of the proportion of elements associated with A at the beginning of each trial.

the first trial and some new ones, and again the result when event A is observed to occur is that all of the sampled elements are labelled A. Thus, if, say, the event A were the reward on a series of uniformly rewarded elementary learning trials, a typical course of acquisition in terms of the irregularly but steadily increasing proportion of elements signifying A as the expected outcome in the situation would be as shown in the graph at the bottom.

It can be seen then that as the proportion of elements labelled A in the population grows, so also will the average proportion included in the new sample drawn on any trial. However, by chance, it might happen that no A-elements would be drawn on a particular trial, in which case the learner would not remember that A was the correct choice. The model combines the growth and all-or-none conceptions of previous theories (for example, Hull, 1943, versus Guthrie, 1935). The learning that occurs on any one trial is an all-or-none matter—only the elements sampled being classified in memory according to the observed outcome—but the result of a sequence of learning trials is an increasing proportion of elements in the whole population so classified and therefore a steadily increasing probability of a particular action—the picture presented by the familiar learning curve of nearly all elementary learning studies.

PROBABILITY LEARNING

The basic model, as just sketched in a very simplified form, may suffice to account for the general course of learning and for the typical pattern of variations among individuals in such standard situations as classical or instrumental conditioning with uniform (100%) reinforcement, or even the acquisition of paired-associates in simple human verbal learning. However, as simple as it appears, the model has implications for considerably more complex situations. Let us look just one step beyond the simplest cases by considering experiments in which the learner must cope with uncertainty, in that the events of interest occur only intermittently with some probabilities, and the learner can adapt to the situation by increasing the frequency of reward or reinforcement only by learning something about the probabilities of the relevant events.

An example would be the T-maze situation with uncertain reward studied by Brunswik (1939), in which animals were given sequences of trials on which turns to one side of the T were rewarded on a fixed proportion of trials and the other side with the complement, for example, left turns leading to food with a probability of .75 and right turns with a probability of .25. With the events of reward on the left and reward on the right denoted A and B, respectively, the course of learning implied by the model is portrayed in Figure 2.2 in a form parallel to Figure 2.1 except that on some

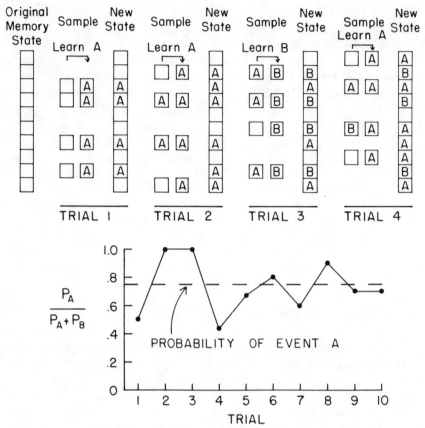

Figure 2.2 Schema for learning when two different reinforcing events, A and B, occur with probabilities .75 and .25, respectively, the format of the upper panel being analogous to Figure 2.1. The lower panel shows the course of learning in terms of the proportion of elements associated with A rather than B.

trials in the T-maze, event B rather than A occurs and thus the elements sampled on the trial are classified as B's rather than as A's. Thus the course of learning in this new situation is indexed by the changing proportion of A- and B-labelled elements in the animal's memory system, and leads over a series of trials to a state of affairs in which the proportion fluctuates around the true probability of an A outcome as portrayed by the graph at the bottom of Figure 2.2.

A new question arises concerning the relation between memory and behavior in the probabilistic situation. Namely, after learning has gotten started and there is a mixture of A- and B-labelled elements in memory, what should we expect to happen if on a new trial the organism samples the situation and draws some elements associated with A and some with B? The assumption adopted for simplicity is that on such occasions the organism scans the sampled elements and responds on the basis of the first labelled element encountered. Thus, in the example, as trials go on, the probability of responding A rather than B will move in the direction of the true probability of an A outcome. Some experiments have shown that under particularly simplified conditions this predicted result (commonly termed *probability matching*) is actually realized quite closely, lending some support to the model (Atkinson, 1956; Estes & Straughan, 1954; Jarvik, 1951; Neimark, 1956; Woods, 1959).

Lest this model seem much too simple in conception to apply to human learners as well as animals, I will mention that, though I didn't realize the fact when I was formulating the model, the mechanism is strikingly close to the scheme developed intuitively a couple of hundred years earlier by David Hume in his classic analysis of the way people form beliefs about causation in situations where multiple causation is the rule and individual causes are uncertain in their effects. His suggestion was that in such typically uncertain situations as forming beliefs about likely changes in the weather, people remember instances in which particular conditions or sets of conditions have led to given outcomes and develop beliefs as to the relative likelihood of one outcome relative to another in proportion to the relative proportions of remembered instances of the two types.

> There is certainly a probability, which arises from a superiority of chances on any side; and according as this superiority increases, and surpasses the opposite chances, the probability receives a proportionable increase, and begets still a higher degree of belief or assent to that side, in which we discover the superiority. . . .
>
> It is more probable, in almost every country of Europe, that there will be frost sometime in January, than that the weather will continue open throughout the whole month; though this probability varies according to the different climates, and approaches to a certainty in the more northern kingdoms. Here then it seems evident, that, when we transfer the past to the future, in order to determine the effect, which will result from any cause, we transfer all the different events, in the same proportion as they have appeared in the past, and conceive one to have existed a hundred times, for instance, another ten times, and another once. As a great number of views do here concur in one event, they fortify and confirm it to the imagination, beget that sentiment which we call *belief*, and give its object the preference above the contrary event, which is not supported by an equal number of experiments, and recurs not so frequently to the thought in transferring the past to the future. (Hume, 1748, reprinted 1947, pp. 383–385)

In the transition from philosophy to experimental psychology, the outlines of the interpretation have not changed at all, but the empirical basis has changed from casual and uncontrolled observation to specific experiments and the informally sketched interpretation to a more formal model within which actual testable predictions about the course of learning and the actions of the learner can be computed.

SUMMARY

After this brief presentation of the essentials of the statistical model, it may be clearer why I took some pains in the introduction to the paper to spell out the general philosophy guiding the work. In a model intended to represent what an individual learns about the relation between a stimulating situation and the outcomes of different actions it may evoke, I have chosen the analytical rather than the holistic side of a longstanding controversy in psychology. In particular I have proposed to represent learning in terms of the states of ensembles of aspects or components of the stimulating situation, more generally elements, that are not explicitly definable in terms of physical or physiological dimensions or properties. Presumably the elements must correspond to some physiological or biochemical events or processes in the organism. However, the strategy is simply to suppose that these elements exist and have properties suggested by various converging empirical and rational considerations, then to gain evidence on the viability of the concept by working out implications of the model that can be tested in various ways by experiments on learning and memory.[1]

NOTE

1. As this paper is being edited in 1981, the strategy spelled out some twenty years earlier still seems sound to me. However, I no longer feel so severely constrained to keep the notion of stimulus elements, or what I might now term memory elements, entirely free of contamination (or enrichment, depending on one's viewpoint) by ideas coming from branches of psychology other than quantitative studies of learning. In particular, it now seems quite in order and probably fruitful to think of the elements not only as carriers of certain abstract quantitative properties but also as corresponding to the outputs of feature detectors, or, more generally, different ways of encoding stimulus information in the perceptual and memory systems.

REFERENCES

Atkinson, R. C. An analysis of the effect of nonreinforced trials in terms of statistical learning theory. *Journal of Experimental Psychology,* 1956, *52,* 28-32.

Audley, R. J., & Jonckheere, A. R. The statistical analysis of the learning process. II. Stochastic processes and learning behaviour. *British Journal of Statistical Psychology,* 1956, *9,* 87-94.

Brunswik, E. Probability as a determiner of rat behavior. *Journal of Experimental Psychology,* 1939, *25,* 175-197.

Eccles, J. C. *The neurophysiological basis of mind, the principles of neurophysiology.* Oxford: The Clarendon Press, 1953.

Estes, W. K. Learning theory. *Annual Review of Psychology,* 1962, *13,* 107-144.

Estes, W. K., & Straughan, J. H. Analysis of a verbal learning conditioning situation in terms of statistical learning theory. *Journal of Experimental Psychology,* 1954, *47,,* 225-234.

Guthrie, E. R. *The psychology of learning.* New York: Harper, 1935.

Hebb, D. O. *The organization of behavior.* New York: Wiley, 1949.

Hull, C. L. *Principles of behavior.* New York: Appleton-Century-Crofts, 1943.

Hume, D. An enquiry concerning human understanding, 1748. Reprinted in S. Commins & R. N. Linscott, *The world's great thinkers: Man and spirit: The speculative philosophers.* New York: Random House, 1947.

Jarvik, M. E. Probability learning and a negative recency effect in the serial anticipation of alternative symbols. *Journal of Experimental Psychology,* 1951, *41,* 291-297.

Lawrence, D. H. The nature of a stimulus: Some relationships between learning and perception. In S. Koch (Ed.), *Psychology: A study of a science,* Vol. 5, pp. 179-212. New York: McGraw-Hill, 1963.

Neimark, E. D. Effects of type of non-reinforcement and number of available responses in two verbal conditioning situations. *Journal of Experimental Psychology,* 1956, *52,* 209-220.

Rashevsky, N. Mathematical biophysics of conditioning. *Psychometrika,* 1937, *2,* 199-209.

Skinner, B. F. *The behavior of organisms: An experimental analysis.* New York: Appleton-Century-Crofts, 1938.

Spearman, C. *The abilities of man.* New York: Macmillan, 1927.

Thurstone, L. L. *The vectors of mind.* Chicago: University of Chicago Press, 1935.

Woods, P. J. The relationship between probability difference $(\pi_1 - \pi_2)$ and learning rate in a contingent partial reinforcement situation. *Journal of Experimental Psychology,* 1959, *58,* 27-30.

Individual Behavior in Uncertain Situations: An Interpretation in Terms of Statistical Association Theory

INTRODUCTION

Group decision processes depend upon the behavior of individuals. For this reason it is to be expected that theories developed in social sciences and theories developed in experimental psychology will not be unrelated. Inspection of certain of the more formalized theories of group behavior, e.g., theories of games and economic behavior, reveals that these theories include, explicitly or implicitly, assumptions concerning characteristics of individual behavior. It is an attractive possibility that the descriptive laws or principles of behavior that enter theories of group behavior as axioms may be deducible from theories of individual behavior.

We note that in a game or an economic situation the individual is called upon to predict or to attempt to control uncertain events. The sequence of events may be random or it may follow a pattern about which the individual has initially incomplete information. We shall discuss in this paper two sets of experiments that have been carried out with adult human subjects (college students) in highly simplified experimental situations. The first set will bring out certain aspects of the behavior of an individual in attempting to predict correctly the outcomes of a series of situations when the alternative outcomes occur in a random sequence (the individual *not* being informed that the sequence will be random). The second set of experiments will bring out certain aspects of the behavior of an individual in attempting to produce an event by choosing on each trial some one of a set of alternative responses, the different responses having different probabilities (initially unknown to the individual) of producing the event. In each case we will show how the data can be handled in terms of a statistical theory of associative learning.

W. K. Estes, Individual behavior in uncertain situations: An interpretation in terms of statistical association theory. In R. M. Thrall, C. H. Coombs, & R. L. Davis (Eds.), *Decision processes*, pp. 127–137. New York: Wiley, 1954. Reprinted by permission.

It is contemplated that these simplified experiments may provide basic paradigms which can be progressively modified in the direction of situations directly relevant to utility theory and game theory. It will also be of interest to consider possible relationships between the model that accounts for the data of these experiments and models that are developed in connection with other decision processes.

CASE I: PREDICTION OF AN UNCERTAIN EVENT

The experiments to be considered in this section all have the same basic design. The activity studied is similar in some respects to that involved in predicting the results of roulette games or horse races; there are two important simplifications, however. In these experiments the outcome of the situation has no utility for the individual (except that of being right or wrong in his guess) and the information available to the individual is restricted to what he can obtain from observing a series of replications of the situation.

In any one experiment, the subject is run for a series of trials. All trials in the series begin with a signal, S. In some experiments S has been onset of a light, in some the onset of a tone, in some simply a verbal signal from the experimenter. A short time (2–5 seconds) following the signal S, one of a set of alternative outcomes, $E_1, E_2, \ldots, E_n$, occurs and terminates the trial. Immediately after the onset of S on each trial the subject writes down his prediction as to which of the events $E_1, E_2, \ldots, E_n$ will occur on that trial; then he is permitted to observe which event actually does occur. The subject is given no information about the conditions of the experiment except that some one of the E_j will follow the signal S on each trial; he is instructed to do his best to make a good score (in terms of correct predictions), and to make a prediction on each trial regardless of how uncertain he may feel about the outcome. The events $E_1, E_2, \ldots, E_n$ actually occur at random with probabilities $\pi_1, \pi_2, \ldots, \pi_n$. No communication between subject and experimenter is permitted once the series of trials has begun. Trials are spaced at intervals of about five seconds ordinarily.

The theory that has been applied to this situation with some success is a statistical model for associative learning that has been developed during the last five years by the writer and others. In this theory the behaviors available to the subject on any experimental trial are categorized into mutually exclusive and exhaustive classes (in the present experiment alternative predictions concerning the E_j) by means of experimental criteria. It is assumed that the change in probability of any response class on a given trial depends upon the momentary environmental situation and upon the state of the individual as defined in the model. When the model is interpreted in terms of the present experiment, it turns out that the rate of learning (systematic change in probability of making a given prediction) depends upon the characteristics of the momentary environmental situation but that over a considerable series of trials the probability of making a given prediction tends to a stable asymptotic distribution with the asymptotic mean, for a group of similar individuals run under like conditions, being independent of the momentary environmental situation, in the present experiment, the nature of the signal, S. The dependence of $\bar{p}_j$, the mean probability (for a group of like individuals) of predicting event E_j, upon n, the number of previous trials in the series, is given by the equation

$$\bar{p}_j(n) = \pi_j - \frac{1}{N\bar{\theta}} \sum_{i=1}^{N} \theta_i [\pi_j - F_{i,j}(0)] [1 - \theta_i]^n \tag{1}$$

where the θ_i represent the probabilities of occurrence on any trial of the N environmental determiners comprising the situation at the beginning of the trial, π_j represents the probability of the outcome E_j on any trial, and $F_{i,j}(0)$ represents the initial probability that the ith element in the set of environmental determiners would, taken alone, lead to a prediction of outcome E_j. This equation is derived from certain primitive assumptions concerning the learning process. The assumptions are given in references [3, 4].

Since the stable course of action arrived at by the individual over a series of trials is the feature of the situation that is apt to be of most interest in relation to group decision processes, we shall consider only the asymptotic distribution of p_j in this paper. It can be seen from inspection of equation (1) that the asymptotic value of $\bar{p}_j$ is independent of the initial state and also of the distribution of θ_i. Therefore we can conveniently simplify the model for our present purposes by assuming all of the θ_i equal to some value θ, which amounts empirically to assuming that all aspects of the environmental situation obtaining at the beginning of each trial are equally likely to affect the subject. Then the difference equations leading to equation (1) in the theory reduce to the following set of linear transformations:

(a) If E_j occurs on trial n, then
$$p_j(n + 1) = p_j(n) + \theta(1 - p_j(n))$$

(b) If E_j fails to occur on trial n, then $\qquad$ (2)

$$p_j(n + 1) = p_j(n) - \theta p_j(n)$$

(c) If E_j occurs with probability π_j, then on the average

$$\bar{p}_j(n + 1) = \bar{p}_j(n) + \theta(\pi_j - \bar{p}_j(n))$$

and we have asymptotically,

(a) $\bar{p}_j(\infty) = \pi_j$

and $\qquad$ (b) $\sigma_{p_j}^2(\infty) = \pi_j(1 - \pi_j)\theta/(2-\theta)$ $\qquad$ (3)

It will be noted that the equations (2) and (3) can be obtained from the linear operator model of Bush and Mosteller [1] if suitable restrictions are imposed upon the parameters.

Data from two experiments of the sort under consideration are summarized in Figure 2.3 below.

The bottom curve represents data collected by James H. Straughan and the writer at Indiana University. Subjects were 30 college stu-

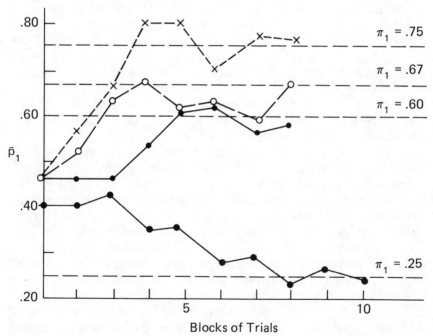

Figure 2.3 Data from prediction experiments plotted in terms of mean proportion of E_1 predictions per trial block.

dents. The signal, S, was a pattern of four lights which flashed for one second at the beginning of each trial. The outcomes E_1 and E_2 were the appearance or non-appearance of a single light two seconds after the signal pattern. The trials on which E_1 appeared were determined in advance of the experiment by a random number table with $\pi_1 = .25$ and $\pi_2 = .75$. Each point on the curve represents the mean relative frequency of predictions of E_1 in a block of 10 trials. The three upper curves represent data from a very similar experiment conducted by Jarvik [7] at the University of California, with π_1 equal to .60, .67, and .75 for three groups of subjects respectively. In Jarvik's experiment the signal at the start of each trial was utterance of the word "now" by the experimenter and the two alternative outcomes, E_1 and E_2 were utterance of the word "check" or the word "plus," respectively, by the experimenter. The Jarvik data are plotted in terms of mean relative frequencies of "check" predictions over blocks of 11 trials. It will be seen that in all cases the mean value of p_1 levels off in the neighborhood of the predicted asymptote by the end of 60 to 80 trials. The agreement of theory and experiment in this instance is especially interesting in view of the fact that the theoretical predictions of $p_1(\infty)$ utilize no degrees of freedom from the data. Similar experiments by Humphreys [6], who originated the experimental design, and Grant et al. [5] report data which are in accord with theoretical predictions insofar as asymptotic means are concerned. The Jarvik, Humphreys, and Grant papers do not report individual data or variance estimates.

The reader may be concerned at this point over the fact that the experimental curves cited represent group performance. The terminal mean probabilities of E_1 predictions by groups of subjects agree with the theory in all instances, but according to the theory, not only group means but also mean response probabilities of individual subjects should approach π_1 asymptotically. We cannot tell from the group data whether this feature of the theory is verified. A mean response probability, $\bar{p}_1(n)$, equal to π_1 could arise if the values of $p_1(n)$ tended to cluster around π_1, but it could also arise if the proportion π_1 of the subjects in a group ended up at $p_1(n) = 1$ while the remainder went to $p_1(n) = 0$. As a matter of fact, inspection of individual data from a number of experiments run in the writer's laboratory shows that the latter possibility can be rejected. To illustrate this point, we have plotted in Figure 2.4 the records of each of a group of four subjects run in one of these experiments under somewhat better controlled conditions than the group studies. The values plotted are proportions of E_1 predictions per ten-trial

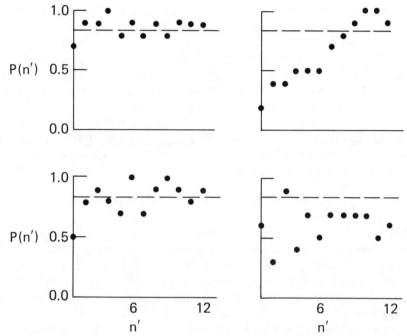

Figure 2.4 Individual records from a prediction experiment plotted in terms of proportion of E_1 predictions, $P(n')$, per block of ten trials, n'.

block. According to theory, these individual curves, regardless of initial value, should tend to approach $\pi_1 = .85$, the relative frequency of E_1, as learning progresses. Three of the four records certainly do this; the fourth record is in some doubt, not having stabilized anywhere by the end of 120 trials.

It may be noted that during the later trial blocks, the plotted values for these subjects tend to fluctuate around the .85 level rather than remaining constant. This asymptotic variability is also in accordance with theory. Since the theoretical asymptotic probability of E_1 predictions is .85, the standard deviation of proportions of E_1 predictions per block of ten trials at the asymptote will be expected to be approximately (neglecting a covariance term)

$$\sqrt{\frac{.85 \times .15}{10}} = .113$$

In the case of the experiment represented in the lowest curve of Figure 2.3, the inter-subject variability around the mean curve decreases steadily throughout the series of trials. In the last two blocks of trials over 60 per cent of the subjects have p_1 values (i.e., proportions of E_1 predictions) in the range .1 to .3 as compared with 33 per cent in the first block, and the proportions of zero and one values do not increase at all during the series.

It will be noted that the course of action adopted by the subjects in these experiments does not maximize the expected frequency of correct predictions. Take, for example, a series with π_1 equal to .25. The subjects settle down to a relatively steady level at which they predict E_1 on 25 per cent of the trials. This behavior secures the subject an expected percentage of correct predictions

$$(25 \times .25 + 75 \times .75)\% = 62.5\%$$

whereas the "pure strategy," in the von Neumann and Morgenstern sense, of predicting the more frequently occurring event on all trials would yield an expectation of 75 per cent correct predictions.

It would be of interest in connection with the broader problem of decision processes to modify the design of these experiments on prediction by introducing systematic variation in the information available to the subject and in the utility attached to the outcomes $E_1, E_2, \ldots, E_n$.

CASE II: ATTEMPTING TO CONTROL
AN UNCERTAIN EVENT

A group of experiments which are closely related, in terms of the theory, to those described above, study the behavior of the individual in attempting to control an uncertain event. In one variation of this experiment, two telegraph keys are available to the subject and he is required to choose one or the other on each trial. On a panel in front of the subject there is mounted a lamp globe. The subject is told that on each trial one key is "correct" and one key is "incorrect" in accordance with some scheme or plan that is entirely unknown to him except for what he can learn during a series of trials, and is led to believe that whenever he chooses "correctly," the light on the panel will flash. Actually the light is operated by a device programmed by means of a random number table so that the light flash will follow choices of key #1 with probability π_1 and choices of key #2 with probability π_2.

As in Case I, a theoretical account of this experiment can be derived from the statistical model [3,4]. For purposes of the present discussion we will give here simply the end result of the derivations. If we again simplify the model by assuming that all components of the situation S have equal probabilities of influencing the individual's response, then the changes in response probability on any trial are described by the linear transformations given in the table below. Let $p_1(n)$ represent the probability of choosing key #1 on trial n.

Key Chosen	Outcome	Expected Change in p_1
1	E_1	$p_1(n + 1) = p_1(n) + \theta(1 - p_1(n))$
1	E_2	$p_1(n + 1) = p_1(n) - \theta p_1(n)$
2	E_1	$p_1(n + 1) = p_1(n) - \theta p_1(n)$
2	E_2	$p_1(n + 1) = p_1(n) + \theta(1 - p_1(n))$

Then under the conditions stated above, we obtain for the expected change in mean probability of choosing key #1

$$\bar{p}_1(n + 1) = \theta(1 - \pi_2) + (1 - 2\theta + \theta\pi_1 + \theta\pi_2)\bar{p}_1(n) \qquad (4)$$

And for the asymptotic mean

$$\bar{p}_1(\infty) = \frac{1 - \pi_2 \,(5)}{2 - \pi_1 - \pi_2}$$

The data reproduced in Figure 2.5 are taken from an experiment conducted at Indiana University by Marvin H. Detambel [2]. Detambel ran four groups of college students under the conditions described above with the following values of π_1 and π_2

Group	π_1	π_2	Theoretical Asymptote, $\bar{p}_1(\infty)$
I and III	100	0	1.0
II	50	50	0.5
IV	50	0	0.67

Predicted values for asymptotic mean probabilities of choosing key #1 are readily computed from equation (5) and the values for Detambel's groups are included in the table just above. In the case of Group IV, which has $\pi_1 = 0.5$ and $\pi_2 = 0$, we see that the course of action to which the subjects tend over a series of trials is far from the "pure strategy" which would be the best solution to the situation from the standpoint of maximizing successes. Over the last half of

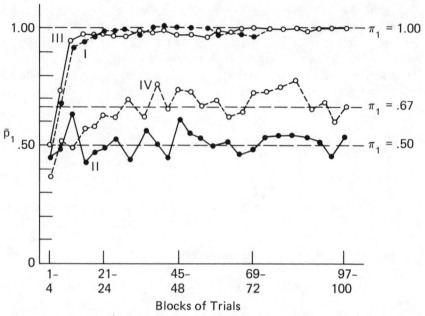

Figure 2.5 Mean proportion of E_1 predictions per four-trial block in Detambel's two-key, contingent reinforcement experiment.

the series the subjects, on the average, select key #1 approximately 67 per cent of the time, in accordance with theoretical expectation. Under the conditions of the experiment, this course of action yields as the expected percentage of successes

$$67 \times .50 + 33 \times 0 = 33.5\%$$

whereas by selecting key #1 on all trials the subjects would have raised their expectation to 50 per cent successes.

The behavior pattern exhibited by these subjects may be better suited, in some respects, to dealing with environmental uncertainties than the strategy of going over to a p value of unity on the more frequently reinforced response. The "pure strategy" would be optimal only if the sequence of environmental events constituted a stationary time series. Actually in this experiment the subjects were not told that the π values would remain constant throughout the series and they had no sound basis for inferring constancy. The compromise solution of the problem arrived at by the subjects would be advantageous if the environmental probabilities were to change at any point in the series so that the formerly unfavorable response became the more favorable. If, for example, the probability of reinforcement on key #2 in the Detambel experiment had been changed from zero to .75 halfway through the series, the subjects would soon have shifted their response probabilities to a level appropriate to the new situation, whereas a "rational" subject operating under a "pure strategy" of selecting key #1 on all trials would not have discovered that the balance of probabilities had changed. It is very doubtful, however, that many individuals in these experiments work out a solution at a verbal level. Probably long experience with environmental uncertainties has developed relatively stable habits of response to reinforcement and non-reinforcement. In this situation it appears that the subject proceeds as though failure of reinforcement on one key means that the other response would have been correct on the given trial, although as the experiment is conducted this actually is not generally true. Subjects might eventually change their behavior pattern, but under experimental conditions they give little evidence of doing so even over series of considerable length.

Both types of experiment seem to support the conclusion that in a simple decision process the human subject tends to behave in accordance with the principles of associative learning and not, in general, in the most rational manner as "rational" is conventionally defined. The suggestion arises, then, that in formulating theories of group decision processes it may be worth while to draw upon the principles of individual behavior revealed by experimental-theoretical research of the kind described here rather than to depend upon common sense notions concerning characteristics of individual behavior.

BIBLIOGRAPHY

1. Bush, R. R. and Mosteller, F., A linear operator model for learning. In preparation.
2. Detambel, M. H., A re-analysis of Humphrey's "Acquisition and extinction of verbal expectations." M. A. Thesis, Indiana University, 1950.
3. Estes, W. K., Toward a statistical theory of learning. *Psychol. Rev.*, 57 (1950), 94–107.
4. Estes, W. K. and Burke, C. J., A theory of stimulus variability in learning. *Psychol. Rev.*, 60 (1953), 276–286.
5. Grant, D. A., Hake, H. W., and Hornseth, J. P., Acquisition and extinction of a verbal conditioned response with differing percentages of reinforcement. *J. exp. Psychol.*, 42 (1951), 1–5.

6. Humphreys, L. G., Acquisition and extinction of verbal expectations in a situation analogous to conditioning. *J. exp. Psychol.*, 25 (1939), 294–301.
7. Jarvik, M. E., Probability learning and a negative recency effect in the serial anticipation of alternative symbols. *J. exp. Psychol.*, 41 (1951), 291–297.

Reinforcement in Human Behavior

Stimulus, response, reinforcement—by proper application of these concepts the contemporary psychologist can mold the behavior of a laboratory animal with astonishing ease. As a first exercise in an operant conditioning laboratory, a student learns how to train a rat or a pigeon to perform a prescribed action, for example to approach and press a switch which activates a food dispenser. He need only make available the *stimulus* to which he wishes the animal to respond, wait for the *response* to occur in the course of the hungry animal's normally variable activity in the situation, and ensure that food reward (*reinforcement*) is given promptly after occurrence of the response. Almost inevitably, and apparently quite automatically, the reinforced response increases in probability (becomes conditioned) and behaviors not leading to reward decrease in probability (undergo extinction).

Up to a point there can be no doubt regarding the practical efficacy of the techniques of reinforcement. By direct extrapolation of the methods of the operant conditioning laboratory to institutional settings, practitioners of "behavior modification" have been able to instill useful habits in the severely mentally retarded and even to begin to modify the behavior of schizophrenic adults in socially desirable directions (Krasner and Ullman 1965; Verhave 1966). But as extrapolation continues, questions and doubts begin to arise.

Does the effectiveness of reinforcement procedures, however impressive within a limited sphere of application, unequivocally attest that we fully understand the processes involved? Do we have adequate grounds for anticipating continuing success if the reinforcement principles are further extended, as some enthusiasts propose, to deal with problems of human behavior arising in the schools, in the prevention of delinquency, in the control of crime? Need we fear that, as a reading of Skinner (1971) might suggest, there is already at hand a behavioral technology which would enable a knowledgeable practitioner to shape the behavior of other people to his will?

W. K. Estes, Reinforcement in human behavior. *American Scientist*, 1972, *60*, 723–729. Reprinted with permission of the Society of the Sigma Xi.

In order to judge the likelihood that a principle can successfully be extended beyond its present domain, we require an understanding of its theoretical status. One view of the reinforcement principle holds it to be no more than an empirical generalization prescribing sufficient conditions for learning in a particular set of experiments (thus the designation "empirical law of effect," McGeoch 1942). If this view is correct, then we have no rational basis for extrapolation beyond situations closely analogous to those already studied. But in another interpretation, reinforcement is a general, abstract principle which closely mirrors an underlying process, and thus may be expected to hold wherever the constituents—stimulus, response, and reinforcement—can be identified (Hull 1943).

The rather widespread resistance on the part not only of laymen but of many psychologists to accepting the reinforcement principle and the techniques of operant conditioning as the main approach to the modification of human behavior is based largely on intuitive distaste for the rather mechanical conception of human action that seems to be implied. But reinforcement theory is based on hard evidence from laboratory studies and applications. Thus, in attempting to decide on the merits of the approach, we should tackle it on its own ground and ask what equally hard evidence there may be from scientific observation and experiments on human learning to provide a basis for judging the adequacy of reinforcement principles when extended to problems of education, training, and therapy of human beings.

I have been deeply concerned with these problems for a number of years, and my efforts to deal with them at a technical level have already been reported (Estes 1969, 1970; see also related work of Atkinson and Wickens 1971, and of Buchwald 1969). Here I propose only to review some of the types of evidence considered and the general nature of the conclusions to which I have been led.

MOTIVATIONAL AND INFORMATIONAL ASPECTS OF REINFORCEMENT

Any reinforcing event which serves as a reward for a learner has both motivational and informational functions. If a hungry rat receives food following a correct choice in a T-maze, or if a pupil is praised for spelling a word correctly, the reward presumably satisfies a motive—hunger in the one case, a need for approval in the other. But also this event may convey information as to what action can be expected to lead to reward in the future.

These two aspects of reinforcement have not been distinguished in traditional formulations of the law of effect, or reinforcement principle, perhaps because reinforcement theory has grown largely out of animal studies. In experiments with animals, contingencies are nearly always arranged so that reward occurs uniformly following some designated response, or at least with higher probability than following other responses (as in the case of "partial reinforcement"). Thus the occurrence of reward always conveys information as to the response most likely to yield further reward. And regularity in the association of a response with reward in its past experience is the sole source of information available to the animal concerning the contingencies likely to prevail in the future.

The human learner, in contrast, has many sources of information available. Thus we can raise the question whether a reward will strengthen the response which produces it if the learner also receives information indicating that the same response will not lead to reward on future occasions. Indications that actually reward consistently fails under such circumstances have come from a pioneering study by Thorndike (1935), who indeed will be found to have anticipated almost every empirical and theoretical development in this entire field, and from an ingenious series of experiments by Nuttin (Nuttin and Greenwald, 1968). However, neither of these investigators employed controls adequate to show whether the same reward might be effective or ineffective in strengthening the same response depending on the learner's state of information. Since the theoretical question at issue is of major importance, we set about constructing in my laboratory an experimental situation which would provide the requisite controlled comparisons.

To ensure interest and motivation for the experimental task, we arranged a situation which was presented to the subject as a simulation of the job of an aircraft controller. During the experiment the subject sat at a Teletype terminal connected to a small computer which controlled the operation of the experiment. As dictated by the experimental program, the keyboard of the teletypewriter could be utilized by the subject for the purpose of typing in messages, or control could be taken over by the computer when messages were to be transmitted to the subject. In either case, whatever was typed was immediately visible to the subject as it was entered on the strip of paper under the window on the terminal.

The subject was asked to imagine that the window with the paper beneath it represented a radar screen, on which from time to time he would see a moving arrow representing a moving airplane. The arrow would first appear at the left of the window and then move rapidly across his visual field to the right. The subject's task was to transmit a message to the hypothetical pilot of the plane in time to permit him to avoid a collision with another plane or an obstacle. Also the subject knew that there were exactly two messages which he might transmit to the pilot; these messages were coded by two letters corresponding to the two keys on the teletypewriter, which the subject could use to transmit a message.

Under what we might term the baseline, or control condition, the events of a trial run as indicated in Figure 2.6. The A and B at the bottom of the figure represent the two keys on the teletype-writer that the subject may use to send messages. At the beginning of the trial the arrow starts to move across the window. Suppose that on this trial the subject decides to send message A and operates the corresponding key. The letter A then appears following the last position of the moving arrow, signifying that the pilot has received the message. If the message chosen is the correct one, movement of the plane stops and the word "SAFE" is typed out as shown in Figure 2.6. If the message is the incorrect one, the arrow continues to move to the end of the line and then the word "FAIL" appears, indicating a collision. Thus the subject is rewarded by a successful outcome (preventing a collision) if he chooses the correct message and punished by his failure to prevent a collision if he chooses the wrong one.

In order to determine the effect of the reward or punishment, the subject was given one experience under the condition described, then was tested a few trials later with the same pair of messages. The effect of a rewarded trial was an increase from .33 to .60 in the

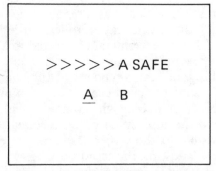

Figure 2.6 Schema for a trial with normal feedback in the aircraft con-troller experiment. The subject typed key A; message A was received by the pilot and led to a successful outcome.

subject's probability of choosing the key which had led to a successful outcome. This effect is quite substantial considering that problems were following one another very rapidly and that within each
trial the subject was operating under considerable time pressure.

But how should this effect be interpreted in theoretical terms?
Can we accept it as simply another example of the action of the law
of effect—that is, the tendency to choose a particular response key
being strengthened when operation of the key is followed by a
satisfying outcome? Perhaps so. But having adopted an analytical
frame of mind, we are inclined to be a bit suspicious and to wonder
whether the same effect would have been observed if the subject's
understanding of the task did not lead him to expect that a message
which was successful on one occasion would also be successful on
another.

In order to permit closer analysis of the relationships between
different aspects of the subject's performance and the rewarding or
punishing outcomes, we contrived a variation of the experiment
which we might term the "conflicting feedback" condition. In this
condition, the subject was told that because of noise in the communication system there might be occasions on which the message
he intended to transmit would not get through clearly and might be
misperceived or misinterpreted by the pilot of the airplane. He would
know that this had occurred if, for example, he hit the A key, but
nonetheless a B appeared in the window, as illustrated in Figure 2.7.
This machination was easy to accomplish in our situation simply by

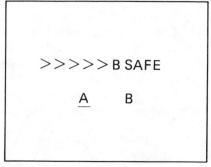

Figure 2.7 Schema for a conflicting
feedback trial on which B was the correct message. The subject typed key
A, but message B was received by the
pilot. Thus the outcome was a success
even though the subject had actually
made an incorrect choice.

appropriate programming of the computer. I might add that problems with normal feedback and problems with conflicting feedback occurred in random sequence during the experimental session (intermixed with other problem types which need not be described here), but with each problem having its own pair of messages so that there would be no carry-over or interference from one to another.

With the conflicting feedback condition available, we were in a position to evaluate the effect of reward on a trial when the subject chose one message key but a different message was received by the pilot, and thus the environmental effect of the subject's action was not the one that he intended. The result in this case was no increase, and in fact a slight decrease (from a probability of .60 to .54) in the subject's tendency to choose the message key which had led to reward.

The substance of these and other results obtained in this experimental situation is to confirm and extend the earlier findings of Thorndike and Nuttin. Evidently we may conclude that success yields increased probability of the correct response and failure decreased probability of the incorrect response only if the stimulus feedback generated by the response signifies to the learner that the given response will have the same consequence on future occasions.

Understanding this limitation on the empirical law of effect as applied to normal human behavior is doubtless of considerable practical import. But what is its theoretical significance? Are we to assume that the extent to which rewards and punishments strengthen or weaken the actions that produce them is limited by the informational state of the learner? Or should we entertain the more radical assumption that rewards and punishments do not directly strengthen or weaken responses at all, but only provide a basis for the acquisition of information which may indirectly influence actions?

The distinction can be elucidated in terms of another experiment conducted in our laboratory (reported in part by Estes 1969). The task set for a group of college students was to earn as many points as possible by learning always to choose the correct members of various pairs of stimuli. The incorrect members of all stimulus pairs were assigned reward value 0, whereas the correct members were assigned positive values.

On each trial of the experiment, the subject was presented with one of the pairs of stimuli, chose the stimulus that he believed to be correct, and then predicted the reward value that he would receive. Whenever the subject chose an incorrect stimulus, he was shown the reward value 0 and received no points. When he chose the correct stimulus, he was shown the value the experimenter had decided to give for that stimulus if it were chosen on a given trial, but only if the subject had predicted the value correctly was the given number of points added to his total.

Two pairs of stimuli were assigned to the condition of primary interest, termed "Never Right" for reasons that will soon become apparent. In one of these pairs, the correct stimulus was assigned reward values 1 and 2, in the other the correct stimulus was assigned values 3 and 4. When the subject chose the correct member of one of the Never Right pairs, and predicted its value, the experimenter (rather diabolically) exhibited always the reward value which the subject had not predicted. Thus if the subject chose the correct member of the pair belonging to the 3,4 Never Right condition and predicted a 3, the experimenter exhibited a 4; conversely, if the subject predicted a 4 he was shown a 3, and in neither case did he receive any reward.

If it should prove that over a series of trials, subjects learn always to choose the correct members of Never Right pairs (which is in fact the result observed), the change in performance must be attributed to their acquisition of information regarding the values associated with various stimuli.

An alert reinforcement theorist might raise the question whether, even though learning occurred in the absence of reward, the learning might have been faster if rewards had actually been received for correct choices. To check on this possibility, we included in the experiment 3,4 Random and 1,2 Random pairs. The correct member of each of the Random stimulus pairs was assigned the same pair of reward values as the corresponding Never Right item. But on trials when a Random pair was presented, the experimenter determined by chance which of the assigned reward values he would exhibit; therefore on correct choices, the subject had a .50-.50 chance of predicting the value the experimenter had selected and thus receiving a reward.

The pairs belonging to the various conditions were mixed up in a random order, and the subject was given training on successive cycles through the list until he reached a criterion of 100% choice of the correct stimuli in all pairs.

In the analysis of the results, our interest centers of course on a comparison of the Random and Never Right conditions. In these two conditions the subject receives the same information with regard to the reward values assigned to the correct stimuli; however, in the Random condition he is rewarded half of the time on the average for correct choices, whereas in the Never Right condition he never receives reward for correct choices (or indeed for any choices).

The data show, first of all, virtually no difference between the Random and Never Right conditions with regard to speed of learning to make 100% correct choices. But still more informative results come from a set of test trials given after the subjects had met the criterion of learning and in which all of the correct stimuli were tested against each other in the various possible pairs. The rather striking outcome of these tests is that all comparisons involving Random and Never Right stimuli yield a uniform picture of almost exact equivalence. For the pooled data of all tests of the Never Right 3,4 stimulus against all others, the Never Right stimulus was chosen 73% of the time; the corresponding comparison of the Random 3,4 stimulus yielded 74%. For the combined results of the two tests in which the Random 3,4 stimulus was pitted against Never Right 3,4 and Random 1,2 against Never Right 1,2, the percent choice for Random was .52. On the other hand, the Never Right 3,4 stimulus was chosen 95% of the time over the Random 1,2 although the subjects had never been rewarded for choosing the former and had been rewarded 50% of the time for choosing the latter.

These results point up the necessity of an informational interpretation of reinforcement, at least in the case of normal human learners. In their experience with a mixture of problems, our subjects had opportunity to learn that, on the average, stimuli with higher assigned values yielded higher rewards. And on choice trials with particular pairs, they had an opportunity to learn the values assigned to the individual stimuli. If any of the subjects noticed that they repeatedly failed to obtain the rewards associated with the Never Right items, they doubtless dismissed these failures as an unlucky happenstance.

Though on first thought this experiment may seem rather artificial, on further consideration one can see close analogies to many situations in everyday life. People are often heard to wonder why the inveterate loser at picking horses or dabbling in the stock market does not profit from his experience and give up his unprofitable ways. The answer is that their view of the individual's experience is too narrowly circumscribed by their habit of thinking in terms of the law of effect. An individual's experience includes not only his own choices and their outcomes but also his observations of the choices of others, some of whom may reap larger rewards. The "unlucky" dabbler in stock continues to respond in accord with his expectations of reward, unaware that his own inferior judgment consigns him to the fate of the subject in the Never Right condition of the experiment.

ANTICIPATION OF REINFORCEMENT
AND STIMULUS SELECTION

The new insights arising from our novel manipulations of normal reward contingencies call for a change in our usual way of looking at the law of effect. We are led to infer that the occurrence of a rewarding or punishing event does not act backward in some sense to strengthen the response which preceded it, but rather provides an opportunity for the organism to learn a relationship between the stimulus which evoked its response and the rewarding or punishing consequence.

This conclusion is supported by a substantial accumulation of evidence showing that a rewarding event need not be contingent upon any particular response in order to produce learning; further, the effect of a reward (or punishment) upon performance is not necessarily specific to the action which produced it. Rather, any stimulus which comes to signal an impending increase in reward becomes a nonspecific facilitator (and one which signals impending punishment a nonspecific inhibitor) of any action sequence whose initiating stimulus occurs during the interval between the signal and reward. These notions can be illustrated in terms of the following experiment on human reaction time conducted in my laboratory (Stillings, Allen, and Estes 1968).

The situation we contrived for our purposes was a variation on the simple reaction time experiment which is utilized to determine the speed with which a person can respond to various types of stimuli. In our experiment the subject sat in front of a visual display screen upon which numerals could be projected. Between the screen and the subject was a response button, and above the screen were four colored signal lights. The subjects, college students, understood that their task was to depress the response button as quickly as possible following onset of the signal lights.

Prior to onset of the signal lights on each trial, a number between 0 and 80 flashed on the screen informing the subject of his reward for the trial. These numbers represented points, and the subject understood that his monetary payment for the session depended on the total number of points he received during the 40-minute experimental period. However, it should be emphasized that the number of points awarded on any trial did *not* depend on the subject's speed of reaction on that trial; rather, the point values of 0, 20, 40, 60, and 80 were delivered in a random sequence.

Examining mean reaction times for trials on which the various rewards were given, we found a small but systematic increase in response speed (decrease in reaction time) as a function of the amount of reward given on a trial. That is, on the average the subjects responded more rapidly when they anticipated a larger reward even though they knew that the amount of reward they received depended in no way on their performance.

One is immediately led to wonder whether the notion of anticipation of reward is meaningful only in connection with human subjects who are capable of verbalizing relationships between previously experienced events or whether it represents a basic behavioral process. Fortunately data are already at hand which resolve this crucial question. A particularly apt example is a study of response speed in monkeys as a function of noncontingent reward which parallels the study just described about as closely as one could ask for (unpublished study by D. L. Medin, cited in Medin and Davis 1974).

On each trial the monkey's task was simply to displace a stimulus object over a foodwell in order to obtain the food reward beneath it. Magnitude of reward was varied by utilizing more and less preferred foods, for example raisins versus bits of carrots or celery. The more and less preferred foods were presented in a random sequence and a red or green light was turned on above the site of the foodwell at the beginning of a trial, one color being associated with availability of the preferred food and the other with the nonpreferred food. Thus the animal had an opportunity to learn to anticipate which reward he would receive on each trial, but the reward received depended in no way upon his speed of response. Nonetheless, just as with the human subjects, analysis of the animals' reaction times over a series of trials revealed a substantial increase in response speed on trials when the colored cue indicated that the preferred food was available as compared to trials on which the colored cue signaled the nonpreferred food. Further, it was found that performance on a given trial did not vary at all as a function of the amount of reward received on the immediately preceding trial. A very similar result has been reported by Bresnahan and Shapiro (1972) for children engaged in a simple motor task.

FEEDBACK MECHANISMS

It seems clear that operationally definable states of anticipation of reward can be established in nonverbal as well as in verbal organisms. What can we say on the theoretically critical question as to the kind of neurophysiological mechanism or process which might link these informational states to variations in performance?

Much new experimental evidence, only a sample of which has been touched on in the preceding pages, indicates that any increase in the input of rewarding stimulation must activate a mechanism in the nervous system which generates facilitative inputs to action centers, and a decrease in rewarding stimulation (or the occurrence of punishment) a reduction in this input. I have referred to the sources of facilitative input simply as *positive feedback mechanisms,* or more suggestively, *stimulus amplifiers* (Estes 1969, 1970). It is tempting to surmise that the positive feedback mechanisms might prove identifiable with the centers in the midbrain which have been found to exert reinforcing effects upon direct electrical stimulation (Miller 1963; Stein 1964).

Specification of the neurophysiological loci of feedback mechanisms is speculative at present, but for the interpretation of reinforcement we require only definite assumptions about their functional properties. (1) These mechanisms are activated by changes in rewarding stimulation. In the innate organization of the nervous system, there must be connections between these mechanisms and stimuli which in the history of the species have been likely to signal impending satisfaction of needs or termination of pain. Thus, for example, even without prior learning we should expect that a sweet taste would lead to increased activity of a positive feedback mechanism. (2) Through classical conditioning, the activity of feedback mechanisms comes under the control of other stimuli. We speak of anticipation of reward if some cue which has preceded reward in the past becomes a conditioned stimulus for increase in activity of a positive feedback mechanism, and of anticipation of punishment if the cue has become a conditioned stimulus for a decrease in such activity. (3) Evocation of a response which, either innately or through learning, is associated with a given stimulus is facilitated by simultaneous input to the action center from the stimulus and from a stimulus amplifier.

The sequences of events embodied in these assumptions are schematized in Figure 2.8 in the manner of a kymograph record. In the upper portion of the figure, onset of a stimulus S gives rise to no anticipation of the rewarding outcome, $E+$, but after an interval it evokes a response R, which produces $E+$. This outcome leads immediately to an increase in positive feedback, $FB+$ in the diagram. As a result of this experience, the activity of the feedback mechanism may be conditioned to the preceding stimulus, S. Then upon a later occurrence of the stimulus S, an increase in activity of the feedback mechanism is produced anticipatorily (Antic. $E+$ in the lower panel of Fig. 2.8), and its facilitative input is available to

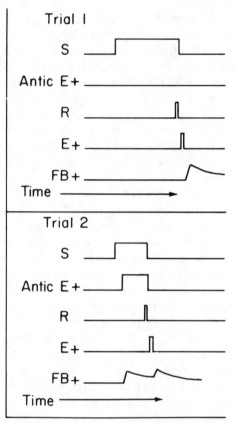

Figure 2.8 Schematic representation of temporal relations between events in feedback model. On trial 1 a novel stimulus S induces no tendency to anticipate the rewarding event $E+$; however, S ultimately evokes response R, and the rewarding event produces positive feedback $FB+$. Activity of the feedback mechanism becomes conditioned to S, so that on trial 2, S gives rise to anticipation of $E+$, which in turn produces $FB+$ and facilitates evocation of response R.

combine with that from the stimulus itself in determining response evocation. The shortening of the arrow between S and R in the lower part of the figure is intended to signify the reduction in reaction time that occurs when positive feedback is available immediately upon occurrence of the stimulus.

REINFORCEMENT AND CHOICE

Though the facilitative effects of anticipation of reward are shown most clearly in especially simplified experiments, the major implications with regard to the control of behavior have to do with choice situations. Suppose that an individual is confronted, not by a single stimulus as in the reaction time experiment, but by a set of stimuli from which a choice must be made. An everyday example would be a restaurant menu. Each stimulus has some probability of leading to reward, but the responses of choosing mutually exclusive items are mutually inhibitory and the individual must resolve a conflict in order to arrive at an overt response.

Extensive analysis of the choice problem has led to formulation of a "scanning model" for response selection (Bower 1959; Estes 1960). The principal assumptions of the model are as follows: (1) The higher the level of anticipated reward associated with a stimulus, the shorter is the average reaction time of a positive response (that is, a response involving approach to or selection of the stimulus). (2) Probability of a positive response to a stimulus within any given interval of time varies inversely with the mean reaction time. (3) When an individual is confronted with a number of stimuli in a choice situation, he scans the stimuli in a random order, except that the one scanned first tends to be the one most recently chosen, and considers each stimulus for some interval of time Δt before going on to another. As a consequence of these assumptions it can readily be seen that the probability that any given stimulus will be chosen during the interval when it is under consideration will be directly related to its associated reward value and that on the average, though not inevitably, a stimulus with a high reward value will be more likely to be chosen than one with a low value.

Quantitative implications of the model are readily derivable by interpretation of the choice process as a Markov chain, as illustrated for the case of two alternatives in Figure 2.9. The parameters σ_1 and σ_2 denote the initial probabilities of observing, or considering, the alternatives S_1 and S_2, respectively; and p_1 and p_2 denote the probabilities of choosing each alternative during an interval when it is under consideration.

One of the most interesting uses for a theory is to predict results which run counter to common sense expectations, or even better, to predictions of other theories. To illustrate in the present context, let us consider a multiple choice situation in which we record the time required by the subject to arrive at his choice among the alternatives. How should we expect choice times to be related to the

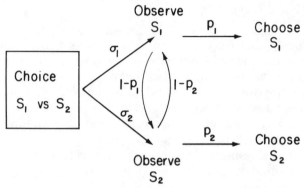

Figure 2.9 Representation of choice process. With probability σ_i ($i = 1, 2$) the individual initially considers alternative S_i. During any interval Δt when the individual is considering S_i, he has probability p_i of choosing it and probability $1 - p_i$ of switching attention to the other alternative.

reward values associated with the various alternative stimuli? Firstly, one might think that if all of the stimuli have equal values, choice time would be directly related to the number of alternatives, since the individual doing the choosing would require a greater amount of time to consider a larger number of stimuli. In terms of the scanning model, however, an individual's probability of making a choice at any moment is determined solely by the anticipated reward value associated with the stimulus he is considering; consequently if all of the stimuli have equal reward values, the predicted choice times will be independent of the number of alternatives present.

An experiment bearing directly on this prediction has been reported by Kiesler (1966). By means of a preliminary procedure involving preferential judgments, Kiesler determined the relative reward values of a number of varieties of candy for each member of a group of school children. Then each child was offered choices among a number of sets of candy bars, and choice time was recorded in each instance. In the comparison of immediate interest, each member of a group of 30 children was offered a choice on one occasion between two and on another occasion among four stimuli of equal value. The result was almost identical mean choice time in the two cases—7.76 sec and 7.72 sec for two and four alternatives, respectively.

In another interesting comparison, Kiesler obtained mean choice times for a set of four alternatives, two of which were of the same reward value as those of the previous comparison and two were of lower reward value. Should we expect choice time to be increased or decreased when we go from an equal to unequal set of reward values? Most people seem to expect intuitively that the time required to choose should be shorter the greater the separation in values among the available alternatives. Further, this is precisely the prediction arising from a number of formal psychological theories (for example, Cartwright and Festinger 1943; Hull 1952, p. 230).

But in terms of the scanning model, our prediction must in some cases be just the opposite. We recall that the predicted speed of response to any stimulus is directly related to the expected magnitude of reward. When two stimuli are presented for a choice, the subject is assumed to scan them in a random sequence until one or the other evokes its associated response and terminates the trial with an observed choice. Assuming that the stimuli are fully discriminable, choice time is predicted to depend most strongly upon the anticipated reward value associated with the higher-valued of the two stimuli. But if this is held constant, the choice time will *decrease* as value of the second stimulus *increases,* and conversely. Thus we must predict that choice time should be more systematically related to the sum than to the difference of the reward values of a problem. Kiesler's result, in agreement with the scanning model, was a substantial increase in choice time when he changed from the equal to the unequal set of alternatives.

Another relevant study with a similar outcome has been reported by Keller et al. (1965). Results of this kind provide supporting evidence, not only for the general idea that the actions of rewards depend on the learning of expectations, but for the particular kind of choice process assumed in the model described here.

TOWARD A THEORY OF REINFORCEMENT
IN HUMAN BEHAVIOR

The sample of studies reviewed here lends some feasibility to the idea that we can further our understanding of human behavior by the same general approach that has led to the development of operant conditioning and reinforcement theory. The principal means in each case is the careful laboratory analysis of simplified situations, supplemented on occasion by mathematical analysis of hypotheses and models arising from experimental results. On the other hand, we have found substantial reason to doubt that the law of effect, or reinforcement principle, can safely be generalized beyond a specific class of experimental situations.

We conclude, first of all, that in the case of a normal human learner a reward does not necessarily strengthen, nor a punishment weaken, the response which produces it. In order to predict the effect in either case we need to take account not only of the relation between the stimulus to which the individual responds and the reinforcing event which ensues but also of any other information available to the learner bearing upon the probability that the same relationship will prevail on future occasions. The immediate relevance of the individual's informational state to his behavior arises from the fact that any stimulus which leads to anticipation of an increase in probability or level of reward exerts a direct facilitative effect upon performance, manifest in decreased latency or increased probability of response to the stimulus. In any choice situation the individual is assumed actively to scan the available alternatives and to be guided to a choice by feedback from anticipated rewards.

Prescriptions for the practical modification of behavior derived from an informational-feedback theory may be expected to agree quite closely with those of operant conditioning when one is concerned with the training of simple habits in highly restricted situations, as for example in dealing with an institutionalized mental defective. But approaches deriving from the two kinds of theory may be expected to differ increasingly as we turn to problems of education and training of normal children and adults, where multiple sources of information are the rule rather than the exception and where the individual typically has almost unlimited latitude in selecting the stimuli to which he will respond.

It is interesting to note that the individuals who are real professionals in the manipulation of human behavior characteristically show an excellent intuitive grasp of the principle of reinforcement that would be dictated by an informational-feedback theory. Most importantly, they concentrate their efforts on the processes of stimulus selection, employing diverse and often ingenious procedures of information (and misinformation) in their efforts to associate high levels of anticipated reward with stimuli they want potential customers or voters to select in choice situations. And like the subjects in my "Never Right" experiment, the individuals subjected to adroitly conceived barrages of advertising or propaganda often continue indefinitely to choose the goods or candidates they have come to associate with high levels of anticipated reward even though they may never experience these rewards themselves.

In contrast, efforts by representatives of society to modify people's behavior in socially desirable directions are all too often conducted in accord with the obsolescent view that rewards directly strengthen actions and punishments weaken them. Further, these efforts to modify human behavior, whether by education, rehabilitation, or psychotherapy, are often conducted in institutional settings isolated from the environments in which the individuals carry on their normal activities. Consequently it is always difficult to establish new expectations concerning the likelihood that particular actions will be followed by reward or punishment outside of the training environment.

On the whole, I think it unrealistic to expect that the effective management of human behavior will be much advanced by direct application of the techniques of the animal conditioning laboratory. It appears that some basic mechanisms and principles do carry over from the animal to the human case, but extrapolations must always take account of the superior capabilities of the human organism as an information processor. The next major advances in treating problems of human behavior will surely be mediated by theories based jointly on neurophysiological investigations, the extensive results of animal conditioning studies, and the direct analysis of human learning. Indeed, the tentative and provisional theories of this type now emerging can already serve to clarify problems that are of social concern and at least to indicate directions in which we must be searching for solutions.

REFERENCES

Atkinson, R. C., and T. D. Wickens. 1971. Human memory and the concept of reinforcement. In R. Glaser (Ed.), *The Nature of Reinforcement*. New York: Academic Press, pp. 66–120.

Bower, G. H. 1959. Choice-point behavior. In R. R. Bush and W. K. Estes (Eds.), *Studies in Mathematical Learning Theory*. Stanford, Calif.: Stanford University Press, pp. 109–124.

Bresnahan, J. L., and M. M. Shapiro. 1972. Learning strategies in children from different socioeconomic levels. In H. W. Reese (Ed.), *Advances in Child Development and Behavior*, Vol. 7. New York: Academic Press, pp. 31–79.

Buchwald, A. M. 1969. Effects of "right" and "wrong" on subsequent behavior: A new interpretation. *Psychological Review* 76:132–43.

Cartwright, D., and L. Festinger. 1943. A quantitative theory of decisions. *Psychological Review* 50:595–621.

Estes, W. K. 1960. A random-walk model for choice behavior. In K. J. Arrow, S. Karlin, and P. Suppes (Eds.), *Mathematical Methods in the Social Sciences*, 1959, Stanford, Calif.: Stanford University Press, pp. 265–276.

Estes, W. K. 1969. Reinforcement in human learning. In J. Tapp (Ed.)., *Reinforcement and Behavior*. New York: Academic Press, pp. 63–94.

Estes, W. K. 1970. *Learning Theory and Mental Development.* New York: Academic Press.

Hull, C. L. 1943. *Principles of Behavior.* New York: Appleton-Century-Crofts.

Hull, C. L. 1952. *A Behavior System.* New Haven, Conn.: Yale University Press.

Keller, L., M. Cole, C. J. Burke, and W. K. Estes. 1965. Reward and information values of trial outcomes in paired-associate learning. *Psychological Monographs* 79 (Whole No. 605).

Kiesler, C. A. 1966. Conflict and number of choice alternatives. *Psychological Reports* 18:603–10.

Krasner, L., and L. P. Ullman. 1965. *Research in Behavior Modification.* New York: Holt, Rinehart, & Winston.

McGeoch, J. A. 1942. *The Psychology of Human Learning.* New York: Longmans, Green.

Medin, D. L., and R. T. Davis. 1974. Memory. In A. M. Schrier and F. Stollnitz (Eds.), *Behavior of Nonhuman Primates,* Vol. 5. New York: Academic Press, pp. 1–47.

Miller, N. E. 1963. Some reflections on the law of effect produce a new alternative to drive reduction. In M. R. Jones (Ed.), *Nebraska Symposium on Motivation.* Lincoln: University of Nebraska Press, pp. 65–112.

Nuttin, J., and A. G. Greenwald. 1968. *Reward and Punishment in Human Learning.* New York: Academic Press.

Skinner, B. F. 1971. *Beyond Freedom and Dignity.* New York: Knopf.

Stein, L. 1964. Reciprocal action of reward and punishment mechanisms. In R. G. Heath (Ed.), *The Role of Pleasure in Behavior.* New York: Hoeber.

Stillings, N. A., G. A. Allen, and W. K. Estes. 1968. Reaction time as a function of noncontingent reward magnitude. *Psychonomic Science* 10:337–38.

Thorndike, E. L. 1935. *The Psychology of Wants, Interests, and Attitudes.* New York: Appleton-Century.

Verhave, T. 1966. *The Experimental Analysis of Behavior.* New York: Appleton-Century-Crofts.

Cognitive and Developmental Aspects of Reinforcement and Choice Learning

Presumably behavior exists as an instrument of adaptation and thus is necessarily sensitive to its consequences. Whatever the processes responsible for such adaptation, they sometimes work extraordinarily well but sometimes conspicuously fail, and the conditions that make a difference between success and failure are far from thoroughly understood. In research addressed to the problem over the past half century, emphasis has shifted between two main themes: the continuing effort to formulate a principle giving the necessary and sufficient conditions for the consequences of an action to lead to increasingly adequate adjustment; and the view that selective learning reflects, not the direct strengthening and weakening of response strengths by aftereffects, but rather the acquisition of information relevant to choices.

In the first of these themes, Thorndike's original Law of Effect gave way to the more elaborate body of rules for relating outcomes to actions offered by Skinner's operant conditioning theory and more recently to the body of applications of the theory termed behavior modification. The advances in this line of research are an enormous achievement, and the resulting understanding of how to manage behavior in many situations will not be overturned by results that may ensue in the future. However, what can change, and has been changing, is the way we look at this body of theory and results.

Curiously, in the same book that included the most complete presentation of his Law of Effect and its supporting evidence, Thorndike (1931) planted the seeds for a theoretical development that would ultimately undermine it as a basic principle of human behavior. Almost in passing, he mentioned as a possible alternative to the Law of Effect a "representative" or "ideational" hypothesis.

This paper is based in part on an address given at the dedication of the Richard M. Elliott Psychology Building at the University of Minnesota, October 12, 1973. The research reported was carried out at Rockefeller University with the assistance of Edith Skaar. The collection and analysis of the data were supported by U.S. Public Health Service Grants MH 16100 and MH 33917.

63

On this idea, a learner would profit from past rewards and punishments by calling up memories ("images" or "ideational equivalents") of them in a later choice situation and allowing these mental events to augment or inhibit tendencies to repeat the previously rewarded or punished responses. Thorndike rejected the ideational hypothesis primarily because reports of the hypothesized memories were rarely elicited from subjects in post-experimental questionnaires. As will be seen later in this paper, Thorndike's conclusions regarding the specific form of ideational hypothesis he considered were probably correct, but he failed to recognize that the hypothesis could take other forms, which might be viable despite his negative findings.

Nonetheless, the weight of Thorndike's authority, together no doubt with the rising influence of behaviorism, resulted in the temporary submerging of representative or ideational theory in any form. Its resurfacing in the 1950s was evidently a joint consequence of the weakening of behavioristic orthodoxy, the precursors of the information processing movement, and a growing appreciation of a missing element in Law of Effect theory—the process of choice that intervenes between situations and action (Siegel, 1959; Tanner and Swets, 1954). From about 1950 to the present, the cognitive theme has led to gradually increasing research efforts premised on the idea that the role of incentives in human learning cannot be fully understood by focussing on the surface structure of correlations or contingencies between situations, actions, and outcomes. It has become generally recognized that we need to go deeper and attempt to understand not only the shaping of behavior by experience, but also the processes that lead to choices of actions and the cognitive operations and knowledge-structures on which these choices depend.

I think we can be sure that the interplay, and even conflict, between the two mainstreams of thought regarding incentives and actions has by no means reached its end. The reason, in brief, is that the issues that divide the behavioral and the cognitive approaches cannot be settled by any one ingenious experiment or even by clusters of experiments. Their relative dominance and influence depend, in part, on a broader theoretical framework in psychology, which necessarily is continually changing. This conclusion does not imply, however, that the choice between the behavioral and cognitive approaches to reinforcement must be purely a matter of philosophical taste or style. Rather, it may be expected that the choice will be conditioned in very specific ways by the value of these approaches in directing new research on major questions of continuing interest. In the following sections I will try to illustrate some research directions in which I find the cognitive approach the more fruitful and perhaps even essential.

FROM RESPONSE STRENGTHENING
TO MEMORY FOR VALUES

Since several detailed reviews of research on the role of information in reinforcement are available (Estes, 1969, 1971, 1981) I shall give here only a brief résumé, limiting attention to essentials of experimental designs and omitting procedural details. The way experimental situations are presented to subjects varies from study to study in this area, but it will be convenient to take as typical one method that has been used in some of my own work (Estes, 1981). A subject is asked to imagine that he or she has to contend with a problem, taking the form of an illness or disability for which alternative treatments are available, by learning from experience which treatment is to be preferred. In any one experiment, the subject understands that when a display presenting a problem appears at the beginning of a trial, a choice is to be made among the alternative treatments offered (characteristically by selecting a key on a response keyboard signifying the treatment selected). Following a choice, the experimenter displays information concerning success or failure in the form of numerical values that represent values of the treatments (for example, percentages of success).

At the time when I first became interested in this topic, the standard experimental design was the one set down by Thorndike and used in many of his studies of the Law of Effect (summarized, for example, in Thorndike, 1931). In this design the subject is presented with a list of symbols one at a time and as each is exposed can choose any one of a known set of alternatives, for example, the digits 1-9, and then receive information as to whether the choice was right or wrong. The symbols and digits correspond to the problems and treatments, respectively, in the current version.

Normal subjects do, of course, learn over a series of trials to select the correct alternatives, and this fact, together with such phenomena as the "spread of effect" (i.e., the finding that the effect of reward tends to generalize to responses temporally adjacent to the rewarded one) were taken by Thorndike to substantiate the idea that learning was a consequence of the automatic action of satisfying aftereffects in strengthening rewarded stimulus-response connections. However, some details, for example the asymmetry of effects of "right" and "wrong" and the effects of variation in the number of alternatives available, were not readily accountable in terms of the simple Law of Effect. Later analyses by Buchwald (1969) supported, rather, the view that subjects acquire information about the various relations between symbol, action, and outcome independently and then use the information in memory to direct choices. A very similar interpretation was proposed by Keller, Cole, Burke, and Estes (1965) for their finding that the effect of differential reward magnitudes on human binary choice learning depends strongly on the way information about reward values is conveyed to the subject.

Thus, by about 1970, it seemed that one might regard the Law of Effect as being limited to lower organisms and adopt a simple cognitive interpretation of human learning based on the idea that individuals simply learn, that is memorize, relationships between their choices and the values of outcomes and then use this information in a rational way to guide future choices (Atkinson & Wickens, 1971). As usual in such instances, however, investigators continued to seek new ways of finding whether such a simple interpretation could really be wholly satisfactory, and, as often happens, the answer proved to be no. In studies reported by Allen (1972) and Allen & Estes (1972), subjects engaged in trial-and-error learning of essentially the Thorndikian variety, but rather than receiving simple announcements of "right" or "wrong" following responses they were given rewards of different quantitative values. Further, during the course of choice learning, the experimenter occasionally interrupted the trial sequence and probed the subjects' memories for the reward values, obtaining the finding, unsettling for the simple cognitive interpretation, that characteristically subjects learned to make uniformly correct choices before they were able to recall the correct reward values. This result was a surprise at the time, but might perhaps have been anticipated on the basis of Thorndike's earlier findings with post-experimental memory probes.

Additional evidence casting doubt on the idea that individuals characteristically memorize outcome values was obtained in a series of studies in which I generalized the traditional paradigm of differential reward learning in a way calculated to make it difficult or impossible for subjects to solve the choice problem by rote memorization (Estes, 1976). In experiments done up to that time, the standard procedure was to assign a specific reward value to each alternative available in the choice learning situation, so that learning specific associations between alternatives and values was at least possible. In the modified design, I assigned to each alternative, rather, a set of values from which the particular reward or payoff given on a particular trial following a choice was determined by random sampling. Thus, as illustrated in the upper portion of Figure 2.10 for a two-choice problem, the values 6, 8, and 9 might be assigned to one alternative in a particular problem and the values 4, 5, and 6 to the other, the procedure being to draw a value at

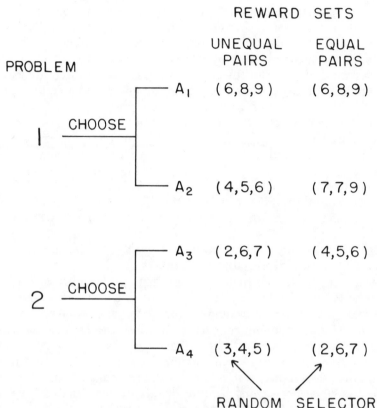

REWARD SETS

Figure 2.10 Schema for binary choice learning with reward sets. When a given problem is presented on a trial, the subject chooses from the pair of alternatives offered, then sees an outcome selected randomly from the corresponding reward set. The reward sets assigned to a problem normally differ in average value (Unequal Pairs), but in one special case are of equal average value (Equal Pairs).

random from the appropriate set whenever that alternative was chosen. Since the average reward value would be higher for one alternative than the other over a series of trials, there was a basis for selective learning, provided that subjects could make use of the probabilistic information. Learning all of the associations between alternatives and assigned values would be possible, but it would be very difficult, because in an experiment a subject would cycle through a number of problems, each having a different pair of alternatives with different reward sets, and on any one trial would obtain information only as to the particular value sampled from the set corresponding to the alternative chosen. Nonetheless, learning proved to be almost as fast as in the simple standard situation, and once subjects had learned to choose with greater than chance probability the higher-valued member of each of several pairs, appropriate choices were made with considerable success when alternatives were re-paired on transfer tests. Further, as in the simpler situation, probabilities of choices on transfer tests proved to be predictable on the assumption that the consequence of learning was the development of a memory representation in which different alternatives are, in effect, represented in a structure akin to a scale of measurement, with differences in average value corresponding to distances between the representations on the scale.

How could a representation of this kind take form if subjects do not start by learning the actual values of outcomes? A hypothesis was suggested by consideration of the situations outside the laboratory, where, except when rewards are calibrated in money, values generally are not expressable in numbers at all. Thus, for example, upon hearing a number of lectures or visiting a number of different restaurants, one might be convinced that the lectures or the meals deserved quite different evaluations on different occasions and might even be able to remember quite well that one lecture was much more informative than another, that one meal was slightly better than another, and so on, even though these memories would not be representable by numerical values. What one can, and probably does, do is to remember enough of the details of an experience such as hearing a lecture or eating a meal so that on the next experience of similar kind one can make a mental comparison and decide whether the second was better or worse than the first. In a model that proved to account quite well for all of the choice learning results up to that time, with either the standard or the novel designs, I assumed that these comparisons are indeed made, that the results of the comparisons are stored in memory just as any kind of event, and that information concerning frequencies of these events comes to be represented in memory just as the frequencies of trial outcomes in probability learning (Estes, 1976).

ANOTHER LOOK AT THE ROLE OF MEMORY

With this model and its supporting evidence in hand, it might have seemed that the issue of information versus effect had been finally settled. Evidently human learning in choice situations is a matter of the individual's making comparisons of the values or utilities attached to events of a given type that occur in close temporal succession, recording the outcomes of these comparisons in memory, and building representations of the relative frequency with which one alternative is valued over another, this memory structure in turn providing a basis for improving choice behavior with experience. Yet again, however, it subsequently proved possible to contrive new variations in procedure that would submit the emerging theory to still more exacting tests and reveal points of inadequacy, or at least incompleteness. In my continuation beyond the studies reported in 1976, the next step was actually quite simple in conception. All experiments to date on differential reward learning had been con- ducted, naturally enough, with the alternatives offered for choice in any particular problem (for example, the different treatments available for a given hypothetical disability), differing in value, at least on the average, over a series of trials. What should we expect to happen if the difference were reduced to zero, so that, for a given problem, the alternatives between which the subject had to choose were of the same average value? With respect to any one such prob- lem, of course, the subject could not increase the probability of higher rewards with experience over a series of training trials. How- ever, if several such problems were experienced concurrently, dif- ferences in value between pairs might, on the cognitive interpretation, be expected to lead to learning that would be manifest on transfer trials.

To illustrate in terms of the treatment analogy, suppose that the subject were offered on some trials a choice between alternatives, A_1 and A_2, each of which had high but equal average values as treatments for a given disability, and on other trials a different pair of alternatives, A_3 and A_4, which had low but equal average values, as illustrated in the lower portion of Figure 2.10. If during training with these, the individual builds up a mental representation of the average value associated with each alternative, then on a subsequent transfer test in which, say, A_1 was presented together with A_3, the individual would have a basis for choosing the treatment of probable higher value.

Just such a design was realized in an experiment conducted with 24 student subjects, the same apparatus and general procedures as those of the choice experiments reported in Estes (1976), and the following design. During training a subject was cycled randomly through a list of three problems, each problem comprising an identi- fying symbol (corresponding to a disability in the analogy) and two alternatives (corresponding to treatments). As illustrated in the upper panel of Figure 2.11, one problem had alternatives A_1 and

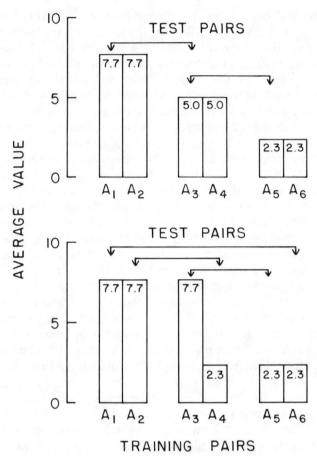

Figure 2.11 Upper Panel: Design of experiment in which training was given with only Equal Pairs. Lower Panel: Design of experiment including both Equal and Unequal training pairs. In both cases, training was followed by the indicated transfer tests.

A_2 each with average value 7.7. The second problem had alternatives A_3 and A_4, each with average value 5.0, and the third problem alternatives A_5 and A_6, each with average value 2.3. The values were calibrated in points, displayed as trial outcomes and cumulated until the end of the experiment when they were convertible to monetary payments.

The proportions of choices within each problem during a training series[1] are essentially meaningless, and all that is of interest is the result when on transfer tests a test pair was made up of alternatives drawn from two different training problems. On the first set of these tests given after the training series, the proportion of choices of the higher-valued members of the test pairs was .52, based on 96 observations, clearly not different from chance. Thus, although the subjects had had the same opportunity to learn the average reward values of the alternatives as in the previous experiments, this information, if indeed acquired and stored in memory, did not lead to greater than chance preference of higher-valued alternatives on the tests.

What could account for this apparent failure to learn, given that the subjects had had equivalent numbers of trials and opportunities to learn associations between alternatives and average outcome values as had characterized the earlier experiments in which learning was uniformly quite rapid? A hint as to a possible answer may be had by referring back to my 1976 model, in which it is assumed that the building of relevant memory representations of value scales depends on the individual's actively comparing current trial outcomes with those remembered from immediately preceding trials and remembering the outcomes of these comparisons. Perhaps in a situation where it is found to be impossible to improve the probability of success of one's choices, individuals either do not make these comparisons or do not rehearse the results of them in the way necessary to enter them in long-term memory. If this idea has substance, learning with respect to equal-valued alternatives might occur if the design were modified just sufficiently to produce comparison and rehearsal strategies more like those of the earlier experiments.

The design of an experiment suggested by this line of reasoning is shown in the lower panel of Figure 2.11. The procedure was the same as before, but, as illustrated in the figure within the three pairs of alternatives, A_1 and A_2 were assigned equal average values of 7.7; A_3 and A_4 unequal values of 7.7 and 2.3, respectively; and A_5 and A_6 equal values of 2.3. The fact that performance on the "learnable" A_3 versus A_4 problem could be improved by control processes of attending to differences in reward values and encoding results of the comparisons in memory might motivate the employment of these processes on all problems throughout training. Further, the high value of the unequal pair was common only to two of the equal-valued alternatives and the low value to the other two. Thus an effective strategy for the subjects would have been to categorize together all of the alternatives with high average values, and similarly those with low values, and to encode only the relative positions of those two categories on a preference scale. If this strategy were followed, the higher-valued alternatives should be preferred on all types of transfer tests.

The results were very clear. Denoting high and low members of the learnable pair by H and L and the members of the high and low equal pairs by E and e, respectively, initial tests of the type H-e (for example, A_3 versus A_5) yielded 92% correct choices, tests of the type E-e (for example, A_1 versus A_6) 90% correct choices, and tests of the type E-L (for example, A_2 versus A_4) 79% correct choices. In brief, the subjects exhibited highly efficient test performance in all cases where they had had opportunity to acquire the necessary information, whether the alternatives involved came from equal- or unequal-valued training pairs.

These findings clearly could not have been predicted from the Law of Effect, nor from an equally simple cognitive principle based simply on the memorization of associations between choices and values of outcomes. Together with other findings discussed above, these results indicate an important role of memory in reinforcement, but not memory in the customary literal sense. Individuals undoubtedly can and do remember rewarding or punishing episodes if the events are recent, or even when remote if they are unique or unusual. However, cumulating experimental evidence indicates that, except in such special cases, people generally form memory structures that suffice to mediate appropriate choices but that do not include information sufficient to enable later recall or reconstruction of the actual values of previous rewards or punishments. Evidently the structure has the properties of a preference scale on which previously experienced alternatives are encoded in relative positions corresponding to the results of earlier comparisons of experienced with remembered values. Further it seems clear that forming such a memory structure in the course of experience in a choice learning situation is not accomplished automatically or effortlessly and that the necessary control processes, presumably having to do with selective attention and rehearsal, are engaged in only if the learner has reason to categorize the situation as one in which relative values of current and remembered outcomes are likely to be relevant to future choices.

Clearly an adequate account of human choice learning requires a rather broadly based theory that takes account of the contributions of a number of aspects of attention and memory. Among these are concepts that, in the current terminology of cognitive psychology, refer to top-down or concept-driven as distinguished from bottom-up or data-driven processes. What an individual learns as a consequence of experiences in a choice situation appears to depend strongly on the way he or she categorizes the situation with regard to the potential relevance of particular kinds of information to future choices (Bandura, 1977; Estes, 1972; Nuttin & Greenwald, 1968). The categorization is determined both by instructions or task orientation and by early experience in the given situation. As a consequence of varied prior experiences, the normal adult evidently comes to an experiment with an assemblage of schemata, or conceptual schemes, containing information as to what events are relevant and what relationships between events require attention in a particular type of learning situation. The way a new situation is categorized then determines which of these schemata is retrieved from long-term memory and provides a basis for organizing attentional and learning processes. But once attention has been directed to the appropriate relationships, characteristically learning proceeds with surprising speed and efficiency even in experimental situations so complex in design that the experimenter needs a computer to keep track of the contingencies. The most significant consequence of the learning is the formation of memory representations with abstract properties well suited to maximize transfer to related situations. This theoretical picture is a far cry from the Law of Effect, or even early cognitive interpretations, but in complexity it seems to be the minimum needed to account for the salient aspects of human selective learning.

ONTOGENY AND PHYLOGENY IN THE INTERPRETATION OF CHOICE LEARNING

If the conclusion is correct that adult learning in specific situations is determined to an important extent by long-term consequences of prior learning in other situations, then we might expect to obtain additional evidence bearing on the theory that has emerged by going beyond particular experiments with normal adult subjects and looking for data on the way characteristically adult modes of learning develop. The kind of research needed falls outside my own competence, but some relevant results can be found in a study conducted in conjunction with my overall program of research on reinforcement by K. W. Estes (1971).

This study started from the supposition that the adult human being is not only an information processor but also a product of a developmental history during which he has acquired through experience the strategies that he brings to problems in or out of the laboratory. Might it be that a relatively primitive mechanism, which allows only for increasing the likelihood of repetition of more highly rewarded responses, gives way in the course of intellectual development to mechanisms that involve the acquisition of information concerning alternatives and outcome values and a more flexible utilization of this information in the determination of performance?

One way to obtain some relevant evidence would be to study children at a series of age levels, utilizing an experimental design that would permit either mode of response. As the experiment was conducted, children at the prekindergarten, kindergarten, first, and second grade levels participated as subjects, with a procedure and apparatus similar in essentials to those used by Zeaman and House (1963) in their many studies of discrimination learning in mentally retarded children.

On each trial a child was presented with a pair of stimuli (colored forms) that covered cups in which different numbers of reward tokens had been placed prior to the trial. The child selected one of the stimuli and received the reward in the cup below it. During the series of training trials the children had experience with two pairs (see Figure 2.12). In the first, Stimulus *A* was associated with a reward of four tokens and *B* with two, whereas in the second problem, Stimulus *C* was associated with one token and *D* with zero. The two pairs were presented in random sequence (with varying left-right positions of the stimuli) until a criterion of seven correct choices on two consecutive 4-trial blocks was met, or 60 trials had elapsed; then transfer tests were given. The entire procedure was then replicated with a new set of stimuli.

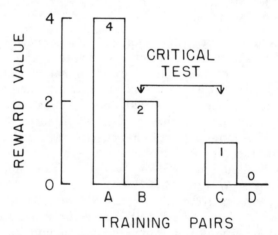

Figure 2.12 Design of K. W. Estes (1971) experiment, conducted with young children. Training was given on the two unequal pairs shown and followed by transfer tests, the one indicated being of special theoretical interest.

The data in which we are particularly interested are those of test trials given at the end of this training, in which Stimulus *B*, the lower-valued member of the first problem was paired with Stimulus *C*, the higher-valued of the second problem. This test was given twice, once in each left-right arrangement of the stimuli, with tests on other pairs interspersed. During the original training the children all learned nearly always to choose *A* over *B* and *C* over *D*. If they simply carried over the acquired approach and avoidance tendencies to the test problem, then they would be expected to choose *C* over *B* since *C* was one that they had learned to select and *B* one that they had learned to avoid. But if they learned associations between stimuli and reward values, then on the test trial they would choose the stimulus of higher value.

The data on this critical transfer trial, given in Table 2.1, show an interesting age pattern. In the first test of the first replication, the children chose the higher-valued alternative less than half the time; in other words they tended to carry over their previous learned approach and avoidance tendencies to the transfer test. On the second test, and throughout the second replication, the choice proportions of the second grade children shifted to a significant preference for the stimulus of value 2 (the former "loser") over the stimulus of value 1 (the former "winner"). The same trend appears in weaker form for the younger children. Thus, as a joint function of age and experience in the situation, we see a progression from what might be termed a more primitive strategy of carrying over specific stimulus-response tendencies to what might be termed a more cognitive strategy of transfer on the basis of acquired information concerning reward values.

However, even for the older children, as for the adults in my experiments and those of Thorndike, there is evidence that choices

Table 2.1 Percentages of Choices of Higher-Valued Alternative in Children's Transfer Tests

Age Group	Replication 1		Replication 2	
	1st Test	2nd Test	1st Test	2nd Test
Prekindergarten	32	40	44	56
Kindergarten	32	41	41	59
First Grade	41	41	45	45
Second Grade	25	63	67	75

Note: Tests were on the stimulus pair *B* vs. *C* after training with the pairs *A* vs. *B* (reward values 4 and 2, respectively) and *C* vs. *D* (reward values 1 and 0, respectively).

could not have been made entirely on the basis of memory for specific reward values. After the transfer tests in each replication, the experimenter held up the individual stimulus blocks one at a time and asked the child how many tokens had been found under the stimulus when it was chosen. The results showed poor recall of the intermediate values (less than 25% for the youngest children and less than 50% even for second graders), better recall of the 0 value (60–70%), and substantial recall of the 4 value (ranging from about 60% for prekindergarteners to 90% for second graders). Of special interest, the children often assigned the value 4 to stimuli actually having other values; and the oldest children did so much more frequently for stimuli of actual value 1, the high member of the 1–0 pair, than for stimuli of actual value 2, the low member of the 4–2 pair, the percentages of these errors being 37% and 21%, respectively. It appears that as the children shift toward the adult mode of transfer with increasing age and experience, they, like the adults, come to respond on the basis of a mental scale of preference rather than on the basis of specific memories of the outcomes of previous choices.

One might interpret these findings as showing that there is a basic reinforcement process whereby events that follow responses exert strengthening or weakening effects proportional to their reward values, but that in the course of development higher-level cognitive processes may come to mask the reinforcement process. Perhaps so, but I believe that there is more to be said for a somewhat different interpretation. I suggest that at all levels of development, the concept of reinforcement refers to a feedback mechanism that guides performance and that the effects of current reinforcement on future behavior always depend on the acquisition of information concerning relations between cues, responses, and outcomes. However, the particular information acquired depends on factors that direct selective attention to some aspects of the situation rather than others. At an early age, the child is preoccupied with his own responses and their immediate consequences. At later ages, the child's attention characteristically shifts to the detection of environmental regularities and the categorization of situations according to the value of using information about these regularities to guide choices.

Reflecting on the whole collection of studies discussed in this and the preceding paper we can see that under sufficiently restricted conditions, organisms at a variety of phylogenetic and developmental levels ranging from rats through children to adult human beings can be induced to learn under conditions that can be described by such simple formulas as the Law of Effect or the principle of conditioning by contiguity. However there is neither logical nor empirical justification for elevating these descriptive formulas to the status of general laws and extrapolating them to all forms of animal and human behavior. Under less restrictive conditions, the same organisms exhibit learning that has not at all the character of automatic strengthening or weakening of responses but that rather lends itself to interpretation in terms of concepts of attention and memory. In understanding learning and the control of behavior at all levels, we may find that the concepts of selective attention and memory are the more general and therefore the more basic, and that principles such as the Law of Effect may prove to be only descriptions of special cases in which information acquired has to do with aspects of the organism's response and its consequences.

NOTE

1. The training series prior to the first test included 20 trials on each problem. In other experiments with the same subject population, apparatus, and procedure, in which the problems comprised unequal pairs having the differences in average reward value within pairs (7.7 vs. 5.0; 5.0 vs. 2.3) equal to differences between pairs in the present experiment, training series of the same length led to performance levels of 80–90% choices of the higher-valued members of test pairs. Hence, if learning were simply a matter of acquiring information about average reward values, there should have been comparable opportunity during training with equal and with unequal pairs.

REFERENCES

Allen, G. A. Memory probes during two-choice differential reward problems. *Journal of Experimental Psychology*, 1972, *95*, 78-89.

Allen, G. A., & Estes, W. K. Acquisition of correct choices and value judgments in binary choice learning with differential rewards. *Psychonomic Science*, 1972, *27*, 68-72.

Atkinson, R. C., & Wickens, T. D. Human memory and the concept of reinforcement. In R. Glaser (Ed.), *The nature of reinforcement*, pp. 66-120. New York: Academic Press, 1971.

Bandura, A. Self-efficacy. *Psychological Review*, 1977, *84*, 191-215.

Buchwald, A. M. Effects of "right" and "wrong" on subsequent behavior: A new interpretation. *Psychological Review*, 1969, *76*, 132-143.

Estes, K. W. Transfer following two-choice, differential reward learning in children. *Psychonomic Science*, 1971, *25*, 317-321.

Estes, W. K. Reinforcement in human learning. In J. Tapp (Ed.), *Reinforcement and behavior*, pp. 63–94. New York: Academic Press, 1969.

Estes, W. K. Reward in human learning. Theoretical issues and strategic choice points. In R. Glaser (Ed.), *The nature of reinforcement*, pp. 16–36. New York: Academic Press, 1971.

Estes, W. K. Reinforcement in human behavior. *American Scientist*, 1972, *60*, 723–729.

Estes, W. K. Some functions of memory in probability learning and choice behavior. In G. H. Bower (Ed.), *The psychology of learning and motivation: Advances in research and theory*, Vol. 10, pp. 1–45. New York: Academic Press, 1976.

Estes, W. K. Cognitive processes in reinforcement and choice. In G. d'Y dewalle and W. Lens (Eds.), *Cognition in human motivation and learning*, pp. 123–140. Leuven: Leuven University Press; and Hillsdale, N.J.: Lawrence Erlbaum Associates, 1981.

Keller, L., Cole, M., Burke, C. J., & Estes, W. K. Reward and information values of trial outcomes in paired-associate learning. *Psychological Monographs*, 1965, *79* (12, Whole No. 605).

Nuttin, J., & Greenwald, A. G. *Reward and punishment in human learning.* New York: Academic Press, 1968.

Siegel, S. Theoretical models of choice and strategy behavior: Stable state behavior in the two-choice uncertain outcome situation. *Psychometrika*, 1959, *24*, 303–316.

Tanner, W. P., & Swets, J. A. A decision-making theory of visual detection. *Psychological Review*, 1954, *61*, 401–409.

Thorndike, E. L. *Human learning.* New York: Appleton-Century-Crofts, 1931.

Zeaman, D., & House, B. J. The role of attention in retardate discrimination learning. In N. R. Ellis (Ed.), *Handbook of mental deficiency*, pp. 159–223. New York: McGraw-Hill, 1963.

The Cognitive Side of Probability Learning

Probability learning has been somewhat eclipsed in the literature of cognitive psychology by an increasing preoccupation with psycholinguistics and the semantic aspects of memory. Nonetheless, it should be recognized that we are scarcely in a position to close the chapter of research on this aspect of human learning. First, the reasons, both theoretical and practical, that were responsible for the wave of interest in probability learning during the 1950s have by no means evaporated. Rather, it continues to be apparent that probability learning constitutes a major interface between cognitive psychology and the practical world. Second, major problems of methodology and interpretation remain unsolved. And third, as I propose to show in the following pages, new findings are emerging that may bring the study of probability learning closer to the mainstream of research on human memory and information processing.

SOME PROBLEMS IN NEED OF A THEORY

A theme expressed earlier by, for example, Cohen (1964) and Restle (1961) is the keynote of a new exploration by Kahneman and Tversky (1972) of the fallibility of human probability judgments: "Subjective probabilities play an important role in our lives. The decisions we make, the conclusions we reach and the explanations we offer are usually based on our judgments of the likelihood of uncertain events" (p. 430).

Among the specific areas where probability learning can be expected to play a central role are economics, clinical judgment and medical diagnosis, and the control of human behavior by reinforce-

W. K. Estes, The Cognitive side of probability learning. *Psychological Review*, 1976, *83*, 37–64. Copyright 1976 by the American Psychological Association. Reprinted by permission of the publisher.

This paper was presented, in substance, as an invited address at the May, 1974 meetings of the Midwestern Psychological Association.

Research reported herein was supported by Public Health Service Grants MH16100 and MH23878 from the National Institute of Mental Health.

I am indebted to Edith Skaar for assistance with every aspect of the experimental work and data processing.

ment. In the area of economics, besides the techniques already available for assessing opinions and beliefs after the fact, a body of theory is required that will enable prediction of changes in people's beliefs and expectations in response to fluctuations in economic variables. In the medical area, it has been shown in both experimental (Estes, 1972a) and clinical (Goldberg, 1970) settings that human judges whose tasks require them to make decisions on the basis of their knowledge of probabilities perform with far from maximal efficiency. In fact, they are often outdone by models which consistently use the same decision strategies that are manifested, though less uniformly, in their own behavior. Thus, a major question remains to be answered by research and theory: Where do the judges fall short—in processing information regarding probabilities of uncertain events or in making choices based on states of information?

With regard to the control of human behavior by reinforcement, the old picture of the human learner being shaped relentlessly by the effects of rewards and punishments via their strengthening and weakening influences on stimulus–response connections or habit strengths has given way to a view of the human organism as an information processor and decision maker using, rather than being driven by, informative feedback from the consequences of his actions. The individual is seen as actively sampling the alternative courses of action available in a choice situation, generating expectations about the probable consequences of the actions based on his past experience, and tending to select the responses yielding the higher expectations of success (Atkinson & Wickens, 1971; Estes, 1969, 1972b; Greeno, 1968). However, in the research that is needed to subject this newer conception to rigorous test, expectations and decisions can only be inferred from performance. Once again, adequate models are needed to provide a framework within which we can effectively study the hypothetical processes and mechansims.

ALTERNATIVE MODELS FOR PROBABILITY LEARNING

The expenditure over several decades of a great deal of effort directed toward the development of such models has led to an extremely mixed picture. Even if we limit attention to models that have evolved within the framework of learning theory, three main types can be identified: (a) incremental learning models, (b) all-or-none coding models, and (c) hypothesis-testing models. In the first category are the familiar linear models of stimulus-sampling theory

(Bush & Mosteller, 1955; Estes & Straughan, 1954); in the second, the pattern model (Estes, 1959) and schema models (Restle, 1961). In the third class are Bayesian approaches, which, in effect, treat the learner as an intuitive statistician (Shuford, 1964), and more psychologically oriented models such as that of Castellan and Edgell (1973).

A curious outcome of numerous applications of these three types of models to data is that each has produced some striking successes. The linear, or stimulus-sampling, models have provided quite satisfactory descriptions of the course and terminal level of probability learning for a wide range of experiments on predictive behavior over limited numbers of trials (typically 1 to 300) and a close account of numerous detailed properties of data in some situations (Estes, 1972c; Friedman et al., 1964; Suppes & Atkinson, 1960). Discrepancies between models and data begin to appear as one deviates from the restrictive boundary conditions and attempts to deal with long sequences of trials, with many alternative choices, or with asymmetric payoffs for correct and incorrect predictions.

Predictions from the pattern model agree with those of the linear model regarding overall learning curves in most situations, but they differ with respect to variances and sequential statistics. In two-choice situations with noncontingent event probabilities, the pattern model has proven superior to the linear model in predicting detailed sequential properties of data and has in fact been notably successful in a few instances (Yellott, 1969).

Hypothesis-testing models have dealt largely with asymptotic behavior. Even the best developed model of this type, that of Castellan and Edgell (1973), does not attempt to account for the course of learning but simply assumes that the learner somehow develops subjective probabilities at least roughly in accord with objective probabilities. Hypothesis-testing models have in a number of cases provided excellent accounts of asymptotic performance even in quite complex situations (Castellan & Edgell, 1973; Friedman, Rollins, & Padilla, 1968), but they have not addressed the details of learning or sequential properties of performance.

Although none of these models comes close to providing a satisfactory account of the broad range of probability learning data, the instances of accurate predictions for substantial bodies of data in particular cases can scarcely be attributed to chance. Evidently, the different models are capturing different aspects of a complex process, some aspects being more prominent in some situations. One would like to replace the collection of locally successful models with one general theory, but this objective may not be within our

capabilities. A more feasible immediate goal may be to try to understand why different models are required to deal with different
situations.

ON THE SEPARATION OF INFORMATION
AND DECISION PROCESSES

Progress toward this goal may depend on better analyses both of
learning and of performance. However closely intermeshed these
may be in the individual's behavior, we can at least conceptually
separate questions concerning the nature of the information an
individual acquires about environmental probabilities and the way in
which he generates choices on the basis of this acquired information.
In the present study I shall concentrate on questions of the former
type for two reasons: First, in the literature of probability learning,
the question of exactly *what* is learned has been relatively neglected;
second, in the current literature of cognitive psychology, there is
much that is new in both methodology and theories of memory
and information processing that might be, but so far has not been,
applied to the interpretation of probability learning.

Extant theories of probability learning are primarily, though to
varying extents, performance rather than learning models. They have
been concerned mostly with what the individual achieves in a choice
situation rather than with the basis for achievement. The so-called
"learning models" have been primarily concerned with the rules for
changes in performance; the hypothesis-testing models, with the
way in which the individual performs when his memory is characterized by various possible states of knowledge. Thus, the basic assumptions of the linear and stimulus-sampling models prescribe how the
probabilities of various predictive responses by the learner change
as a function of outcomes. In the pattern models it is presumed
that the individual succeeds in encoding recurring patterns of stimulation as units; the assumptions of the pattern models prescribe the
probabilities with which the individual attends to different types of
patterns and the predictive responses he makes when these patterns
occur. In hypothesis-testing models, the formal assumptions specify
the probabilities with which the subject selects various stimulus dimensions or cues as relevant to a choice problem; they also specify
the decision mechanism as a process of basing choices on the subjective probabilities of various outcomes occurring when these relevant
cues are attended to (Castellan & Edgell, 1973).

None of the models of any of the three classes comes to grips
with the problem of how information on environmental probabilities

is represented in the memory system. Thus the possibility arises that attention to this neglected problem might prove fruitful in a number of respects. Ideas drawn from current theories of memory and information processing may help to organize both the phenomena and the theories and may provide clues to why such different models seem required under different circumstances.

THE RELEVANCE OF CONCEPTS OF MEMORY

In the experimental analysis of probability learning, research seems often to have proceeded from one study to the next with little attention to reformulating the problems from time to time in the light of theoretical advances in related areas. It may be instructive to step back for a moment and attempt to place the kind of behavior studied in these experiments in the broader context of learning and memory in relation to environmental uncertainties.

In general, we generate predictions by recognizing a new situation as one of a class of situations to which some rule applies. The rules with which we have to deal can be ordered in terms of complexity. For the normal adult, the rules often take the form of laws, principles, or formulas gained from scientific or technical training. For the most part, predictive behavior based on these formal rules is beyond our present capacity for experimental or theoretical analysis; perhaps the one small step beyond sheer description is to be found in the studies of sequence learning (e.g., Myers, 1976; Restle & Brown, 1970; Wolin, Weichel, Terebinski, & Hansford, 1965).

But the predictive behavior of animals and young children, and even much of that observed in adults, is based not on formal rules but only on the experience an individual gains from his observation of recurrences of a given type of situation, together with his faith in the uniformity of nature. In everyday life, as well as in science, we always tend to assume that the repetition of the same combination of circumstances will lead to the same outcome. Concepts of causality and determinism express an idealization of this rule of thumb as an abstract principle, representing a limiting case of our experience rather than a result of direct observation. What we do observe is that, generally, the more nearly circumstances are reinstated, the greater is the likelihood of the same outcome.

When repeated occurrences of apparently the same combination of circumstances yield different outcomes, we form expectations on the basis of relative frequencies. The most frequent outcome in the past is assumed, other things being equal, to be the most likely in the future. The study of the way these expectations develop in simplified situations that provide no other sources of information is the study of probability learning as this concept has evolved in the research literature (Björkman, 1966).

In terms of current cognitive theory, what processes should we expect to play important roles in this type of learning? A logical analysis of the problem of prediction brings out aspects relative to both sides of the distinction between episodic and semantic memory, a distinction which has become increasingly prominent in current research and theory. As introduced by Tulving (1972), *episodic memory* refers to recall or recognition of events in context. Restle's schema theory might be regarded as a direct extension of the concept of episodic memory. Restle (1961) assumes that the full pattern of events occurring on each trial of an experiment gives rise to a schema that is stored as a unit in the memory system; the basis for an individual's predictive behavior in new situations is a comparison of the new pattern of stimulation with the various schemata stored in memory, with the expectation that the outcome of the present situation will be the same as the outcome of the most similar situation represented in the memory store. The pattern model (Estes, 1959) can be given a similar interpretation.

The counterpart to episodic memory in Tulving's classification is *semantic memory*, referring to the long-term representation of concepts and relations between concepts. However, it should be noted that concepts can be defined in terms of classes of events and need not be linguistic in character. Thus, I suggest that a better classification for our purposes would be *episodic* versus *categorical* memory. In the case of probability learning, categorical memory refers to the representation of relative frequencies of classes, or categories, in memory. These representations may be tapped directly in experiments on verbal discrimination learning (Ekstrand, Wallace, & Underwood, 1966) and relative frequency judgments (Hintzman, 1969). It seems pertinent to inquire whether these representations may not also play an important role in predictive behavior and probability estimates.

AN EXPERIMENTAL DESIGN FOR THE ANALYSIS OF PROBABILITY LEARNING BASED ON CATEGORICAL MEMORY

If analysis of the probability learning situation in terms of memory concepts is basically correct, then the data from the standard experiments must represent a mixture of contributions from episodic and categorical memory. On some occasions during a sequence of trials, the subject may recognize a familiar pattern (for example, a run of three consecutive occurrences of the E_1 outcome light in a Humphreys-type experiment) and remember the outcome that previously followed this pattern; on other occasions he may not recognize a familiar pattern but may nonetheless be able to improve his guess concerning the next outcome by using information he has acquired about probabilities of event categories.

In a series of experiments reported elsewhere (Estes, 1976a) I proceeded from this analysis to construct a revision of the usual probability learning experimental paradigm so that one of the component memory processes would be reduced to negligible proportions, thus leaving a clear picture of the other component. The task was presented as a simulation of a public opinion poll preceding an election. The subjects were told that on a series of observation trials they would be presented with simulated data from opinion polls about three pairs of potential candidates (A_1 vs. A_2, A_3 vs. A_4, and A_5 vs. A_6) for a subsequent election. The subjects' task was simply to observe the opinion poll data on the observation trials and attempt to form impressions of the relative likelihood of wins and losses for each of the various candidates. Attending to or rehearsing particular runs of wins or losses would clearly be irrelevant to the task since the subject was tested on his acquired knowledge only on a block of test trials given without feedback following a long series of observation trials. Furthermore, during the test block the subject was also asked to predict election winners from various pairs of candidates (for example, A_1 vs. A_3) that had not been paired during the observation trials. Under these conditions, it was expected that subjects would base their predictions on accrued categorical information concerning the various candidates' relative probabilities of wins and losses.

The results of these experiments seem quite clearly to confirm my conjecture that in the usual probability learning experiment, the subject's performance reflects a mixture of learning categorical frequencies and attempting to learn sequential patterns that actually hinder efficient prediction. With the observation-transfer design, learning proved to be more rapid and more precise than has been characteristic in standard probability learning experiments. Even though the differences in event probabilities among the various alternatives were small compared to those usually studied (.62–.38, .58–.42, and .54–.46 for the three observation pairs, respectively), the subjects' proportions of correct predictions on test pairs lined up as an orderly monotone function of the probability differences between the test alternatives, with performance fully as good on new pairs as on observation pairs.

One might wonder whether the subjects were simply learning an ordering of candidates rather than actually acquiring specific information concerning success probabilities. To find out, I investigated an additional variation of the basic design, illustrated in Figure 2.13. Two subjects were given a series of observation trials on the three pairs of candidates labeled Set A, who had the win—loss probabilities (π values) indicated by the bar diagrams; the subjects were then given observation trials on the three pairs of candidates labeled Set B, these pairs having the same combination of π values

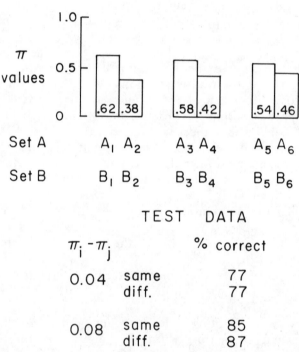

Figure 2.13 Design and results of experiment in which subjects had observation trials on two sets of alternatives, A and B, separately with the π values indicated above, and then tests on new stimulus pairs formed by recombining members of the same set (same) or by pairing a member of Set A with a member of Set B (diff.).

as the corresponding pairs of Set A. Finally, the subjects were given a series of test trials in which test pairs were formed within each set (e.g., A_1 vs. A_2, A_1 vs. A_4) and also across the two sets (e.g., A_1 vs. B_2, A_3 vs. B_5). If the subjects had learned only the ordering within each set they would be helpless on these tests of the A_i versus B_j type.

The test data summarized at the bottom of Figure 2.13 reveal rather impressive performance. When the members of a test pair differed by .08 in π value, the subjects predicted correctly 85% to 87% of the time, and when the members of a pair differed by only .04, subjects were still correct 77% of the time. Perhaps more strikingly, accuracy of prediction was almost exactly as good for between-sets test pairs (A_i vs. B_j) as for within-set test pairs. Clearly, the subjects had not simply learned orderings of the particular stimuli within each set but rather had acquired information about probabilities of outcomes. It appears that the subjects must have formed representations in memory equivalent to a scale on which the various alternatives (candidates) are placed in positions reflecting their relative probabilities of winning.

GENERAL DISCUSSION: INTERPRETATIONS AND APPLICATIONS

Summary of Major Findings

Our preliminary examination of the present state of knowledge concerning probability learning pointed up the need for untangling the varying contributions of learning and performance variables to the patterns of results obtained with different subject populations and different experimental procedures. Accordingly, throughout the present series of studies I have tried to reduce variance attributable to various determinants of performance by simplifying the subject's decision problem, and thus to bring out in clearer relief the information-processing components of probability learning.

The periods within each experiment during which the subjects were able to obtain information concerning event probabilities were segregated from the periods during which they were tested for their ability to predict events, thus minimizing subjects' tendency to treat the experiment as a guessing game. Furthermore, subjects were always fully instructed concerning the probabilistic nature of the task, and they were encouraged to base their choices on the information about event probability that they had accumulated from their observations of sequences of trial outcomes.

Under these circumstances, learning proved to be extremely rapid and precise compared to that usually found in classical probability learning experiments, even though the present experiments generally presented more difficult tasks in terms of the numbers of probabilistic combinations the subjects had to deal with simultaneously.

But at the same time, the results suggest that the term "probability learning" is in a sense a misnomer. I have found nothing to encourage the tendency to think of probability learning as a basic or unitary process or as a direct manifestation of a capacity for perceiving the statistical structure of sequences of events. The subjects clearly are extremely efficient at acquiring information concerning relative frequencies of events. But by appropriately modifying the instructions on how subjects are to respond on individual observation trials, I have shown that they acquire this information selectively about the events to which they attend. The result is that under some circumstances, the information subjects acquire leads them to make judgments that appear to reflect differences in probabilities of events with great fidelity, but under slightly different circumstances, equally efficient operation of the same learning process leads them to make judgments of likelihoods of events that are widely at variance with the actual probabilities.

The apparent trade-off between stimulus frequency and outcome probability observed in a number of the present experiments might be taken to indicate that subjects confuse familiarity of a stimulus with the probability that it leads to a winning outcome. However, appropriate controls showed that stimulus frequency per se does not influence choice probability, the apparent effects being attributable to inefficiency or bias in the process of encoding events in memory.

The best characterization of the learning process I can offer at present is that subjects categorize the events involved in a task and then learn relative frequencies within classes. However, whether owing to lack of adequate training or to limitations of memory capacity, they do not always carry the process of categorization far enough for optimal performance on a given task.

Consider, for example, the situation in which the task involves a simulated public opinion poll with several pairs of candidates for an election running against each other. In acquiring information concerning the results of the simulated preference survey, the subjects clearly categorize the trial outcomes appropriately in terms of wins and losses for individual alternatives, but they generally fail to assign to separate categories the data belonging to the pairs of stimuli that have been pitted against each other during the observation series. If the different pairs are represented equally often during the observation series, which has been almost invariably the case in previous studies of probability learning, this lack of second-order categorization leads to no error. But if we modify the usual procedure and present different pairs with different frequencies, subjects make very large errors of judgment, in some instances predicting that an alternative that has appeared frequently but as a consistent loser will be preferred to another alternative that has appeared infrequently but has been a consistent winner.

Information and Performance

Given our conclusion that probability learning is a derivative of frequency learning, how do we conceive the connection the learner makes between his state of frequency information and his predictive responses, or judgments of probability? I suggest, first of all, that there is no immutable general rule but rather that individuals bring frequency information to bear upon specific problems in accord with task requirements and relevant experience.

In situations of the type investigated in the present series of experiments, it appears that the learner translates the request for predictions based on probabilities into a request for relative frequency judgments. Thus, when an individual has had experience with a series of opinion polls and then is asked to predict the result of a preference test or an election, he predicts success for the alternative that he remembers as having had the greatest frequency of success in his past experience.

If, as in many classical probability learning experiments, the individual is led to believe that he is dealing with a problem situation that has a determinate solution, then I see no reason to assume that his trial-to-trial predictions will reflect trial-to-trial assessments of relative frequency. Rather, in the light of existing evidence on all-or-none learning (Estes, 1964; Restle, 1965), we might better assume that in situations of this type, the learner seeks ways of encoding recurring patterns of events in context, ways that enable him to base predictions on episodic memory of specific circumstances under which a to-be-predicted event occurred in the past.

However, this response system does not remain static or immune to effects of changing experience. During the series of trials in which an individual is responding in accord with these encodings, we might say at a descriptive level that he is using a response *strategy* as this term has been used, for example, by Restle (1962). Nonetheless, learning in the sense of accrual of relative frequency information continues. At some point, most likely following an error or a sequence of errors, the learner might be expected to reassess his state of frequency information and, if necessary, recode the events and thus change his response strategy.

Because the relationships between states of information and response rules are not well understood, it seems quite possible that various comparisons made in the probability learning literature, especially those involving different developmental levels, may be misleading. Consider, for example, the finding that in probability learning experiments younger children tend to show a strategy of maximizing successes, presumably the most rational approach to the situation, whereas older children tend to yield probability matching (Weir, 1964). It is possible, though, that the younger children are actually operating at a more primitive level, tending to ignore negative outcomes and to make choices directly reflecting their impressions of the frequency of positive outcomes, and that the older children are actually operating at a more sophisticated level, attending to both positive and negative outcomes and encoding events in terms of their information concerning relative frequencies of both. If this analysis is correct, then it follows that meaningful developmental comparisons will require experimental procedures that will lead children of different ages to follow similar response strategies and that will thus yield interpretable data reflecting differences in the nature or efficiency of learning in the sense of information processing.

Some Implications for Probability Learning
Outside the Laboratory

In terms of the revised theoretical formulation taking shape as a result of these new investigations, it appears that we can begin to make sense of some of the otherwise puzzling observations on characteristic human behavior in probabilistic situations outside the laboratory (Jenkins & Ward, 1965; Kahneman & Tversky, 1972; Smedslund, 1963; Brehmer, Note 1).

If we accept the idea that probability learning is actually based on the acquisition of information about frequency of various individual events occurring in a probabilistic situation, we can state two general conditions that must be met in any situation if the learning process is to lead to veridical estimates of probability by the learner: (a) The alternative events involved in a situation must have equal opportunities of occurrence and (b) the learner must attend to and encode occurrences of all of the alternative events with equal uniformity or efficiency.

Both of these conditions are probably satisfied quite well, for example, in learning to anticipate changes in the weather. Shifts toward both fair and foul weather have equal opportunities of occurrence, and quite likely both eventualities are clearly perceived and encoded by the human observer. However, in many other situations, these conditions must be uniformly and grossly violated. For example, in the primaries preceding a general election, it is common for different candidates to take part in different numbers of primaries. Similarly, in an individual's experience with alternative treatments or remedies for illnesses, it is probably most common for his experience with different subsets of remedies to be quite unequal, owing to the effects of advertising, hearsay, or simply habits of trying particular remedies. In these situations we must expect that learners will be almost entirely unable to correct for differences in numbers of opportunities and thus will often be misled in the probability estimates they form on the basis of experience. On the whole, they will tend to persist in choosing the more familiar candidate or remedy, not because of its familiarity per se, but because its more frequent occurrence in their experience has given it an opportunity to accumulate a greater total number of successes than its competitors that have been experienced less often.

Just as clearly, the requirement of equivalent attention to alternative outcomes is systematically violated in many practical situations. Conspicuous examples of this occur when individuals form impressions regarding the probability of crime in different localities or the probability of accidents using different modes of transportation. The occurrence of a crime or an accident is a clearly perceptible and readily encodable event that will inevitably leave its residue in the memory system. But a basic problem in each case, from the standpoint of the present analysis, is that there is no correspondingly clear-cut way for the learner to identify the individual occasions when there were opportunities for crimes or accidents to occur but they did not in fact transpire, that is, when there were negative outcomes. Thus, we might expect automobile drivers in a given locality to form very accurate impressions of the relative frequencies of accidents on the thruway and on a nearby city street but at the same time to have grossly distorted conceptions of the probability of having an accident during a given number of miles traveled in the two cases.

In general, we must evidently say that the term *probability learning* characterizes a type of problem situation rather than a type of learning. One and the same set of underlying processes can be expected to lead to highly efficient and veridical probability learning under some circumstances but to systematic and often gross distortions of probability estimates in others. Nothing in our analysis leads us to expect that it should be easy to train people to judge probabilities accurately in a wide range of practical situations, but it may still be possible to make progress in this direction once the nature of the problem and the processes of learning and performance are conceptualized within a satisfactory theoretical framework.

TOWARD A THEORY OF PROBABILITY LEARNING BASED ON CONCEPTS OF MEMORY

Characteristics of the Acquisition Process

In the earlier work on probability learning, the predominant strategy was to apply various highly specific mathematical or, in some cases, computer-simulation models to data, in the hope that one of them might prove to account for the detailed course of acquisition over varying experimental conditions. As I have noted above, it is apparent that many of these specific models do very well under particular circumstances, but none comes close to providing the desired generality. Consequently, in this essay I shall explore the alternative strategy of drawing upon a wide range of data for clues to the *type* of model that might have some generality. In this section I propose only to summarize where we stand in this respect and to present an example of a model that both accounts for the new information we have acquired and may help to bring out some theoretical connections between quite different types of experiments, though at the cost of not providing full and detailed quantitative accounts of the data of any one experiment.

First, let us summarize some of the salient characteristics of the probability learning process that must evidently characterize an adequate model.

1. When the learner is tested in the same contexts in which he has had an opportunity to make observations, and in particular when the situation involves only a few frequently recurring contexts, the learning of associations between outcomes and contextual patterns appears to be all-or-none in character.

2. When tests are given under contextual conditions quite different from those of observation trials (as in the experiments de-

scribed in this article), learning appears to be analog in character, with even very small differences in event probabilities being reflected in subjects' predictive tendencies.

3. Transfer performance following a sequence of multiple-cue probability learning trials has many of the properties that would be expected if the learner had formed a representation in memory of a scale on which different choice alternatives were positioned according to their frequencies of occurrence. These scale values appear not to represent absolute frequencies, but rather the frequencies with which instances of stimulus-outcome categories occur relative to instances of all other categories that occur in the given situation.

4. The event categories whose frequencies come to be represented in memory are those to which the individual is led to attend by the task orientation and training procedures.

5. Changes in scale values following a shift in event probabilities appear to be described by the learning operators characteristic of stimulus-sampling models rather than those of accumulative models such as Luce's beta model (1959) or the frequency counter model of Ekstrand, Wallace, and Underwood (1966).

Modes of Information Storage and Retrieval

As a first step toward formalization, I propose to consider the possibility of meeting the requirements sketched above with an associative theory of memory that takes account of the newer concepts of organization and retrieval strategies. I shall organize this discussion in terms of a particular variant, the associative coding model (Estes, 1973, 1976b). This model shares a number of ideas with Feigenbaum (1963) and Anderson and Bower (1973) with respect to the associative structure, with Johnson (1970) in regard to coding, and with Tulving (1968) concerning the conception of retrieval cues.

The basic information storage process in this model is conceived to be the formation of a memory trace representing the occurrence of an event in context. If an event E occurs in a context x, it is not assumed that an association forms between E and x directly, but rather that they become associated by way of a common control element C, as illustrated in Figure 2.14. This associative structure has the property that future reinstatement of the combination xE will activate the control element and hence any other representation in memory with which this control element is in turn associated. This associative unit may be more compactly represented by the

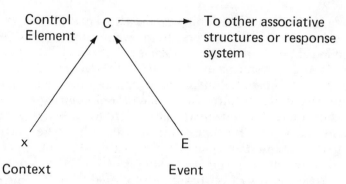

Figure 2.14 Schematic representation of associative memory structure representing the occurrence of an event E in a context x.

notation T_{xE}. In a two-choice probability learning situation, two types of events occur—E_1 and E_2 (which in the simulated preference surveys would be wins and losses, respectively)—and thus two types of traces would be stored, T_{xE_1} and T_{xE_2}. On a test trial, the test context would reactivate a trace of one type or the other and lead to the corresponding predictive response on the part of the subject.

Three types of contextual cues need to be distinguished, together with the possibility that memory storage may occur with respect to any of these, or even to all three types concurrently. These are (a) background cues that remain functional regardless of variations in event schedules, (b) local context, specific to a particular event schedule (including, for example, stimulus patterns associated with runs of like outcomes over successive trials), and (c) stimulation arising from internally generated "coding responses." The second and third types are assumed by virtually all theorists (see, e.g., Myers, 1976) to be of major importance in standard, two-choice prediction experiments; under noncontingent probability schedules, these are typically characterized by a relatively small number of frequently recurring event patterns (e.g., short runs, double alternations) to which subjects are known to attend (Feldman & Hanna, 1966). In the transfer design of the experiments reported in this article, local contextual cues arising from the training event sequences would not be present during transfer tests; therefore, test performance must be presumed to depend on memory traces associating outcome events with background cues.

Furthermore, there is evidence that under some circumstances subjects may shift attention from one type of context to another. Thus, Mandler, Cowan, and Gold (1964) observed that, in a concept learning experiment including correlated, partially valid cues, subjects exhibited probability matching with respect to the partially valid cues during the presolution period, but nonetheless went on to achieve 100% correct responding to the fully valid cues.

It is quite possible, and even likely, that subjects may simultaneously acquire information relating outcome events to both background and local context. This multiple processing may not be apparent during learning under a particular event schedule if subjects typically select one of the available types of context as a basis for responding, but it may emerge with a change in conditions. A case in point is observed when, following a series of trials on a standard two-choice, noncontingent probability schedule, subjects are suddenly shifted to extinction ("blank trials," as in Neimark, 1953) or to a noncontingent success schedule (all responses correct, as in Yellott, 1969). Typically, subjects continue to respond at a probability matching level, even though there is no continuing feedback to support this predictive behavior.

We know that the data for predictive behavior during preshift trials are well described by a pattern model that assumes all-or-none learning of coded patterns of contextual cues that are available during the noncontingent series, but these sequential patterns must suddenly become unavailable after the shift to no-feedback or noncontingent success conditions. Since, nonetheless, probability matching performance continues, evidently we must assume that learning also occurred during the noncontingent series with respect to background cues that remain available following the shift.

Even more direct evidence for memory storage on multiple tracks is available from studies reported by Binder and his associates (Binder & Estes, 1966; Binder & Feldman, 1960) conducted with a transfer paradigm. In these studies, training was given with a modified paired-associate procedure in which patterns of cues were associated with outcome events according to the schema $AB-E_1$, $AC-E_2$, $DB-E_3$, $DC-E_4$, but some of the patterns occurred more often than others so that, for example, $AB-E_1$ might occur twice as frequently as $AC-E_2$ during training. During the learning sequence, conducted with an anticipation procedure, the subjects quickly arrived at an asymptotic level of 100% correct performance, indicating that they had stored memory traces relating the AB pattern to event E_1, the AC pattern to event E_2, etc. and were responding on the basis of retrieval of the corresponding traces.

But on subsequent transfer tests, when for example, Cue A was presented alone, it was observed that the subjects predicted event E_1 with a probability that matched the relative frequency with which

AB and AC occurred during training. Thus, although it was not manifest during the training series, the subjects must also have been storing traces relating the individual cues such as A or B in their background context to the outcome event.

The picture to which we appear to be led is one of multiple-track learning in which memory traces may be formed concurrently at a number of levels of processing or coding of contextual information. Differing test conditions lead to the retrieval of different types of contextual trace patterns and consequently, different patterns of test performance.

Episodic Memory and the Pattern Model

On the basis of a variety of considerations discussed in preceding sections, it seems reasonable to assume that predictive behavior is dominated by episodic memory of patterns of events whenever this mechanism is available. Two cases need to be distinguished, corresponding to short-term and long-term retention. The more obvious but, in practice, less important case is that in which a situation is reinstated following a very short interval, so that the individual has a relatively full representation of the situation and the outcome in short-term memory and simply predicts that the same outcome will occur again. The more important case arises following a longer retention interval, when the individual cannot remember all of the original circumstances but may be able to recall a code or label that he applied to the original episode—therefore, he predicts the outcome that he associated in memory with the given code or label.

With some simplifying assumptions, this latter conception leads to a simple, but still surprisingly powerful, model for predictive behavior in the standard, noncontingent probability learning situation. The special condition for applicability of the pattern model is that the sequence of learning trials include a number of recurring spatial or temporal patterns of stimuli for which the individual has already established coding responses, usually verbal labels. On a trial when a code c is activated and an outcome E_i occurs, a memory trace T_{cE_i} is formed. When the same code is reinstated by the context of a later trial, the trace is reactivated, and any response (in this context a predictive response) associated with the event E_i is evoked.

A complication arises if the same code c is available both on a trial when event E_i is the outcome and on a subsequent trial when a different event E_j is the outcome—it thus enters into two trace structures, T_{cE_i} and T_{cE_j}, that tend to evoke different responses. In previous developments of the associative coding model (Estes, 1973),

I assumed that if the responses to E_i and E_j were mutually exclusive, then the one more recently activated would inhibit the other through an inhibitory association.

On the simplifying assumptions that a fixed set of N coding responses is available throughout an experiment and that the different codes are equally likely to be available on any trial, this special case of the associative coding model is formally equivalent to the pattern model as applied to a number of variants of simple probability learning by Estes (1959), Suppes and Atkinson (1960), and Yellott (1969).

Categorical Memory for Relative Frequencies

Whether coding responses are available or not in a given situation, memory traces must be formed associating background context with stimulus events to which the individual attends. The sample of background cues receiving attention will vary from trial to trial; thus, for example, in a sequence of observation trials in a probability learning experiment, traces T_{xE_1}, $T_{x'E_1}$, $T_{x''E_2}$, . . . might be established ($x^{(i)}$ denoting the sample of background context and E_1 and E_2 denoting the outcomes, e.g., A_1-Win or A_2-Loss).

On a test trial, the subject will be exposed to a sample of contextual cues that, in general, will have elements in common with a number of the different samples that were present on the observation trials. Consequently, a number of the traces may be partially reactivated, but a match between the test context and any of the traces will be impossible since the outcome events are missing from the test context. How, then, can a predictive response (or a probability or frequency judgment) be generated? The answer, I propose, is to be found in the scanning model of stimulus-sampling theory (Bower, 1959; Estes, 1962, 1966).

The Scanning Model for the Selection of Predictive Responses

Interpreted in terms of the present problem, the scanning model implies that in a test situation, the individual interrogates his ensemble of partially activated memory traces by generating probes that take the form of coded representations (labels or the equivalent) of the alternative to-be-predicted events. If the stimulus input from one of these probes, together with the current sample of contextual cues presented by the test situation, matches one of the traces $T_{x^{(i)}E_j}$, then the individual predicts outcome E_j.

If the scanning is done in a random order, then the probability that a match will first occur on a trace including E_j is simply equal to the proportion of traces in the ensemble scanned that have the component E_j. Consider first a special case in which the individual has attended only to winning outcomes. On a test of A_i versus A_j, his probability of predicting a win for A_i would be simply

$$P_{ij}(i) = \frac{W_i}{W_i + W_j}, \tag{1}$$

where W_i and W_j denote the frequencies of winning outcomes for the two alternatives during the observation series. Similarly, if he attended only to losing outcomes, the probability of predicting a loss for A_j, and therefore a win for A_i, would be

$$P_{ij}(i) = \frac{L_j}{L_i + L_j}, \tag{2}$$

where L_i and L_j denote frequencies of losses.

Under some circumstances, it would be reasonable to apply Equation 1 or 2 directly. (See, for example, the treatment of relative frequency judgments in a later section.) However, there is substantial reason to think that in normal adult choice behavior, alternatives are not scanned at random; rather, the individual tends to first scan the alternative he has most recently chosen. With this assumption incorporated, the expressions for choice of alternative A_i over A_j take the forms (cf. Estes, 1960, 1962)

$$P_{ij}(i) = \frac{W_i^2}{W_i^2 + W_j^2} \tag{3}$$

and

$$P_{ij}(i) = \frac{L_j^2}{L_i^2 + L_j^2}. \tag{4}$$

An additional possibility to be considered is that the individual attends to both winning and losing outcomes. In this event, the simplest assumption would be that on a test of A_i versus A_j, the individual scans both alternatives, stopping the scan if he recalls a win for A_i and loss for A_j or a loss for A_i and win for A_j, but continuing if he recalls wins for both or losses for both. The probability of a choice of A_i over A_j would then be

$$P_{ij}(i) = \frac{W_i L_j}{W_i L_j + W_j L_i} .\qquad(5)$$

Before trying to apply these functions to data, we should note that Equations 1 through 5 all assume an asymptotic state of learning in which every possible sample of test context will find a match in the ensemble of stored memory traces. To allow for incomplete learning, it will suffice for our present purposes to introduce a parameter ϕ to denote the proportion of instances in which a match between a test context and a memory trace will be available. The value of ϕ will vary from 0, prior to the first observation trial, to 1, at the asymptote of learning. Thus, on any test trial there will be probability $1 - \phi$ that no memory match will be found and that the individual will have to choose on a chance basis. The predictive equations will take the forms

$$P_{ij}(i) = (1 - \phi)(.5) + \phi\frac{W_i^2}{W_i^2 + W_j^2} ,\qquad(6)$$

$$P_{ij}(i) = (1 - \phi)(.5) + \phi\frac{L_j^2}{L_i^2 + L_j^2} ,\qquad(7)$$

and

$$P_{ij}(i) = (1 - \phi)(.5) + \phi\frac{W_i L_j}{W_i L_j + W_j Li} ,\qquad(8)$$

for the cases when the individual scans on the basis of memory traces for wins, losses, or both, respectively.

Elsewhere (Estes, 1960, 1962), I have discussed more elaborate machinery for dealing with trial-to-trial changes in choice probability during learning. For present purposes, in the case of any experimental application, we need only determine the value of ϕ from the observed choice data on any one pair of alternatives at a given stage of learning; this determination presents no difficulties since all of the other quantities entering into Equations 6 through 8 are observable.

An experimental design that provides an appropriate application of the model is probabilistic paired-associate learning. In a study reported by Voss, Thompson, and Keegan (1959), for example, one of two different response alternatives was assigned to each of nine stimuli. The items so constructed were presented in random order, the π values (ranging from .1 to .9) associated with an item determining which alternative would be presented as the correct response to the given stimulus on any trial. Estimated asymptotic choice proportions (representing averages of the observed proportions over the terminal trial blocks for three replications of their Experiment 3) are plotted as a function of π value in Figure 2.15.[1] The orderly sigmoid function thus obtained seems quite well described by the values predicted from Equation 6 with ϕ set equal to .92. Once again, we find that in the absence of instructions to the contrary, subjects evidently store information only regarding winning ("correct") outcomes and scan the representations of these in memory when called upon to anticipate the outcomes.

Numerous other examples could be given, but those discussed above may suffice to show that the variation in particular formulas required to describe predictive behavior in different situations corresponds to the variation in modes of information processing and response selection induced by different tasks.

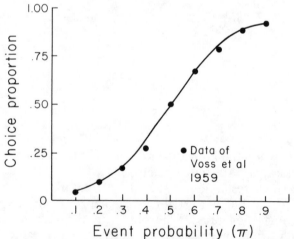

Figure 2.15 Estimated asymptotic choice proportions for the probabilistic paired-associate study of Voss, Thompson, and Keegan (1959) together with the predicted function from the relative frequency model (Equation 6).

[1] I wish to thank James Voss for supplying the numerical data.

Application of the Model to Relative
Frequency Judgments

Beyond providing a framework for the interpretation of various types of probability learning, the assumptions of the model bring out important similarities between the phenomena of probability learning and relative frequency judgments. In research designed to elucidate the relationships between recognition, verbal discrimination learning, and memory for frequency, a number of investigators have employed observation–test designs analogous to that of the experiment illustrated in Figure 2.13. However, these investigators have usually presented stimuli singly, rather than in pairs, on observation trials, and the subject's task on test trials has been to judge which member of the pair of test stimuli occurred more frequently during the observation series.

From the viewpoint developed here, the experiments of these investigators involve an especially simple case of the type of information processing assumed to underlie probability learning. Typically, rather long lists of items are used, and buffer items are inserted between the last occurrence of a to-be-tested item and the first test trial. Consequently, it is unlikely that episodic memory could play any appreciable role, and we must assume that the test responses are based on categorical memory for frequency information. To generate specific predictions from the present model, we need only treat each occurrence of an item as corresponding to a winning outcome in the probability learning situations. Since particular pairs of items usually are not tested repeatedly in these studies, or are retested only infrequently compared to probability learning studies, we should assume that the alternatives of a test pair are scanned in a random order. Thus, the appropriate function for purposes of predicting test performance is Equation 1, but with the parameter ϕ incorporated to allow for intermediate degrees of learning as in Equations 6 through 8; that is,

$$P_{ij} = (1 - \phi)(.5) + \phi \frac{W_i}{W_i + W_j}. \qquad (9)$$

The principal implication of this analysis is that on tests of pairs of items presented at least once,[2] relative frequency judgments should tend to match the actual relative frequencies. This expecta-

---

[2] Tests involving pairings of previously presented items with novel items bring in additional considerations, concerning stimulus generalization, which are beyond the scope of the present study.

tion seems well borne out in the data of a number of studies (Hintz-man, 1969; Radtke, Jacoby, & Goedel, 1971; Underwood & Freund, 1970; Underwood, Zimmerman, & Freund, 1971). In Hintzman's data, for example, actual relative frequencies were

$$.60, .62, .67, .71, .80, .83, .86, .91,$$

and mean choice proportions,

$$.66, .66, .65, .75, .78, .89, .88, .91,$$

respectively. In the data of Radtke et al. (1971), relative frequencies were

$$.60, .67, .75, .80$$

and choice proportions,

$$.62, .66, .74, .80,$$

respectively. When the frequency of repetition of test pairs increases materially in this type of experiment, we should, of course, expect that subjects will begin to scan the test stimuli in the order of their relative frequencies and therefore that choice proportions will shift in the direction of the values predicted by Equation 6.

Probability Estimates

A loose end that at present I can do little to tie into a formal theory concerns experiments in which subjects are called upon to produce numerical estimates of event probabilities. Typically, learning functions for mean probability estimates are very similar to those for proportions of predictive responses, and in the case of simple, noncontingent event schedules, tend to approach probability matching (Bauer, 1972; Neimark & Shuford, 1959).

I assume that estimates, like predictions, are based on categorical memory for frequency information, but the process by which an individual converts the memory representation into a numerical estimate of probability or frequency is something of a mystery. Perhaps the most parsimonious idea suggested by the present theoretical analysis is that the individual resamples the background contextual cues available on the test trial a number of times, generating a sequence of covert predictive responses, and then counts or "subitizes" these (as in reporting frequencies of dots from tachistoscopic displays) in order to generate a numerical response. On this assumption, the learning function for a noncontingent probability learning experiment would take the form of Equation 9, with P_{ij} denoting the subject's mean probability estimate with reference to event E_i, and with π_i (the probability of event E_i) taking the place of $W_i/W_i + W_j$. On the assumption that the parameter ϕ would in this case take the form $\phi = 1 - (1 - \theta)^n$, where n is the trial number and θ the stimulus–sampling fraction, this learning function would quite satisfactorily describe the obtained learning curves in the studies of Bauer (1972) and Neimark and Shuford (1959), with a bit of extra confirmation from the very similar pre- and postshift learning rates observed in the Bauer study.

Whatever the merits of this conjecture regarding the mechanism of response selection, considerable evidence seems to be accumulating to suggest that probability estimates, relative frequency judgments, and predictive behavior all share a common basis in associative memory.

REFERENCE NOTE

1. Brehmer, B. *Inductive inferences from uncertain information* (Umeå Psychological Report 78). University of Umeå, Sweden, 1974.

REFERENCES

Anderson, J. R., & Bower, G. H. *Human associative memory.* Washington, D.C.: V. H. Winston, 1973.

Atkinson, R. C., & Wickens, T. D. Human memory and the concept of reinforcement. In R. Glaser (Ed.), *The nature of reinforcement.* New York: Academic Press, 1971.

Bauer, M. Relations between prediction- and estimation-responses in cue-probability learning and transfer. *Scandinavian Journal of Psychology*, 1972, *13*, 198–207.

Binder, A., & Estes, W. K. Transfer of response in visual recognition situations as a function of frequency variables. *Psychological Monographs*, 1966, *80*(23, Whole No. 631).

Binder, A., & Feldman, S. E. The effects of experimentally controlled experience upon recognition responses. *Psychological Monographs*, 1960, *74*(9, Whole No. 496).

Björkman, M. Predictive behavior. Some aspects based on an ecological orientation. *Scandinavian Journal of Psychology*, 1966, *7*, 43–57.

Bower, G. H. Choice-point behavior. In R. R. Bush & W. K. Estes (Eds.), *Studies in mathematical learning theory.* Stanford, Calif.: Stanford University Press, 1959.

Bush, R. R., & Mosteller, F. *Stochastic models for learning.* New York: Wiley, 1955.

Castellan, N. J., Jr., & Edgell, S. E. An hypothesis generation model for judgment in nonmetric multiple-cue probability learning. *Journal of Mathematical Psychology,* 1973, *10,* 204-222.

Cohen, J. *Behavior in uncertainty and its social implications.* New York: Basic Books, 1964.

Ekstrand, B. R., Wallace, W. P., & Underwood, B. J. A frequency theory of verbal discrimination learning. *Psychological Review,* 1966, *73,* 566-578.

Estes, W. K. Component and pattern models with Markovian interpretations. In R. R. Bush & W. K. Estes (Eds.), *Studies in mathematical learning theory.* Stanford, Calif.: Stanford University Press, 1959.

Estes, W. K. A random-walk model for choice behavior. In K. J. Arrow, S. Karlin, & P. Suppes (Eds.), *Mathematical methods in the social sciences, 1959.* Stanford, Calif.: Stanford University Press, 1960.

Estes, W. K. Theoretical treatments of differential reward in multiple-choice learning and two-person interactions. In J. H. Criswell, H. Solomon, & P. Suppes (Eds.), *Mathematical methods in small group processes.* Stanford, Calif.: Stanford University Press, 1962.

Estes, W. K. All-or-none processes in learning and retention. *American Psychologist,* 1964, *19,* 16-25.

Estes, W. K. Transfer of verbal discriminations based on differential reward magnitudes. *Journal of Experimental Psychology,* 1966, *72,* 276-283.

Estes, W. K. Reinforcement in human learning. In J. Tapp (Ed.), *Reinforcement and behavior.* New York: Academic Press, 1969.

Estes, W. K. Elements and patterns in diagnostic discrimination learning. *Transactions of the New York Academy of Sciences,* 1972, *34,* 84-95. (a)

Estes, W. K. Reinforcement in human behavior. *American Scientist,* 1972, *60,* 723-729. (b)

Estes, W. K. Research and theory on the learning of probabilities. *Journal of the American Statistical Association,* 1972, *67,* 81-102. (c)

Estes, W. K. Memory and conditioning. In F. J. McGuigan & D. B. Lumsden (Eds.), *Contemporary approaches to conditioning and learning.* Washington, D.C.: V. H. Winston, 1973.

Estes, W. K. Some functions of memory in probability learning and choice behavior. In G. H. Bower (Ed.), *The psychology of learning and motivation: Advances in research and theory* (Vol. 10). New York: Academic Press, 1976. (a)

Estes, W. K. Structural aspects of associative models for memory. In C. N. Cofer (Ed.), *The structure of human memory.* San Francisco: Freeman, 1976. (b)

Estes, W. K., & Straughan, J. H. Analysis of a verbal conditioning situation in terms of statistical learning theory. *Journal of Experimental Psychology,* 1954, *47,* 225-234.

Feigenbaum, E. A. The simulation of verbal learning behavior. In E. A. Feigenbaum & J. Feldman (Eds.), *Computers and thought.* New York: McGraw-Hill, 1963.

Feldman, J., & Hanna, J. F. The structure of responses to a sequence of binary events. *Journal of Mathematical Psychology*, 1966, *3*, 371-387.

Friedman, M. P., Burke, C. J., Cole, M., Keller, L., Millward, R. B., & Estes, W. K. Two-choice behavior under extended training with shifting probabilities of reinforcement. In R. C. Atkinson (Ed.), *Studies in mathematical psychology*. Stanford, Calif.: Stanford University Press, 1964.

Friedman, M. P., Rollins, H., & Padilla, G. The role of cue validity in stimulus compounding. *Journal of Mathematical Psychology*. 1968, *5*, 300-310.

Goldberg, L. R. Man versus model of man: A rationale, plus some evidence, for a method of improving clinical inferences. *Psychological Bulletin*, 1970. *73*, 422-432.

Greeno, J. G. *Elementary theoretical psychology*. Reading, Mass.: Addison-Wesley, 1968.

Hintzman, D. L. Apparent frequency as a function of frequency and the spacing of repetitions. *Journal of Experimental Psychology*, 1969, *80*, 139-145.

Jenkins, H. M., & Ward, W. C. Judgment of contingency between responses and outcomes. *Psychological Monographs*, 1965, *79*(1, Whole No. 594).

Johnson, N. F. The role of chunking and organization in the process of recall. In G. H. Bower (Ed.), *The psychology of learning and motivation: Advances in research and theory* (Vol. 4). New York: Academic Press, 1970.

Kahneman, D., & Tversky, A. Subjective probability: A judgment of representativeness. *Cognitive Psychology*, 1972, *3*, 430-454.

Luce, R. D. *Individual choice behavior. A theoretical analysis*. New York: Wiley, 1959.

Mandler, G., Cowan, P. A., & Gold, C. Concept learning and probability matching. *Journal of Experimental Psychology*, 1964, *67*, 514-522.

Myers, J. L. Probability learning and sequence learning. In W. K. Estes (Ed.), *Handbook of learning and cognitive processes* (Vol. 3). Hillsdale, N.J.: Lawrence Erlbaum Associates, 1976.

Neimark, E. D. *Effects of type of non-reinforcement and number of alternative responses in two verbal conditioning situations*. Unpublished doctoral dissertation, Indiana University, 1953.

Neimark, E. D., & Shuford, E. H. Comparison of predictions and estimates in a probability learning situation. *Journal of Experimental Psychology*, 1959, *57*, 294-298.

Radtke, R. C., Jacoby, L. L., & Goedel, G. D. Frequency discrimination as a function of frequency of repetition and trials. *Journal of Experimental Psychology*, 1971, *89*, 78-84.

Restle, F. *Psychology of judgment and choice: A theoretical essay*. New York: Wiley, 1961.

Restle, F. The selection of strategies in cue learning. *Psychological Review*, 1962, *69*, 329-343.

Restle, F. Significance of all-or-none learning. *Psychological Bulletin*, 1965, *64*, 313-325.

Restle, F., & Brown, E. R. Serial pattern learning. *Journal of Experimental Psychology*, 1970, *83*, 120-125.

Shuford, F. H., Jr. Some Bayesian learning processes. In M. W. Shelly II, & G. L. Bryan (Eds.), *Human judgments and optimality*. New York: Wiley, 1964.

Smedslund, J. The concept of correlation in adults. *Scandinavian Journal of Psychology*, 1963, *4*, 165–173.

Suppes, P., & Atkinson, R. C. *Markov learning models for multi-person interactions*. Stanford, Calif.: Stanford University Press, 1960.

Tulving, E. Theoretical issues in free recall. In T. R. Dixon & D. L. Horton (Eds.), *Verbal behavior and general behavior theory*. Englewood Cliffs, N.J.: Prentice-Hall, 1968.

Tulving, E. Episodic and semantic memory. In E. Tulving & W. Donaldson (Eds.), *Organization of memory*. New York: Academic Press, 1972.

Underwood, B. J., & Freund, J. S. Relative frequency judgments and verbal discrimination learning. *Journal of Experimental Psychology*, 1970, *83*, 279–285.

Underwood, B. J., Zimmerman, J., & Freund, J. S. Retention of frequency information with observations on recognition and recall. *Journal of Experimental Psychology*, 1971, *87*, 149–162.

Voss, J. F., Thompson, C. P., & Keegan, J. H. Acquisition of probabilistic paired associates as a function of $S-R_1$ $S-R_2$ probability. *Journal of Experimental Psychology*, 1959, *58*, 390–399.

Weir, M. W. Developmental changes in problem solving strategies. *Psychological Review*, 1964, *71*, 473–490.

Wolin, B. R., Weichel, R., Terebinski, S. J., & Hansford, E. A. Performance on complexly patterned binary event sequences. *Psychological Monographs*, 1965, *79*(7, Whole No. 600).

Yellott, J. I., Jr. Probability learning with noncontingent success. *Journal of Mathematical Psychology*, 1969, *6*, 541–575.

Learning Theory and Intelligence

All scientific measurements of intelligence that we have at present are measures of some product produced by the person or animal in question, or of the way in which some product is produced. A is rated as more intelligent than B because he produces a better product, essay written, answer found, choice made, completion supplied or the like, or produces an equally good product in a better way, more quickly, or by inference rather than by rote memory, or by more ingenious use of the material at hand. . . .

Psychologists would of course assume that differences in intelligence are due to differences histological or physiological, or both, and would expect these physical bases of intelligence to be measurable. . . . Even if one aimed at discovering the physiological basis of intellect and measuring it in physiological units, one would have to begin by measuring the intellectual products produced by it. For our only means of discovering physiological bases is search for the physiological factors which correspond to intellectual production [Thorndike, 1926, pp. 11-12] .

Such was the status of this problem when Thorndike was writing *Measurement of Intelligence* nearly 50 years ago.

Thorndike was well aware that in measuring intelligence we do go further than sampling an individual's current performance in order to predict his potentialities for various types of tasks. To the extent that we can sample performance for different individuals following equal opportunities to learn, we also infer relative rates of gain in performance in the future. In fact,

an obvious hypothesis, often advanced, is that intellect is the ability to learn, and that our estimates of it are or should be estimates of ability to learn. To be able to learn harder things or to be able to learn the same things more quickly would then be the single basis of evaluation. . . . If greater ability to learn means in part ability to learn harder things, we have excluded the vague general valuation of certain products and ways of producing only to include it again. . . . If greater ability to learn means only the ability to learn more things or to learn the same things more quickly,

W. K. Estes, Learning theory and intelligence. *American Psychologist*, 1974, *29*, 740–749. Copyright 1974 by the American Psychological Association. Reprinted by permission of the publisher.

The substance of this article was included in an invited address presented at the meeting of the Toronto Psychological Association, February 1972, and at a symposium on intelligence held at the University of California, Los Angeles, June 1971.

we have a view that has certain advantages of clearness and approximate fitness to many facts. Even less than in the case of truth-getting [insight into reality], however, do our present actual instruments for measuring intelligence measure directly a person's ability to learn more things than another person can, or to learn the same things more quickly. . . . Much evidence will therefore be required before we can wisely replace our present multifarious empirical valuations by the formula that intellect is the ability to learn more things or to learn the same things more quickly [Thorndike, 1926, pp. 17-18].

It seems to me that the preceding paragraphs could almost as well have been written yesterday as several decades ago. Little has changed with respect either to the basic method of measuring intelligence by the sampling of performance or to our inability to improve on this procedure by more direct measurement of learning abilities.

One reason why the great amounts of effort expended on problems of intelligence and its measurement in the interim have produced so little change in basic conceptions may have to do with the fact that from the time of Binet, the primary criterion for measuring intellect has been success in predicting performance in school and other situations requiring intellectual effort. Long ago, efforts to increase the predictive power of intelligence tests began to run into sharply diminishing returns, and it now seems quite possible that we are near the maximum attainable, given the usual limitations on time and expense of testing.

Thus, in raising again the possibility of replacing the characterization of intelligence in terms of performance with a characterization in terms of learning processes, I am not motivated by any expectation that appreciable gains in predictive power could be achieved. One of the motivations for a reappraisal is almost purely intellectual, and, again, I find that I can improve but little on Thorndike:

We have learned to think of intellect as the ability to succeed with intellectual tasks, and to measure it by making an inventory of a fair sampling from these tasks, arranging these in levels of intellectual difficulty, and observing how many the intellect in question succeeds with at each level. . . . Such a definition in terms of tasks accomplishable, and such a measurement in terms of the contents of a graded inventory is sound and useful, but is not entirely satisfying. One cherishes the hope that some simpler, more unitary fact exists as the cause of intellect and that variations in the magnitude of this fact may provide a single fundamental scale which will account for levels and range and surface. Moreover, one realizes the desirability of search for the physiological cause of intellect, regardless of whether that cause be single and simple or manifold and complex [Thorndike, 1926, p. 412].

Thorndike went on to offer a specific interpretation of intelligence in terms of the learning theory of his day:

> The standard orthodox view of the surface nature of intellect has been that it is divided rather sharply into a lower half, mere connection-forming or the association of ideas, which acquires information and specialized habits of thinking; and a higher half characterized by abstraction, generalization, the perception and use of relations and the selection and control of habits in inference or reasoning, and ability to manage novel or original tasks. . . . The hypothesis which we present and shall defend admits the distinction in respect of surface behavior, but asserts that in their deeper nature the higher forms of intellectual operation are identical with mere association or connection forming, depending upon the same sort of physiological connections but requiring *many more of them*. By the same argument the person whose intellect is greater or higher or better than that of another person differs from him in the last analysis in having, not a new sort of physiological process, but simply a larger number of connections of the ordinary sort [Thorndike, 1926, pp. 414–415].

According to this conception, an individual's effective intelligence at any time was thought to be determined jointly by his original intellectual capacity, identified with the number of potential connections available in his brain, and by the number of connections actually formed as a result of training and experience.

Thorndike claimed "almost crucial" evidence for his hypothesis in a collection of correlational data from tests he believed to measure the higher abilities of relational thinking and abstraction (sentence completion, arithmetical problems, analogies) and tests believed to measure lower, "associative" abilities (vocabulary, numerical calculation, information tests). From the finding that intercorrelations of the higher tests among themselves, of the lower tests among themselves, and of the higher tests with the lower tests were all of the same order of magnitude, Thorndike concluded that both the associative and the higher abilities must have "in the main the same cause [1926, p. 470]." And the common cause must lie at the associative level because the lower, associative abilities can be found without the higher (as in the mentally deficient), but the higher abilities are never manifest in the absence of the associative abilities.

Thorndike's conclusion rests on an assumption that we shall find in the sequel to be open to serious question, namely, that one can find subtests of intelligence scales which are relatively pure measures of either the associative or the higher abilities. Nonetheless, the number-of-connections hypothesis has continued to represent for several generations of psychologists and educators the way in which learning theorists would interpret intelligence.

Because of its conceptual meagerness, the hypothesis has never aroused among psychologists much enthusiasm for following up this line of inquiry. Consequently, it remains essentially without a competitor—never a healthy state of affairs in any scientific discipline. It seems most timely, therefore, to ask what form would be taken by a similar effort today, utilizing the richer body of theory that has grown out of several decades of research on learning.

Beyond utilizing conceptual resources that were not available to earlier investigators, I propose to take a somewhat different basic orientation. Thorndike's approach was to look at the learning theory of his day in order to see what concepts or ideas embodied in it might serve to account for differences in intelligence. Like many other investigators in the psychometric tradition, Thorndike seems to have viewed intelligence as a trait or characteristic of the individual that sets the limits on his level of intellectual functioning. An interpretation of intelligence in terms of learning would, then, entail finding some theoretically meaningful quantity with which variations in intelligence might prove to be correlated; his choice, as we have seen, was the number of available associative connections.

In the course of a rather extensive review of the literature on learning theory and intelligence (Estes, 1970), I have come to think that a new effort toward establishing a more significant working relationship between the two research traditions should begin by turning the problem around. Rather than looking to learning or physiological theory for some correlate of intelligence, I should like to focus attention on intellectual activity itself. By bringing the concepts and methods of other disciplines to bear on the analysis of intellectual behavior we may come to understand how the conditions responsible for the development of its constituent processes and the manner of their organization lead to variations in effectiveness of intellectual functioning.

If this approach has appeal in principle, we need next to consider just what behaviors to analyze in order to be sure that the activity we are dealing with is closely related to that involved in measurement of intelligence. The simplest and most direct approach, it seems, is to begin with the specific behaviors involved in responding to items on intelligence tests.

The idea of relating performance on subtests of intelligence scales to various psychological categories or functions is by no means new. In his detailed analysis of the Stanford revision of the Binet scale, McNemar (1942) considered the idea that the various subtests of the Binet that seemed to have something to do with memory (e.g., digit span, repeating sentences, copying bead strings from memory) are alternative measures of a single memory function that might represent a purer manifestation of intelligence than the variegated tests of the scale as a whole. McNemar found the reliability of a pooled "memory" test to be relatively low and took this finding as rather negative evidence. However, he was not entirely satisfied with this basis for a conclusion and added:

> The final answer as to whether variance in measured intelligence is more dependent upon retentivity than upon original learning, or as to the extent of each as a contributor, must be sought in the laboratory. We hazard the guess that securing the answer will involve experimentation rather than wholesale correlational analysis [McNemar, 1942, p. 151].

The experimental analysis that McNemar found so sorely wanting 30 years ago did not follow with unseemly speed. Consideration of the few examples of relevant research that are now available will, I think, make clear some of the reasons for the long delay in their appearance. I suggest that we will find a dominant factor to be changes in the state of theory concerning learning and memory over this period.

In order to give some idea of the kinds of analyses that are immediately within our reach, I would first like to discuss two cases in which the identical task that constitutes a subtest of an intelligence scale has been subjected to laboratory investigation, and then two cases in which only rather modest extrapolation from closely relevant research is required.

ANALYSES OF TEST BEHAVIOR

The Digit Span Test

One of the simplest appearing subtests of the Stanford-Binet is the digit span test. As it occurs in the scales for Year 10, for example, the subject's task is to repeat a sequence of random digits immediately after they have been read aloud by the examiner. Successful recall of a string of six digits in the correct order is scored as passing performance at this level. The test correlates satisfactorily with total score on the Binet scale and with usual validation criteria, so it evidently samples some aspect or aspects of intellectual performance. But if an individual scores low on this test, what measures should we expect to be useful in improving his performance in this kind of task? An obvious possibility would be practice at recalling sequences of digits. But this seems rather narrow and most unlikely to transfer to any other situation. A better plan might be to have the individual practice recalling sequences of items of different types, digits, letters, words, etc.

These suggestions, together with an admonition to carry out the practice in a variety of contexts, would seem to be about all that could be derived from the learning theory available to Thorndike (1926) when he was writing *Measurement of Intelligence*.

If any subtest of the Stanford-Binet measures only the lower, associative abilities, the digit span test must surely qualify. The basis for successful performance would be conceived in classical association theory to be the establishment, or at least the strengthening, of interitem associations so that if, for example, the digit string 691472 were presented, the resulting structure in memory might be represented as 6-9-1-4-7-2. The request to recall would be the stimulus for remembering the first digit of the string, this in turn would lead to recall of the next digit and so on. If an individual failed the test, the interpretation would be either that he was inefficient in forming the required new associations, or that the strength of these associations in memory decayed too rapidly to permit successful recall.

A substantial body of research and theory dealing with short-term memory for sequences of items shows quite clearly that this interpretation in terms of interitem associations is inadequate and is in fact quite possibly entirely wrong.

Perhaps the most basic difficulty is presented by rather direct evidence that the item in position n of a string is not a necessary and sufficient stimulus, or even necessarily part of the stimulus, for recall of the item at position $n + 1$. For example, Jahnke (1970) showed that for most serial positions in a string, an individual's recall of the item at position n is better if he is simply asked to recall the item at that serial position than if he is given the item at position $n - 1$ and asked to recall its successor. This result was obtained with young adults who, it appears, must have established in long-term memory a conception of the sequence of ordinal numbers and must also have available a strategy of relating incoming items of a sequence to ordinal position.

There is considerable evidence to suggest that no effective associations at all may form between adjacent items in a sequence unless the individual has been instructed that he will be required to use individual items as retrieval cues in a subsequent test. Lesgold and Bower (1970) found no transfer whatever from learning of a serial list of items to a subsequent paired-associate task in which the pairs were adjacent items from the serial list unless the subjects had been informed in advance of the relationship between the serial and paired-associate tasks.

Numerous studies that have appeared since Miller's (1956) introduction of the concept of *chunking* have shown that, for strings greater than three or four items, recall is greatly facilitated if the individual groups the items into subgroups of approximately three items each. This procedure of grouping, or chunking, whether done by the experimenter as he presents the material or spontaneously by the subject as he attempts to organize it in his memory, is a powerful determiner of what is and is not learned in a short-term memory situation. Bower and Winenz (1969), for example, showed that when the material is grouped by the experimenter at input, repetition of the string of digits leads to improvement in recall only if the particular mode of grouping is the same upon subsequent repetitions of the string.

Further, grouping is as important a factor with children as with adults, and with mentally deficient or brain-injured children as with normals. Spitz (1966), utilizing a modified digit span test with visual presentations, showed a substantial facilitatory effect of grouping of the digits upon performance of retarded children with an average IQ of 60; the effect was present but smaller with equal mental age normals, perhaps because the grouping (by twos rather than by threes) was not optimal. Notably, it was found that when the retarded children who had been given the grouped presentation were subsequently tested with ungrouped material, their performance declined, whereas that of normal children was unaffected, indicating that the retarded children had not developed the habit of spontaneously grouping material in order to aid recall.

These and related lines of evidence have suggested an interpretation of short-term memory for strings of verbal units in terms of organization and coding. Johnson (1970) developed in detail the idea that grouping facilitates recall because the individual assigns a code to each subgroup of a sequence and maintains in memory only the smaller set of codes until the time of recall, when he decodes these in order to reconstruct the original sequence. When these ideas are taken into account, the simple schema of classical connectionism becomes amplified into a hierarchical structure of representations in memory:

LIST

Chunk 1

Position 1	Position 2	Position 3
6	9	1

Chunk 2

Position 1	Position 2	Position 3
4	7	2

On presentation of the digit sequence 691472, the individual is conceived to subgroup the sequence into two chunks, assigning a code to
each which he maintains in memory, and within each chunk relating
the items of the sequence to the ordinal numbers 1, 2, and 3. On a
request to recall the string, the individual brings into memory his
coded representations of the two chunks; each of these in turn activates recall of the individual digits and their associated serial positions. While this process goes on, the individual must hold the
partially reconstructed sequence in an output response buffer by an
inhibitory process until the decoding is complete and then emit the
digits in the proper order. This schema may seem complex, and certainly in details it is by no means beyond controversy, but numerous
lines of solid evidence in addition to those reviewed briefly in the
preceding paragraphs indicate that something not far from this theoretical picture is required (Estes, 1972).

With the revised schema in mind, we can readily see that there
must be many different ways in which major individual differences
can arise with respect to performance on a digit span test. In the
young or the mentally retarded child, we may find failures occurring
because the individual has not developed sufficient familiarity with
the sequence of ordinal numbers, or enough experience in using the
number sequence to order other materials. An individual of any age
may fall short of standard performance if he has not developed the
strategy of grouping to the extent characteristic of his age group, but
may perform normally when led to utilize grouping by the experimenter or examiner. Another individual may not be able to accomplish the coding process necessary to take advantage of chunking
even when material is presented to him in subgroups. Still another
may be able to recall well enough but may lack the capacity for selective inhibition necessary to order his output properly.

Clearly it would be possible with the advantage of added theoretical insight to augment the standard digit span test in such a way as
to localize the source of difficulty for an individual who fails under
the standard procedure. This augmentation would quite likely do
little to improve the predictive value of the test, but it might be of
considerable help in indicating how deficient performance in this and
related tasks might be remedied.

Digit Symbol Substitution

Although various aspects of the digit span task have been studied in
the laboratory, the fact that it also appears in intelligence scales is
largely coincidental. Motivation and direction for these studies have

arisen from previous theory and research on learning and memory. I have been able to find very few instances in which a task has been taken directly from an intelligence scale and subjected to experimental investigation with a view to elucidating the basis of its clinical usefulness. Of these, the most substantial is the recently reported investigation of the digit symbol task by Royer (1971).

The point of departure for Royer's study was the digit symbol subtest of the Wechsler Adult Intelligence Scale, which has been of special clinical interest because of its steep decrement in performance with age and its sensitivity to various neurological defects. In the standard form of the test, the individual being examined is given a table relating nine symbols to the digits 1–9, as illustrated in the upper two rows of Figure 2.16, and an answer sheet with rows of boxes above which numerals appear in a haphazard order. His task is to place the appropriate symbols in the boxes, and his score is the number of substitutions completed in 90 seconds. The task can just as well be presented in reverse, with numerals being substituted for symbols, and in fact Royer studied both variations.

Royer (1971) noted that the test can be considered to be a mea-

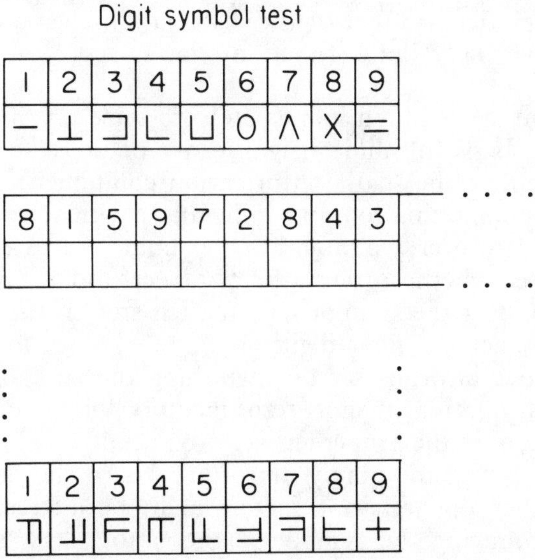

Digit symbol test

Figure 2.16 Assignments of symbols to digits in Wechsler digit symbol scale (first two rows) and in set 5 of Royer's (1971) study (last two rows), together with sample from an answer sheet (third and fourth rows).

sure of information-processing capacity because an index of rate of information processing derived from information theory proves to be linearly related to standardized score on the test. Further, within the set of symbols two types of information which have been significant in perceptual theory may be distinguished. One of these, which for brevity may be termed *spatial information*, serves only to distinguish members of a subset of symbols which belong to a rotational equivalence set, that is, which may be superposed following an appropriate rotation (e.g., the third and fifth figures in the second row of Figure 2.16). The other type of information distinguishes figures that cannot be superposed following any possible rotation.

In his first experiment Royer (1971) varied the distribution of digits on the answer form—balanced (rectangular) versus unbalanced —the latter being the condition obtaining on the Wechsler scale, and relative proportion of content and spatial information in the symbol set. The symbol set from the Wechsler scale was utilized, together with four others which included increasing proportions of symbols that differed only on the spatial dimension. The fifth set, in which all but one of the symbols belonged to the same rotation-equivalence set, is shown in the bottom row of Figure 2.16. Administration of this set of variations to a large group of college student subjects yielded no significant effect of the distributional variable but a substantial and virtually linear function relating score to the similarity condition.

One might be tempted immediately to seize on this function as indicating the basis for clinical significance of the test because difficulties in handling the spatial information component are known to characterize young children and individuals with various neurological disorders. However, we should first examine the task more closely in order to see whether other aspects of performance might covary with the nature of the symbol set. At each step in the task the subject must inspect the next digit, go to the proper location in the table, code the information distinguishing the symbol found, and carry this information in short-term memory long enough to reproduce the symbol in the proper answer box.

Looking first at the purely motor aspects of the task, one must inquire whether one relevant factor might be differences in difficulty in reproducing the symbols in the various sets. Royer (1971) investigated this possibility in a second experiment in which subjects were required simply to copy haphazard sequences of symbols drawn from the various sets. He found a significant trend in the same direction as that obtained for test performance, but concluded that the variation was relatively small compared to that in the substitution task itself.

Probably of considerably more importance are factors having to do with the coding of the information in the symbols. Excluding individuals who can maintain fully adequate visual images, probably a rarity in the adult population, efficient performance must depend on the individual's having available or being able quickly to produce distinctive codes to represent each of the symbols in memory. On this assumption, the task would be the easiest for the Wechsler symbols. Many of these have distinctive labels readily available, for example, a minus sign for the first symbol, an inverted T for the second, and an L for the fourth (second row of Figure 2.16). In contrast, the symbols of Set 5 (bottom row of Figure 2.16) would require the creation of an adequate labeling system in the course of the substitution task.

Once accomplished, coding will obviate the necessity of looking more than once at the symbol required for a given substitution. Further, it is likely that even within the short time involved in the test some individuals will be able to learn some of the digit code associations and thus on many occasions not need to look from the digit to the table at all in order to make the appropriate substitution. It is clear from examining the sets of symbols used by Royer that suitable codes would be least readily available for the set containing the largest number of members of a single rotational equivalence group.

A satisfactory interpretation of Royer's principal results awaits further research which may serve to differentiate the role of relative proportions of content and spatial information from that of availability of distinctive codes. Evidence now available seems rather clearly to point to the latter interpretation. I have in mind, particularly, the extensive data concerning sex differences in performance on subtests of intelligence scales. Generally, girls score higher on verbal subtests, and boys, on those involving spatial manipulations. Digit symbol substitution has usually been assigned to the nonverbal category, and consequently the superior performance by girls (McNemar, 1942) has seemed an anomaly. The explanation, I suggest, is that skill in digit symbol substitution involves a verbal-encoding process as a major component.

Vocabulary

The ubiquitous vocabulary test, appearing, for example, at all of the higher age levels in the Stanford-Binet, is similar to the digit span test both in the deceptively simple appearance of the task and in the substantial growth of relevant theory over the years in which the test has been used, but differs in the lack of directly relevant experimental analysis in the learning laboratory.

Considering how inextricably the vocabulary test has been bound up with the assessment of intelligence over nearly three quarters of a century, it seems remarkable how little is known as to just what aspects of intellectual performance are being measured. In particular, we are largely ignorant concerning the extent to which the test taps vocabulary, in the sense of the stock of words an individual uses or can recognize, as distinguished from the processes involved in constructing a definition or an explanation of the meaning of a word.

Vocabulary tests have been validated extensively, but evidently always against other measures or criteria of intelligence, not against alternative measures of vocabulary. What might these other measures be? One, in particular, is suggested by recent studies of Howes (1971) on the direct estimation of an individual's vocabulary via time-sampling procedures. Howes' method is to record several thousand words of informal discourse from an individual, then, utilizing a statistical model relating word samples to populations, to obtain an estimate of the individual's vocabulary which is quite independent of the other processes involved in answering the usual vocabulary test items.

In terms of contemporary learning theory, what should we expect to be the principal determinants of performance when an individual is presented with a series of words and asked to give definitions or explain their meanings? Most basic, in a sense, must be the long-term memory structures established by previous experience with the words in question. In classical association theory, this result of past learning was conceived of simply as a set of associations between a particular word and others which might be used to convey its meaning. In contemporary thinking, the status of a word in memory is characterized by its values with respect to a set of features or attributes (Anglin, 1970; Underwood, 1969). Accessibility to this representation in memory is determined by the presence of retrieval cues (Tulving, 1968), which may be conceived as learned associations between the cluster of features and the contexts in which the word has been or might be used. But the existence of these associations is not enough; actual performance at any time depends on their availability, which in turn is a function of recency and frequency of usage (Allen, Mahler, & Estes, 1969; Horowitz, Norman, & Day, 1966).

Depending on the specific retrieval strategies that he has learned to use and the availability of retrieval cues, an individual who is asked to give the meaning of a word on a vocabulary test may function at a number of levels, as illustrated in Figure 2.17. The most primitive answer in a sense, and the least efficient, is that of simply giving some other words which are aroused by association. This type of

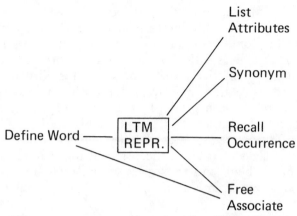

Figure 2.17 Levels of response to a request for definition of a word, all except the lowest requiring activation
of a representation of the word in long-term memory
(LTM).

answer deserves, and in practice receives, only partial credit because
it does not tap the organization of word meaning in memory. If the
coded representation of the word in long-term memory is activated,
the individual can attempt to produce an acceptable answer by recalling specific occurrences of the word and their circumstances, by
recalling a dictionary definition or its equivalent, or by actually expressing the features and attributes that serve both to relate and to
differentiate the word from others in his long-term memory system.

Finally, though by no means least important, production of an
acceptable answer in this as in any other test situation requires that
the individual have in mind a conception of the characteristics of an
acceptable answer, in this instance of an acceptable definition or
explanation of the meaning of a word. For a child who has grown up
in a more or less average home environment with numerous opportunities and occasions to inquire concerning the meanings of words and
to have these explained to him by parents and siblings, this requirement is so automatically satisfied that it may tend to be taken for
granted. Whenever he is able to achieve the necessary information,
the child will be able to generate an acceptable answer by comparing
his own partially formed utterances with the properties he knows
from his own experience to characterize a satisfactory definition. A
child who has not had these opportunities will lack the basis for cor-
rective feedback of his production.

Clearly an individual's successful passing of a vocabulary test provides valuable information as to the extent to which the numerous prerequisites for successful performance have been simultaneously satisfied by his combination of inherent capacities and past experiences. But failure gives little diagnostic information, for it can come about in many qualitatively different ways. Inability to explain or define a word on request may occur because the necessary memory structure has never been established, because of a lack of retrieval cues for an intact memory structure, because words required to express the definition are at low availability owing to disuse, or because the individual lacks a general conception of the required solution to this type of problem and thus gives an answer which is meaningful within his own frame of reference but not within that of the examiner.

I think we must concede that, in comparison to digit span, present learning theory is not so clearly in a position to prescribe directly ways in which conventional tests of vocabulary might be augmented in order to provide more information concerning the different processes involved in test performance. However, it does appear that the line of analysis we have illustrated may go beyond the classical psychometric approach in generating specific kinds of research which might provide bases for remodeling the vocabulary test from a pure instrument for prediction of performance to one more useful in diagnoses of processes.

Word Naming

One's first impression of this task, a subtest of Year 10 of the Stanford-Binet scale, may well be that it scarcely seems to constitute an intellectual task at all. The individual is simply requested to name as many different words as he can in one minute, excluding counting or the use of sentences. Since, however, correlations of this subtest with total test score and with criteria are of the same order of magnitude as those for subtests with more obvious intellectual content, closer examination is evidently called for.

Consideration of the performance required of the individual immediately points to two of the processes intimately involved in the vocabulary and digit span tests, namely, the availability of words as responses and short-term memory, respectively. However, it appears that neither of these can be a major determinant of individual differences in performance. All but the most severely retarded individuals to whom this test might be given must have many more words in a relatively high state of availability than the 28 required as a passing score at Year 10. Short-term memory must be involved to some extent because the individual must keep track of the words he has already given in order to avoid repetitions during output. However, the bulk of available evidence (see Belmont & Butterfield, 1969; Estes, 1970) indicates that rate of short-term forgetting does not vary substantially with either age or intelligence over a wide range.

A more central factor in the word-naming test is manifest if we note that it is in a sense a limiting case of the free verbal recall experiment, in which the subject is read a list of words and then asked immediately to recall as many as possible in any order. A very substantial amount of recent research shows clearly that performance in free recall is largely determined by the organization of an individual's long-term memory system and the way in which he makes use of this organization to guide performance in the testing situation. Data obtained by administration of free-recall tests to various populations show that amount recalled from a given list length increases systematically with age, education, and intelligence and that the tendency of the individual to organize his output in terms of clusters of meaningfully related words exhibits parallel trends. More importantly, the performance of young or mentally retarded subjects can be brought up to substantially higher levels if the individuals are led by the examiner to make use of meaningful categories in organizing their responses (for a review of this literature, see Estes, 1970).

A sharp distinction needs to be made between the extent to which an individual's memory is organized in terms of categories and the extent to which he utilizes these categories in retrieving material in a test situation. For example, on examination with the usual procedures, children belonging to a nonliterate African community appeared substantially inferior to American schoolchildren of similar age in free recall (Cole, Gay, Glick, & Sharp, 1971), and it would be easy to dispose of this not particularly surprising finding as an example of the effects of cultural deprivation on the African children. By means of a painstaking series of researches involving close examination of the subjects' performance and of its relation to their cultural background, these investigators were able to show that when the African children were led by special techniques to respond in terms of meaningful categories their recall performance improved sharply to a level similar to that of American school children.

Mandler (1967) reviewed evidence suggesting that an individual's total vocabulary may be organized into a hierarchy of clusters of meaningfully related words in much the same fashion as the smaller sample of material presented in a free-recall experiment and that efficient performance in a word-naming test depends importantly on the extent to which the individual utilizes this organization. Both the time required to retrieve words and the demands on short-term

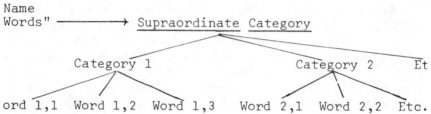

Figure 2.18 Schemata for processes of word naming by chain association (upper portion) and by utilizing a categorical organization of memory (lower portion).

memory are greatly reduced to the extent that one runs through a set of categories in an orderly fashion, enumerating as many as possible of the words belonging to each category in turn. In Figure 2.18, this strategy (lower panel) is contrasted with the less efficient one of chain association.

The data of Cole et al. (1971) indicate that the habit of retrieving material from long-term memory by means of categories depends strongly on amount of schooling, but when amount of schooling is held constant, retrieval is only slightly related to either age per se or other aspects of cultural background. There is clearly a pressing need for still more analytical research to determine just what aspects of school experience are responsible for developing this type of intellectual strategy.

CONCEPTIONS OF INTELLIGENCE AND LEARNING ABILITY: CONCLUDING REMARKS

Now, where do we stand at a theoretical level with respect to the interpretation of intelligence in terms of concepts of learning theory? First, referring back to our starting point, we might ask how, in the light of ensuing developments, we would now evaluate Thorndike's proposal that differences in intellect are manifestations of differences in the total number of available associative connections. Research and logical analyses within the framework of modern learning theory have certainly done nothing to dampen the skepticism that most of us doubtless felt concerning the plausibility of Thorndike's conjecture. In particular, Thorndike's correlational evidence is now seen to be distinctly less than crucial, for our analyses yield no reason to believe that any of the tests he used provide pure measures of either associative or higher cognitive abilities. But, although subsequent events have not supported Thorndike's hypothesis, neither can they be said to have disproved it. What does become clear upon consideration of the complex interaction of biological and environmental events and processes over a prolonged period which are necessary for the development of effective intellectual behavior is that a model of the type Thorndike proposed is incapable of refutation by any methods now at hand or even foreseeable.

To be sure, some contemporary investigators, especially among those seeking to ameliorate mental deficiency by biochemical or psychopharmacological techniques, appear to operate on the tacit assumption that something akin to Thorndike's model is correct. Thus, one sees studies reported in which groups of intellectually deficient animals or children are subjected to new diets or new drugs and then tested to see whether their performance has improved relative to normals. But this strategy seems doomed to be as fruitless in the future as it has been in the past. For even if Thorndike's conjecture were correct, and if someone were to discover a drug that produced a substantial increase in the supply of available connections, the individual who was treated could not be expected to manifest any sudden increase in intellectual performance. The increased potentiality might be there, but a substantial program of reeducation and training would be required to make up for the deficiencies in past learning and to lay the groundwork for the organization of processes needed for efficient intellectual performance. I suggest that to have any rational basis for expectations of fruitful results, research directed toward the amelioration of intellectual deficiencies by physiological and chemical therapy must be conducted in close conjunction with the intensive application of the most sophisticated resources of learning theory to help trace the way through the no-man's land between capacity and performance.

With regard to continuing theory construction, we can begin to see that theories of the form "differences in intelligence are manifestations of differences in x" or "differences between retardates and normals are produced by deficiencies in x" are the wrong kinds of theories to be trying to construct. The urgent need now is not for better means of classifying people with respect to intellectual functioning and correlating these classifications with other variables, but for understanding what brings about specific kinds of competence and incompetence in intellectual activity.

An additional source of motivation for exploring the possibility of characterizing intelligence in terms of learning processes, going beyond the purely intellectual challenge, has to do with the changing mood of society. We are seeing increased resistance to the very conception of testing and measuring intelligence solely for purposes of prediction. If the trend that we see reflected daily not only in the newspapers but in the more erudite journals continues, we may find that not far in the future it will become impossible to measure intelligence, except in white, middle-class children, unless we can demonstrate some direct value to the individual being tested. This demand might be met if, for example, it came to be recognized (and in fact to be the case) that the primary purpose of intelligence testing had become that, not of predicting intellectual performance, but rather of indicating and guiding measures that can be taken to improve intellectual performance.

Little can be accomplished in this direction with present instruments for measuring intelligence because these operate primarily by sampling performance, and in every type of intellectual task any given level of performance can arise in many different ways. One's first thought may be that our present instruments for measuring intelligence need to be replaced by new ones better suited for diagnostic purposes. Aside from the perhaps transient problem that we have no specific idea at present how to proceed in this direction, we face the major difficulty that almost inevitably new tests of quite different design will be less valid predictors of intellectual performance than those now in use.

An alternative route involves not replacing or revising, but rather augmenting present methods of measuring intellect. The desired goal may be achieved if we can interpret the processes involved in test behavior in terms of concepts drawn from learning theory and utilize these interpretations as a basis for developing techniques to localize the sources of the deficits in performance revealed by test scores. This is not to imply that one should expect practical benefits to follow quickly and easily from laboratory analyses of test behavior. At the very least, it will be necessary to go on to the analysis of situations outside the laboratory which call for various types of intellectual activity. However, it does seem that research on intelligence within the framework proposed here might prove as fruitful for theory as that confined to the psychometric tradition and might lead to additional long-term social gains.

REFERENCES

Allen, G. A., Mahler, W. A., & Estes, W. K. Effects of recall tests on long-term retention of paired-associates. *Journal of Verbal Learning and Verbal Behavior,* 1969, **8,** 463–470.

Anglin, J. M. *The growth of word meaning.* Cambridge, Mass.: MIT Press, 1970.

Belmont, J. M., & Butterfield, E. C. The relation of short-term memory to development and intelligence. In L. P. Lipsitt & H. W. Reese (Eds.), *Advances in child development and behavior.* Vol. 4. New York: Academic Press, 1969.

Bower, G. H., & Winzenz, D. Group structure, coding, and memory for digit series. *Journal of Experimental Psychology Monograph,* 1969, **80**(2, Pt. 2), 1–17.

Cole, M., Gay, J., Glick, J., & Sharp, D. W. *The cultural context of learning and thinking.* New York: Basic Books, 1971.

Estes, W. K. *Learning theory and mental development.* New York: Academic Press, 1970.

Estes, W. K. An associative basis for coding and organization in memory. In A. W. Melton & E. Martin (Eds.), *Coding processes in human memory.* New York: Academic Press, 1972.

Horowitz, L. M., Norman, S. A., & Day, R. S. Availability and associative symmetry. *Psychological Review,* 1966, **73,** 1–15.

Howes, D. Vocabulary size estimated from the distribution of word frequencies. In H. Myklebust (Ed.), *Progress in learning disabilities.* Vol. 2. New York: Grune & Stratton, 1971.

Jahnke, J. C. Probed recall of strings that contain repeated elements. *Journal of Verbal Learning and Verbal Behavior,* 1970, **9,** 450–455.

Johnson, N. F. The role of chunking and organization in the process of recall. In G. H. Bower (Ed.), *The psychology of learning and motivation: Advances in research and theory.* Vol. 4. New York: Academic Press, 1970.

Lesgold, A. M., & Bower, G. H. Inefficiency of serial knowledge for associative responding. *Journal of Verbal Learning and Verbal Behavior,* 1970, **9,** 456–466.

Mandler, G. Organization and memory. In K. W. Spence & J. T. Spence (Eds.), *The psychology of learning and motivation: Advances in research and theory.* Vol. 1. New York: Academic Press, 1967.

McNemar, Q. *The revision of the Stanford-Binet scale.* New York: Houghton Mifflin, 1942.

Miller, G. A. The magical number seven, plus or minus two: Some limits on our capacity for processing information. *Psychological Review,* 1956, **63,** 81–97.

Royer, F. L. Information processing of visual figures in the digit symbol substitution test. *Journal of Experimental Psychology,* 1971, **87,** 335–342.

Spitz, H. H. The role of input organization in the learning and memory of mental retardates. In N. R. Ellis (Ed.), *International review of research in mental retardation.* Vol. 2. New York: Academic Press, 1966.

Thorndike, E. L. *Measurement of intelligence.* New York: Teacher's College, Columbia University, 1926.

Tulving, E. Theoretical issues in free recall. In T. R. Dixon & D. L. Horton (Eds.), *Verbal behavior and general behavior theory.* Englewood Cliffs, N.J.: Prentice-Hall, 1968.

Underwood, B. J. Attributes of memory. *Psychological Review,* 1969, 76, 559–573.

3

Memory

Scarcely any field of study in psychology can have changed as drastically over the period being sampled in this volume as the study of memory. Even as recently as 1950, memory was not close to the status of a research specialty, and, in fact, the term *memory* rarely appeared in the research literature except rather casually with reference to studies of retention of learned material or habits. The dominant theoretical framework was associationism, and association theory was still confined almost wholly to the idea of simple interitem connections. Alternative approaches included nothing that could reasonably be termed a theory. Gestalt psychology was dormant except in the field of perception. The ideas of Bartlett (1932), interpreting memory in terms of continual reorganizations of schemata and images, were to become influential when rediscovered later, but they were not so in the research of the 1950s. The idea of dealing in a constructive theoretical way with problems of the form of memory representations or the cognitive processes operating on them had not begun to appear.

In the psychology of the 1980s, memory has moved to center stage, the focus of the new cognitive psychology, which subsumes much of the continuation of earlier research traditions on learning, thought processes, and perception. Association theory has changed almost beyond recognition, the chain of simple interitem connections having given way to structured network models and propositional representations. The conceptions of stages of processing of perceived information and cognitive operations on the consequent encoded memory structures—all within the paradigm of information processing—have been central motifs of the last two decades.

MEMORY IN STIMULUS-SAMPLING THEORY

How does the development of my own ideas fit in with this changing scene? At the beginning of the period just reviewed, my conception of association was essentially the classic one, differing from the norm only with regard to my

127

deeper interest in formalizing and elaborating existing theories. The first specific new development in my own work leading toward models for memory was the recognition that the availability or accessibility of associations must be determined not only by activation from external stimuli buy also by continual spontaneous variation as a function of the fluctuating pattern of internal activities of the organism over time. This idea was implemented in models that proved relevant to the interpretation of phenomena, ranging from spontaneous recovery of conditioned reflexes to a rationale for forgetting curves and spacing effects in learning. The first important presentation of this work occurred in 1955 (Estes, 1955a, 1955b) but the paper included as the first reprint in this chapter (from Estes, 1971) presents the same ideas with a more modern flavor.

During the 1960s, a major change of emphasis from the *how* to the *what* of learning occurred throughout the field of human learning and memory. The focus shifted from the way learning and retention loss occur over time to questions of the form and organization taken by the products of learning and contents of memory. Stimulus-sampling theory seemed well adapted to deal with the former type of question but was not so appropriate for the latter. New and highly fertile lines of research, such as Sternberg's studies of short-term memory scanning (Sternberg, 1966), Conrad's findings on auditory encoding of visually presented materials in short-term memory (Conrad, 1964, 1967), and a burst of work on organization in free recall (for example, Mandler, 1967), were difficult to talk or think about in terms of populations of simple and mutually exchangeable associations or memory units.

ENCODING AND INFORMATION PROCESSING

During the late 1960s, I was one of a number of scientists who were assimilating this flood of new material and responding to it with major enrichments and elaborations of earlier theoretical ideas. Thus, the first papers giving a major extension of my own earlier ideas on memory (Estes, 1972a, 1973) appeared almost simultaneously with those of, for example, Anderson and Bower (1973), Collins and Quillian (1972), and Rumelhart, Lindsay, and Norman (1972). The second paper reprinted in this chapter reviews findings that I had thought compelling with regard to the way stimulus information comes to be recoded in memory and presents in first approximation a family of new models, ranging from a treatment of very short term sensory memory based on reverberatory loops to a hierarchical associative structure for long-term memory. Further development of these ideas and discussions of their relation to the information processing movement and other current approaches to organization in memory are the subject of the third and fourth papers in this chapter.

In these papers, one will find indications of my growing concern with some aspects of the currently most influential approaches to memory—information-processing models in the computer analogy and the network and feature models closely related to case grammars and other linguistic concepts. To my mind, the early work on information-processing conceptions—for example, Atkinson and Shiffrin (1968), Hunt (1962), Simon and Feigenbaum (1964), and Sternberg (1966)—seemed a welcome shift of orientation from the previously dominant functionalism and traditional associationism. Until the emergence of the information-processing analogies, such mental structures as images and such mental operations as memory search had seemed almost mystical ideas, beyond the reach of experimental analysis. With the availability of computer analogies to suggest hypotheses about specific functional properties of such entities, however, and reaction time methods to gain evidence on their time courses, the situation seemed radically changed. By the mid-1960s, I was deeply involved in the new approaches to mental chronometry, but that line of research, largely concerned with visual search and signal detection, is not specifically represented in this volume.

By the end of the last decade, I had begun to wonder whether the information-processing approach and the computer analogy were perhaps being overdone in some respects. The idea that the human being processes discrete packets of information, usually symbols, through successive stages of filtering, manipulation of symbols in short-term memory, transfer to long-term storage, and so on, was proving fruitful but also constraining. Even in studies of my own and my associates (Drewnowski, 1980; Lee & Estes, 1977, 1981) conducted in that tradition, one could see evidence of more analog-appearing properties of the processing system, with memory storage and retrieval based more on the storage and manipulation of information about distributions or on gradients of information about attributes of events than on the passage of discrete items through memory stores. Some new directions in our thinking arising from these considerations may be seen in the third paper in this chapter.

A similar course of interactions can be seen in relation to network models of organization in memory. The appearance of network and feature models of semantic memory and language processing in the early 1970s at first seemed to present a stark contrast between old and new conceptions. Traditional association theory, still grappling with fine points of paired-associate learning, seemed to offer few interesting potentialities by comparison with the new models being used to guide and interpret a variety of research on comprehension and representation of sentences, propositions, and categories. In a sense, however, much of the new model building seemed to go too fast. Just as a quarter of a century earlier I had been concerned over the excessive postulation of unobservable constructs on the part of Hull and Tolman, I now wondered whether the almost uninhibited introduction of qualitatively new kinds of associations (for example, the "is a" relations of Collins and Quillian, 1972, and the linguistically labeled associations of Rumelhart, Lindsay, and Norman, 1972) was encouraging the piling up of new theory at a rate faster than new phenomena could be interpreted. I wondered whether progress could be made by enriching earlier association theories without reifying each newly introduced formal construct. Granted that information in memory about concepts calls for some kind of representation in a network, for example, need it follow that the nodes and links of the network must correspond one-to-one with concepts representing linguistic relations? By simply assuming that syntactic and semantic properties are stored in memory and then creating mental structures to represent them, one may risk giving only the appearance of explanation and discouraging research directed toward explanation in terms of more primitive or general concepts.

At the same time I unreservedly appreciate the accomplishments of the new approaches of Anderson and Bower (1973) and others in breaking new ground, and I recognize keenly that the much needed body of theory that might meaningfully relate work on the processing of sentences, propositions, and larger units to other aspects of and in some senses more basic bodies of research and theory on memory and learning is a large order. At this point, I have done no more myself than explore some possible approaches. A few more specific ideas regarding how we might proceed with more attention to theoretical economy are sketched in the fourth paper reprinted in this chapter.

VISUAL PROCESSING AND READING

During the same period in which these developments in research and theory on memory were occurring, a virtually new psychological discipline, having to do with visual information processing of letters and words, was taking form (Haber, 1969; Neisser, 1967). For me, the new approaches to visual processing provided an ideal ground on the border between perception and memory for working out earlier ideas concerning stimulus sampling in a new theoretical context. The flavor of this new research motif and references to more technical developments will be found in the final paper in this chapter, dealing with the interaction of perception and memory in reading.

I never made a deliberate decision to do research on reading; rather, I found myself turned in that direction in the course of efforts to distinguish the contributions of memory from those of perceptual processes in the identification of individual letters or digits (Estes & Taylor, 1964). That problem has proved difficult enough, so that I have never felt a need to leap ahead to more direct attacks on the full reading process.

Nonetheless, a direction from the simple toward the complex is inherent in the research process itself. In the case of letter identification, as a theoretical account of the interactions among unrelated letters in the visual field began to take shape (Estes, 1972b, 1974; Shiffrin and Geisler, 1973; Wolford, Wessel, and Estes, 1968), it was natural to begin to wonder just how the principles would be modified if the letters were combined into familiar units—a query that, in my case, led into a series of studies of the word superiority effect, in collaboration with Elizabeth L. Bjork (Bjork & Estes, 1971, 1973). We recognized the special properties of letters in words, just as do investigators with more holistic orientations, but we sought explanation of the effects of word context in the way it modifies the combination and interaction of more basic processes. To begin to see how these modifications might occur, we of course had to go beyond the study of individual letters as stimuli and investigate how constraints on the way letters combine in English words constrain, in turn, the decision processes by means of which the outputs of perceptual mechanisms are interpreted. (To give a simple example, if a letter c is perceived in a string of letters that might constitute a word, the reader's threshold, or criterion, for accepting stimulus input from the next location to the right as signifying the presence of an h would be lowered, but that for an n would be raised.) Elucidation of this problem has required progressive expansion of the original theoretical focus to incorporate concepts and methods from signal detectability theory and models of short- and long-term memory (Estes, 1975a, 1975b).

Progress in this line of research seems slow in relation to the ultimately desirable objective of understanding reading, yet the advances over the state of the field as it existed ten or fifteen years ago are rather substantial. Although there are many points of controversy, a considerable consensus has emerged on an overall strategy of going as far as possible toward interpreting reading by way of basic structures and processes of perception and memory. Reading is viewed as beginning with the recognition of visual patterns, the special aspect of reading being not the perceptual processes responsible but the way the material is organized. The very large number of words in the language can be represented by arrangements of a very much smaller number of letters, and, more hypothetically, the letters can be represented, in turn, by arrangements of a still smaller number of visual critical features (Gibson, 1969; Rumelhart, 1970). These characteristics of the alphabetic system are assumed in a family of current models to correspond to a hierarchy of units in the memory system (Estes, 1975a, 1975b; LaBerge & Samuels, 1974; McClelland & Rumelhart, 1981).

In the models developed within this framework, information from visual patterns is conceived to be sifted through a series of memory structures that function as interactive filters (a concept introduced to this field by Anderson, 1977), the outputs being representations of units at the successive levels of the linguistic hierarchy.

My current assessment of this theoretical effort will be apparent in the final paper in this chapter, which includes a sketch of my version of the hierarchical filter model, together with research bearing on the way processes of encoding and decision are modified by both visual and linguistic factors at different levels of the hierarchy. In writing the paper (that is, the lecture on which the paper was based), I was especially concerned with assembling available evidence bearing on the question of whether a reader gains access to information about linguistic properties of text in some way that bypasses the bottom-up filtering and interpretation of information emanating from the printed letter patterns, as conceived in the hierarchical model. The question is raised by an approach to reading in which it is assumed that the reader approaches a text with an assemblage of hypotheses about possible messages and then tests these hypotheses against properties of the input in order to construct an account of what is there. One representative of this view is Smith (1971), who had developed an account of reading in terms of hypothesis testing on the basis of global properties or supraletter features of text. In Smith's terms, "rather than saying that he [the perceiver] discovers order and regularities that are properties of the environment, it is more appropriate to say that the perceiver imposes his own organization upon the information that reaches his receptor systems" (p. 187).

It is scarcely possible to test a global theory of this sort rigorously as a whole, but it is reasonable to look for evidence bearing specifically on major constituent propositions. Following this line of thought, some of my experimental work described in the last paper in this chapter was designed to determine whether a reader can decide whether a briefly displayed string of letters constitutes a word before, or independent of, identification of the individual letters. The results were uniformly negative.

However, the picture of word perception supported by my results is not a feature-analyzing mechanism driven solely by the stimulus input and grinding to a conclusion, independent of other cognitive processes. Rather, the processing clearly is partly concept-driven, in current parlance, and information gained from the perception of text can only be defined and measured relative to the initial informational state of the perceiver. In research continuing beyond that described in this chapter, specific evidence is accruing that not only a priori expectations or hypotheses but also information obtained from early states of processing function to modify the reader's criteria or thresholds for accepting incomplete sensory information (arising, for example, from a letter partially masked by neighbors in indirect vision) as indicating the presence of linguistically significant units in the stimulus input. The interaction of concurrent concept-driven and stimulus-driven processes is becoming an increasingly important motif in other lines of research on memory, continuing beyond the studies discussed in this volume.

REFERENCES

Anderson, J. A. Neural models with cognitive implications. In D. LaBerge & S. J. Samuels (Eds.), *Basic processes in reading: Perception and comprehension,* pp. 27–90. Hillsdale, N.J.: Lawrence Erlbaum Associates, 1977.

Anderson, J. R., & Bower, G. H. *Human associative memory.* Washington, D.C.: V. H. Winston, 1973.

Atkinson, R. C., & Shiffrin, R. M. Human memory: A proposed system and its control processes. In K. W. Spence & J. T. Spence (Eds.), *The psychology of learning and motivation: Advances in research and theory,* Vol. 2, pp. 89–195. New York: Academic Press, 1968.

Bartlett, F. C. *Remembering.* Cambridge, England: Cambridge University Press, 1932.

Bjork, E. L., & Estes, W. K. Detection and placement of redundant signal elements in tachistoscopic displays of letters. *Perception & Psychophysics,* 1971, *9,* 439–442.

Bjork, E. L., & Estes, W. K. Letter identification in relation to linguistic context and masking conditions. *Memory & Cognition,* 1973, *1,* 217–223.

Collins, A. M., & Quillian, M. R. How to make a language user. In E. Tulving & W. Donaldson (Eds.), *Organization of memory,* pp. 309–351. New York: Academic Press, 1972.

Conrad, R. Acoustic confusions in immediate memory. *British Journal of Psychology,* 1964, *55,* 75–84.

Conrad, R. Interference or decay over short retention intervals. *Journal of Verbal Learning and Verbal Behavior,* 1967, *6,* 49–54.

Drewnowski, A. Attributes and priorities in short-term recall: A new model of memory span. *Journal of Experimental Psychology: General,* 1980, *109,* 208–250.

Estes, W. K. Statistical theory of distributional phenomena in learning. *Psychological Review*, 1955, *62*, 145–154. (a)

Estes, W. K. Statistical theory of distributional phenomena in learning. *Psychological Review*, 1955, *62*, 369–377. (b)

Estes, W. K. Learning and memory. In E. F. Beckenbach & C. B. Tompkins (Eds.), *Concepts of communication*, pp. 282–300. New York: Wiley, 1971.

Estes, W. K. An associative basis for coding and organization in memory. In A. W. Melton and E. Martin (Eds.), *Coding processes in human memory*, pp. 161–190. Washington, D.C.: V. H. Winston, 1972. (a)

Estes, W. K. Interactions of signal and background variables in visual processing. *Perception & Psychophysics*, 1972, *12*, 278–286. (b)

Estes, W. K. Memory and conditioning. In F. G. McGuigan and D. B. Lumsden (Eds.), *Contemporary approaches to conditioning and learning*, pp. 265–286. Washington, D.C.: V. H. Winston, 1973.

Estes, W. K. Redundancy of noise elements and signals in visual detection of letters. *Perception & Psychophysics*, 1974, *16*, 53–60.

Estes, W. K. Memory, perception, and decision in letter identification. In R. L. Solso (Ed.), *Information processing and cognition: The Loyola Symposium*, pp. 3–30. Hillsdale, N.J.: Lawrence Erlbaum Associates, 1975. (a)

Estes, W. K. The locus of inferential and perceptual processes in letter identification. *Journal of Experimental Psychology: General*, 1975, *104*, 122–124. (b)

Estes, W. K., & Taylor, H. A. A detection method and probabilistic models for assessing information processing from brief visual displays. *Proceedings of the National Academy of Sciences*, 1964, *52*, 446–454.

Gibson, E. J. *Principles of perceptual learning and development*. New York: Appleton-Century-Crofts, 1969.

Haber, R. N. *Information-processing approaches to visual perception*. New York: Holt, Rinehart & Winston, 1969.

Hunt, E. *Concept learning: An information processing problem*. New York: Wiley, 1962.

LaBerge, D., & Samuels, S. J. Toward a theory of automatic information processing in reading. *Cognitive Psychology*, 1974, *6*, 293–323.

Lee, C. L., & Estes, W. K. Order and position in primary memory for letter strings. *Journal of Verbal Learning and Verbal Behavior*, 1977, *16*, 395–418.

Lee, C. L., & Estes, W. K. Item and order information in short-term memory: Evidence for multi-level perturbation processes. *Journal of Experimental Psychology: Human Learning and Memory*, 1981, *7*, 149–169.

Mandler, G. Organization and memory. In K. W. Spence & J. T. Spence (Eds.), *The psychology of learning and motivation: Advances in research and theory*, Vol. 1, pp. 327–372. New York: Academic Press, 1967.

McClelland, J. L., & Rumelhart, D. E. An interactive model of context effects in letter perception. Part I: An account of basic findings. *Psychological Review*, 1981, *88*, 375–407.

Neisser, U. *Cognitive psychology*. New York: Appleton-Century-Crofts, 1967.

Rumelhart, D. E. A multicomponent theory of the perception of briefly exposed visual displays. *Journal of Mathematical Psychology*, 1970, *7*, 191–218.

Rumelhart, D. E., Lindsay, P. H., & Norman, D. A. A process model for long term memory. In E. Tulving & W. Donaldson (Eds.), *Organization of memory*, pp. 197–246. New York: Academic Press, 1972.

Shiffrin, R. M., & Geisler, W. S. Visual recognition in a theory of information processing. In R. L. Solso (Ed.), *Contemporary issues in cognitive psychology: The Loyola Symposium*, pp. 53–101. Washington, D.C.: V. H. Winston, 1973.

Simon, H. A., & Feigenbaum, E. A. An information-processing theory of some effects of similarity, familiarization, and meaningfulness in verbal learning. *Journal of Verbal Learning and Verbal Behavior*, 1964, *3*, 385–396.

Smith, F. *Understanding reading*. New York: Holt, 1971.

Sternberg, S. High-speed scanning in human memory. *Science*, 1966, *153*, 652–654.

Wolford, G. L., Wessel, D. L., & Estes, W. K. Further evidence concerning scanning and sampling assumptions of visual detection models. *Perception & Psychophysics*, 1968, *3*, 439–444.

Short-Term Memory

STATISTICAL MODEL FOR SHORT-TERM MEMORY

The theory to be presented is psychological rather than neurophysiological in character, in that the overall strategy is to set down assumptions concerning properties of the process of retention loss without hypothesizing physical loci for the events involved. Also, for the present, the merits of the theory are assessed in terms of its demonstrable potentiality for predicting phenomena observed in experiments on memory. Nonetheless, the theory is not unrelated to basic concepts of neurophysiology and neuroanatomy which have been introduced in other chapters.

On the basis of our general knowledge of the structure and operation of the nervous system, perhaps the most salient single characteristic we should expect a model for memory to exhibit is that of multiplicity, or redundancy of basic elements. The earliest work concerned with searching for the anatomical bases of memory was organized in terms of the search for an "engram," the engram being the physical trace presumably laid down somewhere in the nervous system as a result of a learning experience and serving as the carrier of memory for the experience. It was, however, one of the first major accomplishments of physiological psychology, associated primarily with the work of Lashley, to demonstrate convincingly that the engram, whatever it might be physically, was not localized in any one small region of the nervous system. Numerous studies showed that memory for a particular learning experience could not be eradicated by ablation of any one localized area of the brain, and that for the most part impairment of memory for a learning experience was roughly proportional to amount of tissue removed. Thus it seems necessary to assume that not a single engram, but a collection of them, are involved in the establishment of any particular memory. To avoid undesired connotations, we shall speak of the members of this collection simply as elements.

A second major characteristic which must be assumed to char-

Excerpted from W. K. Estes, Learning and memory. In E. F. Beckenbach & C. B. Tompkins (Eds.), *Concepts of communication*, pp. 282–300. New York: Wiley, 1971. Reprinted by permission.

acterize the systems involved in retention is that of spontaneous variation in activity over time. Electrophysiological studies of the nervous system have shown abundantly that at all levels of the brain there is constant fluctuation in activity independent of the changes produced by incoming stimulation. Thus in the model for retention we assume that the memory elements fluctuate between an active and an inactive state, the fluctuation being random with respect to time and independent of learning experiences.

With these basic considerations in mind, we are ready to sketch more specifically the assumptions embodied in a statistical model for short-term memory. This presentation can be accomplished most conveniently with reference to the schematization shown in Figure 3.1.

We should emphasize that if the individual under study, say the receiver in a communication system, has a number of learning experiences involving different events, then the theory defines a different set of memory elements corresponding to each of these experiences. Thus in Figure 3.1 we represent the receiver's memory with respect to message 1 in a series by the rectangle labeled M_1, his memory with respect to message 2 by the rectangle labeled M_2, and so on. For an experiment involving a number of different messages, it is not necessary that the different sets of elements all be of the same size or have the same fluctuation parameters, though for simplicity in

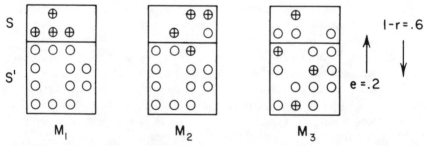

Figure 3.1 Theoretical schema for fluctuation model. The three rectangles represent sets of memory elements, circles above and below the horizontal lines representing elements active and inactive, respectively, at the given time. An element marked with a + sign is positive relative to recall of the message. The parameters e and r determine the rate of fluctuation of elements between the active and inactive states. The diagram represents the states of the systems immediately after initial receipt of message M_1, a short time after initial receipt of message M_2, and a sufficiently long time after receipt of message M_3 for the fluctuation process to have reached the asymptotic equilibrium condition.

the diagram all of the sets have been taken to be of the same size. Taking the set corresponding to one of the messages, say M_1, we note, first, that the system has an active and an inactive state, represented by the upper and lower parts of the rectangle, respectively. Elements above the horizontal dividing line are in the active state at the time represented, and those below the horizontal line are in the inactive state. It is assumed that constant random fluctuation occurs across the boundary, the parameter e denoting the probability that any currently inactive element enters the active state during a short interval of time Δt and the parameter r denoting the probability that any currently active element remains active during the same interval.

The second primary property of a set of memory elements is the state of the elements with respect to the learning of the item of information involved. It is assumed that at any time the elements in a given system are partitioned into those that are positive and those that are negative with respect to memory for the particular message. Positive elements are those that would contribute to a correct response if the individual were asked to recall the message, and elements which are negative are those that would not contribute to correct recall. Our assumptions concerning the way in which the state of learning changes are as follows: Stated in terms of the communication situation, upon receipt of a message, say M_1, all of the elements in the momentarily active set are turned positive for that message.

This change of state is permanent in that it does not decay or otherwise change as a function of time and can be altered only by later learning experiences. A message generally states some relationship, and one tests the individual for his memory of a message by supplying some cue to which a correct response will be taken as evidence of memory for the message. Elements that have been turned positive by an effective learning experience are said to be associated with the correct response. This association persists until and unless some later learning experience produces a change in state of these elements, again on an all-or-none basis, so that they become associated with some different response.

For example, suppose message M_1, were "The temperature is 69 degrees." Upon receipt of this message by the receiver, his currently active memory elements for this item would become associated with the response "69 degrees" and would lead him to make this response if subsequently questioned concerning the temperature. These elements would, then, remain associated with this response unless a later message concerning temperature, say "The temperature is now 75 degrees," should change the state of the currently active elements so that they become associated with the response "75 degrees" rather than the response "69 degrees."

The way in which the individual's recall response depends on the current state of his memory elements may be more fully specified as follows. We assume that when a cue for recall of a message is given, the individual selects one of the currently active memory elements at random and responds on the basis of the state of this element. If the element sampled is positive for a given response, then that response is given. If the element sampled is in the negative state, then the individual is assumed to respond at random. The sense of randomness intended is the following. For simplicity, we consider a situation in which there are N possible messages, all equally likely to be sent over the channel, with the full set known in advance to both the sender and the receiver. Under these circumstances, if the receiver is asked to recall a message and samples a negative memory element, it is assumed that he has probability $1/N$ of making each of the possible responses. Thus probability of recall of the correct response to a given cue is directly related to proportion of memory elements that have become associated with the appropriate response.

Since the state of learning of memory elements is assumed not to change over time, it is clear that observed retention loss must be due to fluctuations over time in the proportions of positive elements which are in the active state. The way in which this fluctuation process will lead to typical functions for forgetting of learned material can readily be seen by reference to Figure 3.1. The rectangle for M_1 shows the state of a system immediately following the first receipt of the particular message. Originally all of the memory elements were negative, but upon receipt of the message all of those in the currently active subset turned positive. If the receiver were asked immediately thereafter to give the message, it is assumed that he would do so with probability 1 since any memory element he sampled would necessarily be in the positive state. Over a subsequent interval of time, however, fluctuation of elements between the active and inactive states would proceed, so that if the individual were tested for recall after an interval, the state of the system would be more like that shown for message M_2 in the figure. That is, some of the positive elements would have become inactive and some of the negative elements would have become active, so that the individual would no longer be certain to sample a positive memory element when asked to recall the message. Thus probability of correct recall would have decreased from its maximum value immediately after the learning experience. As time goes on and fluctuation continues, this "diffusion" of elements across the boundary between the active and inactive subsets continues until a statistical equilibrium is reached at a level at which the density of positive elements is the same in the active and inactive states. From this point on, on the average, no further observed retention loss should occur.

To develop some of the more detailed implications of the model, we require a difference equation expressing the probability f_{t+1} that any particular element is active at time $t + 1$ recursively in terms of the probability f_t obtaining during the preceding time interval and the parameters of the fluctuation process. The desired recursion takes the form

$$f_{t+1} = (1 - f_t)e + f_t r. \tag{1}$$

This difference equation is readily solved by standard methods to obtain the following formula for probability that any given associative element is active at time t:

$$f_t = \frac{e}{1 - r + e} - \left[\frac{e}{1 - r + e} - f_0 \right] (r - e)^t, \tag{2}$$

which may be written more simply

$$f_t = \lambda - (\lambda - f_0)a^t$$

where $a = r - e$ and $\lambda = e/(1 - r + e)$.

With this basic function in hand, we can readily derive the probability ϕ_t that a positive memory element will be sampled by the observer on a recall test at time t following a learning experience. We note, first, that the probability that the element sampled at time t was in the active state at time 0, and therefore necessarily positive, is $\lambda - (\lambda -1)a^t$, whereas the probability that it was inactive at time 0 is $(1 - \lambda)(1 - a^t)$. Denoting by ϕ_0' the probability that any element inactive at time 0 was positive, we have

$$\begin{aligned}\phi_t &= \lambda - (\lambda - 1)a^t + (1 - \lambda)(1 - a^t)\phi_0' \\ &= \lambda + (1 - \lambda)\phi_0' + (1 - \lambda)(1 - \phi_0')a^t. \end{aligned} \tag{3}$$

Finally, utilizing the assumptions stated earlier regarding response determination, we can write for p_t, the probability of a correct recall at time t following receipt of a message in the communication situation with N equally likely possible messages,

$$p_t = \phi_t + (1 - \phi_t)(1/N)$$
$$= [1 - (1/N)]\,\phi_t + (1/N)$$
$$= [1 - (1/N)]\,[\lambda + (1 - \lambda)\phi_0'] + (1/N) \qquad (4)$$
$$\quad + [1 - (1/N)]\,(1 - \lambda)(1 - \phi_0')a^t$$
$$= p_\infty + (1 - p_\infty)a^t,$$

where p_∞ denotes probability of a correct response after an indefinitely long time following receipt of the message. The gist of this result is that, during a period of time following receipt of a message, the probability of a correct response on the part of the receiver will decline exponentially to a limiting value which depends jointly on the parameters of the statistical diffusion process and on the proportion of elements associated with the correct response at time 0.

IMPLICATIONS OF THE FLUCTUATION MODEL
FOR PHENOMENA OF SHORT-TERM MEMORY

Considering the schema of Figure 3.1, together with the functions just derived, we note first that rate of retention loss following the learning experience is predicted to depend on the parameters of the fluctuation process but to be independent of previous experiences. The fluctuation parameters e and r will be different for different situations, even in the case of the same individual, and they may be expected to be modified by such factors as drugs (for example, barbiturates) or even by variations in bodily temperature. These aspects of the theory are compatible with such well-known experimental results as that rate of retention loss for learned material is slowed if a period of sleep follows immediately upon the learning experience, in the case of human subjects, and that retention of conditioned responses in goldfish is inversely related to the temperature of the water. In particular, we have no reason to expect that rate of fluctuation of memory elements, and therefore rate of forgetting, can be modified by practice, rewards, punishments, or motivation.

The situation is quite different, however, concerning the limit of the forgetting process. Thus, in contrast to the rate of change, the asymptote of the retention curve depends not only on the fluctuation parameters but also on the state of learning. To take one extreme, suppose that all of the elements in a memory system, both those currently active and those currently inactive, were positive for a given item of information. In that event, at whatever time the individual was tested for recall, he would necessarily give the correct response and no changes in correct response probability would occur over time. Since only a portion of the elements in a memory system are active at the time of any one learning experience, it follows that improvement in retention in the sense of raising the asymptote of the retention curve can be achieved only by repetition. If a learning experience is repeated a number of times, in general different memory elements will be in the active state on different occasions, and thus the total number of positive elements in the system will increase.

It can readily be seen, further, that the temporal spacing of repeated learning experiences is of the utmost importance with respect to efficiency. Suppose, for example, at one extreme, that a second instance of message M_1 were sent immediately following the first message, thus arriving when the system was in the state shown at the left side of Figure 3.1. Since all of the currently active elements would already be positive at the time of the second occurrence of the message, no gain would result from the repetition, and the resulting course of forgetting would be precisely the same as though only one instance of the message had been received. Suppose, however, a second instance of message M_2 occurred immediately following the point illustrated in the center rectangle in Figure 3.1. At this point, some time after the first occurrence of the message, a portion of the positive elements would still be in the active state but some would have become inactive, and a second occurrence of the message would have the effect of turning positive some elements that were inactive on the first occurrence but were active at the time of the second occurrence. In general, the greatest gain from repetitions of a message will be attained if the time between repetitions is such that the system arrives at the equilibrium condition shown in the right-hand rectangle of Figure 3.1 prior to each repetition. Further increases in the intertrial interval beyond the time needed to arrive at the equilibrium state would, however, add no further advantage.

The optimal procedures are just the opposite if one's purpose is to correct errors in message transmission rather than to maximize retention on the part of the receiver. Suppose, for example, that at the point represented by the left-hand rectangle in Figure 3.1 the sender discovered that he had inadvertently sent the wrong message, say, "The temperature is 50 degrees," rather than the intended message, "The temperature is 69 degrees." The obvious remedy would be to send a correction message replacing the first one. An important implication of the model is that the time at which the correction occurs may be of major importance. If the second, correct, message were sent immediately following the first one, thus arriving at the point illustrated in the left-hand rectangle of Figure 3.1, when all of the elements which had been turned positive for the incorrect response "50 degrees" were still active, then all of these elements would have their state changed to positivity for the correct response "69 degrees," and the damage would be undone. Henceforth the receiver's memory for the correct message would be entirely unaffected by the inadvertent receipt of the erroneous message.

Suppose, however, that the situation were, instead, that illustrated in the middle rectangle of Figure 3.1. That is, some time had been allowed to elapse following receipt of the incorrect message before the correction message was sent. In this situation, the correct message, when it arrived, would produce the desired change of state of the currently active elements, but some elements which had been turned positive for the incorrect message would be inactive at the time of the correction message and thus unaffected by the correction. If the receiver were tested for recall immediately after receipt of the correction message, he would necessarily give the correct response. If, however, he were not tested until some time later, after further fluctuation of elements between the active and inactive states had occurred, his active set would now include a mixture of elements positive for the incorrect and elements positive for the correct message, and he would have some probability of making an error.

The effects of an incorrect message reception can, then, be completely undone in two quite different ways. First, by sending the correct message promptly enough so that it catches all of the elements active at the time of the incorrect message before any have escaped into the inactive state; or, second, by repeated correction messages given at spaced intervals and continuing until all elements that were active at the time of the incorrect message have been turned positive for the correct one.

IMPLICATIONS OF THE FLUCTUATION MODEL FOR INFORMATION TRANSMISSION

By appropriate application of the fluctuation model for immediate memory, it is possible to generate numerous predictions concerning conditions for achieving various desired properties of information transmission. If a series of messages is being sent across a channel to a single receiver, and if some messages are particularly important so that it is desirable to maximize the probability that they will be transmitted without memory loss on the part of the receiver, then the desired objective can be obtained by introducing redundancy into the series of messages. That is, some of the messages should be repeated at the cost of reducing the total number of different messages that can be sent. Referring to Figure 3.1 and the related formal derivations, we readily see that retention loss for any particular item can be reduced by building up the store of positive elements in the temporarily inactive set S', which increases the value of ϕ_0' in the formula for p_t. With a sufficient number of repetitions of a message, ϕ_0' can be driven to unity, and memory for the item on the part of the receiver will then be perfect; that is, there will be no retention loss. Further, we can see that when redundancy is used, the repetitions of a particular item should be spaced rather than bunched in the sequence of messages. This follows from the fact (see Figure 3.1) that if a message is repeated too soon, there will be no interchange of active and inactive elements between S and S' and thus nothing will be gained by the repetition. In general, repetitions are more effective the more widely they are temporally spaced. If several messages are equally important, then maximum efficiency will be obtained if these messages are given in a repetitive sequence $(A,B,C, A,B,C, A,B,C, \ldots)$. This last result is a consequence of a general theorem to the effect that the maximum amount of information transmitted by any one message will be obtained if the message chosen is the one that will add the greatest number of positive elements. Thus if there are many possible messages, maximal information transmission will result if a different message is sent on each trial, with no repetitions. When, however, there is a large population of possible messages and many are to be sent, it would generally be useful to attempt to achieve maximum transmission only if the receiver had a perfect memory. If the receiver is a human operator with a fallible memory, then, according to the theory, it will nearly always be necessary to repeat some messages at the expense of omitting others.

An Associative Basis for Coding and Organization in Memory

Taking together the facts that a great part of what we know about human memory has grown out of research conducted within the broad aegis of association theory and that research on memory is currently flourishing as never before, one might well be led to ask why some new type of theory should be contemplated. One reason, which becomes abundantly clear on reading a number of the other papers in this volume, is that many phenomena, and particularly those falling in the fringe area between learning and psycholinguistics, seem to call for a theory with much richer conceptual structure than that of traditional associationism.

We will doubtless see continuing attempts to meet the changing demands simply by modifying the basic concepts of association theory. But the resulting multiplicity of memory traces and varieties of connections quickly becomes cumbersome to work with and may be basically ill adapted to deal with phenomena of organization. Further, many investigators have been impressed by the number of conspicuous features of perception and memory not readily handled by extant associative models, which suggest the involvement of some kind of coding process.

Take, for example, current work on memory for strings of letters. When retention is imperfect, the confusion errors that occur are highly systematic. But the patterns of substitution errors are predictable, not from analyses of the stimulus inputs on physical dimensions, but rather from analyses in terms of critical features revealed by linguistic research and theory. Indeed many specific predictions can be made simply on the basis of the phonemes that are shared by pairs of letters.

Thus it is clear that of the information input generated when a letter is heard or read, a great part is discarded in the perceptual

Excerpted from W. K. Estes, An associative basis for coding and organization in memory. In A. W. Melton & E. Martin (Eds.), *Coding processes in human memory*, pp. 161–190. Washington, D.C.: V. H. Winston, 1972. Copyright Hemisphere Publishing Corporation, Washington, D.C. Reprinted by permission.

Research reported herein was supported in part by USPHS Grant GM16735 from the National Institute of General Medical Sciences.

144

processing and what is retained is just sufficient to identify the constituent phonemes (and perhaps a few other acoustic features). What is stored in memory is evidently not a multiplicity of connections between all aspects of the complex input pattern and the response made at the time, but rather a coded representation which suffices to specify at the time of recognition or recall which member of the set of possible patterns occurred.

A new question arises. If concepts of coding are as promising as indicated by some of these findings, why should we not simply scratch association theory and construct a new theory based on concepts of coding and information processing, as suggested, for example, by Johnson (1970)? If there is indeed any reason why we should not, it might lie in the possibility that the conception of coding is useful for dealing with what is remembered but has less to offer with regard to dynamics of forgetting. Perhaps the most promising theory would be one drawing upon both associative and coding models. The present paper is addressed to this possibility.

To show more specifically the considerations which seem to demand a new, hybrid theory, I should like now to review in some detail a particular research topic which has been central to some of the developments briefly alluded to above, namely, experimentation on short-term memory for serial order. The three questions to be addressed are: (*a*) Just what do we know about short-term memory for order of events? (*b*) Will any extant theory, based either on associative or on coding principles, handle the range of established phenomena? And (*c*) if the attempt seems indicated, how might ideas of association and coding be combined into a viable theory that amplifies the advantages of both traditions rather than compounding the limitations?

A starting point for much of the more analytical research on coding in short-term memory has been the familiar experiment on memory span for random strings of digits or letters. Without reviewing the considerable earlier literature, I can assume it well known to readers of the present volume that an individual can substantially increase retention for a digit or character string if the string is subdivided into groups or "chunks" of three to five characters separated by pauses, either upon input or during rehearsal immediately following input. Also I shall assume familiarity with Miller's (1956) paper concerning limitations on immediate memory capacity and the concept of chunking, and with the recent substantial review and augmentation of the literature on this concept by Johnson (1970). The special relevance of this line of research for the present volume is the view, developed in most detail by Johnson, that grouping or chunking of character strings simplifies the learner's task by permitting him to assign codes to the subgroups of a sequence, so that he then need only remember the smaller set of codes which can be decoded on a later occasion in order to reconstruct the entire sequence.

Granting the essential soundness of this general conception of coding as a means of organizing material in memory, I wish to direct interest to the question of precisely where in the chain of events constituting a short-term memory experiment the recoding of information occurs. Further, I should like to elucidate the detailed processes involved and their relation to or bases in associative learning processes.

ORDER AND ITEM INFORMATION IN MEMORY FOR CHARACTER STRINGS

Empirical Relationships

As a preliminary to discussion of theoretical issues I should like to summarize what I believe we know at present concerning the separate representation and short-term retention of order and item information. There is no question but that the experimenter can at will score the subject's recall protocol either simply on the basis of the number of items of the input string which are included or on the basis of the number of these which occur in their correct serial positions. But whether or not data obtained by the two scoring procedures reflect different memory processes is presently a controversial question (Bjork & Healy, 1970; Conrad, 1964; Johnson, 1970). One of the most directly relevant sources of information should be a picture of the time course of retention loss for the two types of information. To my surprise I have found little information concerning this basic problem in the literature. Quite likely, others are able to fill out my background in this respect but in the meantime I shall summarize principal results of a series of recent studies conducted in my laboratory employing variations on the experimental paradigm employed by Conrad (1967).

In this experimental paradigm each trial consists in the presentation to the subject of a string of four letters followed by a sequence of random numbers and then a recall test. The letters and numbers are presented visually and appear singly all in the same location, specifically a single Binaview cell. In what I shall term the standard procedure, the characters are presented at a rate of 2.5 characters per second, with no perceptible blank interval between characters; the interval between the last letter of the string and the recall test is filled by a random sequence of digits also appearing at the rate of 2.5 characters per second. The subjects are required to pronounce aloud the name of each letter in the string as it appears and also the name of each random digit. This rate of presentation is sufficiently taxing so that verbal rehearsal of the letter string during the retention interval is virtually impossible.

At the end of the retention interval the subject attempts to recall the four letters of the string and enter these in their proper order in the four boxes on an answer card. In the experiment of Conrad (1967) subjects were required to fill in all four boxes on each trial, guessing when necessary. In the first of our experiments that I shall discuss (Estes, 1969), a replication and extension of Conrad's experiment, the procedure differed only in that subjects were instructed to leave a box blank rather than making random guesses if they had no memory for a particular letter.

The four letter strings used by Conrad and in my 1969 study were all drawn without replacement from a set of 10 consonants which may be categorized into three groups (BCPTV, FSX, and MN) having the characteristic that the letters within each of the subsets are more acoustically confusable with each other than with letters outside the subset.

In treating the data I shall define any overt error as an acoustic confusion error if the letter actually presented at a particular position in a string has been replaced in the subject's protocol by another letter belonging to the same subset and a nonconfusion error as one in which the letter presented has been replaced by any letter outside that subset. Also I shall use an orthogonal categorization of transposition versus nontransposition errors, a transposition error being defined as one in which the letter which was presented at a particular position in a string has been replaced in the subject's protocol by a letter which appeared at some other position in the same string. Transposition errors provide our principal means of tracing changes in retention of order information. Confusion errors may reflect imperfect memory for either order or content, but the combined category of nontransposition-confusion errors specifically measures loss of item information.

In our extension of the Conrad experiment[1] seven subjects, all students or affiliates of Rockefeller University, were tested. For each

---

[1] Conducted in collaboration with Elizabeth Bjork, Alice Fenvessy Healy, Owen Floody, and Peter Waser at Rockefeller University.

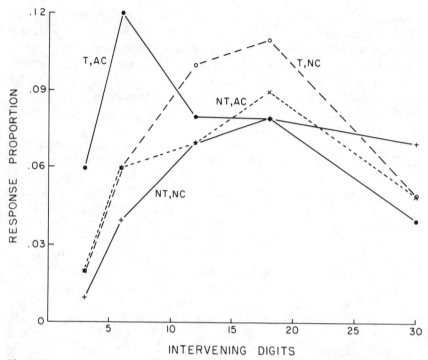

Figure 3.2 Proportions of four types of overt errors (T, AC: transposition, acoustic confusion; T, NC: transposition, nonconfusion; NT, AC: nontransposition, acoustic confusion; NT, NC: nontransposition, nonconfusion) as a function of number of random digit presentations between input and recall (from Estes, 1969).

subject a set of 21 four-letter strings was assigned to each of five retention intervals, the recall test being given after 3, 6, 12, 18, or 30 intervening random digit presentations. The different recall intervals were intermixed in a random sequence for each subject. The aspects of the data of immediate interest are presented in Figure 3.2 in the form of separate retention curves for the four categories of overt errors formed by combining the confusion-nonconfusion (AC, NC) and transposition-nontransposition (T, NT) categories.

In general the retention curve for each type of overt error increases to a peak and then declines, with a clear tendency for the curves for transposition errors within both the confusion and nonconfusion categories to rise more rapidly than the curves for nontransposition errors. Most striking is the sharp early peak for the combined confusion-transposition category. However, within both the confusion and nonconfusion categories considered separately, there is a heavy preponderance of transposition errors, of the order of 2 or 3 to 1, at the shortest retention intervals, shifting gradually over to a slight preponderance of nontransposition errors at the longest intervals. The same trends appeared in an experiment by Bjork and Healy (1970) utilizing the same general procedures but a somewhat different design in terms of confusion sets of letters.

Since it is also the case that the ratio of confusion to nonconfusion errors shifts systematically during the course of retention, from a heavy preponderance of acoustic confusions at the short intervals to a preponderance of nonconfusions at the long intervals, one might wonder whether there is a causal relationship between acoustic confusions and transpositions (as suggested by Conrad, 1964). Some light is shed on this question by a later experiment of mine (Estes, 1970a) which replicated the first experiment in all essentials except that the subjects were not permitted to vocalize the names of the letters or digits as they appeared.[2] In this experiment the ratio of acoustic confusion to nonconfusion errors was constant over retention intervals, but nonetheless within each confusion category the ratio of transpositions to nontranspositions shifted from nearly 2 to 1 at the shortest retention interval to virtual equality at the longest interval.

Although the forgetting of order and item information can be dissociated to a degree by the different time course of retention loss for measures of these two types of information, there is also clear evidence of an intimate relationship between the acoustic confusability of any two letters and the likelihood that a transposition error will occur if they are both present in the same display. This relationship was noted by Conrad (1964), but the study of Bjork and Healy (1970) was much better controlled for purposes of relevant analyses than either Conrad's or my own. Bjork and Healy's data show convincingly, first, that the great majority of acoustic confusion errors involve two letters which were present in the same string; but, secondly, within the small proportion of overt errors occurring at short retention intervals which do not involve transpositions (that is, which reflect loss only of item information), in the great majority of cases the letter substituted for the correct letter in a string belongs to the same acoustic confusion set.

Several experiments utilizing differing materials, procedures, and

---

[2] Instead they were required to say "high" or "low" to each letter according as it fell in the first or second half of the alphabet, and to each digit according as it fell in the first or second half of the digits 0 through 9.

measures have yielded similarly clear-cut interactions between order versus item information loss and other experimental variables. In an experiment reported by Wickelgren (1965) subjects attempted ordered recall of strings of nine consonants presented auditorily at a rate of three per second. Recall was poorer for strings of acoustically similar consonants (those sharing a common vowel phoneme) than for dissimilar strings, but the difference was attributable entirely to the greater incidence of transposition errors involving acoustically similar letters in the phonemically similar strings; the number of letters recalled correctly without regard to position did not differ significantly for the two types of strings. Up to a point an analogous result was obtained for recall of strings of seven consonant-vowel digrams; transposition errors were significantly more frequent for strings in which all the digrams had a common vowel than in dissimilar strings, but item recall was actually significantly better for the similar strings.

Serial position curves provide especially distinct differences in the retention of item and order information both as a function of position and in the way the serial position curve changes with retention interval. We should perhaps expect the simplest case, from a theoretical standpoint, to arise in data from the letter string experiment. Since the relatively rapid presentation rate and the requirement of pronouncing each character effectively preclude rehearsal, and since each letter string is followed by a sequence of random digits, the factors of selective rehearsal and sensory persistence, which have been implicated as major determiners of the primacy and recency segments of the serial position curve in other short-term memory experiments, are eliminated; and we might expect any remaining position function to reflect more intrinsic processes having to do with the storage and retrieval of information.

The experiment by Bjork and Healy (1970), which employed the standard procedure, yields the serial position functions for transposition and nontransposition errors separately shown in Figure 3.3. Clearly the increase in errors at the interior positions two and three of the 4-letter string, yielding the familiar bowed curve, is more accentuated in the functions for transposition errors, which represent solely loss of order information, than for nontransposition errors, which represent solely loss of item information. If we obtain a single composite measure of total item information retained by adding correct responses and transposition errors at each position (thus achieving essentially the same result as rescoring the protocols by a free recall criterion), the functions obtained are conspicuously flat: at the shortest retention interval (3 intervening digits), .97,

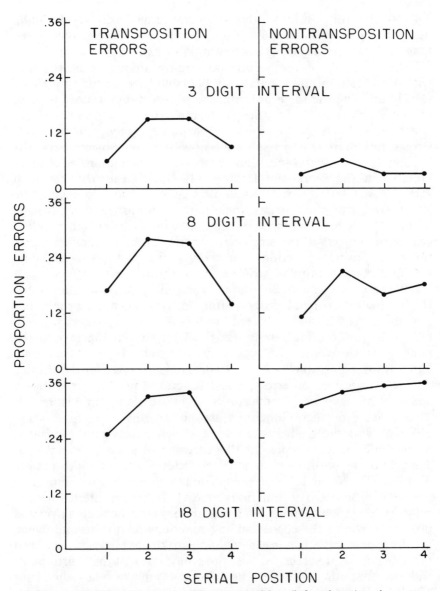

Figure 3.3 Serial position curves for transposition (left column) and nontransposition (right column) errors (from Bjork & Healy, 1970).

.94, .97, .97, for positions 1 through 4 respectively; slightly declining but with no bow shape, .69, .66, .65, and .64, respectively, at the longest retention interval (18 intervening digits).

Confirmation of the picture for transposition errors, together with a useful additional analysis, is available from a study by Healy (1971) utilizing the same procedures and retention intervals as those of the Bjork and Healy study but employing a single set of four consonants which was randomly repermuted to generate the letter strings for all trials; this set was known to the subjects from the beginning so only transposition errors were possible on recall tests. Whereas in the Bjork and Healy study half of the trials for each subject used letter strings containing two acoustically confusable letters and half used strings including no acoustically confusable letters, the same division was obtained by utilizing independent groups of subjects in the single set experiment. In both experiments the serial position functions were very similar in form for the confusable and nonconfusable strings.

For the experiment involving a vocabulary of only four letters, Healy also constructed distance functions showing the probability that the letter which was entered by the subject at a given position in his recall protocol for a trial was the letter which appeared at the same position in the display (hence a correct response) or was a letter from a position 1, 2, or 3 characters removed in the display (hence a transposition error). These functions, pooled over subjects and conditions at each retention interval are shown in Figure 3.4. Two aspects of these functions are noteworthy. The first is the orderliness of the gradients, an error which occurs in any position being more likely to represent the intrusion of a letter belonging at a neighboring position than a letter belonging at a more remote position. The second is the conspicuous symmetry with respect to temporal position. The functions at each retention interval for the third panel, in which position 3 is correct, could be folded over and placed on top of the corresponding functions for the second panel, in which position 2 is correct, yielding strikingly close agreement of the superimposed values. Almost the same is true of the fourth panel and the first, the only deviation from symmetry being the slight across the board difference in correct responses at positions 1 and 4.

The possibility that these relationships involving position are of considerable generality is suggested by the closeness with which they are confirmed in another experimental context differing in numerous particulars. A study reported by Fuchs (1969) required subjects to recall strings of four-letter nouns which were presented simultaneously on slides, the subject reading the words aloud, then counting

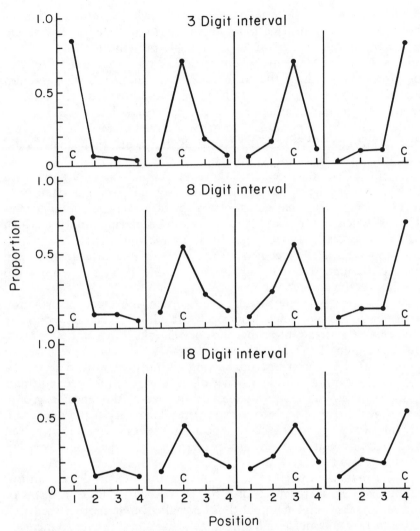

Figure 3.4 Distance functions for Healy (1971) study. The point plotted for position *i* of any panel represents the proportion of instances in which the response occurring in the position marked C on the subject's answer card was the letter appearing at position *i* of the string for the given trial.

backward for the prescribed interval of 4, 8, or 16 seconds before the recall test. Recall was cued by the appearance of a symbol on the screen indicating the position on the previous slide from which recall was to be attempted. Serial position curves for transposition errors, which comprised approximately 56% of all errors, were similar in form to those of the letter string studies, whereas errors reflecting only loss of item information yielded a distinctly shallower gradient when recall was tested following a single presentation of the string and entirely flat gradients when recall was not tested until after two or three repetitions of the string. Distance functions for strings having the correct response at different serial positions showed the same conspicuous symmetry as those of Healy's letter string study. Orderly distance functions have been obtained by Murdock and vom Saal (1967), with three-letter words as items, but their analysis did not provide evidence on symmetry.

It might be remarked that the data of Fuchs's study agree with those of Wickelgren (1967) and Johnson (1970), among others, in exhibiting positional constancy of intrusion errors across strings. That is, when the subject made an error by replacing the word which had appeared at a particular position in a string with a word which had appeared in a preceding string, with significantly greater than chance frequency the incorrect word came from the same serial position as the correct one.

Differences in the handling of order and item information appear also in experiments in which the subject is led to group the elements of a string into subgroups or "chunks." In a study reported by Wickelgren (1967), strings of 8, 9, or 10 digits were presented to subjects at the rate of one per second with instructions to group the digits into chunks of one to five digits under different conditions. Item recall was affected only slightly by size of the rehearsal group, but a measure of order information (the probability that a digit from a string was given at the correct position if recalled at all) increased to a maximum at rehearsal group size three and decreased at group sizes four and five.

The massive supply of data showing that under the conditions of this last study recall tends strongly to be organized in terms of the rehearsal groups will doubtless be well covered in other contributions to this volume. For completeness I would like here to mention only a few aspects of these data that will be particularly relevant to the theoretical interpretation of order effects. Contingency functions for recall of successive serial positions in a string show marked discontinuities at subgroup boundaries. That is, if a subject gives a correct recall response for the item at position i of a string, he has a very low probability of making an error at the next position if it falls within the same rehearsal subgroup, but a much higher probability of making an error if the next position falls in a different subgroup (see for example, Johnson, 1970, and Wickelgren, 1969). Secondly, if a particular string is repeated many times at irregular intervals during an experiment with a single subject, the proportion of letters recalled increases steadily over repetitions only if the mode of subgrouping remains constant from one repetition to the next (Bower & Winzenz, 1969). Finally, Johnson (1969, 1970) has shown that in a number of respects a subgroup which the subject has been led to treat as a chunk tends to behave as a unit in recall. In Johnson's basic paradigm, a sequence of three subgroups of three letters each is presented to the subject, then prior to recall a sequence is presented in which one of the subgroups is unchanged but the others undergo changes, either the substitution of a letter from outside the presented string at some position or the interchange of letters at two positions in the subgroup. When recall of the original string is determined by a modified free recall procedure, retention of the unchanged subgroup is characteristically found to be fully as good as that of a control condition in which there was no interpolated presentation but recall of both changed and unchanged letters in the changed subgroups is severely depressed.

Interpretation of Order Effects

The rather substantial body of clear-cut and replicable factual information concerning order effects in short-term memory now available should, it seems, set the stage for a commensurate effort toward theoretical interpretation. Indeed a number of initial efforts, stemming from quite diverse premises, have appeared in the literature and I should like now to review these briefly and to point out what seem to be the strong points and limitations of each.

Coding

The most explicit and empirically documented coding hypothesis appears to be that of Johnson (1969, 1970). He proposes that in short-term memory for a sequence of characters grouped into chunks, the individual assigns a code to each chunk and then need only retain the codes in memory over the retention interval. The code for each chunk is assumed to be unique and to contain all of the item and order information contained in the chunk, yet at the same time to be "opaque" in the sense that even when the individual has recalled the code for a particular chunk, information about the items in the chunk is not available to him until he has carried out decoding operations. Some of the general features of the chunking of material in memory that are expressed in the idea of coding certainly are well established. In particular, Johnson's own research using his retroactive inhibition paradigm provides considerable evidence regarding the independence of retention loss for material in different chunks and for the selective disruption of chunks by interpolated training procedures.

The all-or-none loss of information by chunks which might be taken to be implied by the coding concept does not entirely come off, however, as witness the substantial differences in recall for changed and unchanged letters within altered chunks (Johnson, 1969).

The principal difficulty I find with the coding hypothesis at present is that the specific processes involved in assigning codes and, even more importantly, decoding at the time of recall are largely unspecified and it is difficult to foresee the extent to which they may turn out to differ from those entailed by, say, an associative theory. It seems beyond question that the retention of character strings involves some process that can be characterized as the assignment of codes to subgroups. But I must confess that at present the additional idea that the code includes all of the information in a subgroup and that the individual carries in memory a set of operations adequate fully to recover all of the information in a chunk given only the code seems to me extremely elaborate and possibly even more complex than the phenomena it is supposed to explain. For the moment I am inclined to use freely when convenient the term "code" to refer to the assignment of a tag or label to a subgroup of a character string but to turn primary attention to the possibility of elucidating the detailed processes involved by concepts drawn from more general theories of learning and memory.

Interitem Association

A rather simplistic rendition of classical association theory would interpret the memory for a letter string in terms of formation of an association between the first letter and the signal for recall, the second letter with the first, the third letter with the second, and so on. The inadequacy of any scheme of this sort as a general theory of serial order was demonstrated to the satisfaction of most psychologists by Lashley in his 1951 paper. With respect to the type of experiment under consideration, one particularly severe difficulty arises from the consideration that the letters in any particular string would already have strongly established associations as a result of previous experience of the subject outside the laboratory and that a single trial in a short-term memory experiment could do little to alter the strengths of these associations.

One might attempt to rescue the theory by appealing to the same distinction between short- and long-term memory that is seen in many contemporary models. It might be assumed that long-term associations are suppressed by an overall set in a short-term memory experiment and that strong but transient associations are set up as a result of a single presentation. A theory of this sort seems, however, to run into a pyramiding of difficulties as one attempts to apply it to specific phenomena. Firstly, the retention curves in the letter string experiments do not appear to approach zero, or chance levels of responding asymptotically; and to the extent that the associations formed within a trial are not entirely transient, the old problems with the theory reemerge. Secondly, one could not account for the orderly distance gradients for intrusion errors as a function of distance from the serial position of the correct letter, except perhaps by complicating the scheme greatly with the assumption of remote associations between the letter in any serial position and those not only adjacent but in more remote serial positions. It is very difficult, however, to imagine how such a scheme could account for the observed symmetry of the distance functions; or how it would be made to predict that repetitions of the string would lead to improved recall only if the mode of grouping of characters was constant from trial to trial (Bower & Winzenz, 1969); or how it could be made to jibe with Johnson's findings that interference with the middle letter of a three-letter group (in a retroactive inhibition paradigm) produces no more impairment in recall of the first and third letters than interference with the first or the third letter produces in the remaining two (Johnson, 1969, 1970).

Finally, there is considerable reason to doubt whether associations of any sort form or are strengthened between adjacent characters in the type of experiment under consideration. The well known experiments of Thorndike (1931) on "belongingness" yielded negative evidence regarding formation of associations between adjacent members of a list when the individual is not instructed to attend to or rehearse relations between them. Similarly, Lesgold and Bower (1970) studied the relation between learning of a serial list and subsequent learning of paired associates in which stimulus and response members of each pair were successive items from the serial list. Positive transfer was found only when the subjects had been instructed concerning the relationship between the tasks.

Coding on a Temporal Attribute

A possibility to be considered is that recall for order of a sequence of items is simply a by-product of the individual's ability to remember the times at which the individual items occurred. The idea that each item which is stored in memory is identified by a "time-tag" has recurred frequently in the literature since it was applied by Yntema and Trask (1963) to the interpretation of a study in which subjects were asked at various points during a session to judge which of two words had appeared earlier in the series being presented. More recently, Underwood (1969) has reviewed the evidence for a temporal attribute in the coding of events in memory and has concluded that it can be distinguished from the concept of strength of a memory trace based on recency.

The conception of time tags, in the sense of positioning events on a continuous temporal attribute, seems never to have been elaborated to the point that one can really come to grips with it. Further, on the basis of available information concerning order effects in short-term memory, this theoretical direction does not appear very promising. Surely any reasonable theory of this type would imply that discrimination is easier between two events with a given temporal separation if both occur more recently, with the implication that serial position functions for order information should be skewed in the direction favoring higher proportions of correct responding at the more recent positions, and a similar skewing should appear in distance functions. However, neither of these effects is manifest in the data of the relevant studies cited above. But, although it seems reasonably clear that direct tagging of items of a temporal dimension could not suffice to account for order effects in memory, the possibility should be kept in mind that a representation of this kind may exist in very-short-term memory, the information being recoded in some other form for longer term storage.

Positional Coding

A conception of "position tags" seems considerably more workable than that of time tags. An associative mechanism to accomplish this coding is immediately at hand, in that the learner might associate each successive item of a sequence with an ordinal number, 1, 2, 3, ... This process, or at least a formal equivalent, appears to be required for Johnson's (1970) conception of coding, in which full information concerning order of items is embodied in the code for a "chunk," and also in Conrad's (1964, 1965) outline of a model for short-term retention. The associations of items of a string with ordinal numbers would immediately account for a number of the qualitative facts about retention of order information; in particular, the assumption of associations between items and ordinal numbers would yield a direct prediction of the tendency for intrusion errors between strings presented on different trials of a short-term memory experiment to occur at the serial position of the intruding item.

However, a number of questions can be raised about the conception of positional encoding which are not easy to answer. Firstly, how could one account for the orderly distance functions, in which probability of an order error involving any two items within a display is inversely related to the number of intervening items? A rather speculative possibility, suggested by Underwood (1969) among others, is that representations of the items of a string might be projected onto a spatial array at some level of the nervous system, so that the encoding of order information would arise from association of each item with its spatial position rather than with an ordinal number. This assumption would immediately have to be augmented to account for Wickelgren's (1967) finding that, whereas retention of item information is relatively constant over size of rehearsal groups, retention of order information varies according to a distinct nonmonotonic function with a maximum at rehearsal group size three. Evidently the spatial representation would have to be of limited informational capacity with only the categories of end and interior positions being clearly discriminable.

This last observation leads in turn to the question of how the different courses of retention loss for item and order information could be handled. Conrad (1964, 1967) has circumvented this question by denying that there is any separate representation of order and item information in memory at all. He suggests that, in effect, the incoming items of a string are coded with respect to position, as though they are deposited in a series of boxes or slots, and that forgetting is solely a matter of loss of item information. Transposition errors arise, according to Conrad, when the items in some pair of positions have suffered partial loss of information so that in choosing his responses for these slots on the answer card the subject guesses either from the two corresponding responses, or at least from a small subset including these and others auditorily confused with them. However, Conrad's scheme seems quantitatively quite inadequate to account for the observed heavy incidence of transposition errors in short-term memory (e.g., Bjork & Healy, 1970) and, further, provides no hint as to why the observed rate of loss of order information should be distinctly faster than that of item information.

Finally, a question which goes to the heart of a positional encoding interpretation is that of why severe impairment of recall should be observed for the unchanged letters in changed subgroups in Johnson's (1969) experiments on recall of grouped letter sequences.

In summary, an adequate interpretation of retention of order information must account for the high accuracy of recall for order at very short intervals, for the differential rates of loss of order and item information, for grouping effects, together with the sensitivity of retention of order information to disruption by changes at any point within a subgroup, and for the orderly serial position and distance functions with their distinctly different forms and different interactions with retention interval for measures of item and order information. None of the types of theory reviewed seems close to achieving this task. Nonetheless, several of them include ingredients which may be needed in an adequate theory.

A PROVISIONAL ASSOCIATIVE MODEL
FOR STIMULUS CODING

Since neither classical association theory nor coding schemes so far developed come close to providing an adequate interpretation of order effects in short-term memory, I should like now to explore the idea of formulating a theory embodying some of the concepts and assumptions of these two hitherto disparate traditions. It is not easy to choose which type of model to make the basis for further development since the ideas of coding seem the more natural for interpreting structural characteristics and those of association theory for interpreting changes as a function of time or trials. Perhaps partly out of habit, but partly also because I can better envisage how to relate the results to other aspects of learning theory, I shall follow the strategy of attempting to revise and augment the concepts of association theory so as to incorporate some of the insights arising from analyses in terms of coding.

Since in the preceding review of empirical phenomena the weakest aspect of association theory appears to be the conception of interitem associations as the basis for organization, this is the point at which I propose to introduce a new conception to bring the associative model more nearly into line with ideas coming from coding theory. The principal new concept to be introduced is that of a *control element*.

Control Elements as the Basis
of Associative Structures

Quite generally in the literature of association theory I believe, and certainly in my own interpretations of human learning (Estes, 1970b), it is assumed that as a consequence of an individual's experiencing a sequence of stimuli, for example, letters or words in a short-term memory experiment, representations of these stimuli are set up in his memory system (presumably somewhere in the brain although I shall not speculate as to specific localization). Associations between these stimulus elements, perhaps more aptly termed memory elements, provide the basis for retention.

The new assumption to be explored is that there is available in the memory system also a pool of elements which we may term control elements. Suppose that an individual experiences in close temporal conjunction two elementary stimuli, say two critical features of an auditorily presented letter. Denoting the representations of these two features in the memory system by f_1 and f_2, the resulting associative structure in terms of classical association theory would be simply

$$f_1 - f_2,$$

whereas in the new theory it would be

where C denotes a control element. The learning which results from the contiguous occurrence of the two stimuli is conceived in the new theory to be, not the establishment of an association between them, but rather of an association of each with a control element. The sense of the term *association* is much the same as in classical theory. If following the establishment of this elementary associative structure, the control element is activated from some motivational source (for example, an instruction to recall), the result is the reactivation of the representations of the two associated features in memory and the evocation of the corresponding articulatory responses. A rather similar structure, but without a specific associational mechanism, has been suggested by Lesgold and Bower (1970) in connection with serial list learning.

Even a minimal short-term memory experiment involves a presentation of a sequence of letters each comprising a number of critical features. In representing the memory structure set up by such an input, I wish to assume firstly that a new control element is established at each discontinuity in the input sequence. The discontinuities may result from the input procedure, as those between letters in a string or between words in a sequence, or they may be generated by the subject when he groups or "chunks" subsets of letters together in rehearsal.

As a result of groupings induced either by the input procedure or by the subject's rehearsal strategy, control elements may be established at successively higher levels, generating a hierarchical organization. For example, suppose two letters are presented in sequence, the first letter comprising features f_1 and f_2 and the second letter the features f_3 and f_4. Two first-order control elements, $C_{1,1}$ and $C_{1,2}$, would be established, one for each letter, and a second-order control element, $C_{2,1}$, for the pair of letters, generating the following structure:

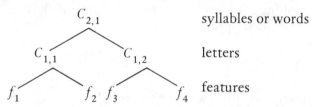

Now activation of either of the first-order control elements would reinstate memory of the particular letter whereas activation of the second-order control element would reinstate memory of the pair of letters.

It will be seen that so far as structural relations are concerned there is a one to one mapping of coding theory onto the association model. Wherever one would speak of the subject's introducing a code for a set of elements, the associative model introduces a control element. For most purposes, in representing the memory representations set up as a result of the input of a single trial in a short-term memory experiment, it will be convenient to simplify the diagram by treating the lower order structures as units. Thus, for example, a short-hand representation of the memory structure for a sequence of four letters would be written

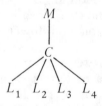

where L_i denotes the representation of the ith letter, C is a control element and M a motivational source which may activate the control element.

When one is presenting a new theory, it is generally best to concentrate on showing how the concepts are to be used, rather than struggling with formal definitions. This is the course I am following with respect to control elements. For the present it will suffice to treat the control element as an abstract construct, on a par with "association," "memory trace," or "habit strength." My general idea is that at the time of input of to-be-remembered items, some element or aspect of the current context serves as a temporary control element. The transient associations with the contextual control element maintain the items in short-term memory by means of a mechanism to be elucidated in the next section. However, the context shifts with the passage of time (see Bower, 1972), and the memory is lost unless control is taken over by a more stable structure. Stability is achieved if some item in long-term memory is activated by the joint effect of its existing associations with some aspect of the context and one or more of the input items. This item establishes new associations with the other input items which are currently in short-term memory, and takes over the control function. Retrieval of the items from memory at a later time will be facilitated to the extent that the permanent control element is associated with cues which constitute part of the context at the time of recall.

Reverberatory Pathways and the Representations of Order in Immediate Memory

The model as presented up to this point provides a basis for representing retention of item information, but so far has nothing to say about the critical matter of information regarding position or serial order of items. I propose to treat the problem of order in terms of two distinct mechanisms, the first having to do with the short-term representation of order information and its loss as a function of time and the second with the stable representation of order in long-term memory which may be established as a result of rehearsal.

Taking together a variety of sources of evidence, which I shall assume to be familiar to readers of this volume, we can sketch the course of events on a typical trial of a short-term memory experiment: (*a*) A stimulus pattern, say a vocally presented letter, arrives at the sensory apparatus; (*b*) much of the information in the pattern is lost within a matter of milliseconds, but during this brief interval subsystems of the perceptual apparatus which may be termed feature detectors are activated and a representation of the letter is set up in short-term memory in the form of a combination of features, phonemes in the case of a spoken letter; (*c*) by an associative process a representation of the letter in long-term memory is activated and the individual is enabled to identify or label the letter. In terms of the work of Posner (1969; Posner and Warren, 1972) we can assume that at an early stage in this sequence the subject is able to make a same-different judgment regarding physical similarity of the input letter to one previously presented but that only at the end of the sequence can he name the letter.

Now we arrive at one of the central problems with respect to memory for serial order. If the retrieval times for various letters, words, or other possible items of a sequence were approximately equal, and had negligible variance, then following the presentation of a sequence of items the listener might be expected automatically to generate a sequence of names in the same order, that is, to remember the input order perfectly. However, the assumption of constant times of retrieval from memory is certainly incorrect. In general the items of an input sequence must have substantially varying retrieval times from long-term memory; and, judging by associative reaction time data, latency distributions even for such familiar items as digits or letters of the alphabet have standard deviations which are substantial relative to their means. Thus if a series of letters or words is presented at a rapid rate, as is frequently done in short-term memory experiments, the order in which representations of these items are retrieved from long-term memory cannot be assumed invariably to agree with the input order.

The organism's way out of this difficulty, suggested by much current research on memory, is to maintain a coded representation of the last few items of an input sequence in a short-term memory store for an interval of a few seconds. The labels or other associations activated by these items in long-term memory can, then, be checked for order against the representation of the sequence in short-term memory and the labels or names rehearsed in their proper order before the short-term representation is lost.

The basic concept of the short-term mechanism in the present model is a reverberatory loop which, for a single element in the stimulus sequence, say a feature f_i of a letter L_{ij}, and a contextual control element, might be schematized as follows:

The idea is that once a representation of the feature f_i has been set up in memory and has established a connection with a control element, the reverberatory loop connecting the two produces a recurrent reactivation of the representation of the feature at a rate determined by the refractory phase of the system. This maintenance of the representation of the element in a state of heightened excitability is the basis of short-term retention. Further, if a sequence of stimulus features has become associated with a single control element as a result of the input of a single experimental trial, a similar reverberatory loop is established for each feature, with the consequence that the features will be reactivated in sequence, thus providing for the initial representation of order information in short-term memory.

If the reverberatory loops were completely deterministic, this memory would be permanent. However, it seems reasonable to assume that there is a certain amount of random error in the recurrence times owing to differences in refractory phases among individual elements and to perturbations arising from other concurrent activity in the nervous system. The result of these random variations is that over a period of time the timing of recurrent activations of the individual elements of a sequence will come to deviate sufficiently from the original relationships so that eventually interchanges in order will begin to appear between adjacent elements.

This cyclic reactivation process is assumed to operate in basically the same way at each level at which perceptual processing of a stimulus input produces units that may enter into short-term memory. With the materials ordinarily used in short-term memory experiments, these units would include at least the critical features which identify visually displayed characters, acoustic features (e.g., phonemes) which identify auditorily presented characters, and semantic features or markers in the case of words as units.

Thus the representation of a sequence of items in short-term memory is not like a string of beads, but rather like sequences of indicators on parallel tracks, each track having to do with a different kind of information about any given item. When, for example, a letter is displayed visually, representations of identifying visual features are activated and begin their reactivation cycles in short-term memory; then when the individual, in response to the visual input, pronounces the character and hears his own auditory feedback, representations of acoustic features are activated and in turn begin their reactivation cycles.

The representations arising from different modalities are assumed to be independent, but they will presumably have different rates of reactivation. Further, it seems quite likely that the visual representation is more sensitive to changes in context than auditory representations and consequently that in the former case the reactivation process would damp out more rapidly as a result of shifts in context;

to the extent that this is so, there would be less time available following input for the activation of associated control elements in long-
term memory in the case of visual than in the case of auditory input.

Even in the case of auditory features, the duration of the short-
term process appears on the basis of considerable evidence to be no
more than 2 to 3 seconds (Bjork & Healy, 1970; Crowder & Morton,
1969; Estes, 1970a). However, even 2 or 3 seconds is a rather long
time on a scale of sensory information processing and short-term
memory. If the sequence of letters is presented at the rapid rate
characteristic of many short-term memory experiments, often 2 to
3 per second, then for a short time following input of the string the
individual, according to the present model, has available in short-
term memory information concerning the order in which various
identifying visual features of the letters and various phonetic features, for example stop and vowel phonemes, occurred in the input
sequence.

According to this conception, loss of order information in short-
term memory results entirely from perturbations in timing in the
reactivation cycles of representations of various features of the stimulus input. Most importantly, these perturbations lead to interchanges in order of the representations of features of characters in
the string which is to be remembered and thus lead to transposition
errors in recall. However, it should be noted that, when the interval
between a presentation of a string of characters and the recall test is
filled with presentations of "noise" characters (as when a string of
letters is followed by a sequence of random digits), perturbations in
reactivation cycles may also lead to interchanges in ordering of the
representations of the characters of the string with characters in
the intervening sequence. Depending on the nature of the material,
this process may lead to intrusion errors at recall, or to errors of
omission if the result of a transposition is to mix into the representation of the string a character of a type which the subject knows
could not be admissible.

Since transpositions of characters of the input string and characters in the sequence intervening between the string and the recall test
will most frequently involve the later items of the input string, a
serial position curve for loss of item information will, on the present
assumptions, be predicted to be monotonically decreasing (that is,
showing only a primacy effect). On the other hand, as will be shown
later in this section, the serial position curve for loss of order information is predicted to be bowed in form and symmetrical.

Concerning the duration of the short-term memory process, I
assume that the limits ordinarily observed result primarily from the

effects of successive inputs. In most experiments the subject receives the new inputs of successive trials at relatively rapid rates, with the result that the feature detectors and other mechanisms involved in setting up representations of one input string in short-term memory are soon captured by the new input from another string. Doubtless the continuation of reactivation cycles for a particular string depend also on maintenance of the input context, but I shall not attempt to deal with this aspect of the process in the present exposition.

In order to make these ideas specific enough to permit some illustrative calculations with the model, I shall utilize for the present the following set of assumptions.

i. Upon input of a string of items, an associative structure is established, with reverberatory loops connecting the representation of each item to a contextual control element. The structure reactivates the representations cyclically, initially following the input sequence.

ii. Let us denote by h the time between reactivations. Then, for any element of the sequence, during any unit time interval following input, there is some constant probability θ of a perturbation in timing which will result in the next reactivation being advanced or delayed by h time units. Advances and delays are assumed to be equally likely.

iii. Whenever the control element is activated from a motivational source, the articulatory responses corresponding to the items of the string will be made in the order determined by the current timing relationships.

iv. When a perturbation in timing results in an interchange of elements between adjacent items that results in producing unacceptable characters (for example combinations of phonemes that do not constitute letters in a letter string experiment), then the items involved are lost from short-term memory and the corresponding response will not be made on a recall test given at this point. Thus both order and item information are lost as a result of disturbances in timing with, in general, order information being the more sensitive.

Some of the general properties of the model will be fairly readily apparent at an intuitive level from consideration of the assumptions. At the time of input of a string of characters, a representation is established in memory incorporating both order and item information. During a subsequent retention interval, particularly if the interval is filled with other input which contributes perturbations to the timing mechanisms, order information is lost at an exponential rate.

Unlike other models, this one assumes that the loss of order information is primary and the loss of item information is derivative. The rate of loss of information is greater the larger the number of items in the string and the smaller the time intervals between presen-

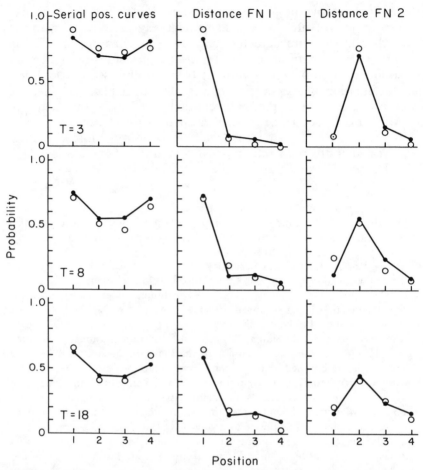

Figure 3.5 Serial position and distance functions from Healy (1971) study (connected points) compared with predicted values from reverberatory loop model.

tations of successive items.[3] Also the rate of loss of order information is directly related to the similarity (communality) between items of the string and, in particular, transpositions are most likely to occur between adjacent similar items.

Within a string, a serial position curve develops in the course of the retention interval which is symmetric, with the highest proportions correct at the initial and terminal positions. The distance func-

---

[3] A finding by Aaronson, Markowitz, and Shapiro (1971), which appeared after this passage was written, seems especially compatible with the present model. These investigators demonstrated a selective facilitation of retention of order information as the ratio of speech-to-pause time in an auditorily presented digit string was decreased.

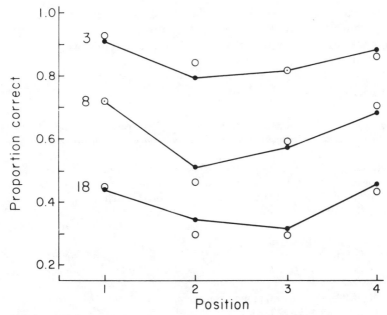

Figure 3.6 Serial position curves from Bjork and Healy (1970) study (connected points) compared with predictions from reverberatory loop model.

tions reproduce at least the main qualitative features exhibited in the data of Healy (1971) and Fuchs (1969), with an orderly decrease in probability of transpositions involving any two items of a string as a function of their distance apart and with these functions being symmetric in the forward and backward directions.

To illustrate these last features, I prepared a computer simulation program by translating assumptions *i-iv* as directly as possible into Fortran statements. Boundary conditions were chosen to simulate Healy's (1971) experiment on recall of order of sequences obtained by randomly permuting a single set of four letters. Then sets of 100 hypothetical subjects were tested on the computer simulation with differing values of the perturbation parameter, θ. Theoretical values obtained for serial position curves and distance functions with $\theta = .10$ are shown in Figure 3.5, together with corresponding points plotted for Healy's data.[4] The same program, with a different choice of θ, provides a comparable description of the serial position curves of the study by Bjork and Healy (1970), shown in Figure 3.6 (distance

---

[4] To increase the reliability of the observed values, the distance functions shown in Figure 3.4 were folded and pooled; thus the middle column in Figure 3.5 represents the pooled data from the first and fourth columns of Figure 3.4 and the righthand column of Figure 3.5 the second and third columns of Figure 3.4.

functions were not available for this study). Even this preliminary and highly simplified version of the model appears to predict the principal quantitative trends in these data reasonably well.

REFERENCES

Aaronson, D., Markowitz, N., & Shapiro, H. Perception and immediate recall of normal and "compressed" auditory sequences. *Perception & Psychophysics*, 1971, **9**, 338–344.

Bjork, E. L., & Healy, A. F. Intra-item and extra-item sources of acoustic confusion in short-term memory. In *Communications in Mathematical Psychology*, Rockefeller University Technical Reports, March, 1970.

Bower, G. H. Stimulus-sampling theory of encoding variability. In A. W. Melton and E. Martin (Eds.), *Coding processes in human memory*. Washington, D.C.: V. H. Winston, 1972. Pp. 85–124.

Bower, G. H., & Winzenz, D. Group structure, coding and memory for digit series. *Journal of Experimental Psychology, Monograph Supplement*, 1969, **80**, May, Pt. 2, 1–17.

Conrad, R. Acoustic confusions in immediate memory. *British Journal of Psychology*, 1964, **55**, 75–84.

Conrad, R. Order error in immediate recall of sequences. *Journal of Verbal Learning and Verbal Behavior*, 1965, **4**, 161–169.

Conrad, R. Interference or decay over short retention intervals? *Journal of Verbal Learning and Verbal Behavior*, 1967, **6**, 49–54.

Crowder, R. G., & Morton, J. Precategorical acoustic storage (PAS). *Perception & Psychophysics*, 1969, **5**, 365–373.

Estes, W. K. Evaluation of some models for acoustic confusion effects in short term memory. In *Communications in Mathematical Psychology*, Rockefeller University Technical Reports, October, 1969.

Estes, W. K. On the source of acoustic confusions in short term memory for letter strings. In *Communications in Mathematical Psychology*, Rockefeller University Technical Reports, April, 1970. (a)

Estes, W. K. *Learning theory and mental development*. New York: Academic Press, 1970. (b)

Fuchs, A. H. Recall for order and content of serial word lists in short-term memory. *Journal of Experimental Psychology*, 1969, **82**, 14–21.

Healy, A. F. Short-term memory of consonant order. In *Communications in Mathematical Psychology*, Rockefeller University Technical Reports, October, 1971.

Johnson, N. F. Chunking: Associative chaining versus coding. *Journal of Verbal Learning and Verbal Behavior*, 1969, **8**, 725–731.

Johnson, N. F. The role of chunking and organization in the process of recall. In G. H. Bower (Ed.), *The psychology of learning and motivation: Advances in research and theory*, Vol. 4. New York: Academic Press, 1970, Pp. 171–247.

Lashley, K. S. The problem of serial order in behavior. In L. A. Jeffress (Ed.), *Cerebral mechanisms in behavior*. New York: Wiley, 1951.

Lesgold, A. M., & Bower, G. H. Inefficiency of serial knowledge for associative responding. *Journal of Verbal Learning and Verbal Behavior,* 1970, 9, 456–466.

Miller, G. A. The magical number seven, plus or minus two: Some limits on our capacity for processing information. *Psychological Review,* 1956, 63, 81–97.

Murdock, B. B., Jr., & vom Saal, W. Transpositions in short-term memory. *Journal of Experimental Psychology,* 1967, 74, 137–143.

Posner, M. I. Abstraction and the process of recognition. In G. H. Bower & J. T. Spence (Eds), *The psychology of learning and motivation: Advances in research and theory,* Vol. 3. New York: Academic Press, 1969. Pp. 43–100.

Posner, M. I., and Warren, R. E. Traces, concepts, and conscious instructions. In A. W. Melton and E. Martin (Eds.), *Coding processes in human memory.* Washington, D.C.: V. H. Winston, 1972. Pp. 25–44.

Thorndike, E. L. *Human learning.* New York: Century, 1931.

Underwood, B. J. Attributes of memory. *Psychological Review,* 1969, 76, 559–573.

Wickelgren, W. A. Short-term memory for phonemically similar lists. *American Journal of Psychology,* 1965, 78, 567–574.

Wickelgren, W. A. Rehearsal grouping and hierarchical organization of serial position cues in short-term memory. *Quarterly Journal of Experimental Psychology,* 1967, 19, 97–102.

Wickelgren, W. A. Context-sensitive coding, associative memory, and serial order in (speech) behavior. *Psychological Review,* 1969, 76, 1–15.

Yntema, D. B., & Trask, F. P. Recall as a search process. *Journal of Verbal Learning and Verbal Behavior,* 1963, 2, 65–74.

Is Human Memory Obsolete?

Will memory continue to be considered an indispensable ingredient of human ability to solve problems, comprehend the environment, and in general function intelligently? That there is room for uncertainty about the answer to this question is suggested by a recent analogous development: the precipitous decline in the importance attached to human calculating skills with the advent of the inexpensive pocket electronic calculator. With regard to memory, technological developments have been even more spectacular. Computer memories based on relays have been successively replaced by those using transistors, then integrated circuits, and perhaps next magnetic "bubble" memories, with ever larger capacities and incredibly short retrieval times (Rajchman 1977). At the same time, like calculators, computers are becoming smaller and cheaper, so that a computer for desktop or even briefcase is now within the means of many households. Here I wish not so much to try to answer the question of whether computers might be nearly ready to take over another human mental function as to use this question to point up what is currently known about the operating characteristics of human memory as opposed to computer memory.

I shall limit my attention principally to what is called "short-term memory" (see, for example, Murdock 1974)—that is, memory for recent events or episodes and for newly learned associations of the kinds tapped in many psychological and neurological tests as well as in most laboratory research on memory from Ebbinghaus to the present. Memory in this sense is both an important and a vulnerable component of our intellectual apparatus. The short-term memory system is important because it must maintain in an active state the items of information, rules, and algorithms required for almost any kind of problem-solving—hence the term "working memory" (Baddeley 1976). And it can be characterized as vulnerable because it is known to be especially susceptible to impairment by neurological disorders, drugs, or simple aging.

Given this vulnerability, the question of whether the functions

W. K. Estes, Is human memory obsolete? *American Scientist*, 1980, **68**, 62–69. Reprinted with permission of The Society of the Sigma Xi.

This article is based on the author's Bingham Memorial Lecture, delivered at Carnegie-Mellon University.

of human short-term memory could be taken over by computers is more than academic. The answer must necessarily depend not only on the technical development of computers but on our understanding of the system to be replaced. In order to gain some perspective on these issues, let us take a look at computer memory and human memory from the standpoint of an engineer concerned with the operating properties of each and with the parallelism or lack of parallelism of these properties that would be critical to any consideration of replacing one system with the other.

FUNCTIONAL PROPERTIES

Comparisons of the structural and functional properties of computer memory and human memory have been attempted often over the years, usually by computer scientists rather than psychologists; but there has been an asymmetry in that engineering specifications for the computer memory are readily supplied, whereas corresponding parameters of human memory have been largely unknown. A computer memory typically consists of two principal components: a core memory, whose contents are very readily available to enter into logical or arithmetical computations, and a larger reservoir of stored information, or "mass storage," usually residing on magnetic tapes or disks, which may be needed at times but is not so readily accessible. In a well-known and widely reprinted paper, Kemeny (1955) gave a capacity of 10^6 bits of information as typical of a core memory and commented that he would not expect computer core memories to get much larger because of the problem of speed of access. I think that with the advent of integrated circuits this figure could be raised somewhat, but it is still representative. Random access to any element in the core memory is extremely rapid by human standards, an item of information being accessible in a single microsecond or even less. The mass storage is virtually unlimited in capacity but access is much slower, an item of information in one of the usual configurations requiring about 1,000 μsec to retrieve. A good deal of research, most of it accomplished since Kemeny's paper, shows human memory similarly to be organized into two principal components (Atkinson and Shiffrin 1968; Craik and Levy 1976). The first of these, commonly referred to as short-term or primary memory, is presumed to have a very small capacity, retaining for a brief interval perhaps half a dozen items such as digits or words or the equivalent in information about a single visual scene (Miller 1956). The second component, called long-term or secondary memory, constitutes both memory for episodes from past experience and organized knowledge about language, the world, and the like. Its capacity is relatively large, perhaps comparable to that of the memory of a sizable computer. Kemeny estimates this capacity to be on the order of 10^8 bits of information, basing his figure not on research but on the idea that sensory patterns can be perceived at the rate of several per second and that all of the patterns perceived during every waking hour of a person's life reside permanently in the long-term memory system.

Although there is some room for skepticism about Kemeny's estimate, there is no reason to doubt that the capacity of the long-term memory is large, running at least to many millions of bits of information. Exactly how large the long-term memory might be is probably an unimportant question, because it seems sure that the speed of access to items in human memory is so slow compared to that of the computer that, even if the memory store were as large as some people have imagined, most of it would be useless because there would never be time to retrieve more than a very small part.

HUMAN RETRIEVAL TIMES

In order to proceed toward a more specific idea of the interchangeability of human and computer memories, we need to replace the very crude characterizations of retrieval time for human memory as "slow" or "very slow" with estimates of actual times. The fact that we can now do this is one of the major breakthroughs of the last ten years of research in this area.

Figure 3.7 illustrates some of the results of the body of research addressed to the problem of estimating retrieval time for items stored in human long-term memory (Estes and Horst 1968). The basic procedure here was simple: subjects were given some items of information to remember and were then tested for their ability to recall these items; the time required for the recall was measured. In preparation for the measurements of reaction times recorded here the subjects were asked to memorize a number of new associations, 6 in the case of the data shown on the left and 24 for the data shown on the right. These associations consisted of arbitrary pairings of words and numbers, for example, the word "room" and the number 62. After the subjects had thoroughly mastered these associations they were given daily sessions in which they were simply tested for their ability to produce the appropriate number when presented with any one of the words. The reaction time was defined as the period elapsing between the presentation of the word and the beginning of the subject's response of typing out the number on a keyboard.

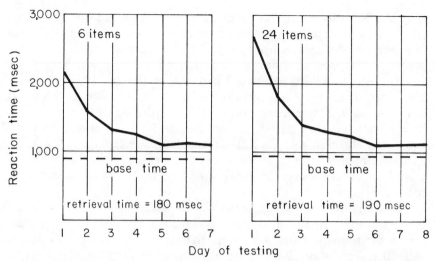

Figure 3.7 Graphs show reaction times for recalling numbers arbitrarily paired with words after these associations had previously been thoroughly mastered. Six such associations were tested at the left, 24 on the right. The base times were established by presenting the numbers on a screen and asking the subjects to type them as fast as they could read them. The difference between the time required to give the associative responses and the time required simply to read and type the numbers provides an estimate of the time required to retrieve an association from the long-term memory, a little under 200 msec in the final days of the experiment. This final level of reaction time is a bit higher for the longer list, but so is the base time, indicating that retrieval time is almost independent of list length. (From Estes and Horst 1968).

It will be seen that even after learning had been so thoroughly accomplished that errors were no longer occurring (Day 1 on the graph), the time required to give a response was really quite long, on the order of 2 to 3 seconds. Over several successive days of further concentrated practice, these reaction times decreased and seemed to level off at a value of 1,100 msec. Now we can't, to be sure, take 1,100 msec as an accurate estimate of the time required for the mental process of retrieving the association, since it includes also the time required both to read the stimulus word and to initiate the overt response of operating a key.

Therefore, following a line of reasoning suggested some hundred years ago by the Dutch physiologist Donders (see Woodworth 1938), we carried out a control procedure in which we simply presented the numbers in question on a display screen and asked the subjects to type them as fast as they could read them. As shown by the base times in Figure 1, about 950 msec were required to make these responses. The difference between these values and the times required to give the associative responses is taken as an estimate of the time required for the mental operation of retrieving a newly learned association, and proves to be just a little under 200 msec. This value agrees quite well with Sabol and DeRosa's estimate (1976) of about 180 msec to identify and retrieve the meaning of a word, which was obtained by a different method. Since in ordinary life people rarely have so much concentrated practice on a small set of associations, we can probably conclude that these estimates are fairly near minimal and that retrieval times for most of the items in a human memory would be rather longer, running up to at least half a second or a second.

Presumably one of the reasons it is advantageous for a human being or other organism, in contrast to a computer, to have a separate short-term memory system is that items currently available in this subsystem may be retrieved more quickly than the much larger number of items in long-term memory. Verification of this supposition has not been easy, however. In a type of experiment that has generally been considered relevant, the high-speed "short-term memory scanning" task originated by Sternberg (1966), the procedure is to present a subject with a small number of items, usually digits or letters, in a random sequence (these being considered the "memory set"). Shortly afterwards a "probe" item is introduced, which may or may not be a member of the set just presented, these cases being denoted "positive" and "negative" trials, respectively. The subject's task is to respond to the probe as quickly as possible by indicating whether or not it was included in the memory set. The reaction time for this response is presumed to include the retrieval time for items currently held in short-term memory together with the time required for encoding the probe and executing the response.

The slope of the function obtained when mean reaction time is plotted against size of the memory set has been taken to measure the combined retrieval and comparison time per item. Sternberg (1966) obtained an estimate of about 38 msec per character for retrieval plus comparison time using this technique, and subsequent studies have yielded figures in fairly close agreement.

With the idea of separating retrieval from comparison time, I contrived the following variation on the Sternberg procedure. In an experiment conducted in my laboratory, half the trials administered to subjects followed the traditional Sternberg procedure. A memory set consisting of 1, 2, 3, or 4 letters was shown, with the letters presented successively on a display screen at a rate of 2 per second. After a short interval a probe letter was introduced. Thus a positive trial with a memory-set size equal to 4 and with *S* as the probe letter would appear as:

$$X \quad S \quad Q \quad V \qquad S$$

The function for mean reaction time versus set size in this experiment is shown in Figure 3.8. Unfortunately, the function is not linear, and we have no direct way of telling whether retrieval or comparison time, or both, change as size of the memory set increases.

Anticipating this problem, we included a procedure designed to allow further analysis. In the other half of the trials, therefore, the subjects were given similar presentations of memory sets and probes under what I shall term a high expectancy, or for brevity, "Ex" condition; these trials were randomly distributed among those employing the standard procedure. To prepare for this variation the subjects were familiarized in advance of the experiment with two subsets of letters, one of which was the set used in the Sternberg trials. The other set, comprising the same number of letters, was termed the Ex set. The subjects were informed that in each of the Ex trials exactly one member of the Ex set would be included in the memory set, and that in a positive Ex trial the Ex member of the memory set was the only item that could appear as the probe. (Thus in half of the Ex trials the Ex member did appear as the probe, and in the other half—the "negative" trials—a letter not belonging to the memory set appeared as the probe.) Since the subject could identify an Ex item as soon as it appeared as the only member of the memory set that could appear as a probe in that trial, I assumed that it would be held in the short-term memory in a state of readiness for comparison. Thus when the probe appeared, this one member of the memory set could immediately be compared with the probe, without any need for search or retrieval from short-term memory.

Given the reasoning I have outlined, reaction time in the Ex trials should include all the components of reaction time in the Sternberg trials except the time needed to retrieve the appropriate member of the memory set from short-term memory upon presentation of the probe. Consequently, if for a given memory-set size we subtract the mean reaction time for Ex trials from the mean reaction time for Sternberg trials, we should have an estimate of the time required to retrieve an element of the memory set. The inset in Figure 3.8 shows the results of this calculation, which yielded an estimate of approximately 25 msec per letter as the retrieval time. Thus we may tentatively conclude that retrieval time for a short-term memory set is appreciably shorter than that for long-term memory, but still very long compared to access time for a digital computer.

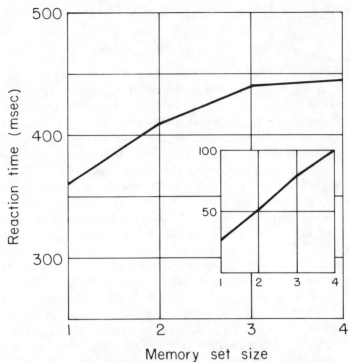

Memory set size

Figure 3.8 In trials using the standard Sternberg procedure, a memory set of 1 to 4 letters was presented to subjects, followed by a probe letter. Here reaction times required for recognition of the probe as a member of the memory set are plotted for sets of various sizes. In order to arrive at a more accurate estimate of retrieval time, an equal number of "Ex," or high expectancy, trials were randomly distributed among the Sternberg trials. In the Ex trials subjects knew that only one member of the set could appear as a probe and thus were able to identify it as soon as it appeared, thereby eliminating retrieval time. As the inset shows, subtracting the mean reaction time for the Ex trials from the mean reaction time for the Sternberg trials yields an estimated retrieval time of approximately 25 msec per letter for the short-term memory.

ORGANIZATION OF SHORT-TERM MEMORY

Up to this point, comparisons seem strongly to favor the computer as a repository for information, and we might seem to be on the way to drawing the moral that we should let computers take over from man as quickly as possible. We need to be sure of our ground, however, in view of the critical role of short-term memory in the "executive" system of any problem solver, human or inanimate, where it performs the essential functions of holding current instructions and assembling data on which current cognitive operations are to be performed. A subsystem of this sort is an important element in models for performance in cognitive tasks, for example those of Gilmartin, Newell, and Simon (1976) and of Kintsch and Vipond (1979).

But if short-term memory is so important, why should its capacity be limited to only a few items? The answer I am going to propose is that the capacity of human short-term memory only appears to be small when we insist on measuring it in terms of discrete items, such as letters or words, in much the way we would assess the capacity of the analogous component of a computer. A consideration of research on short-term memory will indicate, I believe, that the functional properties of human and computer memories differ sufficiently to make the same method of measuring capacity inappropriate in the two cases.

The operating characteristics of a computer memory, or of computer-oriented models for human memory (e.g. Atkinson and Shiffrin 1968), illustrated in the upper portion of Figure 3.9 are well known. Here we suppose that a sequence of characters, represented by the letters A, B, C, and D, has been read into a computer to be retained for later recall. An encoded representation of each of the characters is entered in a memory location, or "slot," the slots typically (though not necessarily) being in adjacent locations, as shown in the figure. Following input, this information will be maintained intact for a period of time unless the contents of some of the locations are overwritten by new input or degraded by hardware failure. In this case, the contents of some locations might no longer be recoverable, but other, intact items would still be associated wth their original positions.

By contrast, the results of research in my laboratory (Estes 1972; Lee and Estes 1977) suggest that human short-term memory is quite differently organized, being oriented toward events and their attributes rather than toward the retention of items as units. In the human memory, forgetting is characteristically a progressive loss of precision of information about an event rather than a matter of total recall or total loss of a stored item. Following input of the items A, B, C, and D, the state of the individual's information about the relative position of any one of the items can best be described by an "uncertainty distribution," with the horizontal axis representing time elapsed during the interval in which the items were presented

Item-in-slot model

Event model

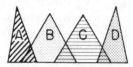   

Figure 3.9 Fundamental organizational differences distinguish human memory from computer memory. As shown in these schematic drawings, computer memory can best be represented as an "item-in-slot" model, retaining encoded items of information—here the letters A, B, C, and D—in separate memory locations or slots and maintaining them intact except where they are overwritten by later input or degraded by hardware failure. Even when this takes place, as shown at the right for the items B and C, adjacent items remain intact. By contrast, the human memory is organized around events as they occur in time and is best depicted as a series of "uncertainty distributions," with the vertical axis indicating the probability that the individual will recall, for example, the locations of the items A, B, C, and D at various points within the interval in which they were presented. Unlike the computer, which has only the alternatives of total recall or total loss of information, the human memory forgets by a gradual process in which the gradients of these distributions become less steep and the overlap between pairs of gradients increases as precision of information about an event is slowly lost, as shown at the right for the items B and C.

and the vertical axis the probability that the subject will remember the occurrence of an item as being localized at any particular instant within the interval.

Typically, it is most likely that an item will be recalled at its correct position relative to others in the sequence, slightly less likely that it will be recalled as having occurred a little before or after its actual point of occurrence, and so on. These gradients are relatively steep for items occurring at the beginning and end of a sequence, where memory for position is relatively precise, and less steep for items occurring at interior positions. Furthermore, these gradients overlap, so that if, for example, the hypothetical individual whose memory is illustrated were to consult his memory at some particular moment regarding the relative positions of items C and D, he might incorrectly recall them as having occurred in inverse order, the likelihood of this error being proportional to the overlap of the uncertainty distributions for items C and D. As time progresses, these gradients become less steep, and the overlap between pairs of gradients increases, meaning that precision of information about the ordering of the original input sequence is gradually being lost.

What reason do we have to believe that this apparently more complex model organized around events is closer to the truth about the workings of human short-term memory than the "slot" model characteristic of the computer? Perhaps the most direct source of information comes from specially designed experiments in which subjects were presented with a sequence of items—letters or digits— and were then asked not only to recall as many of the original items as possible in the appropriate order but also to indicate on a diagram the remembered position of each item within the presentation interval. From these data it is possible to construct empirical uncertainty distributions corresponding to those shown in Figure 3.9. The findings presented in Figure 3.10 (Lee and Estes 1977) demonstrate that the empirical gradients resulting from such an experiment resemble the hypothetical ones in all essentials. Numerous replications of this experiment have uniformly yielded similar configurations of data. We evidently can conclude with some confidence, then, that a person's memory for elements of a sequence of items such as letters, digits, or words is best represented by uncertainty gradients portraying the way information about the remembered position of each item is distributed over an interval of time, rather than by a series of boxes or slots containing items of information.

Since the relative location of an item is apparently represented in short-term memory as a quantitatively graded attribute, would the same be true of other properties of the event of seeing or hearing a letter or word? There is in fact a great deal of evidence that the answer to this question is yes, at least in the case of auditory properties. If, for example, an individual who has heard the letter sequence $X \, T \, Q \, R$ is unable to recall the sequence perfectly in a later test and makes an error, say, regarding the second member of the sequence, the error is likely to take the form of remembering that item to be a letter such as P or C, which has the same vowel sound as the correct

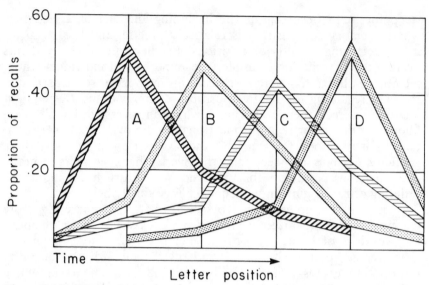

Figure 3.10 When subjects were presented with a sequence of 4 items (in the relative temporal positions indicated by the letters) and asked both to recall the items in the order in which they appeared and to indicate on a diagram the remembered position of each item, the resulting gradients, shown here, closely resembled those of the hypothetical uncertainty distributions depicted in Figure 3.9. Repeated replications of the experiment yielded similar configurations (Lee and Estes 1977).

letter T, rather than a letter such as M or K, which has a different vowel sound (Conrad 1964; Estes 1973; Bjork and Healy 1974). Drewnowski and Murdock (1980) have observed an analogous phenomenon with respect to stress patterns in memory of sequences of spoken words.

The attributes represented in short-term memory are not limited to auditory properties. In analyzing the data illustrated in Figure 3.10, it occurred to us, for example, that we had an excellent opportunity to look for evidence of memory storage of an attribute corresponding to the difference between letters and digits. In an ensuing experiment, subjects were presented in each trial with a sequence of 12 characters, 4 of which were letters to be remembered while the remainder were random digits, the letters and digits being intermixed in various arrangements. In the recall test of each trial the subject was asked not only to try to recall the 4 letters but also to indicate where they had occurred in these 12 possible positions. We were thus able to look for evidence as to whether, when subjects failed to remember the letters presented, they nonetheless retained some information as to the positions in the sequence in which letters rather than digits had occurred.

The results (Fig. 3.11) show that even in cases where the subjects made errors, they still strongly tended to assign the erroneously recalled items to the positions in the sequence that had actually been occupied by letters. In other words, they remembered something about the temporal distribution of items belonging to the category "letter" even when they could not remember what the individual letters were.

Taking together the results of these and related analyses, it appears that short-term memory for even so apparently simple a sequence of events as the occurrence of a series of letters or a string of digits takes the form of an assemblage of uncertainty distributions, each representing what the individual knows about the distribution of a particular attribute over the interval of time in which the sequence was presented. Thus if letters occurred in the middle 4 positions of a sequence of 8 characters (Fig. 3.12), the short-term memory system would contain a distribution of information about the locations containing letters, a distribution of information about phonological properties over position, and distributions for information about still more abstract properties. Recall is evidently a matter of scanning this array and—for each cross section in time (a vertical slice in Fig. 3.12)—utilizing information from each of the distributions to narrow down uncertainty concerning the character that occurred at that point, ideally to the correct item, but even when memory is imperfect often to a small subset including the correct item and others similar to it in some respects.

Specific models embodying these ideas may differ in some technical details, but roughly speaking the predicted likelihood that the subject would recall the letter T in the fifth position, for example, would be proportional to the sum of the heights of the uncertainty curves in the slice above the letter T; the likelihood that an X would be incorrectly recalled as presented at position 5 would be proportional to the sum of the heights of the curves above X in the diagram; and so on. Even without filling in the uncertainty curves for the other positions, it is possible to see that many testable implications follow. For example, we would predict that the letters P and T (which sound alike and therefore both have high values on the auditory feature function) would be more likely to be interchanged in recall than, say, T and R. On the other hand, among letters with dissimilar sounds T would be more likely to be interchanged with R, which is closer to it in the input sequence, than with X, which is

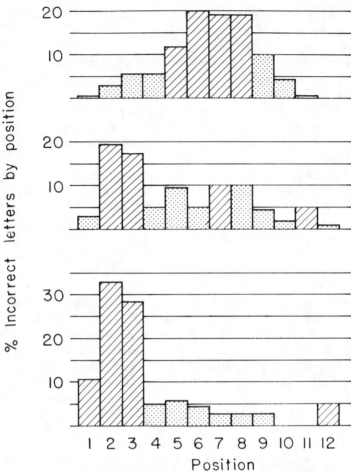

Figure 3.11 Attributes stored in the short-term memory are not limited to relative location or auditory properties. In an experiment testing evidence of memory storage of an attribute corresponding to the difference between letters and digits, subjects were presented with a sequence of 12 characters—4 letters to be remembered, randomly interspersed with 8 digits—and were then asked to recall the 4 letters and to indicate their correct positions in the sequence. This graph showing the percentage of cases in which an incorrectly recalled letter was assigned to one of the positions that had actually been occupied by letters in three replications of the experiment indicates that even when subjects could not recall letters accurately they nevertheless retained some information about the temporal positions in which letters, as opposed to digits, had occurred. (The positions actually occupied by letters are cross hatched).

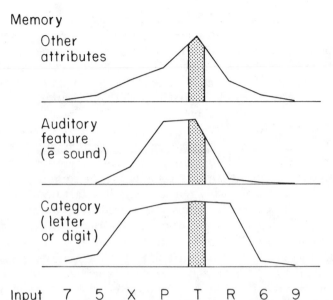

Input   7   5   X   P   T   R   6   9

Figure 3.12 For a sequence of 8 characters in which the middle 4 positions are occupied by letters, the short-term memory would contain distributions of information about locations containing letters, phonological properties, and other, more abstract attributes. To recall a letter, the human memory scans this array for each cross section of time (indicated for the letter *T* by a bar) and then uses information from each distribution to narrow down uncertainty about the character that occurred at this point, either to a small subset of similar characters or (ideally) to the correct character. The probability that the subject would recall the correct position of the letter *T* would therefore be directly related to the sum of the heights of the uncertainty curves in the slice above the letter *T*.

farther away. And any two letters would be more likely to be interchanged than a letter and a digit, for example *R* and 6, where the sharp break in the category function separates the two characters. All of these implications have been well supported by experimental findings (Bjork and Healy 1974; Lee and Estes 1977).

THE NATURE OF FORGETTING

It should be emphasized that the attributes for which we have cited specific evidence probably far from exhaust the list of those that are actually stored in short-term memory, even when the experience in question is one as apparently simple as seeing or hearing a single letter or digit. New instances are continually appearing as research methods are progressively refined. Thus we can conclude that human short-term memory of a single verbal item is not an exact encoded representation of that item stored in a slot in memory, as would be characteristic in a computer memory, but rather takes the form of a large amount of less precise information about various properties or attributes of the sensory experience. As a consequence, forgetting characteristically takes quite a different form in the short-term memories of human beings than in the memories of computers. In computers a stored item typically remains wholly intact until its location is overwritten by some new input or erased as a consequence of a hardware failure (for example, the burning out of a transistor element), in which case all record of the item is irretrievably lost.

In the human being, by contrast, forgetting must be assumed to begin immediately following any sensory experience and is a consequence of many factors, among them internal noise in the nervous system resulting from spontaneous neural activity, fluctuations in body chemistry, and the capturing of the human short-term memory system by new inputs. However, in the human the forgetting takes the form of a progressive loss of precision or completeness of information about the original experience; even after considerable forgetting has occurred the individual may remember something about the events or items making up the original experience, for example the approximate position of an item, as illustrated in Figures 3.11 and 3.12.

It would seem, then, that whereas the digital computer has characteristically been designed to preserve with a high degree of fidelity a very large number of discrete items of information, and to do so in a way that makes precise calculations possible, the short-term memory system of the human being (and doubtless other organisms) has been designed, so to speak, to sacrifice high fidelity in favor of a capacity to maintain large amounts of approximate information, much of which may never be needed, but some of which may be essential as a guide to actions when a situation previously experienced recurs with some variation.

HUMAN VS. COMPUTER MEMORY

Perhaps we can begin to generalize a little about the comparison between man and computer. Everyone working with computers is familiar with the fact that they began as devices with an extremely specialized application. Since that time, however, they have become so diversified that it is now possible to obtain, on the one hand, a mini- or even micro-computer dedicated to some very specific task or, on the other hand, a general-purpose computer capable of dealing with a very wide variety of problems indeed. On this continuum from specialized to general-purpose it begins to appear that the human memory system belongs somewhere off the top, having been developed with the strongest premium on general-purpose capability. This attribute runs through comparisons that can be made between various aspects of human and computer memories, some of which are summarized in tabular form in Figure 3.13.

With regard to efficiency, as we have noted previously, the computer appears far superior to human memory as long as we make the comparison on the basis of information defined as a computer would deal with it, as bits or items. However, we have seen that the human memory system typically does not limit itself to discrete representations of discrete items, but may retain information about properties of items or events and their distribution over time that would not be taken into account in programming a computer or a computer model.

In the same vein, although analog computers can be and have been built, the computer revolution has been characterized mainly

	Human Memory	*Computer Memory*
Preferred storage mode	analog; time-oriented	digital; list-oriented
Retention of information	graded	all-or-none
Efficiency (bits/sec.)	low	high
Capacity	dependent on experience	independent of experience
Retrieval		
relative to context	strongly, dependent	independent
relative to previous retrievals	dependent	independent
Purpose	general purpose; open set of functions	special or general purpose; closed set of functions

Figure 3.13 A tabular comparison of the functional properties of human and computer memories shows the rapid access and high precision of computer memory to be balanced by the robustness and general-purpose capability of human memory.

by the proliferation of digital computers, which are strongly list-oriented and record discrete bits or items of information on an all-or-none basis with provision for high-speed random retrieval. By contrast, the human memory seems strongly to prefer an analog mode in which information of varying degrees of precision or levels of specification concerning attributes of events is stored with relatively high redundancy, so that at least partial retention of information about an experience is likely even if the system is grossly disturbed, as by disease or injury.

The memory of a computer is relatively independent of time; it generally is indifferent to the absolute times at which various items of information come in, and it maintains information in such a way that the bits or items are left undisturbed when the memory is interrogated or when a given item is retrieved. Conversely, human memory tends to be strongly dependent on time, taking account of actual temporal intervals between input events. It does not maintain information in a fixed format, but rather is continually reorganized as a consequence of the processes of interrogation and retrieval (Bjork 1975; Estes 1979).

Indeed, the more we learn about the human memory, the less it seems to fit the stereotyped idea of a simple repository. It seems to be not at all like a storeroom, a library, or a computer core memory, a place where items of information are stored and kept until wanted, but rather presents a picture of a complex, dynamic system that at any given time can be made to deliver information concerning discrete events or items it has had experience with in the past. In fact, human memory does not, in a literal sense, store anything; it simply changes as a function of experience.

The storehouse analogy often does no harm, and can be a convenient metaphor when the emphasis is on some narrow aspect of performance. But it can be pernicious in a consideration of where research efforts should be concentrated, or of how intellectual function can be improved in some general way. It is possible to specify fully the set of functions realized on any computer; it is feasible not only to understand fully the operation of the computer but also to arrive at an objective evaluation of how near at hand such an understanding lies. But for human memory, there seem to be no grounds for believing that we are close to knowing what the full set of functions is. Thus comparisons between man and computer may be quite instructive in pointing up what is and is not known about the human side of the comparison, but as yet they probably have little to tell us about the possibility that computers might one day be capable of outstripping human beings as general-purpose thinking machines.

IS HUMAN MEMORY REPLACEABLE?

Although the efficiency of modern digital computers in storing and retrieving information is awe-inspiring to human beings, with their all-too-fallible memories, the comparisons we have made suggest that the idea of a race between man and computer is inappropriate. Even serious consideration of the possibility that computers could soon take over important functions of human memory seems premature. It is true that computers can successfully take over some intellectual functions from human beings, in particular calculation, but in these cases both computer and man are required to deal with the same inputs and produce the same outputs.

The situation with regard to short-term memory proves on close inspection not to be closely analogous. Items put into a computer are simply deposited in a coded form, and can later be reproduced by decoding. When items are presented to a human being, information *about* the events is recorded in memory, but the precise nature and extent of this information are still incompletely understood. These items may or may not be reproducible (recallable) at a later time, but some information about the items or the occasion on which they were presented can nearly always be recovered. This capability of retaining large amounts of relatively imprecise information regarding past experiences, though less than optimal for the special purposes of calculations and logical operations, is evidently important to organisms that must constantly adapt to their environments. Witness, for example, how helpless people become when their memory systems fail as a consequence of disease, injury, or aging.

A long-term goal of research on human memory is to develop ways of remedying these failures of the human memory systems. Conceivably, the development of "mental prosthetics," in which computers take over some of the functions of the human memory system, may prove to be one way in which this is accomplished. The results of the vast increase of research on human memory during the past two decades seem at this point to make the goal ever more remote, in view of the complexities revealed regarding the organization of human memory. However, these same results have brought about an appreciation of how much remains to be learned, and have led to the development of useful methods for moving toward the deeper understanding that must be reached before the products of advanced technology can take over functions of failing components of the human memory system.

REFERENCES

Atkinson, R. C., and R. M. Shiffrin. 1968. Human memory: A proposed system and its control processes. In *The Psychology of Learning and Motivation: Advances in research and theory*, ed. K. W. Spence and J. T. Spence, II, 89–195. New York: Academic Press.

Baddeley, A. D. 1976. *The Psychology of Memory.* New York: Basic Books.

Bjork, E. L., and A. F. Healy. 1974. Short-term order and item retention. *J. of Verb. Learning and Verb. Behav.* 13:80–97.

Bjork, R. A. 1975. Retrieval as a memory modifier: An interpretation of negative recency and related phenomena. In *Information Processing and Cognition,* ed. R. L. Solso, pp. 123–144. Hillsdale, NJ: Erlbaum Associates.

Conrad, R. 1964. Acoustic confusions in immediate memory. *Brit. J. of Psych.* 55:75–84.

Craik, F. I. M., and B. A. Levy. 1976. The concept of primary memory. In *The Handbook of Learning and Cognitive Processes,* ed. W. K. Estes, IV, 133–175. Hillsdale, NJ: Erlbaum Associates.

Drewnowski, A., and B. B. Murdock, Jr. 1980. Stimulus attributes and memory span. *J. of Exper. Psych.: Human Learning and Memory* 6:319–332.

Estes, W. K. 1972. An associative basis for coding and organization in memory. In *Coding Processes in Human Memory,* ed. A. W. Melton and E. Martin, pp. 161–190. Washington, DC: Winston.

Estes, W. K. 1973. Phonemic coding and rehearsal in short-term memory for letter strings. *J. of Verb. Learning and Verb. Behav.* 12:360–72.

Estes, W. K. 1979. Role of response availability in the effects of cued-recall tests on memory. *J. of Exper. Psych.: Human Learning and Memory* 5:567–73.

Estes, W. K., and D. P. Horst. 1968. *Latency as a Function of Response Alternatives in Paired-Associate Learning.* Technical Report 135, Institute for Mathematical Studies in the Social Sciences, Stanford University.

Gilmartin, K. J., A. Newell, and H. A. Simon. 1976. A program modeling short-term memory under strategy control. In *The Structure of Human Memory,* ed. C. N. Cofer, pp. 15–30. San Francisco: Freeman.

Kemeny, J. G. 1955. Man viewed as machine. *Sci. Am.* 192:58–67.

Kintsch, W., and D. Vipond. 1979. Reading comprehension and readability in educational practice and psychological theory. In *Perspectives on Memory Research,* ed. L. -G. Nilsson, pp. 329–65. Hillsdale, NJ: Erlbaum Associates.

Lee, C. L., and W. K. Estes. 1977. Order and position in primary memory for letter strings. *J. of Verb. Learning and Verb. Behav.* 16:395–418.

Miller, G. A. 1956. The magical number seven, plus or minus two: Some limits on our capacity for processing information. *Psych. Rev.* 63:81–97.

Murdock, B. B., Jr. 1974. *Human memory: Theory and Data.* Hillsdale, NJ: Erlbaum Associates.

Rajchman, J. A. 1977. New memory technologies. *Science* 195: 1223–29.

Sabol, M. A., and D. V. DeRosa. 1976. Semantic encoding of isolated words. *J. of Exper. Psych.:Human Learning and Memory* 2:58–68.

Sternberg, S. 1966. High-speed scanning in human memory. *Science* 153 625–54.

Woodworth, R. S. 1938. *Experimental Psychology*. New York: Holt.

Structural Aspects of Associative Models for Memory

THE CONCEPT OF STRUCTURE

What do we mean by the structure of memory? If the terms are taken literally, the answer may be nothing at all. Often we speak of memory as though it were a warehouse in which things to be remembered are kept in some arrangement like goods on stockroom shelves. But we know that memory actually is not such an entity, in fact, not an entity at all, but rather an aspect of the functioning of a complex information-processing system (Reitman, 1965). This aspect is somewhat analogous to the functioning of libraries or warehouses. Items of information—words, numbers, propositions—are fed into the system and, in a sense, are later retrieved. However, we have no reason to think that between input and output the words, numbers, or propositions are stored in specific locations somewhere in the head. What is inside the head is a fabulous conglomeration of interconnected nerve cells. One property important to the functioning of the system is that the input of a message, say a printed word, generates a change in the state of excitability of some portion of the ensemble of cells with the result that the system responds differently to later input of the same or related messages.

To clarify what we mean when we speak of the structure of memory, we need first of all to understand that we refer actually to the structure of a theory or model within whose framework we are trying to interpret how memory functions. We may try to express our ideas concerning some aspects of memory function in an analogy, for example, by pointing to the similarities of input-output relations between an individual's performance and the functioning of a library. If in this context we ask whether the individual's memory is hierarchically organized, we mean to ask whether the best-fitting

W. K. Estes, Structural aspects of associative models for memory. From *The structure of human memory*, edited by Charles N. Cofer. San Francisco, Calif.: W. H. Freeman and Company. Copyright ©

Preparation of this paper was supported in part by Grant MH23878 from the National Institute of Mental Health.

model (the closest analogy) is a library in which the classification of volumes follows a hierarchical scheme. But we may try instead to comprehend the individual's performance by assuming that it reflects the operation of a network of logical elements, like the switches and connectors in a telephone system or computer. Then our remark about hierarchical structure refers to the arrangement of logical elements that must be assumed in order to explain performance.

In either case, successful predictions lend support to the assumptions of a model but cannot be taken to mean that the structure of the organism's memory is like that of the pictorialization. Many properties of the transmission of impulses through the nervous system can be nicely illustrated in terms of the well-known, iron-wire analogy (Lillie, 1925), but one would not care to go on to infer that the structure of a nerve fiber resembles that of a corròded segment of iron wire.

Even though a model describes a system up to a point, the model may be grossly misleading if taken too literally. We need to allow for the possibility that the concept of structure as applied to memory in computers is inappropriate when applied to the memory of a living organism. Even with computers, we find at least two senses of structure. The most literal meaning of structure in the case of computers refers to the hardware, that is, to the components such as magnetic cores that have a fixed capacity in terms of the number of words of information they can store, or to the registers that are permanently connected by means of cables to other registers or devices. This meaning of structure seems to be the one intended in the "stores" of certain current memory models.

However, a computer programmer need not know the details of the hardware structure of his machine. In writing his programs he deals with logical blocks of memory locations, logical pages, and logical devices, and when running the programs he creates a file structure for the information that must be held in memory. He generally creates and runs his programs with no direct reference at all to the hardware of the machine. It is the logical structure generated by programs that the user of the system has to understand. Structure in this second sense refers to the way in which the information entered in the system is organized relative to the procedures available for operating on it.

When concepts of structure are carried over from computers to human memory, one often sees an almost overpowering tendency to construct diagrams resembling those that picture the hardware components of a computer and to speak as though human memory had a preexisting structure into which items of information can be placed. I think it is fair to say that structural concepts of the hardware variety have served on occasion as useful devices to aid in the communication of general ideas about memory (for a good current illustration, see the "conveyer-belt" model of Murdock, 1974, chapter 10), but their usefulness is being challenged by recent theoretical developments. In the Atkinson-Shiffrin (1968) system, for example, the short-term buffer becomes, not a stack of locations into which items can be entered, but rather a component of the memory system by virtue of which representations of recently presented items are kept in a highly available state through repeated rehearsal. Further, there are clear symptoms in the current literature of a growing disenchantment with the whole conception of fixed memory stores (see, for example, Craik and Lockhart, 1972). Thus in the remainder of the present article I shall confine attention to the concept of logical structure, the structure that takes form as incoming information is transformed and organized under the rules of operation of the memory system.

The first point to emphasize about logical structure is that it need not, and in general does not, correspond in any direct way to the structure portrayed in the block diagrams or flow diagrams that are used to illustrate the general workings of the memory system within any particular theory. Structure takes form as information is processed and therefore cannot be discussed in relation to any specific theory until the flow diagrams have been implemented in terms of a model that actually processes and organizes information. One type of implementation is a computer program that simulates the behavior of an individual whose memory operates in accord with the premises of a given theory. By actually running a program one can ascertain the structural properties that the system imposes on the information it deals with. Perhaps the best example of this procedure that has yet been proposed in theoretical treatments of memory is Feigenbaum's elementary-perceiver-and-memorizer (EPAM) model for verbal learning and retention, within which structure takes the form of a network of images and test nodes, or comparators (Feigenbaum, 1963). Another route to implementing diagrams is by way of the formulation of a mathematical model that defines states of information with regard to prior inputs of event sequences and postulates rules for transition among states (Bower and Theios, 1964; Greeno, 1974). A third route is by way of a model formulated in more primitive terms, that is, in terms referring not to information or information processing but rather to abstract elements and the logical relations among them. This last route is epitomized in association theory, older and newer versions of which will be the main focus of attention in later sections of this chapter.

Being clear about what we mean when we use terms like structure of memory has quite material implications for the way we do research. For one thing we can save much fruitless effort in trying to answer unanswerable questions. A most important class of these in current cognitive psychology considers the relative merits of the two principal theoretical approaches to memory—information-processing theory and learning theory. We shall see that these theories derive from different levels of analysis of the phenomena of memory; it is thus better to regard them as complementary rather than competitive.

WHAT ARE INFORMATION-PROCESSING MODELS?

It is hard to define information-processing models constructively, but it is easy to do so by complementation, for the information-processing approach arose in psychology primarily as a reaction against the behavioristic framework of learning theory and especially as a reaction against stimulus-response association theory. Viewed apart from any philosophical commitments, the study of learning is the study of the ways in which organisms' behavioral dispositions change as a function of experience. I think that nearly all who have thought about the matter deeply would agree that, in principle, all laws of learning could be expressed in stimulus-response terminology. The question is whether they should be. The hazard in confining ourselves to a stimulus-response terminology is not the possibility of being proved wrong, but rather the danger of being too particularistic and thus unable to arrive at principles general enough to be useful in solving problems or interpreting new situations.

Beginning in the early 1950s a number of investigators, including Attneave (1954), Hovland (1952), and Miller (1953), noted that if an individual's response tendencies change with experience then observations of his behavior yield information as to what experiences he has had. Thus we can objectively speak of information being stored in an individual's brain and retrieved by way of tests of memory. This view has had a number of fruitful consequences in research. First of all, an approach oriented in terms of informational concepts allows an investigator to escape from the confines of stimulus-response descriptions and encourages attempts to arrive at a more abstract characterization of the information stored and retrieved (formally, the task of information theory). Further, this approach suggests the value of analyzing the detailed sequence of both the observable and the inferred operations performed by an individual engaged in a cognitive task, that is, engaged in the process of taking in, storing, transforming, and retrieving information. Finally, the task of carrying out these analyses is facilitated by methods developed in connection with information-processing systems oriented around digital computers rather than human brains.

This kind of information-processing theory has some obvious advantages. It necessitates close attention to the information-processing requirements of a task and thus is often useful in uncovering constraints on the learner that would not otherwise be apparent. Further, one can embody the theoretical notions in a program and thus ensure that the implications claimed for the ideas actually follow— the proof being obtained by running the program.

As presented in the current literature, information-processing models often have a very different look from, say, the mathematical models of stochastic learning theories. Rather than equations and matrices, we see block diagrams picturing sequences of memory stores and devices such as comparators that operate on the information as it passes through the sequence. It is tempting, but probably incorrect, to infer that the structure of these diagrams portrays the structure of memory.

To clarify our thinking, we might note that the constituents of the information flow diagrams, like those of mathematical models, are merely symbols used to express assumptions as to how the cognitive system works. To verify the implications of an information-processing model with regard to memory structure, one must implement the flow diagram in terms of a computer program or an appropriate alternative logical or mathematical formalization. Then one can discover by simulation or derivation how items of information that are input to the system become organized in memory.

The essence of the information-processing approach is that the component processes and mechanisms of the system operate on items of information, not on stimuli or responses. Consequently, in this type of model, the structural properties of material stored in memory are independent of the mode of input. In contrast, if one treats problems of memory within the framework of learning theory, one views the organism, not as operating directly on items of information, but rather as responding to stimulus situations that carry information. As a result, concepts that are taken for granted (treated as primitives) in an information-processing model must be derived from more elementary assumptions in a learning model. The task of relating concepts of stimulus and response to concepts of information has fallen to the lot of association theory.

WHAT IS ASSOCIATION THEORY?

Association theory originated in the concept that experiences are represented in an individual's memory as separate units which become linked so that reactivation of one unit leads more or less automatically to reactivation of those with which it is associated. But precisely what becomes associated? In various versions of association theory the answer ranges from ideas to stimuli and responses to abstract linguistic entities.

In the writings of the British associationists (e.g., David Hartley, 1749; James Mill, 1829) it was presumed that the laws of association operate on ideas, entities that are accessible to objective scientific investigation through introspection and not through any other means. The concept of association made its way into experimental psychology through two routes. One of these led through the first experimental research on human memory, the other through the conditioning laboratory.

Ebbinghaus and his successors in the investigation of simple laboratory phenomena of memory, and later, the American "functional psychologists" left little room in their work for niceties of definition, but they all tacitly assumed that the elements of association are direct representations in memory of the items (such as nonsense syllables and adjectives) presented to a subject as part of the experimental task. The earliest experiments on memory (Ebbinghaus, 1885), and indeed most of those performed for many subsequent decades, involved extremely simple materials. A typical experiment required the memorization of a list of unrelated words or nonsense syllables, the task being taken to represent in its essentials the kind of learning that goes on in the memorization of vocabulary items or the like. To explain how memorization occurs, early investigators postulated that traces of the individual items of a list must be laid down in some form in the brain; these traces, or *engrams* as they were termed, would originally be unrelated, but connections or associations would form among them as a consequence of repeated experience with the items of the list. Then on later occasions, activation of one member of a pair of associated engrams would lead to activation of the other and thus provide a basis for recall of the corresponding item.

Experiments on conditioning were quite different in form from those on list-learning, but they posed a similar conceptual problem. A stimulus that originally does not evoke a given response comes to do so after the stimulus and response have been experienced together. The standard interpretation, following Pavlov (1927) and Thorndike (1931), was that an association or connection is formed between representations of the stimulus and the response. This concept of stimulus-response association was basic to the learning theories of Guthrie (1935), Hull (1943), and Skinner (1938). It seemed to solve the problem of the testability of the theories by virtue of the close correspondence between associations and observed stimulus-response relationships.

Only in quite recent times have researchers come to appreciate that rigorous testability of a theory does not depend on conceptual elements being mapped in a one-to-one fashion onto observable events. Thus, in the statistical theory of learning proposed by the writer (Estes, 1950, 1959), the units of association are abstract elements whose function is solely to enable one to derive testable propositions regarding relations between behavioral events.

Clearly, what is common to association theories is not their choice of units but rather their logical form. Any specific association theory comprises a definition of units and relations and a set of assumptions regarding the conditions under which the relations hold. In classical association models only one relation is assumed, that of a one-to-one connection between elements, although these connections might vary in strength. The interpretation of learning in terms of these associative connections is accomplished almost entirely by means of a single logical relation, the exclusive OR. Thus in the case of the conditioned reflex, an original stimulus evokes (is connected to) either its original response or the to-be-conditioned response; strengthening of one connection implies weakening of the other. Or, in paired-associate learning, the result of an effective training trial is to establish, or strengthen, a connection between the stimulus and response members of an item. Consequently, the structure of memory in association models takes the form of an ensemble of pairwise connections between stimuli and responses, representations of items, or homogeneous abstract elements.

This theoretical structure seemed too meager conceptually to offer any promise of interpreting the complex organizational aspects of human memory. Consequently, although during the first five or six decades of this century researchers continually refined association models to predict details of performance in a limited number of laboratory tasks, concurrently, they were setting the stage for the exuberant response of psychologists during the seventies to new approaches that seemed better equipped to cope with problems of structure and organization in memory (Miller, Galanter, and Pribram, 1960; Tulving and Donaldson, 1972).

These new approaches, well represented in other chapters of this volume, have had salutory effects on research, and their orientation in terms of information-processing concepts and computer analogies has encouraged psychologists to attack problems of memory that are much more complex than those that appeared tractable within the conceptual framework of stimulus-response associations.

Nonetheless, it is important to distinguish the intrinsic from the connotative properties of models. From the standpoint of a logical analysis, there are no limits on the complexity of information-processing structures constructed on the basis of associative concepts. Further, it is worth keeping in mind that association theory has guided the greater part of the research that has been done on human learning and memory, and thus is the type of theory that we are best equipped by experience to work with effectively. We need not be surprised to see that association theory is responding with its usual resilience to new challenges and in the process is generating new models quite different in appearance from those identified with connectionism.

In one current line of development, the elements of association are redefined in terms of linguistic concepts (Anderson and Bower, 1973). Another strategy is to maintain a close correspondence between the elementary units and the independently observable behavioral events while at the same time augmenting the very limited set of logical relations among elements that is utilized in classical theories (Estes, 1972, 1973). In the remainder of this chapter, I shall briefly review some of the specific shortcomings of earlier association theories that prompted researchers to develop new theoretical bases for investigation, and I shall outline a reformulation of association theory that combines classical concepts with currently influential ideas concerning the role of coding in memory.

REVISING ASSOCIATION THEORY:
FROM CHAINS TO HIERARCHIES

While it is obvious that new theoretical ideas have been needed to deal with the comprehension and retention of meaningful verbal material, it is also true, though less obvious, that new theoretical developments have been just as much needed to provide adequate interpretations of simpler experimental phenomena.

For several decades, much of the research conducted under the mantle of association theory (in this country, at least) was concerned either with paired-associate learning, the experimental analogy of the acquisition of vocabulary items, or with the learning of lists or other items in serial order. The interpretation of the learning of a vocabulary item (for example, of the acquisition of the ability to give a foreign word as a response to a corresponding English word as a stimulus) was simply that a directional association forms in the memory system leading from the representation of the stimulus to the representation of the response. By direct extension, researchers interpreted the memorization of a list of items, as for example the digits of a telephone number, in terms of directional associations between the successive items in the list. They maintained that once these associations are established, seeing or hearing any one item as a stimulus causes a person to give the name of the next item as a response. To account for the fact that memory for a list does not disintegrate entirely if one item is omitted during recall, these early theorists had to assume that remote associations exist between nonadjacent items.

This version of association theory, which we call the chain-association model, is descriptive of simple experimental phenomena up to a certain point, but even within its original sphere of applicability, it ultimately ran into difficulties. Even in the simplest case of a paired-associate item, an interpretation in terms of a single association proved inadequate. Findings concerning backward recall, that is an individual's ability to recall the stimulus member of an item when given the response member as a cue, produced the addition of the concept of *backward associations*. Furthermore, continued testing of the implications of the chain-association model for the learning of lists resulted in several observations that challenged the validity of the model. For example, one might have expected that preliminary training on pairs of items in a list (on A-B, C-D, and E-F in the list ABCDEF) would, by establishing a portion of the required associations, result in a substantially accelerated speed of learning of the list as a whole—a prediction that has by no means been uniformly borne out in practice (Murdock, 1974). Even the idea that successive repetitions of a list cause the automatic strengthening of interitem associations ran afoul of the finding that such repetitions produce no increase in recall if the items are grouped differently on successive presentations (for example, AB, pause, CD, pause, EF on the first repetition, but ABC, pause, DEF, on the second) (Bower and Winzenz, 1969).

But perhaps the greatest single source of dissatisfaction with the chain-association model arose as a result of the flourishing of studies of free recall. In the typical free-recall experiment a subject is presented with a list of items, most often unrelated words, and then asked to recall them in any order. As illustrated in the top section of Figure 3.14, the classical association model could account for recall on the assumption that successive items of the list become connected by learned associations. Thus, if the list presented comprised the sequence of words *hat, star, dog, . . .* , the starting signal would become associated with *hat*, *hat* with *star*, and so on. The signal to start recall would lead to reactivation of these associations in the same order.

An immediate problem for the model is that in the typical experiment the items are presented in a different order on every repetition of a list and this variation in order produces no obvious difficulty for subjects, whereas according to the chain association model it should raise prohibitive difficulties.

One could revise the model by assuming that each of the list words becomes independently associated with a common cue that serves as a label for the list, as illustrated in the center section of Figure 3.14. Now a signal to start recall would activate all of the

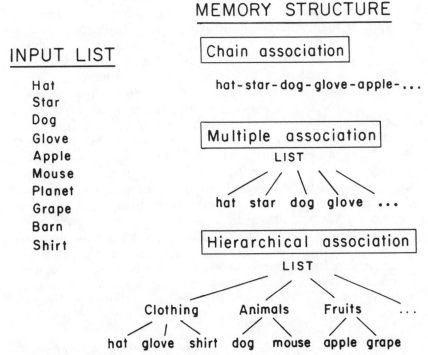

MEMORY STRUCTURE

INPUT LIST

Hat
Star
Dog
Glove
Apple
Mouse
Planet
Grape
Barn
Shirt

Chain association

hat-star-dog-glove-apple-...

Multiple association

LIST

hat   star   dog   glove   ...

Hierarchical association

LIST

Clothing   Animals   Fruits   ...

hat glove shirt   dog   mouse   apple grape

Figure 3.14 Three alternative association models for the memory structure mediating free recall of a list of words.

associations simultaneously. Variations in the order of presentation of the list words from trial to trial would raise no difficulty for this version of the model. However, consideration of the properties characteristic of recall protocols in free-recall experiments brings forth a new problem. Typically, subjects do not recall words in random order but rather tend to produce groups or clusters of semantically related words in their response protocols, a phenomenon termed *secondary organization* or *categorical clustering* by Tulving (1968).

These and other aspects of recall data suggest that the memory structure responsible for free recall takes the form neither of chain associations between individual items nor of independent multiple associations, but rather of a hierarchical structure in which related items are associated with a common category label and the category names are associated with a common cue for the list, as illustrated in the bottom section of Figure 3.14.

In order to handle the numerous facts indicating that free recall reflects a hierarchical organization of material, we clearly require a richer model than can be supplied by classical association theory. The problem is how to arrive at the type of model required. A direct approach, and the one most often exemplified in the contemporary literature, is simply to formulate a new model embodying the assumption that the basic structure of memory is such as to impose a hierarchical organization on remembered material, just as the wooden forms used by a builder dictate the form that the building under construction will take on once the poured concrete has hardened. Thus a number of currently influential models, for example, those of Collins and Quillian (1969) and of Mandler (1968) begin with the presumption that the memory system is organized in a tree structure of interconnected nodes and that incoming, to-be-remembered, material is assimilated into this preexisting structure.

However, this direct postulational approach is not in the spirit of association theory. From the associationist viewpoint, a major aspect of our task should be to find more primitive assumptions from which we can derive predictions that a particular organization of recall behavior will emerge under particular conditions. Our first step must be to reexamine the basic units and operations of association theory to see if we can modify the basic assumptions though an independent rationale that will enable us to derive the organizational properties of recall.

In classical association theory the predominant strategy is to seek units, for example stimuli and responses or elementary ideas, that do not vary from one individual to another and to represent the information an individual gains as a result of his experiences by means of the associative relations or connections established between units. Various specific association theories generally recognize one basic relation, the associative connection, and only one or at most only a few basic units. Thus, in classical conditioning theory, the result of an effective learning experience is represented in terms of an S-R association or a chain of such associations; in the connectionism of Ebbinghaus and Thorndike, an individual's memory for an experience is represented in terms of a chain or network of associations between ideas, and so on. We can divide recent attempts to elaborate and extend association theory to deal with the more complex phenomena of semantic memory into two principal categories, one which I shall term *psycholinguistic association theory* and another which I shall term *associative coding theory*.

PSYCHOLINGUISTIC ASSOCIATION THEORY

In their extremely influential book, *Human Associative Memory*, Anderson and Bower (1973) present a thoroughgoing revision and extension of association theory that retains the idea of simple and general units but introduces a variety of associative relations between units. In order to permit accounts of semantic memory and sentence comprehension, Anderson and Bower draw on psycholinguistic concepts as the basis for an array of labeled associations.

To illustrate the way in which memory for an event is represented in Anderson and Bower's model let us assume that a subject in an experiment has observed the display of two single letters in succession on a closed-circuit TV screen. Anderson and Bower maintain that the subject draws upon his familiarity with the language to construct a proposition describing the events he has observed and then stores this proposition in long-term memory.

The form of the associative structure suggested by the presentation in Anderson and Bower's volume is illustrated in the upper panel of Figure 3.15. The nodes in the associative network, labeled by small letters, are abstract entities which correspond to concepts and exemplars of concepts. Those in the bottom row (*d–h*) correspond to instances of the concepts of past, screen, and so on in the subject's long-term memory system. The topmost node, *a*, corresponds to the individual's idea of the whole proposition. The arrow labeled *C*, extending from *a* to *d*, represents an associative connection signifying that the context in which the episode occurred existed at some time in the past. The arrow labeled *F* signifies a

I. Psycholinguistic Association Model

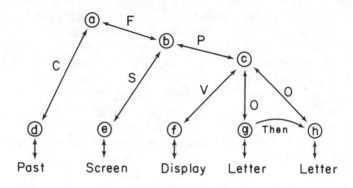

2. Associative Coding Model

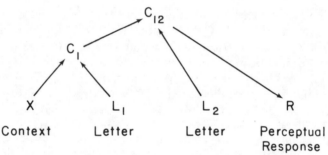

Figure 3.15 Comparison of the mnemonic representations of a hypothetical episode (observation of the successive display of two letters on a TV screen) in the models of (1) Anderson and Bower, 1973; and (2) Estes, 1972.

factual relation between some event and the given context. The arrows labeled S and P, leading downward from node b, signify that something is predicated (P) of a subject (S), which in this instance is the display screen. From the predicate node, c, there extend in turn a labeled association V, signifying that the verb is an instance of the subject's concept of display, and the arrows labeled O, which signify that the object corresponds to instances of the subject's concept of letter. This description may seem somewhat involved, but the concepts are easy to grasp. The rules assumed by Anderson and Bower for the process whereby an individual generates the associative structure are straightforward enough to be incorporated in a computer program that can simulate the behavior of an individual who is exposed to various kinds of events and then queried as to his memory for them.

The significance of the network structure is that it serves as the basis for either recognition or recall. Suppose, for example, that after the hypothetical individual had observed the letter displays in the above example and stored the episode in his memory, he was asked whether he had seen the given letters appear on the screen. He would construct a representation of the test sentence in memory and then compare the representation of the test sentence with the various networks already existing in his memory system; if he found a match, as would be the case in this example, he would answer yes, signifying that the test question described an episode he had actually experienced. Empirical testing of the model has proceeded largely by the generation and testing of various predictions concerning the relative reaction times that should be observed when, following a given experience, a subject's memory is probed by various test sentences that bear varying degrees of correspondence to the proposition he has presumably incorporated into his memory system.

Using this system, Anderson and Bower have been able to make impressively rapid progress in analyzing the way in which people retrieve from memory information concerning relatively complex verbal material. But rapid progress always involves a price, and in this instance the price has been the necessity of postulating *de novo* many elaborate properties of the memory system, for example, the various types of labelled associations. Further, these properties have been suggested primarily by psycholinguistic rather than psychological theory. Consequently, there is a gap between the research and theory formulated within the framework of the psycholinguistic association model and the well-established bodies of research and theory concerning perception and short- and long-term memory in simpler contexts. To fill this gap is a basic objective of the second approach to the revision of association theory, to which we now turn.

THE ASSOCIATIVE CODING MODEL

Basic Units and Relations

In developing the model with which I shall be largely concerned in the remainder of this chapter, the strategy has been to retain simple associative relations while modifying the assumptions about storage processes so that the associated units carry more information than in the classical models. This approach has been influenced primarily by conceptions of coding in memory (see, for example, Melton and Martin, 1972; Johnson, 1970). A basic assumption of the associative coding model is that when a behavioral event (stimulus or response) occurs in a background context, a *trace* of this experience is laid down in the nervous system. The trace may be reactivated later by similar stimulus inputs to generate a full or partial reinstatement of the original experience from the standpoint of the individual. This conception of a trace corresponds quite closely to that of the *image* of a stimulus or response in the EPAM model of Feigenbaum (1963).

The significance of the trace in the functioning of the memory system is that it acts as a *control element* (Estes, 1972) or *interactive filter* (Anderson, 1973), with the primary function of serving as a gate in a network of associations. It is assumed that the neural message arising from any stimulus input takes the form of a multi-dimensional vector, as does the memory trace left by any previous input. When a new message arrives at a control element in the associative network, the input and trace vectors are compared; if a match occurs, the message is transmitted intact, whereas if there is a mismatch, transmission is blocked; and for intermediate degrees of correspondence between input and trace vectors, the message is transmitted with some degradation. Thus the trace vector provides a logical *AND* function.

An immediate consequence of introducing the *AND* function is that we have a basis for recognition. Suppose that an individual has experienced an event, which we denote by E, in a background context, which we denote by X. The memory trace can be represented by a vector (T_{XE}). If, now, the same event recurs in the same context, the new stimulus input vector matches the trace vector, thus reactivating the latter and generating an output which we interpret as a recognition response. But if the test input comprises the same event E in a new context X' or a new event E' in the old context X, then there is a mismatch between input and memory vectors, and the control element is not activated to the point of yielding a recognition response.

Once an organism has had a number of experiences, a number of these trace vectors will have been laid down in the memory system. The result is that as new situations are encountered, the stimulus input from each in turn is directed to the system of trace elements and only if a match of the new input to one of the trace elements occurs is the input transmitted on through the system and allowed to activate associative connections of the matching control element with other elements in the memory system or the response system.

A second important property of the associative coding model is that of *recursiveness*. By this term I refer to the assumption that the output of a memory control element constitutes an event which may enter into the memory trace laid down upon the occurrence of a subsequent event. This property can be conveniently illustrated in terms of the same example used to illustrate the psycholinguistic model. If an individual observes the display of a letter on a TV screen, we can denote the letter by L_1, the context in which the letter appears (including the screen) by X, and the representation in memory by the trace vector (T_{XL_1}). If immediately following the display of the first letter, the individual sees a second letter, L_2, on the same screen, the context for the second letter presentation includes the trace of the first; the memory trace for the second presentation can be denoted $T_{[XL_1]L_2}$. If, now, the first letter is presented again, the input will match the trace T_{XL_1}, and thus tend to reinstate the original response (perhaps naming the letter). However, since T_{XL_1} is a constituent of the trace $T_{[XL_1]L_2}$, the latter would also be partially activated, thus leading to some probability of reinstating the original response to the second event (that is, the individual would be likely to recall the second letter upon again seeing the first).

One consequence of these assumptions is that the associative structure generated by an experience can be represented by a hierarchical tree structure, as illustrated in the lower panel of Figure 3.15 for the example of the two-letter display. In this structure, the control element C_1, which is activated by the occurrence of the letter L_1 in the context X, corresponds to the memory trace T_{XL_1} and the control element $C_{1,2}$ corresponds to the memory trace $T_{[XL_1]L_2}$. Reactivation of the control element $C_{1,2}$ leads to reinstatement of the response R which occurred on the occasion of the original letter display.

A particularly important property of the *AND* function is that it leads immediately to the generation of higher-order units. If an organism encounters a situation that simultaneously activates two trace elements whose outputs occur concurrently in the memory system, a new trace element is established which henceforth will be activated only if the two, associated, lower-order elements receive inputs simultaneously. Thus we have a basis for organized systems of memory traces.

An intensively studied example of an organized trace structure is the memory system involved in the identification of letters and

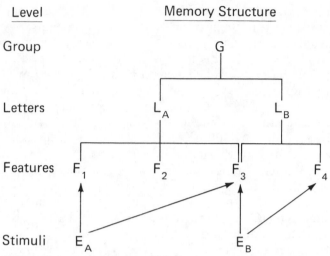

Figure 3.16 Schematic account of the generation of progressively higher-order associative units. The bottom row represents letters presented in a stimulus display; these activate combinations of critical features, which in turn activate control elements in memory for letters, and finally, at the highest level, familiar letter groups.

higher-order perceptual units in reading (see, e.g., Estes, 1975a, 1975b; LaBerge and Samuels, 1974). This system is illustrated in Figure 3.16. The elements at the successively higher levels in the figure denote memory trace elements corresponding to the critical features of letters (the Fs with subscripts), the letters themselves (the Ls), and letter groups (G). We assume that each F_i represents a trace element established by the stimulus input associated with a particular critical feature of a printed character. Each letter is associated with a specific combination of critical features, and hence the memory trace element corresponding to the abstract representation of a letter is activated only when inputs are received from the trace elements corresponding to the appropriate combination of features.

Thus in the situation illustrated in Figure 3.16, if a stimulus event occurs that involves the display of a printed letter A, this input activates feature elements F_1 and F_3 which in turn activate letter element L_A. If the display also includes a printed letter B, feature elements F_3 and F_4 are activated and their output activates L_B. If and only if the display includes both of the letters A and B will the system activate the trace element G, which corresponds to a representation of a letter group.

Interpretation of Free Recall

It will perhaps be evident, at least at an informal level, that the combinatorial and recursive properties posited for the memory-trace mechanism can readily account for the apparently hierarchical organization of memory that is manifest in free-recall experiments. Let us sketch the way in which the system would operate if an individual in list context X were presented with a sequence of words $(W_1, W_2, \ldots, W_N)$ in which words W_1 and W_2 belong to a familiar category a, words W_3 and W_4 to category b, and so on, as in the case illustrated in Figure 3.14. In terms of the example, W_1 and W_2 are the words *hat* and *glove, a* is the category clothing, and so on. Although in many experiments the lists of words to be recalled are selected from familiar semantic categories, it should be noted that even when a list is uncategorized from the standpoint of the investigator, clusters of list words may nonetheless fall into categories from the standpoint of the subject, owing to his idiosyncratic previous experience and his rehearsal activities during list input.

In either case, we assume that recall is mediated by the several types of memory trace vectors listed in Table 3.1. In the case of a categorized list, the individual would already have stored memory trace vectors of the type $T_{W_1 a}$, $T_{W_2 a}$, which represent occurrences of the category label a in conjunction with the words W_1 and W_2. Now, as the list is presented, new trace vectors of several types

Table 3.1 Characterization of Memory Trace Vectors Established during Various Phases of Acquisition of a Free-Recall List

Phase of Experiment	Units Associated	Trace	Effect on Recall
Prior to list presentation	List words (W_i) with category names (C)	$T_{W_i C}$	Word stimuli evoke recall of category names
During list presentation	List words with list context (x)	$T_{x W_i}$	List context (weakly) evokes recall of list words
During rehearsal	List words with traces of category names in list context	$T_{[xC] W_i}$	List context plus recall of category names evokes recall of list words

would be established. Firstly, perception of the stimulus words in the given context during input of the list would give rise to traces T_{xW_1}, T_{xW_2}, ... But also, the perception of W_1 and W_2 would in each case tend to reactivate the preexisting traces T_{W_1a}, T_{W_2a}. As a result, the individual would recall category a thus establishing a trace T_{xa}. Further, rehearsal of the related list words in conjunction with this recall would generate additional trace vectors $T_{[xa]W_1}$ and $T_{[xa]W_2}$.

Upon reinstatement of the list context during a later test for recall, there would be two associative routes for recall of the list words. Firstly, the recurrence of the original context would tend to reactivate the elements T_{xW_1}, but only weakly, since input from x alone would not yield a close match to any of the trace vectors. However, the context would also tend to reactivate trace T_{xa}, which corresponds to recall that the category label a has previously occurred in list context x; this in turn would tend to reactivate $T_{[xa]W_1}$ and $T_{[xa]W_2}$.

These multiple sources of reactivation of control elements for the list words would increase the probability of recall in comparison with the case of an uncategorized list and would result in clustering, that is, in a tendency for words associated with a common category to occur together during recall. Further, as observed in the study of Mathews and Tulving (1973), if list words are presented in conjunction with category labels, the probability of recall of a category should depend only on the frequency with which that category name has been activated in the list context (and not on communalities or differences in the particular exemplars of the category that were involved on different occasions). Thus, free-recall data from an individual whose memory system operates in accord with the assumptions of the associative coding model would accord with the conception of a hierarchical organization of items in long-term memory.

In order to demonstrate just how the associative-coding system would operate in various situations, we will of course have to go beyond informal remarks and formalize the assumptions in either a mathematical or a computer-simulation model, a task much beyond the scope of this article. For present purposes I shall conclude this brief sketch of the coding model by indicating how the model can deal with the critical question of why, during free-recall tests, response output generally ceases before all of the list words have been produced.

According to the model, upon partial reinstatement of the list context at the time of a recall test, the input vector from the context partially matches the trace vectors T_{xWi} of list words. The consequent weak activation of these traces yields outputs sufficiently stronger than those of the inactive traces of nonlist words to provide a basis for recognition, and words thus recognized as members of the input list enter the response output. But then a complication arises. As a consequence of prior experiences, recall of some of the list words, in some instances, activates memory traces of category names that have not previously entered into the organization of the input list (a version of *encoding variability*), and these traces cause recall of nonlist words.

The activation of memory traces of nonlist words affects output in two ways. Firstly, it reduces the similarity between the list context present during recall and that present during list input, thus reducing the probability of activation of additional traces T_{xWi} of list words. At the same time, the indirect recall of nonlist words raises an additional problem for the subject who must attempt to discriminate nonlist from list words on the basis of differences in level of trace activation. Similarly, if subjects are presented with nonlist, "distractor" words at the time of a free-recall test, as in the experiments of Tulving and Thomson (1971), detrimental effects on recall are expected on the basis of essentially the same processes.

Interpretation of Paired-Associate Learning

Other standard experimental paradigms that are readily susceptible to interpretation in terms of the associative coding model include ordered recall of digit or letter strings and paired-associate learning. I have discussed the former elsewhere, especially with reference to the phenomena of grouping and *chunking* (Estes, 1972, 1974). It will be instructive to consider briefly here the acquisition of paired associates in order to point up the contrasts between the present approach and the S-R association model that seemed reasonable at one time (Estes, 1959; Spence, 1956).

In the earlier model, which was based on an analogy to classical conditioning, it was assumed that upon presentation of the two stimuli, S_1 and S_2, of a paired-associate item, the response, R_2 originally evoked by S_2 became associated with, or conditioned to, S_1. The course of acquisition could be accounted for well enough, but there was no direct way of handling backward association or of interpreting the distinction between recall and recognition.

In the associative coding model, it is assumed that the consequence of an effective study trial is the establishment of a memory trace $T_{xS_1S_2}$ (conveniently abbreviated $T_{x_{12}}$) representing the joint occurrence of stimuli S_1 and S_2 in a list context, x. This trace vector provides the basis for recognition if either S_1 or S_2 or both are later presented again in the same context. Further, the evocation or rehearsal of R_2 while the trace $T_{x_{12}}$ is active results in the establishment of a trace $T_{[x_{12}]R_2}$, the basis for later recall of R_2 upon presentation of S_1 in the list context. Similarly, rehearsal of R_1, the response originally evoked by S_1, effects the establishment of an independent trace $T_{[x_{12}]R_1}$, which then mediates recall of R_1 upon presentation of S_2 in the list context. Such phenomena as "forward" and "backward" recall can be interpreted in a manner generally compatible with that of Wolford's *directional-association* model (Wolford, 1971). Wolford assumes that distinct associations form between S_1 and R_2 and between S_2 and R_1 during study of an item, and that these associations form the basis for forward and backward recall, respectively, and for various types of recognition performance. In the associative coding model, it is assumed that a single trace $T_{x_{12}}$ may be reactivated by the recurrence of either S_1 or S_2 in the list context, but that the output of this trace enters as a constituent into those involving R_1 and R_2 which may be formed during rehearsal. Predictions of the kind considered by Wolford (e.g., predictions of old and new recognition from forward- and backward-recall scores after one list presentation) appear to be indistinguishable for the two models, but differentiation might be possible when data from repeated acquisition trials are considered.

The associative-coding approach to paired-associate learning is similar in a number of essentials to that of Humphreys and Greeno (1970). Analyzing acquisition data within the framework of a discrete-state, Markov model, Humphreys and Greeno obtained evidence supportive of a two-stage conception in which the first stage is the establishment of a representation of the S_1–S_2 presentation in memory and the second stage is the discovery of a retrieval strategy that enables a subject to recover response R_2 once the representation is reactivated. The only material differences between my interpretation and theirs seem to be that the trace vector $T_{xS_1S_2}$ in the associative coding model takes explicit account of context and that the recursive property of the coding model, leading to the establishment of the second-order trace $T_{[x_{12}]R_2}$ during rehearsal, does away with the need for a qualitative distinction between encoding and retrieval strategies. Furthermore, the latter mechanism represents a formalization of the concept of a *retrieval cue*, which has been fruitfully applied to numerous phenomena of verbal memory by Tulving and his associates (e.g., Tulving and Thomson, 1971; Watkins and Tulving, 1975).

ON THE STRUCTURE OF MEMORY THEORY

The foregoing, summary examples of my own efforts to delve into structural aspects of memory, together with the many interesting examples brought forward by other contributors to this volume, lead me to think that the enormous range of problems confronting investigators of human cognitive activity requires a commensurate range of types and levels of theories. No one of the current approaches—information processing, psycholinguistic theory, associative coding theory—can be sufficient by itself. One reason is that the structural and organizational properties of memory are manifest in quite different ways at different levels of analysis. Owing to our inability to comprehend all aspects in a single manageable formalism, we find ourselves working with a number of different bodies of theory, and a particular investigator's choice of plots in this array depends on both his theoretical predilections and the empirical problems he happens to be addressing.

Looking over the assemblage of models that receive attention in this book, we can discern a semblance of order. As illustrated in Table 3.2, we can arrange a number of the models in order of increasing abstraction of theoretical elements or units and increasing complexity of subject matter. We start at what seems to be for our purposes the ground floor of this structure with Anderson's interactive-filter model for memory, in which the elements are traces left in the nervous system by patterns of sensory input and the principal theoretical relation or function is computation of correlations between new input patterns and traces of old inputs. To date

Table 3.2 Levels of Memory Theory

Model	Elements	Relations	Special Area of Competence
Computational linguistics	Abstract concepts	Syntactic and semantic	Comprehension of language
Psycholinguistic association	Concepts and instances	Labeled associations	Semantic memory
Associative coding	Representations of events in context	Associations	Role of frequency, recency, grouping
Interactive filters	Traces of neural input patterns	Correlations	Recognition

the model has been applied in detail only to a limited class of experiments on recognition memory (Anderson, 1973).

At the next level we have the associative coding model, which I have discussed in the present paper. The basic structural units in this model are representations of events and contexts in memory. However these units need not be taken as primitive assumptions; rather they appear to be derivable from the elements of Anderson's model by a simple logical operation. The same logical operation applied to the elements of the coding model generates higher-order units that correspond to such psychological notions as words, categories, and concepts. The associative coding model is most directly applicable to phenomena having to do with the frequency, recency, and grouping of relatively simple events in memory.

But theories that build directly on concepts of sensory inputs and memory traces, even though considerably enriched conceptually as compared with traditional association theories, have theoretical resources that are too limited to keep up with the cognitive psychologist's voracious appetite for ever more complex and naturalistic phenomena. In order to investigate the comprehension of language, or memory for information conveyed by linguistic expressions at the level of sentences or even paragraphs, a number of current researchers have turned to a new level of theory that employs some of the relational structure of association theory but takes concepts as its basic units and distinguishes classes of concepts and classes of associative relationships among them according to semantic and syntactic properties. This type of theory, here termed psycholinguistic association theory, is represented in the recent work of Anderson and Bower (1973), Kintsch (1974), Rumelhart, Lindsay and Norman (1972). It is able to deal with questions like "Will it take longer to comprehend Sentence A than Sentence B?" or "Can a subject recall Sentence A if element p is presented as a cue?" Finally, at the top level of our structure we find a group of theoretical approaches deriving from computational linguistics, represented for example in the work of Schank (1972) and Winograd (1972); in these top-level theories, the elements are abstract concepts and the theoretical relations are derived entirely from linguistic rather than psychological theory.

Working in terms of these higher-level theories and relying increasingly on computer simulation rather than on experimentation, current investigators have obtained interesting results with reference to aspects of linguistic performance that would have been far out of the reach of research based on traditional association theory. These efforts will doubtless continue to flourish, for it is often an excellent idea to tackle complex problems with new techniques, unfettered by the constraints of older theoretical frameworks. However, if we seek not only to simulate successfully various types of data but also to understand the cognitive functioning of the living human being, we need to devote some attention to the problems of developing links between the various levels of theory. We must not only fill in the gaps between older and newer theoretical approaches, but also devote some of our efforts to deepening our understanding of simpler empirical problems that have been bypassed rather than solved in some of the newer and higher flights of cognitive psychology.

REFERENCES

Anderson, J. A. A theory for the recognition of items from short memorized lists. *Psychological Review*, 1973, *80*, 417–438.

Anderson, J. R., and Bower, G. H. *Human associative memory.* Washington, D.C.: Winston, 1973.

Atkinson, R. C., and Shiffrin, R. M. Human memory: A proposed system and its control processes. In K. W. Spence and J. T. Spence (Eds.), *The psychology of learning and motivation: Advances in research and theory* (Vol. 2). New York: Academic Press, 1968.

Attneave, F. Some informational aspects of visual perception. *Psychological Review*, 1954, *61*, 183–193.

Bower, G. H., and Theios, J. A learning model for discrete performance levels. In R. C. Atkinson (Ed.), *Studies in mathematical psychology.* Stanford, Calif.: Stanford University Press, 1964.

Bower, G. H., and Winzenz, D. Group structure, coding, and memory for digit series. *Journal of Experimental Psychology Monograph*, 1969, *80* (2, Pt. 2), 1–17.

Collins, A. M., and Quillian, M. R. Retrieval time from semantic memory. *Journal of Verbal Learning and Verbal Behavior*, 1969, *8*, 240–247.

Craik, F. I. M., and Lockhart, R. S. Levels of processing: A framework for memory research. *Journal of Verbal Learning and Verbal Behavior*, 1972, *11*, 671–684.

Ebbinghaus, H. [*Memory*] (H. A. Ruger and C. E. Bussenius, trans.). New York: Teachers College, 1913. Reprint, New York: Dover, 1964. (Originally published in 1885.)

Estes, W. K. Toward a statistical theory of learning. *Psychological Review*, 1950, *43*, 94–107.

Estes, W. K. The statistical approach to learning theory. In S. Koch (Ed.), *Psychology: A study of a science* (Vol. 2). New York: McGraw-Hill, 1959.

Estes, W. K. An associative basis for coding and organization in memory. In A. W. Melton and E. Martin (Eds.), *Coding processes in human memory.* Washington, D.C.: Winston, 1972.

Estes, W. K. Memory and conditioning. In F. J. McGuigan and D. B. Lumsden (Eds.), *Contemporary approaches to conditioning and learning.* Washington, D.C.: Winston, 1973.

Estes, W. K. Learning theory and intelligence. *American Psychologist,* 1974, *29,* 740–749.

Estes, W. K. The locus of inferential and perceptual processes in letter identification. *Journal of Experimental Psychology: General,* 1975, *104,* 122–145. (a)

Estes, W. K. Memory, perception, and decision in letter identification. In R. L. Solso (Ed.), *Information processing and cognition: The Loyola symposium.* Hillsdale, N.J.: Erlbaum, 1975 (b).

Feigenbaum, E. A. Simulation of verbal learning behavior. In E. A. Feigenbaum and J. Feldman (Eds.), *Computers and thought.* New York: McGraw-Hill, 1963.

Greeno, J. G. Representation of learning as discrete transition in a finite state space. In D. H. Krantz, R. D. Luce, R. C. Atkinson, and P. Suppes (Eds.), *Contemporary developments in mathematical psychology* (Vol. 1). San Francisco: W. H. Freeman and Company, 1974.

Guthrie, E. R. *The psychology of learning.* New York: Harper & Row, 1935.

Hartley, D. *Observations on man. His frame, his duty, and his expectations.* London: Bath, Leake and Frederick, 1749.

Hovland, C. I. A "communication analysis" of concept learning. *Psychological Review,* 1952, *59,* 461–472.

Hull, C. L. *Principles of behavior.* New York: Appleton-Century-Crofts, 1943.

Humphreys, M., and Greeno, J. G. Interpretation of the two-stage analysis of paired-associate memorizing. *Journal of Mathematical Psychology,* 1970, *7,* 275–292.

Johnson, N. F. The role of chunking and organization in the process of recall. In G. H. Bower (Ed.), *The psychology of learning and motivation: Advances in research and theory* (Vol. 4). New York: Academic Press, 1970.

Kintsch, W. *The representation of meaning in memory.* Hillsdale, N.J.: Erlbaum Associates, 1974.

LaBerge, D., and Samuels, S. J. Toward a theory of automatic information processing in reading. *Cognitive Psychology,* 1974, *6,* 293–323.

Lillie, R. S. Factors affecting transmission and recovery in the passive iron nerve model. *Journal of General Physiology,* 1925, *7,* 473–507.

Mandler, G. Association and organization: Facts, fancies, and theories. In T. R. Dixon and D. L. Horton (Eds.), *Verbal behavior and general behavior theory.* Englewood Cliffs, N.J.: Prentice-Hall, 1968.

Mathews, R. C., and Tulving, E. Effects of three types of repetition on cued and noncued recall of words. *Journal of Verbal Learning and Verbal Behavior,* 1973, *12,* 707–721.

Melton, A. W., and Martin, E. *Coding processes in human memory.* Washington, D.C.: Winston, 1972.

Mill, J. *Analysis of the phenomena of the human mind.* London: Baldwin and Cradock, 1829.

Miller, G. A., Galanter, E., and Pribram, K. H. *Plans and the structure of behavior.* New York: Holt, Rinehart & Winston, 1960.

Murdock, B. B., Jr. *Human memory: Theory and data*. New York: Wiley, 1974.

Pavlov, I. P. *Conditioned reflexes* (G. V. Anrep, trans. and ed.). Oxford: Oxford University Press, 1927.

Reitman, W. R. *Cognition and thought: An information processing approach*. New York: Wiley, 1965.

Rumelhart, D. E., Lindsay, P. H., and Norman, D. A. A process model for long term memory. In E. Tulving and W. Donaldson (Eds.), *Organization of memory*. New York: Academic Press, 1972.

Schank, R. C. Conceptual dependency: A theory of natural language understanding. *Cognitive Psychology*, 1972, *3*, 552–631.

Skinner, B. F. *The Behavior of organisms*. New York: Appleton-Century, 1938.

Spence, K. W. *Behavior theory and conditioning*. New Haven, Conn.: Yale University Press, 1956.

Thorndike, E. L. *Human learning*. New York: Century, 1931.

Tulving, E. Theoretical issues in free recall. In T. R. Dixon and D. L. Horton (Eds.), *Verbal behavior and general behavior theory*. Englewood Cliffs, N.J.: Prentice-Hall, 1968.

Tulving, E., and Donaldson, W. *Organization of memory*. New York: Academic Press, 1972.

Tulving, E., and Thomson, D. M. Retrieval processes in recognition memory: Effects of associative context. *Journal of Experimental Psychology*, 1971, *87*, 116–124.

Watkins, M. J., and Tulving, E. Episodic memory: When recognition fails. *Journal of Experimental Psychology: General*, 1975, *104*, 5–29.

Winograd, T. *Understanding natural language*. New York: Academic Press, 1972.

Wolford, G. Function of distinct associations for paired-associate performance. *Psychological Review*, 1971, *78*, 303–313.

On the Interaction of Perception and Memory in Reading

The recent surge of interest in reading on the part of experimental psychologists doubtless has at least two sources of motivation. One of these has to do with the urgent social problems of dealing with literacy and reading disabilities, the other with the fact that reading embodies a number of aspects of perception and memory that are of much current interest in their own right. The psychology of reading had a flying start near the turn of the century with the pioneering work of Cattell (1886) and Huey (1908), using ingenious experimental techniques and instrumentation for the measurement of eye movements in reading and the analysis of perception during single fixations—work that thas been improved upon but little down to the present. The slow development of the psychology of reading as a specialty within cognitive psychology, following that auspicious beginning, must be attributed, I think, to the fact that for many decades the state of theory lagged behind the advance of experimental methodology, and as a consequence concepts and models were not available to interpret the findings that laboratory techniques were capable of delivering.

Perhaps the first important accomplishment of experimental psychology in this area was to clarify the nature of the problem that the task of reading presents to an individual's cognitive processing system. The problem turned out to be quite different, and distinctly more complex, than might have been anticipated on the basis of impressions gained from everyday experience. If the reader of this chapter allows his eyes to run along the line of type at the top of Fig. 3.17, he may have the impression that his eyes move smoothly along the line, allowing him to see all of the letters, and that once he has seen the letters, he recognizes familiar words, then remembers their meanings and as a consequence comprehends the message conveyed by the passage of text. But the facts are quite different. In actuality, as every psychologist now knows, the eyes do not move

W. K. Estes, On the interaction of perception and memory in reading. In D. LaBerge & S. J. Samuels (Eds.), *Basic processes in reading*, pp. 1–26. Hillsdale, N.J.: Lawrence Erlbaum Associates, 1977. Reprinted by permission.

continuously and the letters are seen with varying degrees of distinctness (to the point where some may be missed altogether). Further, no discrete successive stages of sensation, perception, and comprehension can be marked off; rather, processes of perception and memory interact in complex ways throughout the succession of stages of visual processing that lead from the original sensory experience to comprehension of the text.

If, rather than allowing his eyes to move along the top line in Fig. 3.17, the reader fixates his gaze for a few moments at each of the points marked by an arrow, he can satisfy himself that what he is able to make out during each of these fixations has much the character of the illustrative displays on the lines below, these having been constructed, on the basis of tachistoscopic research, to represent approximately what we would expect a person to be able to report from each fixation. Only a few letters on either side of a fixation point can be distinguished at all: those at the center in general clearly, and sometimes also those more remote if they come at the end of a word. The arrows in the figure represent the points at which fixations actually occurred in the case of an experimental subject whose eye movements were photographed in a study cited by Woodworth (1938). It can be assumed that the eyes moved from one of these fixation points to the next so rapidly that nothing could be seen during the movements. The first task of the processing system during reading, then, must be to accept this typically fragmented and irregular stimulus input, clean it up, fill in gaps in a

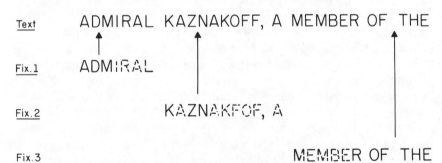

Figure 3.17 Illustration of the sequence of fixations (indicated by vertical arrows) made by an individual while reading the line of text at the top. Below each fixation point is shown a hypothetical reconstruction of effective stimulus input during the fixation, letters near the fixation point being seen clearly and those further away less clearly, but always with an advantage for letters adjacent to spaces.

reasonable way, and generate a representation of the letter sequence that gave rise to the input at a level more abstract than that of the physical stimulus pattern. The second task entails an interaction between this representation and other informational inputs either from the background context or from the long-term memory system to enable the recognition of words and their meanings.

PROVISIONAL CHARACTERIZATION OF THE INTERACTION OF PERCEPTION AND MEMORY: THE HIERARCHICAL FILTER MODEL

At a very general level, the way in which memory must enter into reading may seem almost obvious. Visual processing of text gives rise to representations of stimulus patterns, which are then compared with representations in memory of patterns previously experienced. Familiar patterns constituting syllables, words, or even larger units are recognized and by way of associative processes activate components of the semantic memory system that constitute or generate the meaning of the material perceived. The fundamental problem for a theory of reading is to prescribe more specifically just how this process of comparisons between sensory input and memory is accomplished.

Consider, say, the word "Admiral" in the top line of Fig. 3.17. Presumably, there exists in the memory system of each reader a representation of this word with which the sensory input could in some sense be compared—perhaps several representations, since the word may have been encountered in different type styles. But this word is only one among many thousands represented in the mental lexicon. Although it would be possible for each incoming sensory pattern to be compared successively with all of the word patterns in memory in search of a match (and just this procedure is followed in some primitive computer programs for pattern recognition), such a process seems exceedingly cumbersome in the light of the relatively slow rates of transmission of messages in the nervous system. It is conceivable that words are classified and encoded primarily in terms of a limited number of attributes or features having to do with overall shape and the like, but although this suggestion has been put forward many times, it has not yet adduced any substantial empirical support. Some specific relevant evidence will be presented in connection with an experiment to be described in a later section. In the meantime, I shall proceed on the assumption that global attributes of words play only a subsidiary role in word recognition.

A more promising approach arises from the observation that the word "Admiral," like any other, is not simply an arbitrary pattern of contours but, rather, is generated by a system of alphabetic elements. A recognition system that makes use of the properties of the alphabet can capitalize on the very large differences in frequency of occurrence of elements at different levels. The word "Admiral" occurs rather seldom in ordinary English text, but the constituent letter "*A*" occurs very much more often, and the horizontal bar in the *A* more frequently still. Cognizance of this important property of the alphabetic system led psychologists to the observation that the letters of the alphabet can be generated by combining in appropriate ways a smaller set of frequently occurring constituents, or "critical features," just as the large number of words in the lexicon can be generated by combining in appropriate ways the very much smaller number of letters (Geyer & DeWald, 1973; Gibson, 1969; Lindsay & Norman, 1972; Rumelhart, 1971).

The next step toward a model was the hypothesis that to these elementary constituents of letters there correspond organized subsystems in memory, "feature detectors," whose function is to sift the sensory input and transmit messages to higher levels of the system whenever their critical features are recognized.

In the current work of Estes (1975a, b) and LaBerge and Samuels (1974), it may be seen that a model incorporating a hierarchical arrangement of detectors can efficiently take advantage of the frequency properties of the alphabetic system and begin to provide a plausible account of some properties of letter and word recognition.

In this model, as illustrated in Fig. 3.18, it is assumed that detectors with similar properties are organized at the levels of critical features (F), letters (L), and letter groups such as syllables and words (W). A detector at any level may be regarded as a memory trace or engram built up as a consequence of the individual's past experience with a particular frequently recurring subpattern. This trace structure functions as an interactive filter (Anderson, 1973), or logical gate, in the communication channel from the peripheral sensory mechanisms to higher cognitive centers. It is activated by an incoming pattern of information from the photoreceptors only if the input pattern matches the one that gave rise to the trace structure: When a match occurs, the detector is activated and transmits a pattern of excitation to the next higher level in the system; but when no match occurs, transmission through the given channel is blocked.

Efficiency is obtained at the first stage of processing in that the sensory input pattern need be directed only to a small number of

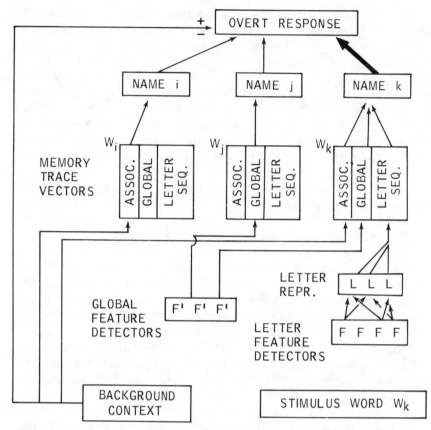

Figure 3.18 Schematization of the hierarchical filter model for letter and word recognition. Visual input from a stimulus word is filtered initially through global feature detectors (F') and letter feature detectors (F). Output of F-combinations activate representations of letters (L); these in turn transmit to letter-sequence components of the memory trace vectors of words (W), through which are filtered all sources of information (including background context) contributing to activation of a letter-name response.

feature detector units rather than to a very large number of detectors for letters or words. The process of comparison and selective transmission is assumed to continue through the higher levels of the system. If the combination of features corresponding to a particular letter is activated by the input on a given occasion, then the excitation transmitted from these in turn activates the representation of the corresponding letter.

One might ask whether efficiency is not lost as the system passes from the letter to the word level in that the pattern of excitation from a group of simultaneously activated letter detectors would have to be transmitted to all of the word patterns at the next level in order not to miss the possibility of a match. The answer, I suggest, is twofold. First, it is likely that the representations of the letter sequences of words are not accessed randomly but, rather, are so organized that excitation from the letter detectors is directed to subsets of word representations that have attributes in common, as, for example, the initial letter.[1] Second, and perhaps more important, the representation of a word in long-term memory must be assumed to incorporate more information than a particular letter sequence. Rather, as illustrated in Fig. 3.18, the memory trace vector for a word includes several components: (1) traces of verbal contexts in which it has frequently occurred (in effect, associations with other words); (2) global attributes of the printed word (outline shape, relative length, etc.); and (3) the letter sequence.

The sources of sensory and associative input to the components of a word trace vector in memory must be assumed to operate independently, often asynchronously, and with differing degrees of specificity. Input via associative paths from the background context provided by other words or letters perceived prior to or simultaneously with a given stimulus word will in general lead to partial activation both of the stimulus word and of many other words that share semantic attributes with it. Similarly, input from the global feature detectors excited by a stimulus word will partially activate the trace vectors of that word and others with similar visual patterns. Only the representation of the letter sequence of a stimulus word, activated by way of the critical feature system, generates input solely to the trace vector of that word. As a consequence of the convergence of inputs from the several sources on the trace vector of the stimulus word, its naming response will be more strongly and quickly activated than those of other words that share its associative or global attributes. Whether or not an overt response will occur on a given occasion depends also on nonspecific input from the background context (including the general task environment and instructions) to the response system.

If the stimulus displayed were a nonword letter string, or an isolated letter, processing through the critical feature system to the level of letter representations would proceed similarly. The output of the letter level would find no match at the word level, but would be

---

[1] Since this passage was written, a study by Smith and Jones (1975) has appeared, presenting some empirical evidence for the hypothesis that verbal memory is organized in terms of the initial phonemes of words.

transmitted to letter name and overt response mechanisms (by paths not shown in Fig. 3.18). Again, the actual occurrence of an overt response would depend on concurrent excitatory input from the background context to the response system. An important difference between word stimuli and random letter strings is that for the latter the naming response would not receive concurrent input from associative paths and global feature detectors. Consequently, if, say, a word and a random string were simultaneously displayed for a brief interval, a likely outcome is that input from the word would capture the naming response system and gain access to short-term memory while that from the random string would be lost.

EVIDENCE BEARING ON THE MODEL

The critical question demanding consideration at this point is the state of evidence for the type of model envisaged here. It is easy to imagine elaborate mechanisms that might account for the reading process, much more difficult to provide evidence that sharply distinguishes one possible interpretive schema from another. I shall try to address this problem in the remainder of this chapter by considering in turn a number of principal aspects of letter and word recognition as they are presumed to occur in reading, and presenting illustrations of what at present seems to me the most cogent evidence in each case bearing on the adequacy of the hierarchical, interactive filter model.

Sensory Channel Interactions

Although in the study of reading one's concern is primarily with the recognition of meaningful units such as words, an orderly account of the process must begin with consideration of factors that influence the perception of letters per se, whether or not they occur in meaningful contexts. As we have already noted, the eye, when registering the contents of a segment of text, does not act at all like a camera but, rather, transmits to the central processing mechanisms an uneven and often fragmented representation of the stimulus pattern that falls on the retina.

A typical result, from the standpoint of the observer, of viewing a string of letters for a brief interval is portrayed in the serial position functions in Fig. 3.19. These data are taken from a study by Estes, Allmeyer, and Reder (1976) in which subjects were presented with random strings of four consonant letters displayed in horizontal arrays in locations either near the fixation point (Positions 1-4) or

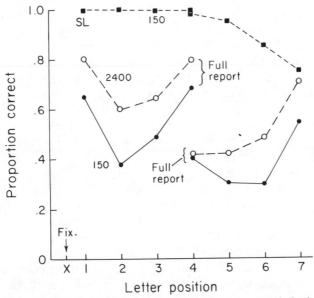

Figure 3.19 Serial position functions for report of single letters (*SL*) or elements of multiletter arrays displayed at different distances from the fixation point (data from Estes, Allmeyer, & Reder, 1976).

further toward the periphery (Positions 4–7) of the visual field. The observer's task was to report as many letters as possible from each display, and the plotted points represent proportions of correct reports from each letter position. In the experiment, letter strings occurred also in corresponding positions to the left of the fixation point, but for convenience the serial position functions have been "folded" so as to extend only to the right of the fixation point. If we consider first the functions for 150-msec exposures and the full-report procedure, we see just the picture that would be expected on the basis of the hypothetical illustration in Fig. 3.17. On the whole, correctness of report falls off from the center toward the periphery of the visual field, but even more conspicuously, perceptibility is poor in the interior positions of a string and much better at the ends.

The proper interpretation of these effects is, however, not immediately obvious. In fact, in the literature running back over many decades, explanations of two alternative types have been in continuing competition (Woodworth, 1938; Coltheart, 1972). One recurring hypothesis is that the apparent variations in perceptibility are actually due to limitations of memory; the observer actually sees the entire display of letters clearly for a brief instance, but is unable to hold all of the items in short-term memory long enough to report them. On this hypothesis, the form of the serial position function would have to be accounted for on the basis of the individual's strategy in tending to report the end items before the middle items. The alternative mode of explanation refers instead to properties of the visual system such as acuity and lateral inhibition.

At the time of Woodworth's (1938) review, it was difficult to choose between these interpretations, but a substantial body of data now available seems to point quite clearly to the conclusion that the serial position effects primarily represent degradations of input owing to properties of the visual system. This point can be illustrated by two other sets of curves from the Estes, Allmeyer, and Reder study, also included in Fig. 3.19. At the top of the figure are seen the results of a variation in which letters were presented at the same locations and for the same duration but singly rather than as components of multielement strings. Here memory limitations could scarcely have been a factor, but, as might have been expected on the basis of what is known concerning acuity at central and peripheral regions of the retina, the serial position function falls off smoothly with the distance from the fixation point to the periphery. However, the decrease is small compared to that observed in the 150-msec multielement displays.

To pin down the role of viewing time per se, four-letter displays were presented with the full-report procedure for very long exposures of 2,400 msec, but with the observer's eyes monitored so that they could not stray from the fixation point during stimulus exposure. Under this condition, limitations of memory should again have been negligible, since four letters is well within the memory span and 2,400 msec is adequate time to permit pronunciation of four letters. Nonetheless, the level of report is far below that of single letters and the forms of the serial position curves are very similar to those obtained with full report at the shorter exposure.

It is difficult to escape the conclusion that in the case of the multielement display, input is degraded at some early point in visual processing as a consequence of interactions between the processes initiated by adjacent letters. I have suggested elsewhere (Estes, 1972) that the entire pattern of results can be conveniently conceptualized in terms of the notion of input channels from the periphery to central feature detector mechanisms, the density of these channels being greatest near the fovea and decreasing toward the periphery, and with the magnitude of the lateral inhibitory interactions between concurrently activated channels varying inversely with the distance between them.

A question that comes to mind in connection with these results on serial position effects is why a reader under ordinary conditions is not normally aware of these patterns of degradation of input. One part of the answer, no doubt, is that the severely degraded inputs from segments of text remote from the fixation point simply are habitually ignored, but can readily be perceived if one's attention is directed to them. A more interesting question concerns the basis of the practiced reader's ability to recognize words that fall within a few degrees of the fixation point even though there must often be imperfect information available to higher processing centers concerning some of the interior letters. The answer suggested within the framework of the hierarchical model is based on the properties of the interactive filter mechanism. As illustrated for a particular example in Table 3.3, it is assumed that earlier occurrences of a clearly perceived stimulus pattern, the word *HAT* in the table, have established a trace structure, $[W_H]$, in the long-term memory system. On later occasions, stimulus inputs from a newly presented instance of the word (Occasion 2 in the table) are transmitted to the location of this trace structure, and if a match of the input pattern to the trace pattern occurs, then the trace structure activates continuing pathways responsible for the conscious experience of having seen the given word and also activation of the response mechanism responsible for its pronunciation. A partially degraded stimulus input (Occasion 3 in the table), as might arise from a brief exposure or a presentation in peripheral vision, would activate the response mechanism less strongly, whereas an incompatible input (Occasion 1) would not be transmitted beyond the level of memory vectors at all. The output of the comparison process is assumed to be all or none, in the sense that an input closely matching the memory trace leads to activation of the output pathways with probability near unity, a slightly degraded input has a slightly lower probability of

Table 3.3 Possible Response Outcomes Resulting from Comparisons between Various Stimulus Inputs and the Memorial Representation (W_H) of the Word *Hat*

Occasion	Stimulus	Memory Vector	Response
1	HAX	$[W_H]$	—
2	HAT	$[W_H]$	"HAT"
3	HAT	$[W_H]$	"HAT"

activating the output pathways, and so on, but operation of the response mechanism is the same whether it is activated by a closely matching or an imperfectly matching input.

Interactions between Perceptual and Linguistic Factors

The Word Advantage

One of the bodies of data that gave rise to the filter model, at least the version I have presented, has been generated by the many studies showing advantages for the perception of a letter embedded in a word as compared to a letter embedded in a nonword display of letters (for reviews, see Baron, 1978; Estes, 1975a; Massaro, 1975; Smith & Spoehr, 1974). According to the model, the extent of the "word advantage" should be expected to depend on the way task parameters of a particular experiment constrain the level of processing of display information that provides the basis for the subject's response.

If the subject's response depends solely on a difference at the level of critical features between the target included in a display and the alternative target that might have been present, then the linguistic properties of other letters present in the display should have no effect. This condition is most closely realized in forced-choice detection studies in which the subject knows in advance of a block of trials the set of target letters (usually exactly two alternatives) that may be presented (e.g., Bjork & Estes, 1973; Thompson & Massaro, 1973). These studies have indeed yielded no trace whatsoever of an advantage for word over nonword contexts.

The results just cited presuppose the use of the *WW–NN* control introduced by Reicher (1969). The control refers to the construction of the displays used in the series according to a plan such that a subject who perceives some of the context letters but not the target in a display and chooses his response so as to complete a word will be unable to improve his likelihood of a correct response. The *WW* strings include a target letter embedded in a word with the property that substitution of the alternative target letter will also complete a word. If, for example, targets *L* and *R* were used equally often during a series of tasks, an acceptable *WW* string would be *RENT*, in which the target letter is *R* but in which another acceptable word would be produced by replacing *R* with *L*. Analogously, *NN* strings have the property that a target letter is embedded in a nonword string that remains a nonword if the alternative target letter replaces the one presented.

The *WW–NN* condition is negatively oriented in that it is sufficient only to rule out certain effects. One can, however, make progress toward distinguishing and monitoring the facilitating effects of context at different levels of processing when they do occur by combining the *WW–NN* with a *WN–NW* condition, as done by Bjork and Estes (1973). In this design, which might be termed *W–N* factorial, half of the trials conform to the *WW–NN* constraint. Of the remaining trials, half employ *WN* strings, the target letter being embedded in a word such that substitution of the alternative target letter would convert the word into a nonword; the other half employ *NW* strings, the target being embedded in a nonword so composed that substitution of the alternative target would convert the string into a word. On the trials on which the *WN–NW* condition is in effect, a subject who perceives some of the letters of a display but misses the target and responds on the basis of a bias for forming words will always be correct on *WN* displays and never on *NW* displays.

With this design we can expect to ascertain whether a word context facilitates detection of a target letter, and, if there is an effect, whether it should be attributed to a perceptual interaction, which would be revealed by a difference between *WW* and *NN* trials, or to an effect of redundancy, which would be revealed by a difference between *WN* and *NW* trials.

To show how these potentialities can be exploited, I shall develop some specific implications of the filter model for both detection and identification of letters in experiments conducted with the *W–N* factorial design. It will be convenient to continue to use the example in Table 3.3 for illustrative purposes. Suppose, first, that we are dealing with a forced-choice detection experiment with the *WW–NN* control, A and I being the alternative targets and HAT the display on a given trial. If the *H* and *T* are clearly perceived, but only some features of the *A*, it is likely that a representation of *HAT* at the word level in the memory system will be activated, since, of the word representations partially activated by the *H–T*, (HIT, HAT, HOT, HUT), HAT is favored by the partial feature information from the *A* in middle letter position. However, this event will confer no advantage on correct detection of the *A* embedded in HAT as compared to an *A* embedded in an *NN* string, say XAG; for the same partial feature information would in the latter case, as well as in the former, lead directly to a choice of *A*, rather than *I*, from the set of possible targets.

If, however, the displays were of the type *WN* (e.g., HAT displayed with the same alternative targets) versus *NW* (e.g., HOT displayed with the same alternative targets), the result would be quite different. If, again, all of the features of the first and third letters were detected, then even if no features of the middle letter were detected, a subject would necessarily be correct on the *WN* but incorrect on the *NW* display if he followed the strategy of selecting from the word representations partially activated the only one compatible with one of the target alternatives and responding accordingly.

The key point in terms of the model is that the partial feature information obtained from a stimulus letter may suffice to bias the individual's choice between known alternative targets or between partially activated memorial representations of words in the direction of a correct detection response, but at the same time may be insufficient to evoke a letter name response. Further, an advantage for a word context is expected to appear only on trials when context letters are better perceived than the target letter. Under ordinary circumstances, this state of affairs obtains on some unknown fraction of the trials of an experimental series, thus rendering predictions of context effects somewhat indeterminate. However, by appropriate experimental manipulations, it is possible to bring the relationship between perceptibility of target and context under experimental control.

Experimental Manipulations of Stimulus Asynchrony between Target Letter and Context

A procedure that achieves the desired objective was used by Estes (1975b) in a *W-N* factorial experiment in which the exposure durations of target and context letters of a display were varied independently, as illustrated in Fig. 3.20. Four-letter displays were presented on an oscilloscope screen controlled by means of a computer with programming that enabled the exposure durations of the target and the context letters of a display to be varied independently. The subject knew in advance the two possible targets, *L* and *R*, that would be used throughout a block of trials. On each trial, following a warning signal, a four-letter display including one or the other of the target letters was exposed for an interval of 15–25 msec, followed by a row of mask characters resembling dollar signs that remained in view until the subject made his response. In making up the display strings, the targets *L* and *R* were used equally often, and each was embedded equally often in word (*WW* or *WN*) and nonword (*NW* or *NN*) strings.

Previous studies (e.g., Bjork & Estes, 1973; Estes, Bjork, & Skaar, 1974) had used only the standard condition, shown at the top, in which both the target letter and the context letters making up the

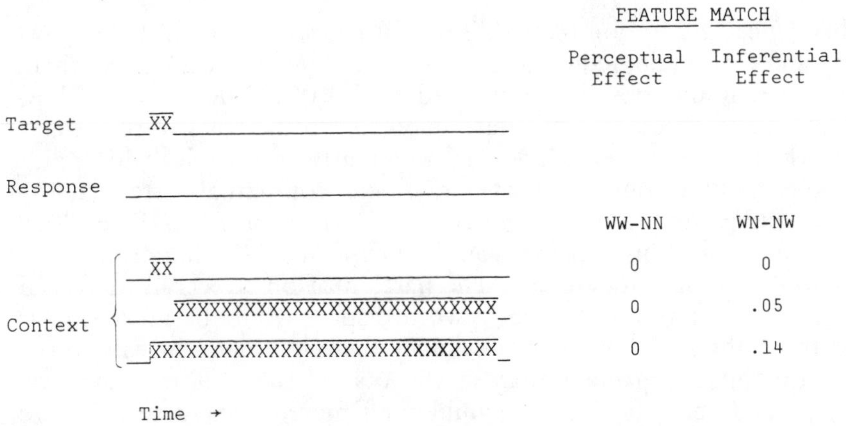

FEATURE MATCH

	Perceptual Effect	Inferential Effect

Target   ___XX_____

Response _____

		WW-NN	WN-NW
Context {	___XX_____	0	0
	____XXXXXXXXXXXXXXXXXXXXXXXXXX_	0	.05
	___XXXXXXXXXXXXXXXXXXXXXXXXXXX_	0	.14

Time →

Figure 3.20 Schematization (at left) of temporal relationships between onsets and offsets of target and context letters within a trial, together with summary data (from Estes, 1975b) for differences in detection probabilities between word and nonword displays under two control conditions.

word or nonword string all appear together; under this condition, no difference had been reported in percentage of correct detections between word and nonword strings. In the second and third conditions illustrated in Fig. 3.20, the target letter appears for the usual brief exposure, but the context letters of the display are available for a much longer interval, their onset being simultaneous with either the onset or the offset of the target letter, and in either case continuing until the subject makes his response, typically an interval of 1,000-2,000 msec. Thus, in the second and third arrangements, we can be sure that the subject perceives all of the context letters and the question is what the effect will be upon detectability of the target.

Under these circumstances, as anticipated on the basis of the preceding analysis, there were no differences in accuracy of detection between *WW* and *NN* displays under any condition, but in both of the conditions involving prolonged display of context letters, an advantage appeared for *WN* over *NW* strings.

The large difference in effectiveness between the Following and Continuing conditions fits well with an account in terms of the matching process of the filter model, but would not seem easily interpretable in terms of the principal alternative explanation—some form of sophisticated guessing. It should be noted in this connection that the diagrams at the left of Fig. 3.20 illustrating the temporal conditions of contextual display are not drawn to scale and that the difference in duration of the display of context between the Following and Continuing conditions is extremely small (10-25 msec where the overall duration is on the order of 1,000-2,000 msec). Thus, the opportunities for deliberate guessing on the basis of redundant information are essentially equal. Evidently, the critical difference is the simultaneous onset of target and contextual letters in the Continuing condition as compared to the asynchrony in the Following condition. This variable would be expected to be important only on the matching hypothesis. The pattern of on-effects in the visual pathways at the beginning of a word display would be more similar to those the individual had previously experienced in the case of the Continuing arrangement than in the case of the Following arrangement, and thus the former would tend more strongly to facilitate the matching process.

It is of interest also to examine the time course of the development of the word advantage within a trial. To this end, I have presented in Table 3.4 an additional analysis of the portion of the Estes (1975b) data representing detection of target letters in word versus nonword displays with the Following and Continuing contexts. Proportions of correct detections (corrected for guessing) are categorized in accordance with the reaction times of the detection responses. It will be seen that when responses occurred within 500 msec there is no trace of a word advantage. A difference between the W and N contexts begins to emerge for responses taking from 500 to 1,000 msec, and becomes very large for responses occurring at still longer reaction times. There would seem to be no support here for the perennially recurring suggestion that the word advantage depends on the perception of global features prior to the perception

Table 3.4 Proportion of Detections[a] of Target Letters in Word and Nonword Displays as a Function of Reaction Time and Context

Reaction Time (MSEC)	Context			
	Following		Continuing	
	W	N	W	N
0–500	.71	.85	.65	.64
500–1000	.74	.66	.71	.63
1000–1500	.63	.50	.48	.25
1500–2000	.23	.10	.42	.15

[a]Corrected for guessing.

of individual letters. But on the other hand, the data follow just the pattern expected on the assumption that the faster responses are based on matches between input and memory at the level of individual features of the target letter whereas the slower responses represent cases when such matches did not occur and responses were based on decisions between partially activated letter groups at a later stage of processing.

Levels of Processing in Relation to Pre- and Postcue Conditions

In summary, all available evidence indicates that when recognition can be accomplished on the basis of a feature difference between familiar targets known in advance, a word context influences performance only by contributing redundant information. When conditions permit, this information enters into the decision process; otherwise it exerts no effect on recognition of a target letter. But although feature extraction evidently proceeds independently of linguistic context, we should expect, within the framework of the filter model, that the same would not be true of full identification. If a task requires the encoding of a target letter to the point of evocation of a naming response, then there are several avenues · through which context may influence the process. First, properties of the context may alter the individual's criterion for generating a naming response on the basis of incomplete feature information. Second, regularities in the context may reduce the amount of positional information that must be encoded in order to synthesize a representation of a letter in its proper spatial relationship to other elements of a display (in particular, other letters and indicators used for response cueing). Third, the context determines whether or not the target letter is a constituent of a familiar letter group that is readily accessible from long-term memory and maintainable in short-term memory by rehearsal.

The first of these modes of influence seems to have been quite clearly implicated in the advantage sometimes observed for letters of words as compared to the same letters displayed alone in tachistoscopic studies (Estes, 1975b). The second and third should presumably be more important in comparisons between word and nonword letter strings as context for a target letter. In the remainder of this chapter, I should like to illustrate experimental paradigms that may permit detailed evaluation of our analyses both of the role of task requirements and of the process whereby context influences identification.

For the first of these examples, I shall present some data from an exploratory study conducted in my laboratory.[2] The apparatus and general procedures were the same as those used in the experiment on detection and context previously cited (Estes, 1975b). Subjects viewed 50-msec exposures of 4-letter displays preceded and followed by pattern masks and were cued either before or after the display with a probe letter that was the basis for their response decision.

Groups of 12 subjects were assigned to each of three conditions:

1. *Precue–Item:* On each trial, a single letter was presented on the oscilloscope screen prior to the target display and the subject's task was to decide whether or not the probe letter appeared anywhere in the display.
2. *Postcue–Item:* The task was the same except that the probe letter was presented immediately after the target display.
3. *Postcue–Position:* This condition differed from the Postcue–Item condition only in that the probe letter was displayed directly below one of the four letter positions of the target display, and the subject's task was to decide whether the probe letter had appeared in that position of the display.

One-third of the trials involved single-letter displays, which will not be considered here. Each of the remaining displays comprised four letters, half being common words and half strings of unrelated letters. On 48 of the 4-letter trials, the target letter was either an *L* or an *R* (equally frequently and exactly one per display), and these displays were constructed in accordance with the *WW–NN* constraint. On the remaining trials, other letters were probed, but without the *WW–NN* control, and those will be treated simply as filler trials. Immediately following each display, the subject indicated on a scale of 1–4 his confidence that the probe letter had been in the display (Precue–Item and Postcue–Item) or had been in the indicated position (Postcue–Position).

The data from the *L*- or *R*-cued trials were treated in two ways. First, with a correct response defined as a rating of 3 or 4 if the probe letter was in the display and 1 or 2 if it was not, the proportion of correct recognitions was computed for each condition. Second, the d' measure of signal detectability theory was obtained in the usual way (see, e.g., Murdock, 1974) to provide an index of recognition that might be relatively free of criterion effects. Both measures are included in Table 3.5.

In terms of the model, we expect the Precue–Item condition to permit correct recognition at the lowest processing level, for to the

---

[2] Edith Skaar assisted with this study.

Table 3.5 Measures of Discriminability (d') and Proportion of Correct Recognitions as a Function of Cuing Procedure and Context (*WW* versus *NN*)

Procedure	Discriminability		Proportion Correct	
	WW	*NN*	*WW*	*NN*
Precue item	1.05	.98	.70	.71
Postcue item	1.30	.96	.73	.70
Postcue position	1.29	.87	.76	.71

extent that subjects become aware of the frequent recurrence of the *L, R* target pair, they can respond on the basis of feature differences on *L-* or *R-*probed trials. The virtual equality of both recognition measures for *WW* versus *NN* displays in this condition bears out the analysis. In contrast, both of the other conditions were assumed to require full identification of the target letter and hence to reflect an advantage for a word context. Here again, the statistics shown in Table 3.5 are confirmatory, small advantages in proportion correct and more substantial advantages in the d' measure appearing for the *WW* displays. This result is of interest in demonstrating within a single experiment the pattern that has previously been observed to hold across experiments with differing stimulus material and subject populations.

Categorical Properties of Words

Converging evidence for the interpretation of the word advantage in terms of the hierarchical model, as opposed to hypotheses assuming global features of words, is forthcoming from a recent study conducted by Allmeyer and myself (Estes & Allmeyer, in preparation). We compared the recognition of letters in word, pronounceable nonword, and unpronounceable nonword letter strings with four subjects who were already highly practiced in standard tachistoscopic report and detection methods. The apparatus and display conditions were the same as those of the study reported by Estes, Allmeyer, and Reder (1976). On each trial, a patterned premask appeared, then an exposure of a horizontal array of four letters either to the left or to the right of a fixation point, and finally a patterned postmask. The words were four-letter English nouns with a single vowel in either the second or the third position. Each of the pronounceable nonwords was generated by changing the vowel in one of the word strings, and the unpronounceable nonwords were obtained by permuting the letters so as to produce an unpronounceable sequence. Following a practice series each subject yielded data on 16 lists, each of which comprised 24 words, 12 pronounceable nonwords, and 12 unpronounceable nonwords presented in random sequence. One-fourth of the trials of each type for each subject were conducted at each of the exposure durations: 25, 60, 95, and 200 msec.

One purpose of the study was to give yet another chance for the appearance of evidence revealing the use of global features of words as a basis for recognition. To this end, the subject's first task following the display of the letter string on each trial was to indicate whether he believed it was a word or a nonword. After giving the categorization response, the subject filled in an answer card with the letters he had been able to identify from the display. We wished to see whether subjects would be able to categorize a word string correctly as a word either at durations too short to permit identification of the constituent letters or, at any duration, on trials when too few letters were identified to permit recognition of the particular word.

The answer to both questions is apparent in Fig. 3.21, in which I have plotted the probability of categorizing a display string of either of the three types as a word at each exposure duration, with the number of letters identified as a parameter. Considering the solid curves, representing data for the W strings, it may be seen first of all that when fewer than all four of the letters of a string were identified, the probability of correctly categorizing it as a word was less than chance. Further, under these circumstances, the probability of correct categorization did not increase as a function of exposure duration even though information concerning any type of overall features of words would surely have become clearer with increasing durations. In sharp contrast, when all four letters of a word were identified, the probability of correct categorization was near unity, independently of exposure duration. (The missing point for the shortest exposure duration on the topmost curve of Fig. 3.21 simply reflects the fact that the subjects were never able to identify all four letters at the shortest exposure). The data for nonword strings, omitted from the figure since they are not especially germane to the present problem, showed better than chance accuracy in categorizing the P and N strings as nonwords at all durations.

The Dependence of Word on Letter Recognition

A more constructive picture of the way in which recognition of a letter depends on information concerning other elements of the

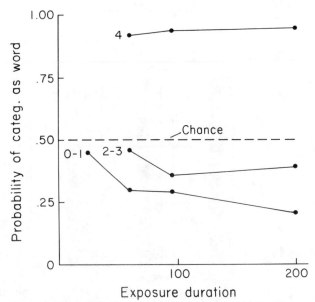

Figure 3.21 Proportions of instances in which 4-letter word displays, intermixed with nonwords in random sequence over trials, were categorized as words when 0-1, 2-3, or all 4 of the constituent letters were correctly identified. The independent variable is exposure duration in milliseconds.

same display is presented in Fig. 3.22. The leftmost set of bars represents the proportions of instances in which at least one letter was correctly reported from a *W*, *P*, or *N* display, the data being pooled over exposure durations. Clearly, the overall or global properties of words as distinguished from either type of nonword confer no advantage whatsoever with respect to the likelihood that at least one letter is identified from a display. Further, nearly the same is true for the probability of identifying a second letter from a display given that at least one has been correctly reported—the second set of bars in the figure. But when at least two letters have been identified from a string, the probability of recognizing a third is substantially higher for the word and pronounceable nonword strings. The fact that the results for these two types are so similar suggests that the critical variable is that the three letters identified constitute a pronounceable trigram. Pronounceability per se should not be overemphasized, for orthographic regularity is inevitably confounded with pronounceability in our displays. However, the confounding is

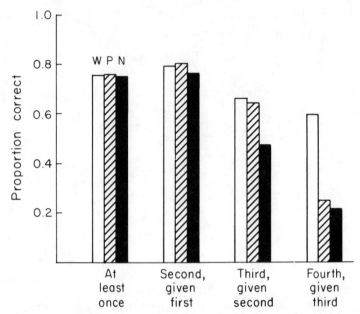

Figure 3.22 Proportions of reports of at least one letter from word (*W*), pronounceable nonword (*P*), or unpronounceable nonword (*N*) displays, together with proportions of these instances in which a second letter was reported, proportions of a third reported given at least two, and proportions of a fourth reported given at least three.

of no great import with respect to our interest here. From the standpoint of the hierarchical model, the crux of matters is that an orthographically regular and/or pronounceable trigram would be a frequently recurring unit in English text and therefore likely to be represented in a readily accessible form in the memory system. When the input from a segment of a display closely matches such a representation, the output of that level of the filter system may be expected to yield a correct report of the given trigram.

In a final aspect of these data, the proportions of correct recognition of the fourth letter of a string given that three have been identified (the rightmost set of bars in Fig. 3.22) show for the first time a substantial difference between the *W* and *P* strings. This result also conforms precisely to expectations on the basis of the hierarchical filter model, for four-letter words certainly have representations in the memory system, whereas four-letter pronounceable nonwords (as we constructed them) generally must not. Thus, for example, the word WORD would have a readily accessible representation in memory. When it is converted into a pronounceable nonword by changing the *O* to an *E*, the segment WER is a frequently recurring trigram that might have an accessible representation in the memory system, in contrast to the full string WERD, which might well have never been previously encountered.

SUMMARY REMARKS ON VISUAL PROCESSING IN READING

It will be apparent, if not from this chapter, then certainly from others in this volume, that an adequate theory of reading will be a towering, multistoried edifice. My concern in this brief essay has been the situation on the ground floor, with attention to the lines of communication running further downward to visual theory and upward to semantic memory.

The Feature–Letter–Word-Processing System

An overall characterization of the view of reading developed here is one of a continual interaction between sensory inputs and memory structures. Input from text is filtered through successive levels of memory trace structures, eventuating in the recognition of letters, letter groups, or words, but with information from other sources combining with outputs of the higher levels to determine the various aspects of the individuals's response to printed material—perception, comprehension, and decision. Differing degrees of specificity of response are associated with different sources of information: Linguistic context acts, often in advance of a target letter or word, to partially activate memorial representations of subsets of words with common semantic attributes; global features of words activate smaller subsets; letter sequences are the most specific, normally leading to the activation of only a single word.

In the case of several examples considered in some detail, we have seen that the multilevel filter model, even in an incomplete and provisional form, helps provide a coherent account of a variety of findings that otherwise would appear unorganized and sometimes even contradictory. Perhaps most has been accomplished with regard to interpretation of the "word advantage," that is, the facilitated recognition of a letter embedded in a word as compared to a letter embedded in a random letter string or presented alone. Among the facts that seem both quite well established and well accounted for in terms of the model are the following:

1. No word advantage appears for forced-choice detection of targets known in advance when the *WW–NN* control is in effect; neither is there an effect in *WN–NW* comparisons if the target and context letters are displayed simultaneously for a brief interval, but a word advantage appears if the context letters remain in view beyond offset of the target, the effect growing systematically as a function of processing time.

2. When letter identification is examined by means of a single-letter probe appearing before or after a brief display, the word advantage increases as conditions require full identification of the target letter rather than simply a response on the basis of feature differences between alternative targets.

3. In the full-report task, words and random letter strings do not differ with respect to the probability that some information (typically, one or two letters) can be extracted from a brief display; but given that some subset of the letters is recognized, the probability of the accrual of additional letters to the report is greater for pronounceable than for random strings and much greater still for words.

In general, the advantage of words and word-like letter sequences appears to lie in the attributes that provide alternative routes to the activation of representations of higher-order letter groups in the memory system and therefore alternative routes to identification of the constituent letters. Among the critical attributes that have been clearly identified are pronounceability, orthographic regularity, letter redundancy, and positional redundancy.

Reaction time data are more difficult to interpret theoretically than measures of accuracy of recognition because of the always complex determination of overt responses by stimulus, context, and often motivational variables. Up to a point, reaction time comparisons for responses to targets embedded in word versus nonword strings fit quite well with expectations from the filter model. In a forced-choice detection task with known targets, we expect response to be based on feature differences between the alternative targets and thus to be relatively immune to effects of context. This implication of the model is well born out by the results of Bjork and Estes (1973), showing virtually identical reaction times for detection of letters embedded in words versus nonword strings (1.02 and 1.00 sec, respectively), a result that was closely replicated (though the data were not included in the published report) in the study of Estes, Bjork, and Skaar (1974).

When the experimental task requires naming of a target letter, then a number of other factors must be expected to enter, including positional uncertainty and response competition. One cannot claim to predict from the filter model, at the present stage of development, such results as the common observation that a common word can often be named more rapidly than an isolated letter, or the finding of Johnson (1975) that a word can be named faster than a particular constituent letter. But neither do these phenomena appear to raise special problems for the model. I think that an understanding of comparisons of this kind will at the very least require much more extensive study of long-term practice effects. After all, accomplished readers must have had great amounts of practice at suppressing naming responses to constituent letters when reading words, and we know little about the ease with which these performance tendencies can be modified or reversed on the basis only of instructions or very limited practice.

Higher-Order Attributes and Auxiliary Information

Inevitably, the model outlined here will have to be modified in details as research continues, but what can we say at present with regard to evaluation of our basic assumptions and overall organization? The principal issue in the literature at present seems to be one dividing models like the one discussed here, which assume reading to be primarily a process of sifting sensory information through a succession of levels of memory comparisons, and more holistic models, which assume that a reader normally goes more directly from stimulus pattern to meaning and only secondarily, when a task requires it, proceeds through more analytic operations to the identification of individual letters. The latter view is represented, for example, by Osgood and Hoosain (1974) and Smith (1971).

The issue concerning the role of higher-order attributes of words or even syntactic units is not whether but how they enter into the reading process. Unfortunately, there has not been a great deal of research bearing sharply on the question of whether information from higher-order attributes of a segment of text actually becomes available earlier than that from individual letters. However, the several attempts, discussed earlier, to approach this question from different angles in our own research program have yielded a consistent pattern of results. When we follow the time course of accrual of information during individual trials in a letter recognition task, we find that information from context enters later, not earlier, than information from the target letters themselves. When we look for direct evidence that the outline shape or other overall attributes of letter strings can enable an individual to determine whether the string is or is not a word prior to the point at which he can identify the letters, the results are negative. Rather, we obtain quite direct evidence that the function of auxiliary information from orthographically regular or meaningful sequences is to enable individuals to complete imperfectly perceived letter groups.

Taking together the large literature showing facilitating effects of context on word and letter recognition with the more analytical experiments discussed here that reveal sharp limitations on the role of context, we may be led to some useful generalizations about the current state of methodology. In particular, it becomes clear, I believe, that experiments in this area need always to take full account of the character of reading as a communication process whose function is to alter the prior state of information of the reader, whether he is perusing a page of text, searching columns of stimuli for targets, or responding to tachistoscopic displays.

The important yet limited role of global features of words such as length and outline can be understood in this framework. Information concerning these features may be stored with the representation of a word in memory, but just as clearly this information does not in general suffice to identify a word uniquely, or even to distinguish words as a class from nonwords that have some orthographic regularities. Thus, if an individual is entirely uncertain as to the nature of a to-be-displayed letter string, he evidently obtains no useful information from the global attributes. If he knows that the string is to be a word, these attributes narrow down the possibilities; if he knows that the word is to be chosen from a limited set of alternatives, the global features may even suffice to enable him to select the correct word uniquely. Consequently, we must expect that comparisons made without regard to the individual's state of information prior to exposure of a stimulus display can yield any possible result. Theoretically significant interpretation of experiments in this area must always depend on adequate specification of prior information and accurate monitoring of the points in time during or following exposure of stimulus material at which information from various aspects of the target stimulus and context exert their effects.

The special importance of the hierarchically organized critical feature–letter–word filter system in reading is that, without interfering with the individual's ability to take account of other sources of information, it sifts sensory information largely independently of the context and thus enables the reader to "see what is there" regardless of his prior expectations. Unlike the information obtained from various sorts of redundancy or from higher-order attributes of words and syntactic units, that obtained through the feature–letter system is nearly independent of the individual's prior state of information and consequently provides an almost fail-safe mechanism for response to printed messages that occur in unexpected circumstances.

Individual Differences

Although firm evidence is scanty, there seems little reason to doubt that both in tachistoscopic experiments and in ordinary reading, individuals have considerable flexibility in their ability to shift their degree of reliance on different types and levels of information. The filter system is always available, and, since it leads to unique identification of letter sequences, must be heavily relied on whenever accuracy is valued. In ordinary reading, where considerable accuracy can safely be sacrificed to gain speed since redundancy provides correction of gross errors, doubtless many letters of a printed line never yield inputs capable of activating their critical features and individual letter recognition is supplemented by considerable reliance on other attributes.

Studies providing comparisons between reading speed and performance in more controlled laboratory situations (e.g., Jackson & McClelland, 1975) suggest that there may be relatively little variance among reasonably accomplished readers with respect to the operation of the filter system for letter and word recognition, but much wider variation in the utilization of auxiliary information. Whether the more important differences between slow and fast readers lie in their states of prior information concerning the material, in the degree to which they have stored in memory higher-order attributes that are useful in discriminating words and syntactic groups, or in habits or strategies for accessing these auxiliary sources of information remains to be determined.

ACKNOWLEDGMENTS

Research reported in this chapter was supported in part by Grants GB 41176 and BNS 76-09959 from the National Science Foundation and MH 23878 from the National Institute of Mental Health.

REFERENCES

Anderson, J. A. A theory for the recognition of items from short memorized lists. *Psychological Review*, 1973, **80**, 417–438.

Baron, J. The word-superiority effect: Perceptual learning from reading. In W. K. Estes (Ed.), *Handbook of learning and cognitive processes*, Vol. 6. Hillsdale, N.J.: Lawrence Erlbaum Associates, 1978. Pp 131–166.

Bjork, E. L., & Estes, W. K. Letter identification in relation to linguistic context and masking conditions. *Memory & Cognition*, 1973, **1**, 217–223.

Cattell, J. M. The time taken up by cerebral operations. *Mind*, 1886, **11**, 220–242, 377–387, 524–538.

Coltheart, M. Visual information processing. In P. C. Dodwell (Ed.), *New horizons in psychology*, 2. Baltimore, Md.: Penguin Books, 1972. Pp. 62–85.

Estes, W. K. Interactions of signal and background variables in visual processing. *Perception & Psychophysics*, 1972, **12**, 278–286.

Estes, W. K. Memory, perception, and decision in letter identification. In R. L. Solso (Ed.), *Information processing and cognition: The Loyola symposium*. Hillsdale, N.J.: Lawrence Erlbaum Associates, 1975. Pp. 3–30. (a)

Estes, W. K. The locus of inferential and perceptual processes in letter identification. *Journal of Experimental Psychology: General*, 1975, **104**, 122–145. (b)

Estes, W. K., & Allmeyer, D. H. Word recognition in relation to the identification of constituent letters and lexical features. Manuscript in preparation, Rockefeller University, 1977.

Estes, W. K., Allmeyer, D. H., & Reder, S. M. Serial position functions for letter identification at brief and extended exposure durations. *Perception & Psychophysics*, 1976, **19**, 1–15.

Estes, W. K., Bjork, E. L., & Skaar, E. Detection of single letters and letters in words with changing versus unchanging mask characters. *Bulletin of the Psychonomic Society*, 1974, **3**, 201–203.

Geyer, L. H., & DeWald, C. G. Feature lists and confusion matrices. *Perception & Psychophysics*, 1973, **14**, 471–482.

Gibson, E. J. *Principles of perceptual learning and development*. New York: Appleton-Century-Crofts, 1969.

Huey, E. B. *The psychology and pedagogy of reading*. Cambridge, Mass.: MIT Press, 1908.

Jackson, M. D., & McClelland, J. L. Sensory and cognitive determinants of reading speed. *Journal of Verbal Learning and Verbal Behavior*, 1975, **14**, 565–574.

Johnson, N. F. On the function of letters in word identification: Some data and a preliminary model. *Journal of Verbal Learning and Verbal Behavior*, 1975, **14**, 17–29.

LaBerge, D., & Samuels, S. J. Toward a theory of automatic information processing in reading. *Cognitive Psychology*, 1974, **6**, 293–323.

Lindsay, P. H., & Norman, D. A. *Human information processing*. New York: Academic Press, 1972.

Massaro, D. W. Primary and secondary recognition in reading. In D. W. Massaro (Ed.), *Understanding language: An information processing analysis of speech perception, reading, and psycholinguistics*. New York: Academic Press, 1975. Pp. 241–289.

Murdock, B. B., Jr. *Human memory: Theory and data.* Hillsdale, N.J.: Lawrence Erlbaum Associates, 1974.

Osgood, C. E., & Hoosain, R. Salience of the word as a unit in the perception of language. *Perception & Psychophysics,* 1974, **15**, 168–192.

Reicher, G. M. Perceptual recognition as a function of meaningfulness of the stimulus material. *Journal of Experimental Psychology*, 1969, **81**, 275–280.

Rumelhart, D. E. A multicomponent theory of confusion among briefly exposed alphabetic characters. Tech Report. Center for Information Processing, University of California, San Diego, 1971.

Smith, E. E., & Spoehr, K. T. The perception of printed English: A theoretical perspective. In B. H. Kantowitz (Ed.), *Human information processing: Tutorials in performance and cognition.* Hillsdale, N.J.: Lawrence Erlbaum Associates, 1974. Pp. 231–275.

Smith, F. *Understanding reading.* New York: Holt, 1971.

Smith, P. T., & Jones, K. F. Phonemic organization and search through long-term memory. In P. M. A. Rabbitt & S. Dornic (Eds.), *Attention and performance.* Vol. V. London: Academic Press, 1975. Pp. 547–562.

Thompson, M. C., & Massaro, D. W. Visual information and redundancy in reading. *Journal of Experimental Psychology*, 1973, **98**, 49–54.

Woodworth, R. S. *Experimental psychology.* New York: Holt, 1938.

4
Mathematical Psychology

This chapter provides a very small sampling of papers reflecting an interest, which has run through a great part of my research from before 1950 down to the present, in the value of efforts to employ mathematical reasoning in the solution of psychological research problems and to develop increasingly powerful models—either mathematical or, currently, of the computer-simulation variety.

In my view, the development of increasingly formal models is neither an esoteric specialty nor a kind of optional garnishing of the research process but rather is an integral constituent of the combination of rational and empirical methods that has provided the vehicle for progress in science for centuries. It has come to be generally accepted, I think, that scientific research is not a matter of producing unadorned facts but rather one of systematically comparing phenomena observed under controlled conditions with informed expectations. A continual recycling of this process leads to progress toward significant theories.

It is essential, however, that the expectations that are to be compared with research results be based on something beyond intuition and general experience, in which case failures to confirm expectations can rarely be given any informative interpretation. It is the function of models to assemble and organize past experience and generate testable predictions. The most fruitful purpose in testing the predictions is not the possibility of obtaining confirmations, which can be rewarding but rarely instructive, but rather to make use of disparities between predictions and observations to guide continuing research and model construction.

The formal models may be categorized somewhat loosely into two main categories—one that may be termed deductive or a priori rational and the other that may be termed inductive or descriptive. The labels can be misleading, but they convey the flavor of the distinction. In the first category, the form of a model is sometimes dictated purely by formal theoretical considerations, sometimes imported by analogy from other domains. In either case, the hope is not ordinarily to provide descriptions of what will actually occur in psychological experiments but rather to provide baselines against which to compare actual performance. An excellent example of this type of model in psychological

247

research of the past few decades is signal detectability theory, originally developed in connection with the engineering of communications systems for the purpose of describing the behavior of an ideal observer faced with the task of detecting signals in noisy backgrounds.

As the detectability model was taken over by psychologists (for example, Tanner and Swets, 1954) there could have been little reason to think that it might represent actual mental processes in decision tasks. Nonetheless, it was immediately seen to provide an extremely valuable baseline model. In many psychological situations, individuals have to make decisions under conditions such that what is perceived might represent an instance of some target category (for example, an image of an aircraft on a radar screen, a shadow signifying a diseased condition on a radiographic plate) or might be in some sense a distractor, having arisen from some irrelevant source or simply a noisy stimulus background. Interpreting the actual behavior of human observers in such situations is a complex matter, for performance might be limited by discriminative capacities, knowledge of relevant decision strategies, motives or expectations that bias judgments, or imperfections of memory. The idealized observer of signal detectability theory faces the same problems and also has limited discriminative capacities, but has perfect memory and operates with a known decision strategy. Thus, comparing the performance of actual observers with the idealized performance generated by the model, one has a basis for narrowing down the possible sources of the errors of judgment made by actual human observers.

Many times I have found comparisons of this type to be instructive, and several specific instances are illustrated in the first two papers in this chapter. In some cases, I have had occasion to go beyond comparisons of observed behavior with a rational model to a three-way comparison of a rational model, observed behavior, and behavior predicted by a substantive model.

By *substantive*, I mean simply to denote models whose assumptions and formal properties have been dictated or suggested by research experience in a particular domain. In a study discussed in the first paper reprinted in this chapter, for example, performance of subjects in a gamelike interactive learning situation is compared with that prescribed for wholly rational participants by the mathematical theory of games (Von Neumann and Morgenstern, 1947), and both the observed behavior and that prescribed by the rational model are compared with predictions from statistical learning theory. In another study summarized in the same paper, performance of subjects in an experiment designed to simulate some aspects of medical diagnosis is compared both with predictions from statistical learning theory and with optimal performance from the standpoint of Bayesian decision theory. These multiple comparisons enable one to progress at the same time toward the theoretical objective of predicting the subject's behavior and the more practical objective of understanding why the behavior falls short of what would be considered optimal on some rational criterion. This motif is exemplified further in the second paper reprinted in this chapter.

In my research, mathematical psychology has never had a special, distinct status; rather, it has been a way of thinking that has entered into all my lines of research, ranging from conditioning to human learning, memory, perception, and decision making. It is in the nature of scientific investigation, however, for theoretically oriented work to yield as important by-products an accumulation of methods that can be used more widely than for the originally intended purposes. These by-products constitute relatively abstract models or constituents of models that can enter into theoretical interpretations of many domains.

There are several aspects to this methodology of model construction, and each may be seen to be salient in the work of some of the investigators who were actively promoting the development of mathematical psychology during the 1950s. One aspect—the one I think is most often taken to be my specialty—is the task of finding fruitful ways of representing psychological processes or characteristics of them. Among these formal contributions arising in my earlier work were the set-theoretical method of representing stimulus sampling, diffusion models for representing variations in availability or activity of subsystems over time, the interpretation of processes of learning and memory as Markov chains (especially important in the investigation of all-or-none aspects of these phenomena), and probabilistic models for relating states of learning or memory to observable response measures.

Another aspect of mathematical psychology is the identification of formal methods or devices that can be abstracted from their original context and given wide application. In the learning theory of the 1950s, Bush and Mosteller (1951) exemplified this tactic. They were perceptive enough to see that a variety of apparently diverse models, ranging from stimulus sampling to models of drug dosages, employed a formal device of a common form, which in their hands came to be known as the "linear operator." As a consequence of the vigorous program of investigation of the properties of these models by Bush and Mosteller and their associates, the linear operator has become perhaps the most widely used conceptual device for representing trial-to-trial changes in behavioral probabilities during learning.

Both of the aforementioned aspects of model development have a common orientation, which is not to attempt to propose assumptions or postulates about the nature of psychological processes so much as to develop formal methods for expressing and testing the consequences of any hypotheses about these processes that may arise in the course of research. A distinctively different approach is that of attempting to set down axioms about properties that ought to hold for psychological processes on a priori rational grounds, as represented by the work of Luce (1959) on axiomatic models for choice behavior.

These distinctions having been made, it should be emphasized that the approaches rarely remain entirely distinct and that the investigators working with them are rarely purists. Thus, Bush and Mosteller (1955) digressed from the main line of their work to show that a combination of their operators and ideas drawn from stimulus-sampling theory could provide an interpretation of stimulus generalization. Similarly, Luce has sometimes turned his attention to the formulation of models for specific empirical domains (Luce, 1963). Though at heart a theoretically inclined experimental psychologist, I have sometimes spent considerable periods, with much pleasure and at least some scientific profit, in systematically investigating (often in collaboration with Patrick Suppes) properties of models or of families of models, with no immediate empirical interpretations in mind (for example, Estes, 1959; Estes & Suppes, 1957, 1959, 1974).

The specialties in psychology—as, I suppose, in any science—that require especially rigorous training and offer only long-term payoffs require some public relations work in order to flourish in the science as a social enterprise. Although mathematical methods and attempts at model construction go back beyond the earliest days of scientific psychology (for example, Fechner, 1860; Helmholtz, 1881), they have never been widely popular, and competence in quantitative methodology has always been limited to a relatively small number of investigators in an increasingly large field. Thus, it is of some importance not only to find ways of doing useful quantitative work in psychology and doing it, but also to find ways of teaching the methods and explaining to psychologists and other scientists—especially those just entering or taking an interest in the field—how mathematical reasoning can enter into psychological research and theorizing, what its purposes are, and how it needs to be employed in order to yield fruitful results, especially with regard to furthering rather than hampering creativity.

During the period from about 1950 to the present, a number of investigators—including all of those mentioned in the preceding paragraphs as well as several others, notably Clyde Coombs and his associates (for example, Coombs, Dawes, & Tversky, 1970) and George A. Miller (Miller, 1964)—have had a hand in this social side of the enterprise. My own efforts in this line are represented in all three papers reprinted in this chapter, the first two of which provide what have seemed to me some relatively striking examples of instances in which relatively simple mathematical methods are found to yield useful insights or to bring out relationships between groups of phenomena that would not be readily perceived without the broadened perspective provided by mathematical abstraction. The third of these papers turns to some of the persisting problems of method in the evaluation of models and some of the problems arising in the competition between traditional mathematical approaches and the newer computer simulation approaches. Throughout, I have tried to convey my view that mathematical models and mathematical reasoning are to be regarded not as a narrowly defined set of cookbook techniques to be used in the refinement and formalization of knowledge in well-worked areas but rather as a mode of theorizing that belongs at the forefront of research. Mathematical thinking should by no means be confined to working with well-defined and restricted problems in standardized situations; rather, it is most needed for its contributions in dealing with problems too complex to yield to purely empirical approaches, however imaginatively conducted.

REFERENCES

Bush, R. R., & Mosteller, F. A mathematical model for simple learning. *Psychological Review*, 1951, *58*, 313–323.

Bush, R. R., & Mosteller, F. *Stochastic models for learning*. New York: John Wiley, 1955.

Coombs, C. H., Dawes, R. M., & Tversky, A. *Mathematical psychology*. Englewood Cliffs, N.J.: Prentice-Hall, 1970.

Estes, W. K. Component and pattern models with Markovian interpretations. In R. R. Bush & W. K. Estes (Eds.), *Studies in mathematical learning theory*, pp. 9–52, Stanford, Calif.: Stanford University Press, 1959.

Estes, W. K., & Suppes, P. Foundations of statistical learning theory, I. The linear model for simple learning. Tech. Rep. No. 16, Contract NR 171–034, Stanford University, 1957.

Estes, W. K., & Suppes, P. Foundations of statistical learning theory, II. The stimulus sampling model. Tech. Rep. No. 26, Contract NR 171–034, Stanford University, 1959.

Estes, W. K., & Suppes, P. Foundations of stimulus sampling theory. In D. H. Krantz, R. C. Atkinson, R. D. Luce, & P. Suppes (Eds.), *Contemporary developments in mathematical psychology*, Vol. 1, pp. 163–183. San Francisco: W. H. Freeman, 1974.

Fechner, G. T. *Elemente der Psychophysik*. Leipzig: Breitkopf & Härtel, 1860.

Helmholtz, H. *Popular scientific lectures* (E. Atkinson, trans.). New York: Appleton, 1881.

Luce, R. D. *Individual choice behavior. A theoretical analysis*. New York: Wiley, 1959.

Luce, R. D. Detection and recognition. In R. D. Luce, R. R. Bush, & E. Galanter (Eds.), *Handbook of mathematical psychology*, Vol. 1, pp. 103–190. New York: Wiley, 1963.

Miller, G. A. *Mathematics and psychology*. New York: Wiley, 1964.

Tanner, W. P., & Swets, J. A. A decision-making theory of visual detection. *Psychological Review*, 1954, *61*, 401–409.

Von Neumann, J., & Morgenstern, O. *Theory of games and economic behavior*. Princeton, N.J.: Princeton Universtiy Press, 1947.

Of Models and Men

We psychologists like to think of ourselves in the role of seekers after truth. Granting that this role is both appropriate and commendable, I should like nevertheless to point out one danger. It is that in the excitement of pursuing new truths we may neglect the equally important task of questioning old ones.

In the hope of mitigating this hazard, I am going to suggest a simple imaginative exercise which has proved a useful antidote to smugness in many spheres of scientific activity. To do this exercise, we consider some fact which we absolutely know to be true and try to imagine what the world would be like if it were false.

A suitable fact for our purposes is the vaunted complexity of human behavior. Practically all psychologists are absolutely sure that attempts to analyze and quantify human behavior will be frustrated by complexities of higher order than any encountered in the natural sciences. If some callow student ventures to doubt this truth, we have a standard argument ready to bring him into line. Look at our present theories, we tell him. Look at Hull's system or at the probabilistic models that are multiplying like overexcited paramecia. Although already too complicated for the average psychologist to handle, these theories are not yet adequate to account for the behavior of a rodent on a runway. Projecting forward the evolutionary arrow of behavioral theories, we can see that the future holds, not a system of simple quantitative laws, but a final stalemate in which the theories further exceed our powers of comprehension than the behavior itself.

For our exercise, we proceed to deny these self-evident propositions. We imagine that the behavior of a mouse or a man is no more difficult to analyze that that of a thunderstorm or a comet. We imagine that psychological theories are actually becoming simpler, the technical complications signifying merely that recondite means are sometimes needed to attain simple ends. We imagine that general quantitative laws, comparable say to the laws of motion or the phase

W. K. Estes, Of models and men. *American Psychologist,* 1957, *12,* 609–617. Copyright 1957 by the American Psychological Association. Reprinted by permission of the publisher.

Presidential address, Midwestern Psychological Association, Chicago, May 3, 1957.

rule, are already visible in outline through the superficial complexities of behavior.

The strenuous part of the exercise is now to place ourselves in the position of a hypothetical psychologist who has never been told whether his world is the imaginary one we have just constructed or the real one in which a psychologist can not be sure what is too complex for what. Remember, the behavior of organisms appears exactly the same in both worlds, only the potentialities for theory construction differ. How can the psychologist find out which world he lives in? Suppose we look at some real behavioral situations through his eyes as he seeks for the general laws that may lie just beyond his grasp. We can at least gain some appreciation of our perplexed psychologist's problem. Perhaps we will even see how he can solve it, and therefore how we, in his place, could do the same for ourselves.

Should any simple laws be found, they will surely be couched in terms of simple descriptive concepts. If, for example, there were a simple and general law of learning, the roles of dependent variables might well be taken by probabilities of observed behaviors. There would also have to be some concept representing a class of events which change the behavioral probabilities. In order to see whether any remote approximation to such a concept exists in the verbal behavior of American psychologists of learning, I have carried out a small linguistic study. The most interesting result is shown in Fig. 4.1.

To prepare it, I have examined every paper on learning published in the *Journal of Experimental Psychology* during the indicated years (an educational experience in its own right) and have plotted the proportions of studies in which the term "reinforcement" is used in the description of procedures or results. This figure may be of historical interest as the first learning curve ever obtained with the psychologists of learning serving as subjects.

Needless to say the most careful search yielded no single element common to the theoretical orientations of all the users of "reinforcement": they ranged from the most devout followers of Hull or Skinner to the most disillusioned eclectics. Neither did there appear to be any physical property common to all of the reinforcing events or operations. It is still possible, however, that all types of reinforcing events exert quantitatively identical effects on learning in spite of their phenotypic differences.

To see what the common quantitative effects might be, let us try the unfashionably direct expedient of looking at some data. Preferably data from an experimental situation that has been especially

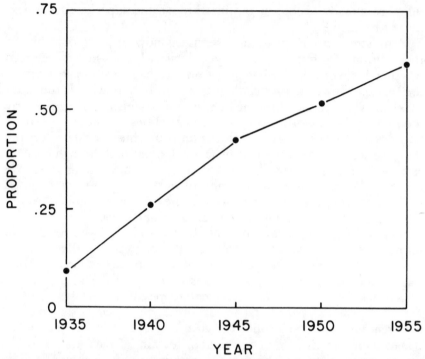

Figure 4.1 Relative frequencies with which papers on learning published in the *Journal of Experimental Psychology* employ "reinforcement" as a descriptive term. Because the *N* for 1945 was very small, the proportion shown has been computed for the 1945 and 1946 volumes combined.

simplified to bring out the effects of reinforcement as clearly as possible.

The design of a verbal conditioning experiment from which I have obtained a sample of data especially suited to our purposes is schematized in Table 4.1. In this table, and throughout the remainder of the paper, the letters *A* and *E* represent actions and reinforcing events, respectively.

The subject's task on each trial was to select one or the other of two response words. The reinforcing events were signals from the experimenter indicating which word was correct. The experimenter determined the word he would designate as correct on each trial by means of a random device which, for any one series, had fixed probabilities—in the example .66 and .34, respectively—of generating E_1 and E_2 events.

Table 4.1 Responses, Reinforcing Events, and Probabilities of Reinforcement for a Single 25-Trial Series

	E_1 (KUW correct)	E_2 (ZUF correct)
A_1 (KUW)	.66	.34
A_2 (ZUF)	.66	.34

One subject would have sufficed for our present purposes, but in order to prepare for a following experiment, which will be described shortly, we secured the services of two. Both were Indiana University undergraduates selected only on the grounds of experimental naivete and availability for a series of experimental sessions. Each was run for 2000 trials. The pair of alternative response words and the probabilities of the reinforcing events were changed every 25 trials, ten different probabilities being used eight times each in the course of the series.

The effects of individual reinforcing events are illustrated in Fig. 4.2. To prepare this graph, I extracted from the protocol of each subject for trials 501–2000 all trial blocks on which the indicated sequence of reinforcing events occurred and pooled the data to obtain the proportions of A_1 responses indicated by the solid horizontal lines in the figure. We can see that, upon occurrence of an E_2, the probability of an A_1 response drops to about 75% of its current value, while upon occurrences of E_1 it increases by about 25% of the difference between its current value and unity.

These observations suggest that perhaps throughout the series the effects of the two reinforcing events upon probability of the A_1 response can be described by the simple formulas given at the top of the figure, with the parameter θ equal, for these particular subjects, to .25. The dashed lines represent the trial-to-trial changes in response probability for an idealized subject whose learning is perfectly described by these rules. In can be seen that the learning of the real and the idealized subjects follow rather similar courses. In other words, we have arrived at a mathematical model.

The alert observer will inquire at this point why the particular formulas shown here were selected when others could undoubtedly be found that would describe these data as well or better. The answers are that these formulas have a rational basis in stimulus sampling theory (2) and that these same formulas have been suggested by many other sets of data. There are, indeed, so many independent

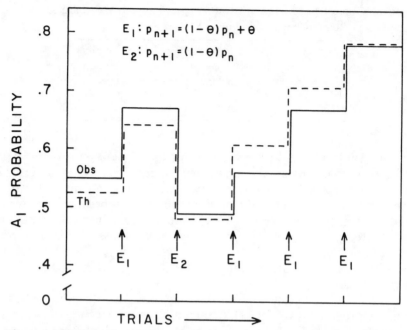

Figure 4.2 Observed and theoretical proportions of A_1 responses per trial for 78 trial blocks on which the indicated sequence of reinforcing events occurred.

sources of support for this pair of quantitative rules that the liberty is taken of referring to them henceforth as laws of reinforcement.

If they could be shown to describe the effects of all varieties of reinforcing events, these laws would satisfy any reasonable criterion of generality. As written, however, the formulas are difficult to apply. Only in especially contrived situations can we evaluate the changes in response probabilities on single learning trials. Convenient experimental tests will be possible only if we can deduce some quantitative properties which characterize the learning of the idealized subject, i.e., the model, over an extended series of trials.

Under the conditions of this experiment, the deductions turn out to be easy and fruitful. By means of a little algebra one can show that, if response probabilities of real subjects continue to vary randomly around those of idealized subjects, then the proportion of A_1 response occurrences per series must be a linear function of the proportion of E_1 reinforcing events. In Fig. 4.3, I have plotted the proportions of A_1 responses and E_1 events per 25-trial series. Data are pooled for all series run under each of the ten reinforcement

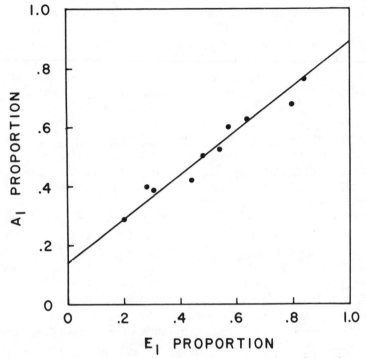

Figure 4.3 Proportion of A_1 responses vs. proportion of E_1 reinforcing events. Each point represents all 25-trial series run under a particular fixed probability of reinforcement.

schedules. Comparison of the observed and predicted trends suggests that the behavior of our two real human subjects may bear a more than casual resemblance to the behavior of the mathematical model.

A second deduction from the model is the following. If the probabilities of reinforcement are constant throughout a series of trials, a subject's response probability will drift upward or downward until it reaches a value equal to its probability of reinforcement, then will continue indefinitely fluctuating around this matching value. The prediction has been confirmed by so many published studies of the ·Humphreys guessing situation and numerous variants that the writer will refrain from adding redundancy by bringing in still more examples.

Instead the writer will try to answer a question that bothers every behavior theorist who strays this far from his Skinner box or T maze. Namely, can theory growing out of human learning data safely be extrapolated to the rat? This is a big step to take, it is realized, and when the question came up around our laboratory, several years ago, the pessimists expressed a very bleak view of the possibility. Rat behavior, they argued, is simply too complex to be described by our simple equations. However, Donald Lauer and the writer felt that the issue had to be faced, so we undertook the task of designing an appropriate experiment. A bit of theoretical analysis indicated that we should expect learning in a simple T maze with correction procedure and food reinforcement to yield the same "probability matching" phenomenon as the studies of verbal conditioning. We predicted then, before securing the rats or constructing the maze, that, under a 75% random reinforcement schedule, the probability of the more frequently reinforced response would tend exponentially to .75 as an asymptote.

The rigors of approximately 180 days of preliminary training, designed to stabilize goal box behavior and eliminate position habits, were survived by a group of 16 rats (not to speak of the two experimenters). Then the rats were given 56 days (one trial per day) of training with the 75% schedule. The closed and open circles in Fig. 4.4 represent cumulative relative frequencies of the more frequently reinforced response and the corresponding reinforcing event, respectively, over the last 28 days. The animals seem to have done about as well as one could reasonably ask at matching their response probabilities to the probability of reinforcement. And, since the random number table which generated the schedule conformed fully as well as the rats to the laws of probability, both of the observed proportions converge nicely to the predicted value of .75. These data can offer little solace to theorists who would like to interpret the "probability matching" phenomenon as an expression of guessing habits mysteriously built into human subjects rather than as an outcome of the laws of reinforcement.

The "probability-matching" principle appears to be quite well established for a particular class of human and animal learning experiments. Still it does not measure up to all we expect of a general empirical law. It can predict nothing whatever about new learning situations in which there is no obliging experimenter to hold event probabilities strictly constant. Unless the matching principle can be shown to be a special case of some more general law, it will be, for everyone but the learning theorist, merely an interesting oddity.

How is one to find out whether a particular law is a special case of some more general one? As one solves any problem: by doing experiments. In this case, we need mathematical as well as empirical experiments. The mathematical experiments consist in finding out how idealized organisms who always behave precisely in accordance

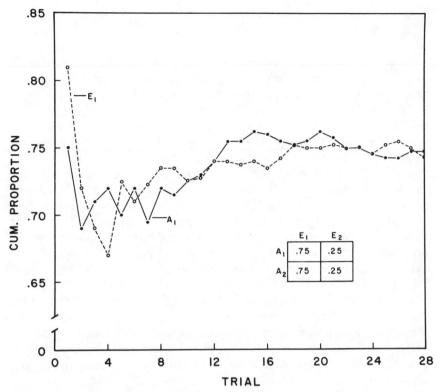

Figure 4.4 Proportions of the more frequently reinforced response and its reinforcing event cumulated over the last 28 days of a 56-day T-maze series.

with the model will learn under all imaginable reinforcement schedules. For the problem at hand, the paper-and-pencil experiments have revealed a gratifyingly general uniformity, a general matching law, of which "probability-matching" is simply a special case (1).

The general matching law requires no restriction whatever on the schedule of reinforcement. It applies whenever the organism's behavior in a recurring stimulus situation can be described in terms of two (or more) mutually exclusive response classes, one of which is reinforced on each trial.[1] The gist of the law is that, beginning at any point in a learning series, the cumulative proportions of a given

---

[1] Application of the law to experiments involving nonreinforced trials, e.g., T-maze learning with noncorrection procedure or bar pressing with fixed ratio reinforcement, requires a more detailed consideration of response units than can be given here.

response and corresponding reinforcing event tend to equality.[2] In other words, the organism keeps accurate books and in the long run pays out an average of exactly one response per reinforcement.

For the particular case of the T-maze study, the law obviously implies the observed asymptotic matching of response and reinforcement proportions. A more interesting test arises with the experimental design represented in Table 4.2. Here the E_1 event, a signal indicating response A_1 is correct, appears with one probability on trials when that response has occurred and with a different probability on trials when the other response has occurred. Since the A_1 response always receives the lion's share of the reinforcement, one might think that eventually its probability would go up to unity. But we can show by simple arithmetic that a unity asymptote is out of the question. If A_1 probability remained at unity over a series of trials, the proportion of A_1 responses would approach unity, but the proportion of E_1 reinforcing events would not exceed .66. Therefore, we must predict that response probability will stabilize at some level below unity where the net effects of the two reinforcing events over a series of trials permit the matching law to be satisfied. It happens that, for the particular case illustrated, the permissible asymptote is approximately .75. We see in Table 4.3 that a group of 12 human subjects run in a modified prediction experiment by Arthur Brody and the writer had no difficulty in finding the proper asymptote by the end of a 180-trial series.

Table 4.2 Probabilities of Reinforcement for Simple Contingent Case

	E_1 (A_1 correct)	E_2 (A_2 correct)
A_1	.66	.34
A_2	1.00	.00

[2] Stated in mathematical terms,

$$\lim_{n \to \infty} \frac{p_j(n)}{\pi_j(n)} = 1.$$

The variable n represents the number of trials in a series counted from an arbitrary origin. The terms $p_j(n)$ and $\pi_j(n)$ represent the relative frequencies of a given response A_j and its reinforcing event E_j over the n trials.

Table 4.3 A_1 and E_1 Proportions over Last 40 Trials of Series with Simple Contingent Reinforcement

	A_1	E_1
Theory	.75	.75
Experiment	.74	.75

In view of the presumed generality of the matching law, it is our duty to confront it with still more strenuous tests. We might, for example, make the probability of reinforcement not only contingent upon the subject's response, as in the last experiment, but contingent in a manner which changes from trial to trial. To investigate such a case, some data were collected, with the assistance of Marcia Johns, for two groups of 10 human subjects in a situation similar to that of the preceding experiment except that probabilities of reinforcement were specified by the rules exhibited in the lower right portion of Fig. 4.5. The conditional probabilities of reinforcing events following A_1 and A_2 responses varied in magnitude as different linear functions of n, the number of trials. (Probabilities of E_2 events are obtainable by subtracting those of the E_1 event from unity.) In a manner of speaking, the probabilities of reinforcement were continually running away from the subjects; but, as can be seen graphically in the figure, not fast enough to prevent the subjects from bringing their proportions of responses and reinforcing events together as required by the matching law.

It begins to appear that, at least for the kind of reinforcing procedures used here, our subjects will continue to satisfy the matching law under any schedule of reinforcement we can manage to contrive. This conclusion has even more far-reaching implications than immediately meet the eye. It follows, for example, that the model should also describe learning in social situations which involve dependencies of one individual's reinforcement schedule upon the behavior of others.

The potentialities of learning theory for elementary forms of social interaction are illustrated on a modest scale in Fig. 4.6. With the assistance of Marcia Johns, data were obtained from two well-practiced subjects (the same two who were introduced to you a few experiments ago) under the conditions of the simple competitive game schematized by the payoff matrix in the lower right corner of the figure. The game requires a series of trials. On each trial, one

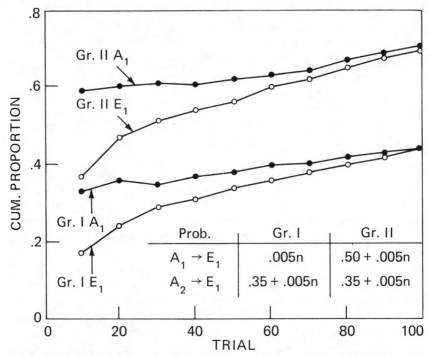

Figure 4.5 Cumulative proportions of A_1 responses and E_1 reinforcing events for series in which conditional probabilities of reinforcement vary linearly with trials.

player chooses a row, the other a column. If their choices are the first row and the first column, the experimenter signals a win for the column player; if their choices are the first row and the second column, the experimenter determines the winner by means of a random device with probabilities of .5 for each player; and so on. The players are not told the payoff probabilities and can learn about them only by observing the consequences of their choices over a series of trials.

This situation has several interesting aspects. For one thing, it represents one of the simple games of strategy that have been exhaustively analyzed by Von Neumann and Morgenstern (5). Thus we can compare the optimal strategies prescribed by game theory for the rational man familiar to students of economics with the course of action prescribed by learning theory for the idealized individual who learns strictly on the basis of the reinforcing effects of his successes and failures. According to game theory, the particular game shown in

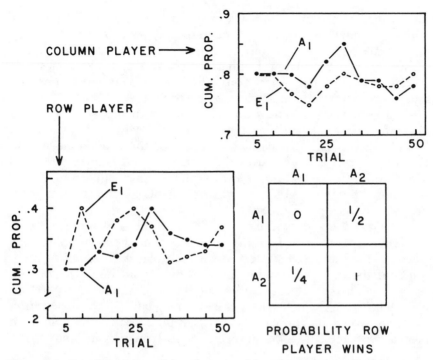

Figure 4.6 Payoff matrix and data for two subjects learning in a simple competitive situation which, from the standpoint of game theory, admits "sure-thing" minimax strategies. The A_1 and E_1 proportions are cumulated over the last 50 trials of a 75-trial series.

Fig. 4.6 exemplifies the famous minimax principle. Assuming that both are strictly rational, the row player should always choose A_2 and the column player, A_1.

According to learning theory, the laws of reinforcement should apply to the response probabilities of both players. But the fact that each player's reinforcement schedule depends on his opponent's behavior introduces serious mathematical complications. It turns out that for most games, including the one shown here, there is no known way to solve the basic equations and predict the course of learning.

Despite these complications, however, the general matching law should apply to both players, and, inspecting the plotted data, we can see that the cumulative proportions of responses and reinforcing events do indeed converge nicely by the end of the series. This observation gives us some real leverage on the problem, for, assuming the validity of the matching law, simple arithmetic enables us to set limits on the possible asymptotic response probabilities for both players. We find, for example, that the minimax solution would not satisfy the matching law for either player. The A_1 probabilities, and therefore cumulative proportions, for both players must approach asymptotes intermediate between zero and unity.

Our subjects, who know nothing of either theory, show a callous disregard for the rational solution, but never stray far from the bounds set for them by learning theory. For the column player, the empirical curves fluctuate around the permissible terminal value of .8 throughout the series. For the row player, they appear to be approaching, but have not quite reached, a permissible level slightly below .4 by the end of the series.

In Fig. 4.7 are shown data for the same subjects in a game with a different payoff matrix. This time the game-theoretic solution is what is called a mixed strategy, with each player choosing A_1 two-thirds of the time in a random order. Looking at the data plots, we see again that the subjects exhibit an almost uncanny ability to find probability levels which satisfy the matching law. On the assumption that this would be the case, it was possible to calculate in advance of the experiment that proportions for the row player would settle

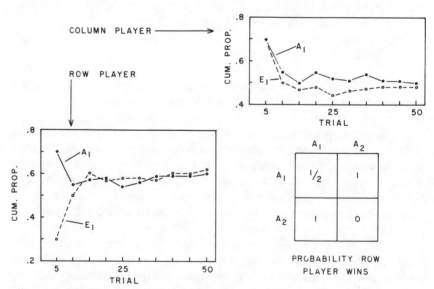

Figure 4.7 Replication of the experiment represented in Fig. 4.6 with a new payoff matrix which admits only mixed minimax strategies.

somewhere between .50 and .75 and that those for the column player would approach .5. The row player is free to satisfy both theories, and appears quite likely to do so; the column player has to choose between the two, and toes the line steadfastly for learning theory.

The writer would be the last to deny that game theory may furnish us excellent tips on how to make our bankrolls last in poker or business. But our results suggest that game theory will be no substitute for an empirically grounded behavioral theory when we want to predict what people will actually do in competitive situations.

For a final attempt to test the limits of the laws of reinforcement, this time in a setting clearly of practical as well as theoretical interest, consider the problem of clinical vs. statistical prediction. Suppose we look at this problem as it arises in the life of a young PhD in clinical psychology who has just been launched into practice from an APA-approved training program. This particular young PhD is atypical only in that he has missed Meehl's book (3) and starts his career as a psychological diagnostician putting his faith wholly in clinical intuition, fed of course with test scores and case history data, but uncontaminated by actuarial methods.

What can we predict about his success in diagnosis? The empirical studies reviewed in Meehl's book suggest that the clinician will do rather more poorly in many situations than a competent clerk using actuarial methods. However, the empirical studies do not answer all of our questions. Is the clinician inferior only in situations where he is handicapped by inferior sources of information? Or is he simply less efficient than the actuary at utilizing information for purposes of prediction?

We might gain further insight into the problem by comparing the clinician and the statistician in a controlled diagnostic situation, if necessary even in an artificial laboratory situation. There we will know exactly what items of information are available to both the clinician and the statistician and how the items of information correlate with the diagnostic criterion. With these restrictions imposed we will doubtless lose some of the rich detail of the "real" clinical situation, but in return we will have a problem clearly enough defined so that we will at least know when it has been solved.

To be concrete, let us suppose the clinician is assigned the task of making differential diagnoses between schizophrenia and manic-depressive psychosis in a hospital population for which these two disorders occur with equal frequency. And suppose further that there are available to the clinician a finite number, say exactly three, items of information which may occur in any combination and which correlate significantly with the criterion according to which the clinician eventually decides whether a diagnosis is correct. The items designated a, b, and c in Table 4.4 might be deviant test profiles, relevant items of case history data, or the like; for brevity, they will be referred to simply as symptoms or, in an experimental context, as cues.

As in the case of the two-person games, we cannot hope that our mathematical model will immediately generate predictions about the complete course of learning for the diagnostician. But if we confine our attention for the present to long-term success rates, we may be able to derive some useful results by applying the general matching law.

In Table 4.5 have been assembled the success rates which are of a priori interest for the particular set of symptom probabilities shown in Table 4.4. They range from the chance level of .50, that would obtain if the clinician learned nothing at all, to the maximum attainable by an actuary using statistical decision theory.

Provided only that the clinician perceives both the symptoms and the informational feedback concerning correct diagnoses, we can immediately rule out the chance value. On each trial the probability of the correct diagnostic response to the symptom pattern presented will increase as a function of reinforcement, and learning will continue at least until the success rate reaches what has been labelled the first plateau. It is the asymptote that would be predicted by statistical learning theory if individual symptoms functioned as stimulus elements (2). At this level, the probability that any symptom taken alone will evoke a given diagnostic response equals the true probability that the symptom will be followed by that diagnostic outcome. However, the symptoms usually occur, not alone, but in combinations, and the matching law would not be satisfied for response proportions in the presence of the various possible symptom patterns or for the overall series.

Table 4.4 Diagnostic Situation

Symptom	Correlation of Symptom with Schizophrenia	Probability of Symptom	
		Schiz.	M-D
a	.26	$\frac{3}{4}$	$\frac{1}{2}$
b	.17	$\frac{1}{2}$	$\frac{1}{3}$
c	-.42	$\frac{1}{4}$	$\frac{2}{3}$

Population: $\frac{1}{2}$ schizophrenic and $\frac{1}{2}$ manic-depressive

Table 4.5 Proportions of Correct Diagnoses under Alternative Models

Maximum (statistical decision theory)	.736
Predicted asymptote (learning theory with pattern model)	.628
Predicted first plateau (learning theory with component model)	.545
Chance	.500

Consequently we must predict that learning will continue until the .628 asymptote is reached. At this level, the conditional probability of a given diagnostic response, say schizophrenia, to each possible pattern of symptoms will match the true conditional probability of schizophrenia in the presence of the pattern; and the matching law will be satisfied for all stimulus patterns that can occur during a series.

The writer had arrived at this point in the analysis about a year ago, during a period of reflection and theoretical activity at the Center for Advanced Study in the Behavioral Sciences. But this set of sharply defined empirical predictions for the diagnostic problem clamored so persistently for an empirical check that the meditative life had to be interrupted long enough for an experiment. With the cooperation of the center, the Stanford Psychology Department, and in particular of Juliet Popper who processed the subjects, it proved possible to collect some data in an experimental situation set up to mimic the conditions of the diagnostic problem as closely as possible.

Data from the last 300 trials of a 600-trial series, presented in Fig. 4.8, show how well the subjects (43 students of psychology and education at Stanford University) succeeded in conforming to the matching law. The chart at the upper right of the figure reviews the probabilities of each of the three cues (symptoms) in the presence of each of the two diagnostic outcomes. The shaded rectangle above each cue pattern represents the true population proportion of outcomes corresponding to the A_1 diagnostic response, and the open rectangle represents the obtained proportion of A_1 responses.[3]

Finally, in Fig. 4.9 we see the entire curve of learning. The successive plotted points represent mean success rates over the first 50 trials, first 100 trials, and so on out to 600 trials. The horizontal lines labelled "component model" and "pattern model" represent the early plateau and the asymptotic level, respectively, which we calcu-

---

[3] The diagnostic responses and outcomes corresponding to Schiz. and M-D in Table 4.4 are henceforth designated simply A_1 and A_2, respectively.

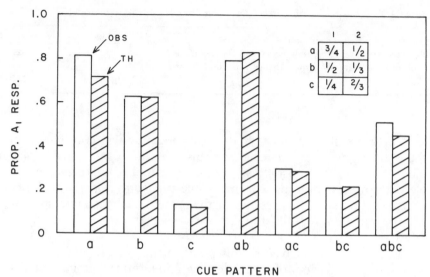

Figure 4.8 Observed and theoretical proportions of A_1 diagnostic responses to each combination of cues (symptoms) over the last 300 trials of a 600-trial series.

lated from the model and which the subjects seem to have had no trouble finding without any calculations at all.

One might suspect that, if the number of different symptoms were to increase, the efficiency of the intuitive clinician relative to the statistician would also increase, so that in sufficiently complex situations the clinician would be able to give reasonably good diagnoses after a short period of observation while the statistician would be lost in a sea of calculations. However, the model says no. As the number of symptoms increases, the statistician will keep his task down to manageable proportions by sampling methods, while the clinician will find it increasingly difficult to get past the first plateau, a level at which information from configurations of symptoms is not being utilized and consequently efficiency is far from optimal.

One might ask whether perhaps the terminal level of the learning curve in Fig. 4.9 is not simply a second plateau, from which the curve would eventually take off again and climb to the maximum level. In reply, we can predict with some confidence that, so long as the learner is restricted solely to the information conveyed by the observed correlations of cues with outcomes over a series of trials, he will not proceed beyond the indicated asymptotic level. In fact, if we calculate the amount of information in the series by the methods of information theory (see, e.g., 4), we can demonstrate that the

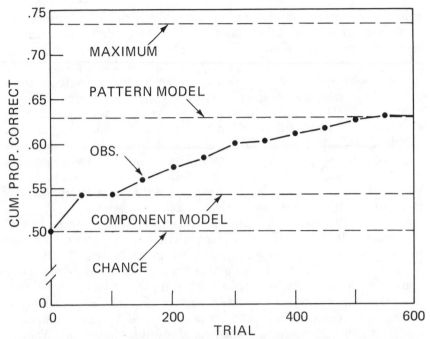

Figure 4.9 Cumulative proportions of correct diagnostic responses for 43 human subjects. The dashed horizontal lines represent the theoretical values of Table 4.5.

pattern-model solution is precisely the one for which the information in the cue-outcome system is transmitted without gain or loss to the cue-response system.[4] In other words, the learner in our experiment, and presumably the intuitive clinician, manages to extract all of the information contained in the series of events he observes, but he adds none to the total.

If our analysis is correct, the clinician can further improve his diagnostic or predictive accuracy only if he draws upon principles or theories which are based upon outside sources of information and which in turn enable him to use more effectively the information he gains from his own observations.

We must now conclude our turn around the outposts of learning theory. In the course of it, we have watched a mathematical model

---

[4] More specifically, we can show that asymptotically: (*a*) the information in the sequence of diagnostic responses equals the information in the sequence of diagnostic outcomes, and (*b*) the uncertainty of the outcome given the cue pattern equals the uncertainty of the response given the cue pattern.

emerge by almost imperceptible steps from the raw material of experimental data and then take on a guiding role in the planning and interpretation of further experiments. We have looked for correspondences between properties of the model and properties of human behavior as both model and man were confronted with a series of increasingly novel and complex learning situations. We have seen the model extended to new situations, not by the addition of elaborate mathematical superstructures, but by the derivation of simple quantitative laws relating classes of observables. Perhaps we have even caught ourselves in moments of uncertainty wondering whether we might indeed live in a world where all natural phenomena yield alike to the analytical weapons of mathematics and experiment and where models yield insight into the behavior of men.

For his own part, the writer can imagine no happier outcome of this exercise than to find that we have all had our uncertainties about the nature of our science increased by a bit or two. In his own experience, the writer has found that the steepest obstacle to theory construction in psychology is not the complexity of behavior. It is the mountain of stereotypes deposited by centuries of prescientific attempts to comprehend behavior and capped by the pronouncements of the academicians who have always known in advance, apparently by divine inspiration, exactly what kind of theory is possible and proper for psychology. This barrier must be undermined by uncertainty before it can be toppled by experiment. Once it is down, our experimental subjects will be able to tell us, through the medium of their behavior, what kind of theory psychology is entitled to.

REFERENCES

1. Estes, W. K. Theory of learning with constant, variable, or contingent probabilities of reinforcement. *Psychometrika,* 1957, **22**, 113–132.
2. Estes, W. K., & Burke, C. J. A theory of stimulus variability in learning. *Psychol. Rev.,* 1953, **60**, 276–286.
3. Meehl, P. E. *Clinical vs. statistical prediction.* Minneapolis: Univer. Minnesota Press, 1954.
4. Miller, G. A. What is information measurement? *Amer. Psychologist,* 1953, **8**, 3–11.
5. Von Neumann, J., & Morgenstern, O. *Theory of games and economic behavior.* Princeton: Princeton Univer. Press, 1944.

Human Behavior in Mathematical Perspective

To outsiders it may well seem that mathematical psychology must be an extremely narrow specialty, that human behavior on the whole must be too complex for mathematical analysis, and that research involving mathematical approaches to behavior must be artificial and remote from practical problems. But a good case can be made that in each instance the truth is precisely the opposite. Mathematical methods in fact have proved essential research tools in many fields of psychology. The very complexity of human behavior presents such difficult problems that we can expect to make progress toward understanding it—if at all—only with the combined efforts of mathematical and experimental analysis. And although principles arising from psychological research rarely are directly applicable to social problems, sometimes fruitful applications can be accomplished once the way has been paved by appropriate mathematical analysis.

The beginnings of experimental psychology saw attempts to establish scales of measurement for subjective quantities—in particular, sensation—comparable to familiar scales of measurement of physical quantities. Psychophysics, the branch of psychology arising from this interaction between psychology, mathematics, and physics, has evolved over the past century into a substantial body of theory that helps us both to understand the way in which human beings process information from the environment and to solve many types of human engineering problems. During and following World War II, an important branch of psychology focusing on human performance

W. K. Estes, Human behavior in mathematical perspective. *American Scientist*, 1975, *63*, 649–655. Reprinted by permission of the Scientific Research Society of North America, Inc.

This article was prepared for the Symposium on Mathematics in Social Science at the January 1975 annual meeting of the AAAS.

arose, largely as a result of the importation into psychology of mathematical theories of information, communication, cybernetics, and control systems (Miller 1964). Most recently, substantial progress in developing a theory of human problem-solving has been catalyzed by an infusion of ideas from the rapidly growing science of information processing systems and the possibility of simulating human behavior on digital computers (Elithorn and Jones 1973; Newell and Simon 1972).

The role of mathematics is apt to be of special importance in the extension of psychological principles and methods to problems arising in the economy or in political or social institutions. All the processes studied by economists, sociologists, geographers, and political scientists arise from the behavior of individuals. And just as the behavior of individuals is elucidated by information and theory arising from studies of the structure and function of the brain and nervous system, we may expect that phenomena concerning the behavior of groups may be elucidated by theories and principles arising from the study of the individual. In this connection, as economist (Haavelmo 1958) has remarked, "I think most of us feel that if we could use *explicitly* such variables as, e.g., what people *think* prices or incomes are going to be, or variables expressing what people *think* the effects of their actions are going to be, we would be able to establish relations that could be accurate and have more explanatory value."

In practice, however, the theories of the other social sciences have generally been developed with little reference to the facts or principles of the psychology of individuals. Theories in economics and political science tend to rely on an intuitive conception of a rational man rather than on the picture of man generated by a century of research in scientific psychology. I would suggest that, to a great extent, the reason is the enormous eclecticism of psychology over most of its history. The main harvest of psychological research has been a vast collection of facts and local principles that are largely specific to particular types of people in particular situations. Hope of contact between this mass of material and the construction of social science theory depends on our ability to abstract from the mass of fact and local theory a characterization of properties of human behavior that is general enough to have wide applicability and can be presented in a form that will interface with the models of economics, government, and other social sciences. The task of producing this abstract characterization of behavior falls squarely in the province of the mathematical psychologist.

In the remainder of this paper I propose to take a look at the picture of the behaving human individual that emerges from current work in mathematical psychology. This picture will describe no specific individual and no concrete situation but rather will delineate some features common to wide ranges of human activity. I shall consider specifically some of the problems and questions that arise when a human being takes on the role of a link in a man-machine system—for example, a communication network—or in a multiperson interaction, as occurs in economics or population dynamics.

Certain functions of the human component of these systems are of special importance. First, regardless of the amount of instrumentation, at some point in any system there must be an observer, and his ability to transmit information depends on his perceptual capabilities, skills, and beliefs. Yet the individual serving these functions cannot be described by a set of fixed parameters; his beliefs are always modified by experience, and his current beliefs affect his subsequent actions. When more than one individual is involved in a system, the beliefs of each are modified through interactions which also must be accounted for. Summarized so briefly, these functions sound abstract, and I should like now to illustrate the way each of them appears in the picture of the human component seen through the eyes of mathematical psychology.

THEORY OF THE HUMAN OBSERVER

The function of the individual as an information filter can be conveniently illustrated in terms of a problem common to all the sciences—namely, the behavior of an observer. Consider a situation in which an observer is attempting to discern the image of a faint star in a telescope or on a photographic plate or to detect a radar signal in the output of a piece of telemetric equipment. In any scientific experiment, the observer's purpose is to be as accurate as possible and to make his observations independently of his own opinions, expectations, or biases.

At one time the problem facing a well-indoctrinated observer seemed extremely simple. If incoming energy from a visual or auditory signal was too weak, it of course would not excite receptors in the eye or ear, and the signal would go unobserved. In terms of earlier psychological theories, we would say that the sensory signal was below the observer's threshold for discrimination. The solution to the problem of weak signals also appeared to be simple: amplify the incoming energy until it reaches the observer's threshold. But in the course of interactions of psychology with physics and engineering, it became apparent that no such solution was available.

In the first place, research revealed that transmission of information through human receptors is inextricably associated with statistical uncertainties of the sort bound up with events at the molecular and atomic levels. The detection of a weak signal by the eye, ear, or nose may involve the effects of only a few photons, in the first case, or the motion of a few molecules, in the second and third (de Vries and Stuiver 1961). There is no way to screen the observer from all influences other than the source of the signal of interest. Incoming energies from other sources may trigger activity in the same receptors used to detect the signal. In general, patterns of excitation in sensory receptors and neurons leading to the central nervous system which are produced by a particular signal can also be produced by noise, defined as energy coming from the environment which happens to mimic the receptor pattern produced by the signal.

In the kind of situation we are considering, the observer is faced with the problem of distinguishing signal from noise. All he can learn by experience is which sensory patterns are most likely to reflect a signal from the source he is trying to detect and which patterns are more likely to arise as a consequence of noise.

In current theory of the behavior of the human observer, it is assumed that the observer has stored in his memory system a representation of the signal for which he is watching. As illustrated in Figure 4.10, this representation in memory can be characterized by a vector—that is, an array in which each element corresponds to one of a large number of binary-valued dimensions; the + 1s and –1s indicate which of the two values on each dimension has been characteristic of the signal in the past experience of the observer. When each observation is made, an input is received by the sensory system, and this input can be similarly represented by a vector in which the pattern of +1s and –1s indicates the degree to which each dimension of the signal is represented in the input. The observer judges whether a signal has taken place by comparing the input vector to his memory vector.

In an analysis of this problem from the standpoint of the neurophysiology of the perceptual and memory systems by Anderson (1973), the comparison takes the form of a computation of the inner product of the input and memory vectors. (That is, corresponding values in the two vectors are multiplied together and the products are summed.) The result yields an output (illustrated at the right of the memory vector in Fig. 4.10) which is a large value if comparison yields a close match between input and memory and a low value if there is a mismatch. The figure illustrates a ubiquitous characteristic of this process: the result of a series of comparisons is a distribution of outputs with the larger values found on trials when signals actu-

Input vectors Filter (memory vector) Filter output values

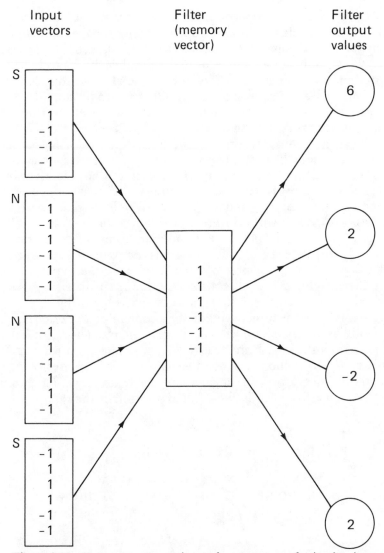

Figure 4.10 Vector representations of a sequence of stimulus inputs from signal (S) and noise (N) sources are compared in turn to a memory vector which serves as a filter. The degree of correspondence between each input and the memory vector determines the filter output value, shown at the right.

ally occurred and lower values on occasions when the input represented noise alone. However, there are occasions on which an output produced by noise is as large as some of the outputs produced by signals.

Over a series of many observation intervals, the result is the generation of two distributions of output values for the filter system, as illustrated in Figure 4.11. One distribution characterizes intervals during which only noise is present and the other distribution, intervals during which there is a signal. Because the two distributions overlap, it is clearly impossible for the observer to be certain on any occasion whether he perceives signal or noise. He can, both in practice and in theory, establish a criterion, or filter-output value, such that whenever an observation yields a value equal to or higher than this criterion, he will report a signal. For observations yielding lower values, he will report noise alone. The criterion is not dictated solely by the objective environmental situation; rather it is influenced by the individual's training and attitudes as well as the payoffs or penalties associated with different outcomes of his observations (Tanner and Swets 1954). If the observer is induced to adopt a sufficiently low criterion, he will never miss any signals but will often yield "false alarms," reports of signals when none actually took place. Conversely, if the observer's criterion is sufficiently high, he will eliminate false alarms, but at the cost of missing many signals.

There is no way to get around the problem of the criterion; all we can do is to try to understand it. As a consequence, we have a substantial body of mathematical theory resulting from the analysis of this type of psychological problem in terms of theories of signal detectability developed in engineering contexts. (See Green and Swets 1966 and Swets 1964 for a full exposition of the theory.)

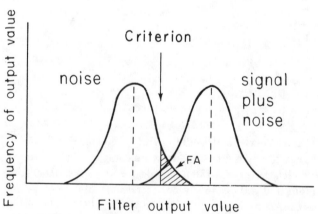

Figure 4.11 Perceptual filter outputs are distributed between two types of trials, those in which the subject hears noise alone and those in which a signal is present in a noise background. *FA* = false alarms.

It should be noted that the problem faced by an observer who tries to distinguish signal from noise—like that posed for the theorist who seeks to determine the role of the criterion and to develop means of allowing for it in specific situations—is not limited to simple tasks like detecting elementary visual or auditory signals. The same problems and the same considerations arise when, for example, a sociologist or anthropologist is making observations of human behavior in social situations. In these situations, even though the properties of observed events do not necessarily fall on simple quantitative dimensions, mathematical reasoning has proved useful.

If quantitative values can be specified for the utilities of outcomes (that is, the payoffs for correct detections and the costs of false alarms) in a given situation, then it is possible, by applying statistical decision theory, to determine the criterion which should be adopted by an ideally efficient observer. Of course, in many practical situations ranging from astronomical observation to medical diagnosis, utilities are difficult to specify. But if we have reason to suspect that observers or diagnosticians are performing at less than ideal efficiency, we might, by arranging training in situations for which the true signal and noise distributions are known, determine how the individuals adjust their criteria in response to changes in experimental parameters and perhaps help them to approach optimal performance.

The problem of understanding the scientific observer does not end here. As a consequence of his experiences in a given type of situation, an observer will inevitably form expectations about what he is likely to see or hear. Experimental studies carried out under the influence of mathematical learning theory have demonstrated the interesting yet unsettling fact that an individual's expectations influence his observations of events (Atkinson, Carterette, and Kinchla 1962; Estes 1971; Estes and Johns 1958). Once again, there are no grounds for thinking that the problem can be circumvented; we can only attempt to understand the situation and, by combined experimental and mathematical analysis, arrive at ways of allowing or correcting for the influences of expectations on the behavior of an observer.

This situation raises an interesting problem for philosophers of science. If an individual's observations are necessarily always influenced by his beliefs and expectations, how can we attain true objectivity? This end, it would seem, can be achieved, if at all, only in a framework of theory in which mathematical reasoning helps us rise above the limitations that nature has placed on our capacities for objective empirical investigation of phenomena.

MODELS FOR CHANGES IN EXPECTATIONS

We turn now to the question of how an individual's expectations are modified by the outcomes of his observations. Theory bearing on this type of learning is relevant not only to the problem of interpreting the behavior of an observer but also to a major aspect of the behavior of a human being in any social context—namely, the way in which his beliefs and attitudes are influenced by information coming to him from other individuals. In any social context, an individual is continually bombarded by messages from other people—or from communication media such as newspapers, television, billboards—that are intended to influence his beliefs or expectations. The way in which these messages exert their effects has been intensively studied by experimental psychologists, and the results enable us to give a rather simple characterization of the way in which an individual's beliefs are modified.

Consider the simplest case of an individual's expectations or beliefs about some single issue. He may be regarded as the receiver in a simple communication situation in which the source, another individual or a group, delivers a sequence of messages, some of which are intended to influence him positively and some negatively, as schematized in Figure 4.12. Let us consider a sequence of occasions in which messages favorable to a particular belief occur with probability λ and messages unfavorable with probability $1 - \lambda$. A description of the effects of the individual messages which has proved quite accurate in many experimental situations is provided by a special case of the "linear operator" model of statistical learning theory (for a summary presentation of the model, see Coombs, Dawes, and Tversky 1970; for a full account, Estes and Suppes 1959).

The gist of the model is that each positive message produces a linear increment and each negative message a linear decrement in the individual's probability of manifesting a positive attitude or expectation on the issue in question. Denoting this probability just prior to receipt of a message by p, and letting θ be a constant with a value between 0 and 1, we see in Figure 4.12 that a positive message increases p by a fraction θ of the difference between its current value and unity, whereas a negative message decreases p by a fraction θ of its current value. Since, on any trial n of a sequence, these operators are applied with probabilities λ and $1 - \lambda$, respectively, it is easy to show that on the average

$$p_{n+1} = \lambda[p_n + \theta(1 - p_n)] + (1 - \lambda)(p_n - \theta p_n) = p_n + \theta(\lambda - p_n) \quad (1)$$

That is, on the average, the probability, p_n, of a positive expectation

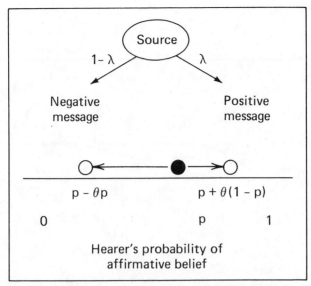

Figure 4.12 In a simple communication situation, a hearer's probability of holding an affirmative belief is represented by a point (*solid circle*) which moves to a higher or lower position (*open circles*) depending on whether the source sends a positive or negative message (these occur with probabilities λ and 1-λ, respectively).

is driven toward λ—the probability of a positive message—and this process will continue until the difference between p_n and λ approaches 0. Thus the model has the interesting property that, asymptotically, the probability of a positive expectation on the part of the hearer is equal to the probability of a positive message being generated by the source. This asymptotic result has given rise to the term *probability matching*, signifying a tendency of human observers to adjust their expectations so as to match the true probabilities of events they have had an opportunity to observe (Estes 1972).

Further, in considering the effectiveness of particular sequences of positive and negative messages, we need only apply the incremental or decremental operators in the appropriate order to predict the effectiveness of particular distributions. Thus in Figure 4.13 we see that if three positive and three negative messages are included in a series, the probability of a positive attitude on the part of the hearer at the end will be higher if the positive messages are concentrated in the latter part of the series than if they are concentrated in the earlier part.

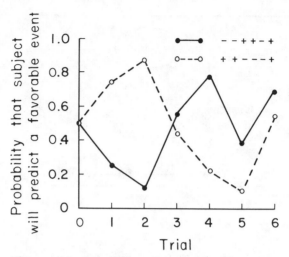

Figure 4.13 Two different sequences of favorable
(+) and unfavorable (−) events produce different
probabilities that, following a sequence of trials, a
subject will predict a favorable event.

We are now in a position to illustrate the interaction between
observation and expectation referred to above. When an observer is attempting to detect a signal, the "messages" he receives are simply
occurrences or nonoccurrences of the signal, and the quantity p_n
in Eq. 1 denotes his probability of expecting a signal following n observation trials. To take account of the fact (Broadbent 1958, 1971)
that the observer's degree of attentiveness will inevitably fluctuate
over time, we introduce a parameter ϕ, denoting the probability on
any trial that the observer is in an attentive state and can correctly
detect the presence or absence of a signal. With probability $1 - \phi$, the
observer is in an unattentive state and fails to detect the signal; in
this state, he makes judgments in accord with his expectations rather
than on the basis of what actually takes place. A straightforward
probabilistic argument shows that, on the average, the observer's
probability, j_n, of judging that a signal occurred is related to his probability of expecting a signal by the expressions

$$j_n = p_n + \phi(\lambda - p_n) \tag{2}$$

and

$$p_{n+1} = p_n + \theta(j_n - p_n) = p_n + \phi\theta(\lambda - p_n) \tag{3}$$

By inspection of Eq. 3, we note that, as in the simpler form of the model, p_n asymptotically approaches λ, the true probability of a signal. Consequently, as n becomes large, the factor $\phi(\lambda - p_n)$ on the right of Eq. 2 tends to 0, and we see that asymptotically the probability of judging that a signal took place on any trial is equal to the probability of expecting a signal, regardless of the value of the parameter ϕ (provided only that it is greater than zero).

CHOICES AND "IRRELEVANT ALTERNATIVES"

In all the experiments discussed in this section, the individual must make a choice from a specified set of alternatives. This feature is common to a broad range of experimental paradigms ranging through those of psychophysics, social psychology, and also many nonlaboratory situations involving choice or preference (for example, opinion polls and consumer preference surveys). In addition to studying the ways in which preferences among alternatives develop through learning, it is of interest to investigate the way an individual's behavioral dispositions, or choice tendencies, are organized at any given time. This problem has been the subject of analysis, first within the context of scaling theory (Thurstone 1927) and more recently in the context of theories of learning (Bower 1959; Estes 1960) and choice (Luce 1959).

A broad class of models, including Bower's Markov model for choice-point behavior and Luce's axiomatization of the static aspects of choice, share an interesting property which has been termed *independence of irrelevant alternatives*, or, following an experimental demonstration by Clarke (1957) in connection with articulation tests, the *constant-ratio rule*. The gist of this property is that the relative probabilities of choice between any two alternatives are independent of the number and value of other alternatives available for choice.

A related, but more general, property that characterizes a still broader class of choice models is the *product rule* (Estes 1960). The substance of the product rule is that, for any three members a, b, and c of a set of alternatives, if we define $p_{ab}(a)$ as the probability of choice of alternative a from the pair ab and so on, then the following relation holds:

$$\frac{p_{ab}(a)}{p_{ab}(b)} \times \frac{p_{bc}(b)}{p_{bc}(c)} = \frac{p_{ac}(a)}{p_{ac}(c)}$$

Application of the product rule for predictive purposes can be illustrated in terms of a study conducted by the author (1960). In an experiment simulating a consumer preference survey, college-student subjects were asked to choose among three color combinations for automobiles: (1) red and white, (2) blue and gray, and (3) yellow and black. The proportions of students choosing combination 1 over 2 and 2 over 3 proved to be .71 and .73, respectively. To predict the proportion choosing 1 over 3, we need only substitute .71 and $1 - .71 = .29$ for the numerator and denominator of the first factor on the left side of the product rule and .73 and .27 for the numerator and denominator of the second factor, obtaining

$$\frac{.71}{.29} \times \frac{.73}{.27} = \frac{.87}{.13}$$

The numerator on the right, .87, is the predicted proportion of students choosing 1 over 3, and comes quite close to the observed value, which was .89.

ELEMENTARY SOCIAL INTERACTIONS

The simple system of a source plus a hearer need only be modified in one respect to bring us to an elementary interactive situation that may provide a conceptual building block for the analysis of many types of social interactions. This alteration requires taking account of the fact that, in social contexts, the listener of our last example usually is not a passive receiver of messages but rather may make active efforts to modify the attitudes of the other individual or group acting as the source.

Thus let us consider the slightly more complex case of two individuals, S_1 and S_2, who are taking part in a dialogue that has the characteristics of an argument or negotiation. Again, for simplicity, let us assume that there is only one issue involved and that at a given time individual S_1 has probability p and individual S_2 has probability p' of manifesting a positive attitude on the issue. For simplicity we shall consider a sequence of occasions on which the two individuals exchange messages. Also we assume that the effects of a message produced by one individual on the attitudes of the other are described by precisely the same operators that appeared in our previous example of a hearer and a source, as summarized in Table 4.6.

A geometrical representation of the learning process can be given in terms of a point moving in two-dimensional space, as shown in

Table 4.6 Schematization of a two-person interaction in terms of the probabilities that each participant sends a message for (+) or against (–) an issue on a given trial, and the new probabilities that participants S_1 and S_2 favor the issue; a and b are parameters of rates of learning

			New Probability of Positive Attitude	
Source	Message	Message Probability	S_1	S_2
S_1	+	p	p	$p' + b(1 - p')$
	–	$1 - p$	p	$p' - bp'$
S_2	+	p'	$p + a(1 - p)$	p'
	–	$1 - p'$	$p - ap$	p'

Figure 4.14—direct generalization of the one-dimensional representation of a single individual's learning (Fig. 4.12). Because the two individuals may differ with respect to the ease of modifiability of their positions, the parameter θ of Figure 4.12 and Eqs. 1–3 has been replaced by the parameters a for participant S_1 and b for S_2 in Table 4.6. If S_1 transmits a positive message, the effect on S_2's attitude is a linear increment in his probability of manifesting a positive attitude. When S_1 sends a negative message, however, the result is a decrease in S_2's probability of manifesting a positive attitude, and just the converse describes the effects of S_2's messages on S_1.

The consequences of such continuing interaction on a series of occasions can now be described by a system of difference equations. From Table 4.6 it follows immediately that, on the average,

$$\begin{aligned} p_{n+1} &= p'_n \left[p_n + a(1 - p_n) \right] + (1 - p'_n)(p_n - ap_n) \\ &= p_n + a(p'_n - p_n) \end{aligned} \tag{4}$$

and

$$\begin{aligned} p'_{n+1} &= p_n \left[p'_n + b(1 - p'_n) \right] + (1 - p_n)(p'_n - bp'_n) \\ &= p'_n + b(p_n - p'_n) \end{aligned} \tag{5}$$

This pair of simultaneous difference equations can readily be solved by standard methods (Goldberg 1958; Jordan 1950). The solutions are somewhat cumbersome, but they exhibit a number of simple properties, as illustrated in Figure 4.15, for four special cases that differ only in the values of the constants a and b, which represent the rates of learning or, if you prefer, the degrees of rigidity of the two interacting individuals.

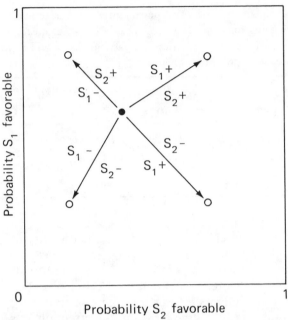

Figure 4.14 The arrows denote possible results of a single exchange of messages in a negotiation between two individuals, S_1 and S_2. The solid circle denotes the original probability of favorable opinions by the two individuals on the issue at stake, and the open circles represent their new positions after the various possible combinations of positive and negative messages.

The model predicts that in all cases the two individuals converge to a final, common level that depends on both the initial values and the slope constants. The common asymptote is given by

$$p_\infty = p'_\infty = \frac{ap'_1 + bp_1}{a + b} \tag{6}$$

From this expression it is clear, in particular, that the asymptote must always fall between the initial values, p_1 and p'_1, of the two participants.

Comparing the two upper panels of Figure 4.15, we see that the final level is closer to S_1's initial position for the case in which S_1 is the slower, or more rigid, learner; it moves in the direction of S_2's

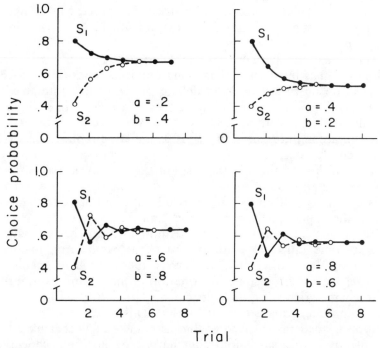

Figure 4.15 Learning-rate constants *a* and *b* control the average probabilities of positive responses by two individuals, S_1 and S_2, engaged in an argument or negotiation. For each combination, S_1 starts with probability .8 and S_2 with probability .4 of manifesting a positive attitude on the issue in question.

original position when S_2 is the more rigid of the two. Comparing the upper and lower panels, we note the interesting property that the sum of the learning-rate parameters determines whether the process is a uniform drift from the initial positions of the two participants to the final level or an oscillatory process. When the learning rates are relatively low, or the rigidity is high—as in the upper panels—there is a monotone drift from the initial to the final position; but when the learning rates are high, or the rigidity low, as in the lower panels, the process is oscillatory.

It should be noted, however, that, although the curves plotted in Figure 4.15 show the trends that would be expected on the average, they do not necessarily typify the course of the interaction that would be predicted for any pair of individuals. In fact, study of the system of difference equations derivable from Table 4.6 reveals that we are dealing with a non-ergodic stochastic process in which the only possible asymptotic states for any individual pair of participants are $p_\infty = p'_\infty = 1$ and $p_\infty = p'_\infty = 0$.

Thus the model implies that, regardless of their initial tendencies, both individuals must end up agreeing on either a positive or a negative position on the issue under debate. However, the rate at which this absorption in the extreme states takes place depends strongly on the values of the parameters a and b. When we programmed the model on a computer and ran off 500 simulated replications of the experiment for each combination of parameters represented in Figure 4.15, we found that, in the cases of the two lower panels, nearly all the simulated pairs of participants had reached one of the extreme states $p_\infty = p'_\infty = 1.00$ or $p_\infty = p'_\infty = 0.00$ by the end of 20 trials. In the cases of the upper panels, none of the simulated pairs had done so.

The point we wish to illustrate is not so much that we have arrived at some universal truths about participants in arguments or negotiations but rather that we have a method which enables us, whenever we are given some information or make some assumptions about characteristics of the participants, to derive definite predictions about the process that will ensue. This machinery is precisely the type needed in order to enable us to take facts that have been demonstrated, or assumptions that have been justified, concerning individual behavior on the basis of psychological research and bring them to bear on problems of social behavior about which we wish to make predictions. Substantial efforts of this kind have been reported by Rosenberg (1968) and Suppes and Atkinson (1960). But although, given suitable data, exact predictions are possible, it is best not to overemphasize this aspect of the enterprise. The main contribution to be expected from mathematical psychology is not the provision of exact numerical predictions concerning human behavior in practical situations, but rather the ability to analyze situations and arrive at an understanding of how the individual will contribute to the system.

The examples we have considered illustrate only two branches of current research in mathematical psychology, one arising out of the tradition of work in psychophysics and signal detectability and the other evolving from research on the application of stochastic processes to the interpretation of human learning and simple social interactions. A new and major development in the field—which can only be mentioned—is the advent of computer simulation models that are, in a way, intermediate between concrete empirical studies and the mathematical analysis of hypothetical, abstract individuals. I think we may expect to find that computer simulation models will provide a major route for examining the way in which the abstract individual enters into still more complex systems. Thus I foresee a continuing interaction between the mathematical analyses of processes in depth and the integration of results via computer simulations of problem situations (Estes, 1975).

REFERENCES

Anderson, J. A. 1973. A theory for the recognition of items from short memorized lists. *Psychol. Rev.* 80:417–38.

Atkinson, R. C., E. C. Carterette, and R. A. Kinchla. 1962. Sequential phenomena in psychophysical judgments: A theoretical analysis. In *Institute of Radio Engineers Transactions on Information Theory: Transactions of the 1962 International Symposium on Information Theory,* vol. IT-8, pp. 155–62.

Bower, G. H. 1959. Choice-point behavior. In R. R. Bush and W. K. Estes, eds., *Studies in Mathematical Learning Theory.* Stanford, Calif.: Stanford University Press, pp. 109–24.

Broadbent, D. E. 1958. *Perception and Communication.* Oxford: Pergamon Press.

——. 1971. *Decision and Stress.* N.Y.: Academic Press.

Clarke, F. R. 1957. Constant-ratio rule for confusion matrices in speech communication. *J. Acoust. Soc. Am.* 29:715–20.

Coombs, C. H., R. M. Dawes, and A. Tversky. 1970. *Mathematical Psychology.* Englewood Cliffs, N.J.: Prentice-Hall.

de Vries, H., and M. Stuiver. 1961. The absolute sensitivity of the human sense of smell. In W. A. Rosenblith, ed., *Sensory Communication.* Cambridge, Mass.: MIT Press, pp. 159–67.

Elithorn, A., and D. Jones, eds. 1973. *Artificial and Human Thinking.* San Francisco: Jossey-Bass.

Estes, W. K. 1960. A random-walk model for choice behavior. In K. J. Arrow, S. Karlin, and P. Suppes, eds., *Mathematical Methods in the Social Sciences, 1959.* Stanford, Calif.: Stanford University Press, pp. 265–76.

——. 1971. Learning and memory. In E. F. Beckenbach and C. B. Tompkins, eds., *Concepts of Communication.* N.Y.: Wiley, pp. 282–300.

——. 1972. Research and theory on the learning of probabilities. *J. Am. Statis. Assoc.* 67:81–102.

——. 1975. Some targets for mathematical psychology. *J. Math. Psychol.,* 12: 263–82.

Estes, W. K., and M. D. Johns. 1958. Probability-learning with ambiguity in the reinforcing stimulus. *Am. J. Psychol.* 71:219–28.

Estes, W. K., and P. Suppes. 1959. Foundations of linear models. In R. R. Bush and W. K. Estes, eds., *Studies in Mathematical Learning Theory.* Stanford, Calif: Stanford University Press, pp. 137–79.

Goldberg, S. 1958. *Introduction to Difference Equations.* N.Y.: Wiley.

Green, D. M., and J. A. Swets. 1966. *Signal Detection Theory and Psychophysics.* N.Y.: Wiley.

Haavelmo, T. 1958. The role of the econometrician in the advancement of economic theory. *Econometrica,* 26:351–57.

Jordan, C. 1950. *Calculus of Finite Differences.* N.Y.: Chelsea.

Luce, R. D. 1959. *Individual Choice Behavior: A Theoretical Analysis.* N.Y.: Wiley.

Miller, G. A. 1964. *Mathematics and Psychology.* N.Y.: Wiley.

Newell, A., and H. A. Simon. 1972. *Human Problem Solving.* Englewood Cliffs, N.J.: Prentice Hall.

Rosenberg, S. 1968. Mathematical models of social behavior. In G. Lindzey and E. Aronson, eds., *The Handbook of Social Psychology* (2nd ed.), vol. 1. Reading, Mass.: Addison-Wesley.

Suppes, P., and R. C. Atkinson. 1960. *Markov Learning Models for Multiperson Interactions.* Stanford, Calif.: Stanford University Press.

Swets, J. A. 1964. *Signal Detection and Recognition by Human Observers.* N.Y.: Wiley.

Tanner, W. P., and J. A. Swets, 1954. A decision-making theory of visual detection. *Psychol. Rev.* 61:401–09.

Thurstone, L. L. 1927. A law of comparative judgment. *Psychol. Rev.* 34: 273–86.

Some Targets for Mathematical Psychology

It is just about 25 years since mathematical methods and theory began to spread in a major way from their long established niche in psychological measurement and scaling into broader areas of experimental psychology, and a little over 10 years since the term "mathematical psychology" became current with the appearance almost simultaneously of the *Handbook* (Luce, Bush, & Galanter, 1963) and the first issues of the *Journal.* How can we characterize the current state of the field? In some respects very well. Certainly the volume and variety of research and the level of technical and methodological virtuosity far exceed anything that might have been reasonably anticipated a couple of decades ago. But at the same time it is clear that many investigators in our field are not entirely happy with their current situation.

A rather pointed documentation of this last remark is to be found in the introduction to the just published *Contemporary Developments in Mathematical Psychology* (which was forced into two volumes by the current pace of research): "It is easy to point to excellent work in mathematical psychology, past and present. But in retrospect, cumulative progress is less easy to find . . . without apologizing for the past, we do need to ask ourselves whether we can do better in the coming decades. Is it possible that the lack of cumulative progress is partly due to that goal being subordinated to others, such as originality or technical mastery? If so, then that goal needs to be formulated more directly, and seeking it needs to be encouraged" (Krantz, Atkinson, Luce & Suppes, 1974, xi–xii). This view is doubtless shared by many investigators in our field, but even if it were not, it would need to be taken seriously since it evidently represents the consensus of four of our most eminent contributors.

A number of comments come to mind concerning this rather sobering self-appraisal. First of all, one might note that if we lack a

W. K. Estes, Some targets for mathematical psychology. *Journal of Mathematical Psychology*, 1975, *12*, 263–282. Reprinted by permission of Academic Press, Inc.

This paper is based on an address given at the seventh annual Mathematical Psychology Meetings, Ann Arbor, MI, August, 1974.

sense of cumulative progress, the fault may to some unknown extent lie in our ability to appraise progress rather than in the state of the field itself. We are handicapped by not knowing what the end result of cumulative progress is going to be, and thus, we are not in an ideal position to evaluate the rate at which we are approaching this unknown goal. Second, we might note that cumulative progress need not necessarily be continuous. Robinson Crusoe had to fashion himself some tools before he could begin to build a house. In our case we need to accumulate a repertoire of small mathematical systems and devices that we understand before we can hope to proceed far in the building of theories. Third, and perhaps most important, I think that in discussions of this sort it is well to distinguish two aspects of mathematical psychology—development of mathematical techniques and models in conjunction with specific researches and development of mathematical psychology as a distinct specialty. The unevenness of progress in these two aspects may be a major source of some of the pains that give rise to critical self-examinations.

With regard to the first aspect, surely no one could complain about the accomplishments of the last quarter century. During the period of the early 1950's, when presentations of mathematical models were just beginning to appear as regular fare in the *Psychological Review* and the first workshops in mathematical psychology were just getting organized, what most of us wanted more than anything else was acceptance of our small subdiscipline as an integral part of experimental psychology or, more broadly, psychological research. The incorporation of mathematical psychology into various research areas, in fact, has proceeded so fast that already one finds it necessary to plod his way through a dozen journals to bring himself up to date on current mathematically oriented research in any of a large number of specific research topics, ranging from lateral interactions among receptor elements to the scanning of short-term memory, to the verification of propositions.

With regard to the second aspect, the editors of *Contemporary Developments* are not alone in looking for something beyond the ever-changing collection of methods and specific models that arise in particular research areas. It is here that we feel a lack of cumulative progress in any well-defined direction. We can note a number of symptoms of this mild malaise.

First, let us scan the overall picture of the contemporary literature. One is struck first of all by the succession of introductory textbooks with a wide range of special emphases (Atkinson, Bower, & Crothers, 1965; Coombs, Dawes, & Tversky, 1970; Restle & Greeno,

1970; Laming, 1973). It would appear that a good number of people must be learning about our field. But students or outsiders can evidently do so only at a fairly elementary level. There is a fairly steady appearance of advanced volumes but these are suitable only for specialists in specific areas. Volumes of contemporary developments, not only ours but similar collections appearing in other countries (for example Poland—Kozielecki, 1971) present a wide variety of topics, but again the individual chapters tend to be addressed only to specialists. The conspicuous lack is any body of common problems in which any major fraction of investigators in the field share concern. A sampling of the *Journal of Mathematical Psychology* over its 11-year history yields a similar picture. Articles on measurement hold constant at 10–20% of the total output, contributions to methodology and treatments of rather general processes somewhat less; about 70–75% of the articles each year are devoted to models for specific experimental areas or other treatments of topics that require expert knowledge of the details of a particular research area for comprehension.

Either gaining a foothold on this literature or keeping up with it once aboard is a difficult task even for the specialist. But consider the plight of the outsider. I have rather frequently had occasion to talk to individuals with backgrounds in mathematics, computer science, or the like, who have heard a little about mathematical psychology and would like to participate. We certainly should welcome such potential contributors, but how can we get them started? All too often, one of these individuals attends a meeting or a few seminars and then gives up, realizing that he would need a Ph.D. in some specific research area to follow the conversation, let alone to begin to participate. Typically these people wander off into genetics or economics, two fields that have in common only the characteristic that they present rather well-defined problems for mathematical attack, problems that are comprehensible to one with only a modest acquaintance with the subject matter and research methods.

Finally, some of us are finding occasion to worry a bit about a problem that mathematical psychology shares with all behavioral science disciplines with respect to their potential contributions to problems of social welfare. Many of us have hoped that mathematical psychology would prove a major vehicle for developing theoretical interrelationships between psychology and the various social sciences, thus facilitating both theoretical developments and applications. But as things have actually gone, the flourishing of new mathematical models and methods has profited various specific research areas greatly but has contributed less than we would like toward bridging the gaps between disciplines or mediating applications of social science to social problems.

What we wish for is clear enough. We would like mathematical psychology to continue to aid in the direction and interpretation of various specific lines of research. But at the same time we would like to see more cohesion and more cumulative development of mathematical psychology as a distinct specialty among the behavioral science disciplines. We would like to see it begin to present a common body of methods and problems that are understood and appreciated by nearly everyone in the field. We would like to invite participation from talented outsiders who are better skilled than we in special aspects of mathematics, computer science, or linguistics, but who are little acquainted with specific research procedures. We would like to see some common body of theory begin to take form at a more abstract level than that involved in the interpretation of memory scanning studies or lateral inhibition in the limulus—theory that might serve to promote useful interconnections between psychology and other social sciences. What could we hope to do that might help some of these wishes begin to come true?

Let me hasten to remark that I am not going to offer any firm prescriptions and most certainly I shall not propose anything of the nature of planning committees, or the turning of our meetings into sessions of agonizing self-appraisal. The substantial progress we can point to in our field, as in other areas of science, is attributable to individual enterprise and evolutionary processes. Thus, I shall suggest only that we might want to look a little harder as individuals for specific things that we might do to put our house in better order. I will offer a few comments under a number of categories.

THE DELINEATION OF PROBLEMS

Most of the time we quite naturally work on and report the results of research on relatively specific problems, having faith that in the long run generality will emerge. Faith is well enough, but it can stand supplementation on occasion by more direct efforts. One thought I have on this note is that our journals might well not only accept but even encourage articles that do not report either mathematical contributions or new empirical results, but rather report efforts to prepare problems for mathematical approaches. It is difficult enough for the specialist and impossible for the outsider to make his way through the typical welter of conflicting empirical findings and discover what pattern of quantitative relationships he should be attempting to account for in almost any of our research areas. But often it would be possible for an investigator with competence in a specific area to review the accumulation of studies, abstract the functional relationships that appear to stand up, and present an organized pattern of results that appears to call for mathematical interpretation. A timely example would be the accumulated work on spacing effects in studies of memory that was the topic of a recent symposium.[1] Although there are problems to be resolved at an empirical level with respect to various specific kinds of experiments on spacing, there also appears to be emerging a rather intriguing pattern of relationships which holds over a variety of materials and invites a more general mathematical interpretation (Glenberg, 1974; Murdock, 1974).

Reviews of this sort might on occasion lead, if not directly to theoretical efforts, to the carrying out of studies designed simply to provide the substantial body of reliable parametric data required to test and extend models. Referring again to the symposium on spacing effects, it is clear that we now have a major need for one or more studies designed simply to collect a substantial quantity of reliable data with the principal parameters varied within a single experimental situation in the fashion needed to provide adequate tests of theoretical efforts that are already under way. Further, just as is now done routinely with programs in computer science journals, the parametric data could readily be made available to mathematical psychologists. It is now so easy and inexpensive to reproduce and transmit quantities of data to interested users by means of tapes or cards that it seems a pity to continue to require every would-be quantitative theorist to serve also as his own data collector.

ON THE EVALUATION OF THEORIES AND MODELS

What problems, some will ask, can you see in the matter of testing mathematical theories? Does not one simply construct a model, apply it to data, and accept or reject on the basis of goodness of fit? Well, that is indeed a standard procedure—perhaps *the* standard procedure. The problem I wish to raise is that the procedure nonetheless may not be good enough.

---

[1] Symposium on Spacing Phenomena in Memory, Mathematical Psychology Meetings, 1974. Participants: Robert A. Bjork, Arthur Glenberg, Douglas L. Hintzman, Thomas K. Landauer, Douglas L. Medin.

It is true, up to a point, that models should describe data, and at one time achieving this purpose was no small task. I can remember the excitement when some functions derived from the early learning models of Bush, Mosteller, and myself turned out to provide reasonable descriptions of empirical learning curves for several situations with only one or two fitted parameters. Also, I can remember full summers of effort devoted to working out methods for estimating parameters in learning models, typically running to horrendous algebraic derivations, endless hours at a hand calculator, and whole chapters in books devoted to methods of estimation. All of this will seem quaintly antiquarian to students who have learned mathematical psychology during the last few years, for in major respects our field has been revolutionized by a development none of us could have anticipated 25 years ago, namely, the fantastically accelerated evolution, proliferation, and widespread use of digital computers. I think that learning to live with computers is perhaps the single most difficult and critical task facing mathematical psychology as a discipline.

The Computer Revolution

The problems raised by computers are of two different types, both having to do with the evaluation of models and theories. The first is simply that the matter of fitting models to data has suddenly become so easy that it no longer constitutes a useful method of tracing theoretical progress. Virtually any learning experiment or group of learning experiments, for example, can be described by a Markov chain model with a sufficient number of states. The fitting of the model to data is accomplished via computer programs with 4, 8, 12—virtually unlimited numbers of parameters being evaluated by computer search of the parameter space—almost completely bypassing both the opportunities for ingenuity and the quantities of blood, sweat, and tears that used to go into this enterprise. It has become almost literally the case that the fitting of a model to a set of data is primarily a test of the technical competence of the investigator and has little to do with the adequacy of the model for interpreting empirical phenomena. I do not propose that we stop fitting models to data; that we will never do. But I do believe that intensive efforts should be directed toward finding additional bases for evaluating quantitative theories.

The second aspect of the computer revolution which has raised new and, to say the least, challenging problems for us is, of course, the advent of computer simulation models—models that can be fitted to data just as readily as the more familiar mathematical models but that have no specifiable mathematical form and for which we are generally unable even to formulate, let alone solve, the problem of testing goodness of fit.

Some enthusiastic proponents of computer simulation models seem to have taken the view that if a program can be written that generates protocols closely mimicking those generated by actual experimental subjects, the problem of goodness of fit is solved and the program must be accepted as an adequate theory for the phenomenon. But despite the persuasiveness with which they are advanced, these arguments are not going to continue to satisfy us for long. If these premises had been accepted and the technology had been available, computer simulation models for the motions of the planets based on the conception of epicycles, or for the process of combustion in terms of phlogiston could never have been rejected. In learning to live with computer simulation models, it may be even more important than in the case of conventional mathematical models to find ways of augmenting the traditional conception of goodness of fit as a means of judging theoretical progress.

Predictive Power of Models

It is easier to pose the problem than to solve it, but I do think we can perceive some directions in which inquiry might be useful. The first suggestion is more serious exploration of an information-theoretic approach to model testing as distinguished from the conventional one based on statistical tests and goodness of fit. This approach has been outlined in an article by Hanna (1969) in which he brings out a number of interesting points, for example, that statistically rejected models may prove more adequate in the sense of providing information about the empirical variables influencing behavior, than statistically accepted models. The coefficient of predictive power of a model relative to a set of data that Hanna proposes is not ready for ubiquitous everyday use in that it can be directly applied only in situations where one can compute likelihood functions. Nonetheless, it might be useful to begin thinking in terms of predictive power as a complement to goodness of fit.

Sequential Model-Fitting Strategies

More generally, to the extent that our objective is a description of data in terms of models, we need to develop better means of assessing progress. A first step toward this end might be an attempt to characterize our overall strategies. It seems to me that two rather different strategies are apparent in current practice. The first of these constitutes an attempt to achieve explanatory and predictive power with respect to a class of phenomena by means of a nested sequence of experiments together with fits of a model, or more often of successive elaborations of a model, to the accumulating data. In the initial stage, a model is found that provides a satisfactory description of the data of a particular experiment. Then a new experiment is conducted involving some variation on the first and an attempt is made to fit the same model to the new data. When the attempt is unsuccessful, the model is modified or elaborated as necessary until a fit to the new data is obtained, usually with the constraint that a special case of the new model should fit the data of the original experiment.

This procedure seems to be motivated, at least in part, by the hope of reaching a point where further elaborations will be unnecessary and the model will prove capable of anticipating the results of new manipulations. In practice, however, this goal is rarely, if ever, attained; the cycle simply continues until the model becomes too cumbersome to be tractable or until the whole development is made obsolete by some new approach to the same material.

A more practical purpose of sequential model-fitting is to obtain a check on the adequacy with which our theoretical conceptions take account of the determiners of the phenomena we wish to predict. We cannot expect to achieve this end by fitting the data of a single experiment. We do research only when we lack complete understanding of a situation, and in the absence of complete understanding we may unknowingly hold constant some factors that would produce major effects if allowed to vary. In the hope of ensuring to some extent against this hazard, we do not rest with an account of one experiment, but follow the iterative procedure of introducing variations into the experiment and attempting to refit the model.

A major drawback to this sequential strategy is that we lack any fully satisfactory stopping rule. When is a description of data in terms of a model good enough? A common answer is "when deviations of observed from predicted statistics of the data fail to reach statistical significance at some conventional level." Unfortunately, this criterion depends so strongly on the power of the experiment that it is all but useless in practice. Almost any model can be accepted if the experiment is sufficiently insensitive and almost any model can be rejected if the experiment is sufficiently powerful.

The Competition Strategy

Realization of this evidently insoluble problem has led to increasing reliance on the second common strategy—competition in which a number of alternative models are compared with regard to their ability to describe the same set of data (good examples would be Atkinson & Crothers, 1964; or Bush & Mosteller, 1959). This strategy certainly has its uses, and in many instances may be the best we have available. When alternative models are available, comparisons of them on the same data nearly always prove illuminating, but they rarely lead to a choice of a single model which then continues to prove superior over the subsequent course of investigation (as witness the two examples cited above among many others which could be cited).

The principal fruits of the competition strategy are to be found in the comparison process itself, which provides an invaluable aid to the testing of scientific hypotheses. Continually we find ourselves posing questions that cannot be answered directly because the processes or mechanisms referred to cannot be supposed to act in isolation. Do drive and incentive combine additively or multiplicatively in their effects on performance? Are the items of a free recall list organized in memory in accord with a chain association or a hierarchical schema? Is a set of items maintained in a short-term memory buffer searched by a self-terminating or an exhaustive scan? To deal with such questions, one must make assumptions concerning other factors that are operative in the test situations. These assumptions, taken together with alternative hypotheses concerning the question at issue, constitute alternative models for the situation. And by determining which model provides the better fit to the test data, we can gain some evidence bearing on the merits of the alternative hypotheses.

One of the drawbacks to the competition strategy is the extreme meagerness of the literature concerning statistical testing of the relative goodness of fit of alternative models to the same data. Wholly satisfactory solutions seem to be available only in a few rare instances where maximum likelihood tests are possible or in which the models being compared are nested in such a way as to permit χ^2 tests (see, e.g., Young, 1971). Further, as in the case of the nested sequence strategy, there is no rationale to lend confidence that a succession of applications of the strategy in a given area should be expected to lead toward models of increasing generality. Most acutely, we lack any methodology for statistical testing of the descriptive adequacy of alternative computer simulation models.

To the extent that our problems in the evaluation of models arise from deficiencies in statistical methodology, there may be little that most investigators in the field can do other than to point up these problems as targets for investigations by mathematical statisticians. However, we should recognize that even if the statisticians did all that could be asked of them our problems would not all be solved. For a statistical goodness of fit is not the only criterion of descriptive adequacy of models and descriptive adequacy is not the only measure of the fertility of a model or theory in relation to research.

Categorization in Terms of Models

Pursuing this line of thought I would like to suggest another concept, which we might term the *sharpness* of a model, that is almost the antithesis rather than the complement of the standard concept of goodness of fit. We commonly speak of one of the major purposes of model construction as being that of describing data, but I do not believe that we really mean what we say. The purpose of constructing models is not to describe data, which must be described before models can be applied to them, but rather to generate new classifications or categorizations of data. It is true enough that a model that fits observations well may on occasion achieve a substantial amount of data reduction—many examples are to be seen for example in Coombs' theory of data (1964) and quite spectacular ones in applications of the constant ratio rule associated with Luce's choice model (1959). But compactness of description, however useful, is at most a facilitator of theoretical advance.

What we hope for primarily from models is that they will bring out relationships between experiments or sets of data that we would not otherwise have perceived. The fruit of an interaction between model and data should be a new categorization of phenomena in which observations are organized in terms of a rational scheme in contrast to the surface demarcations manifest in data that have only come through routine statistical processing. But it is a truth that seems obvious yet is not widely appreciated that models will not force us to new categorizations of phenomena if they are so flexible that they can always be made to fit each new experiment by suitable choices of parameter values.

Given a particular collection of observations, we generally advance our understanding but little if we find a model that will describe the entire collection with a suitable choice of parameters. But we feel that we have made a considerable advance if we find that when the collection of observations is categorized into two or more subsets along lines dictated by a particular model, we can achieve good fits to the observations within one or both categories by appropriate submodels, whereas the observations uncategorized or wrongly categorized from the standpoint of the theory remain refractory. A classical example from physics would be the categorization of phe-

nomena having to do with the propagation of light into those described by wave versus those described by corpuscular models. A
similarly familiar example occurred in the early development of the
Mendelian models in genetics where it proved necessary to categorize data into those representing the principle of random assortment
and those involving linkage. An illustration from psychology would
be Stevens' (1957) categorization of prothetic versus metathetic sensory dimensions in relation to scales of measurement.

The immediate background for these fruitful categorizations, or
recategorizations, of phenomena generally comprises a combination
of conditions: (1) A model that yields definite testable predictions;
(2) sufficient agreement with data to lend confidence that up to a
point the processes involved are understood; and (3) specific errors
of prediction that prove diagnostic of inadequacies in the conceptual
structure and point the way to theoretical advance.

ON MODELS FOR PROCESSES
VERSUS MODELS FOR EXPERIMENTS

We have observed that a principal hazard associated with an over-
preoccupation with the fitting of data is that our available strategies
for the fitting and evaluation of models provide no assurance of progress toward models that are progressively more general and more
useful in disclosing new relationships among previously isolated phenomena or theories. To move toward generality, we need deliberate
and explicit efforts to increase our understanding of variables and
processes one step more abstract than those involved in the interpretation of specific experiments. Perhaps the outstanding success story
for this approach in contemporary psychology is the development
of signal detectability theory, with its widespread applicability to
problems of perception, judgment, and memory (see, e.g., Murdock,
1974; Swets, 1964; Tanner & Swets, 1954). A still more current example would be the flourishing of scanning models both for perceptual processing and for memory search (Estes & Taylor, 1964;
Shiffrin, 1970; Sternberg, 1966) and the systematic investigation of
these processes at an abstract level by Townsend (1974) with the
resulting clarification of much-clouded issues concerning parallel
versus serial scanning processes.

There is little point in speculating as to just where in the field
the next major developments of this sort may appear, but we can
point to one where such developments are acutely needed. I refer
to research on learning and memory of verbal material, particu-

larly in relation to models for the optimization of instruction. Efforts toward the development of theoretical bases for optimization of instructional schedules (Atkinson, 1972; Chant & Atkinson, 1973; Dear, Silberman, Estavan & Atkinson, 1967) have yielded useful and even impressive results, but the applicability of the models resulting from these efforts remains severely restricted to some rather simple varieties of list learning. The reason, I believe, arises from a corresponding limitation in our models for learning and memory that, with respect to dependent variables, are almost entirely limited to a few elementary empirical measures such as frequencies or latencies of correct responses to individual items of a list. However difficult the task may be, I suspect that the attainment of optimization models of much greater generality will have to wait upon our achieving more effective ways of measuring the amount of information stored and retrieved in the course of typical experiments in learning and memory and the formulation of models in terms of transformations of information rather than changes in state of representations of individual items in memory.

MEASUREMENT, SUBSTANCE, AND ORGANIZATION

Undoubtedly the most elegant formal accomplishments of mathematical psychology are those having to do with models of measurement (see, e.g., Krantz, Luce, Suppes & Tversky, 1971). One motivation for the heavy concentration of attention on measurement has been the intrinsic interest of the mathematical problems and the possibility of finding solutions, always a winning combination. A second motivation is more substantive. From the first efforts toward psychological measurement, investigators also seem to have had in mind the goal of making progress toward generality in psychological theory by developing quantities analogous to mass, charge, and the like in physics and showing that laws and principles formulated in terms of these derived quantities would have greater generality than those formulated in terms of observables. But although there have been some substantial accomplishments in the measurement of sensory magnitudes and some strenuous, though to date not conspicuously successful, efforts to do the same for such "psychological magnitudes" as utility and subjective probability (Lee, 1971; Luce & Suppes, 1965), by and large this approach has not yielded a rich harvest in psychological research.

One reason for the relative paucity of connections between measurement theory and substantive theory in psychology may arise from the fact that models for measurement have largely been developed independently as a body of abstract formal theory with empirical interpretations being left to a later stage. The difficulty with this approach is that the later stage often fails to materialize. A fertile interaction between measurement theory and research seems more likely to evolve when a measurement model is part and parcel of a theory developed for the interpretation of a process as, for example, has been the case with Luce's (1959) model for choice behavior and Krantz's (1972) approach to magnitude estimation.

Although the classical approaches to measurement deserve and will no doubt continue to receive attention, it seems likely that in the immediate future the center of action is going to shift from the measurement of simple magnitudes and dimensions to the measurement and representation of organization in behavior. The indicators in this direction are perhaps most conspicuous in the area of human memory and language where organization and structure are the order of the day (see, e.g., Tulving & Donaldson, 1972). But although there is much talk in the current literature about organization of processes in memory and many new techniques for the testing of hypotheses about organization, there have been as yet only the most rudimentary beginnings of formal theory.

Many lines of research point to the need for hierarchical models of the organization of material in memory (e.g., Anderson & Bower, 1973; Collins & Quillian, 1972; Estes, 1972; Mandler, 1972) and one would expect that in consequence we should soon begin to see the emergence of formal theories of the type needed to interpret hierarchical relationships. Tentative suggestions have been put forward (e.g., Allen, 1971; Greeno, 1972) that graph theory may provide a natural medium for the representation of structural aspects of memory, but the suggestions seem not to have taken.

One reason, I would surmise, for the slowness with which these suggestions have borne fruit is the tendency for separation of structure and function in models for organization in psychology. Simply assuming that certain types of structures exist in memory does not in itself help to interpret processes of acquisition, retention, and retrieval of information. The challenge is to produce theories that include assumptions as to how elements of hierarchical memory structures are laid down and how the structures are transformed as a function of experience. So far, efforts of this sort have been confined largely to computer simulation models, but it does not seem

that the harnessing of structure to process need be the sole preroga-
tive of the computer simulation approach. A complementary approach that may prove fruitful is illustrated by the recent work of
Hogan (1975) who assumes that properties of a directed graph representation of memory are subject to a Markov learning process and
shows that the assumed process can be monitored in a free recall
situation by means of overt rehearsal.

A CASE HISTORY: MATHEMATICAL AND COMPUTER MODELS FOR PAIRED-ASSOCIATE LEARNING

A number of points discussed in the preceding sections can be conveniently illustrated in terms of the development of models for
paired-associate learning that flourished during the 1960's. This line
of research was projected almost instantaneously into a position of
high visibility by the discovery that extremely simple two-state
Markovian, "one-element," models could provide strikingly accurate
accounts, not only of the course of acquisition, but of numerous
fine-grain statistics (e.g., variances, distributions of success and error
runs, serial correlations) of the data of certain paired-associate learning experiments (Bower, 1961; Estes, 1961).

For the experiments initially treated, there was literally almost
no room for improvement on the closeness of fit of models to data.
However, the sequential strategy of modifying the experimental
paradigm and refitting the model was set in motion and it soon became apparent that the models were adequate only for a limited
class of experiments involving lists of dissimilar stimuli with exactly
two response alternatives. It was shown, for example, by Estes and
DaPolito (1967) that with more than two response alternatives, the
one-element model provided an adequate account of recognition
data but broke down in the case of recall data. Continuing efforts to
achieve descriptive adequacy for a broader range of conditions then
branched into two quite disparate courses, one utilizing mathematical
models and the other computer simulation techniques.

In the first branch, a study by Polson, Restle, and Polson (1967)
generated a useful categorization, based on a specific deviation of
data from the baseline model. These investigators included pairs
of confusable items in a list of distinctive items. They found that the
data for the distinctive items were adequately handled by the one-
element model but the confusable items required the addition of a

discrimination process, which again could be described by a two-state Markov model.

Investigators who attempted to deal with the learning of longer lists with multiple response alternatives and varying degrees of confusability on both stimulus and response dimensions almost unfailingly found it necessary to elaborate the one-element model by incorporating one or more forgetting processes. Thus, there appeared the "long-short" models proposed by Atkinson and Crothers (1964), and a related model explored by Greeno (1967), all including both short- and long-term memory states deriving from the Atkinson and Shiffrin (1968) system; a "forgetting model" advanced by Bernbach (1965) which bypassed the long-short distinction but included an intermediate state of partial learning; and then a four-state "general forgetting theory" (GFT), first presented by Bjork (1966) and subsequently shown by Rumelhart (1967) to include all of the others as special cases.

The GFT enlarged the empirical scope of this family of models by providing for the representation of spacing effects. However, Young (1971), after satisfying himself that no variant of GFT could account both for the nonmonotone effect of interval between study trials and the advantage of interspersing study with test trials, brought this line of model construction to its presently maximal height of complexity. His five-state, seven-parameter model, incorporating multiple short-term memory states, does bring the two vagrant empirical relationships into the fold, though at the cost of a strenuous and intricate procedure of parameter estimation.

Now, how can we evaluate the theoretical progress associated with this sequence of elaborations on both experiments and models? If we take a full description of data in terms of a model as the primary goal, the answer is uncertain. On the one hand, the GFT and Young's extension provide rather impressive accounts of a considerable range of data. On the other hand, as the number of parameters has become large, the pattern of estimated values has tended to vary over experiments in an uninterpretable fashion and the tradeoff between parameters has lessened the value of discrepancies between observed and predicted data for diagnosing the contributions of underlying processes. Further, we can exhibit no tangible grounds for believing that we have reached a point of convergence of theory and observed phenomena such that we can expect the next variations on the experimental paradigm to be accommodated without still additional elaborations of the models.

If, however, we take the main purpose of developing models to be that of aiding in the identification of processes and generating significant classifications of phenomena, then the picture is brighter. We have mentioned the role of specific shortcomings of the one-element model in pointing to a separation of associative and discriminative processes. Similarly, the pattern of discrepancies between theory and data that was generated by the rather massive effort of Atkinson and Crothers (1964) to treat a collection of some eight experiments in terms of long-short models led to the hypothesizing of a trial-dependent forgetting process. The nature of the dependence is a direct relationship between the probability of forgetting of an item between two presentations and the number of intervening items that are in an unlearned state. This idea was followed up by Calfee (1968), who showed that beyond a lag of zero items, spacing effects on paired-associate acquisition were negligible if the number of unlearned items currently being processed was taken into account. And on still another tack, Humphreys and Greeno (1970) utilized a special case of GFT effectively in conjunction with an experiment in which both stimulus and response difficulty were varied for the purpose of testing alternative hypotheses concerning the stages of paired-associate acquisition. Interpretation of their data within the framework of the model yielded evidence favoring the hypothesis that the subject first stores a representation of a stimulus–response pair as a unit in memory, then in a second stage learns a retrieval route to the stored representation.

The goal of encompassing a still wider range of paired-associate data within a single model certainly is not in sight, and begins to appear not so much unattainable as unattractive. The Markovian models have served rather effectively in the generation and interpretation of research on paired-associate learning, but their usefulness in these respects has not been obviously furthered by increasing complexity of the models.

There is less to be said about computer simulation models for paired-associate learning since the literature to date is largely confined to work associated with the EPAM model originated by Feigenbaum (1963). The basic model includes two learning processes, image building and discrimination [closely parallel to the associative and discriminative processes identified by Polson, Restle & Polson (1967)] and a sorting mechanism that generates recognition by sifting input stimuli through the network of images of stimulus-response pairs laid down during preceding acquisition trials. In general, the course of successive variation of experimental paradigms and elaborations of the model proceeds in much the same way as with the more traditional mathematical models. In one of the few studies that has been reported in detail, a third edition of EPAM was applied to several paired-associate experiments involving variations in similarity and meaningfulness of items (Simon & Feigenbaum, 1964) and statistics computed for simulated protocols proved to yield quite satisfactory fits to the group data.

As with the Markovian models it is difficult to give any formal evaluation of the goodness of fit that has been achieved, and the more interesting fruits of the approaches are to be found in byproducts of the data-fitting. Thus, Simon and Feigenbaum concluded that a satisfactory interpretation of results on intralist similarity requires the assumption that subjects recode CVC's in terms of auditory features. And in the course of fitting other data, Simon and Feigenbaum arrived at an interesting hypothesis (which seems not to have been definitively followed up) to the effect that both meaningfulness and familiarity of items, as manifest in paired-associate learning, are generated by the same familiarization process.

Finally, by means of an interesting variation on the usual protocol-fitting procedure, Hintzman (1968) showed that one can work within the framework of a computer simulation model, just as has been more commonly done with mathematical models, to explicate properties of a single process that is assumed to be operative in many situations. Hintzman simplified the EPAM model, retaining only the discriminative mechanism and subsuming other aspects under random error. Then he was able to provide a useful evaluation of the adequacy of the assumed discriminative process by generating qualitative accounts of the pertinent empirical relationships in a rather extensive range of paired-associate experiments.

Trends In Paired-Associate Models

Judging by the dates in the reference list of this article, the wave of concentrated effort directed toward the interpretation of paired-associate learning in terms of formal models has somewhat subsided. How should we appraise the present state and the likely lines of continuation?

As a consequence of the various efforts toward model construction, it begins to seem clear that formal theory must continue to develop at several distinct levels—at the least those associated with individual items, lists, and vocabularies. Prior to the emergence of Hull's behavior theory, research on paired-associate learning was oriented toward measures of performance on a list of items, for example, trials to reach a criterion of an errorless cycle through the list. Progress toward theory was retarded by the lack of any rationale relating these measures to the systematic dependent variables of either association or conditioning theory.

The first major breakthrough was Gibson's (1940) interpretation of the acquisition of paired-associate items in terms of reinforcement concepts. The association between the stimulus and response terms of an item was the unit of analysis and the effects of similarity and interference among items were treated in terms of generalization and differentiation. The sequence of mathematical models running from the simplest one-element and linear models through GFT all were developed within the same framework, assumptions concerning both acquisition and retention being formulated with reference to memory and performance states of individual items.

Only with the advent of the EPAM model have we seen a major departure from the focus on the item as a unit. Paired-associate acquisition has come to be conceived of in terms of the growth of an associative structure in which the information represented concerning any item depends on the properties of the list in which the given item is embedded. This assumption of list-dependent accrual of item information has not been incorporated into mathematical, as distinguished from computer simulation, models, no doubt owing to considerations of tractability. Whether such a development is feasible at all may turn on the possibility of formulating process assumptions in terms of higher-order dependent variables, as, for example, some measure of the total amount of information stored or the amount retrievable concerning a list of items as a whole.

But new challenges to the construction of theories do not end here. Anderson and Bower (1973) have criticized the EPAM models on the ground that they do not take adequate account of the relationships of new items to the learner's current state of semantic memory. In Anderson and Bower's simulation model (dubbed HAM) the theoretical frame of reference is again broadened and what is learned about a new item on a paired-associate acquisition trial depends on the entire associative network built up during the individual's previous relevant experience, for example, his entire vocabulary in the case of acquisition of words of a second language.

Although the concepts and assumptions of Anderson and Bower's model, or the related one of Rumelhart, Lindsay, and Norman (1972), present too complex an ensemble to invite attempts at comprehensive mathematical formulation, it is too early to predict the further course of theoretical development with much assurance. It may prove that aspects of the memory structures conceived in these models can be represented and studied effectively in terms of branches of mathematics, for example, topology or graph theory, that are so far largely untried in this context. More immediately, investigators may find that computer models sufficiently elaborate to encompass syntactic and semantic aspects of verbal learning will not provide an adequate substitute for mathematical models as a medium for reasoning about abstract relationships among phenomena. Thus, we may see increasingly frequent application of a strategy in which a simulation model provides the framework for investigation and then fragments or subsystems of the model are expressed in mathematical form to permit deeper analysis of the dynamic properties of real-time processes. An excellent illustration of this strategy is to be seen in the treatment of sentence memory by Anderson and Bower (1973, Chap. 10).

Models or Theory?

Numerous rather impressive results have been achieved at the level of formulating models that provide close accounts of specific empirical relationships in situations where many other factors are held constant. Efforts toward a broader synthesis have largely been limited to the development of more complex models that include simpler predecessors as special cases. These efforts have taken two somewhat complementary forms. The stochastic models of the family dubbed "general forgetting theory" and the Atkinson-Shiffrin system incorporate processes having to do with the dynamics of acquisition and retention. Computer simulation models of the EPAM-HAM family embody processes having to do with the encoding and discrimination of information concerning similarities and semantic relationships among items.

In what direction should we look for further progress toward a theory, as distinguished from a collection of models? Still more complex models of either type can, and well may, be constructed, but it is not clear that these will effectively serve the purposes we have identified as the principal *raison d'etre* for formal models in research. More might be accomplished by systematic efforts to organize the information that has been gained from model-oriented research concerning constituent processes and to generate a theoretically significant classification of the phenomena of paired-associate learning in terms of the combinations of processes implicated in various situations.

CONCLUDING COMMENT

It might seem that mathematical psychology has had problems enough trying to gain a foothold in terrain that as yet offers only meager material for formal theory. But on top of these, our discipline finds itself confronted with a state of affairs which in clinical quarters might be termed an identity crisis. Suddenly, the all but omnipresent computers are taking over one after another of the functions formerly served only by mathematics. It seems that many of the things mathematical psychologists have learned to do with much effort the programmer can already do faster and better. Is mathematical psychology in danger of becoming obsolescent before reaching maturity?

A review of the current situation suggests rather that there are more than enough problems to go around and that mathematical and computer simulation models may prove more complementary than competitive. The computer program offers means of working with ideas that are insufficiently explicit for mathematical expression and techniques for simulating behavioral protocols that are too complex to be fitted by tractable mathematical models. But mathematics remains our principal vehicle for the flights of imagination that smooth our experiences and extract from varying contexts the relationships that would hold among events under idealized noise-free conditions. These abstract representations are not necessarily closely descriptive of data obtained in real noise-filled environments, but in the course of interactions with data they generate the reorganizations of our ideas that constitute new theory.

We cannot be sure that we have identified all of the reasons why mathematical psychology falls short of realizing our most ambitious aspirations with regard to cumulative impact on the field. But it does seem apparent that one major reason has to do with the fact that our long-term objectives are rarely kept sufficiently in mind during the course of our day to day research to have much influence on our choice of actions.

Although it is unrealistic to hope for changes on a grand scale, small measures that might yield tangible benefits are surely within our hands. We might, for example, cultivate just a bit more dissatisfaction with the assumption that if we attend devotedly enough to the fitting of models to data the problem of generality will take care of itself. Or with the assumption that, if we devote most of our efforts to dealing in isolation with measurement or with substance, with structure or with process, these strands will magically come together to form harmonious theories. Perhaps we need to shift the allocation of our processing capacity from virtually 100% concentration on tactics to a division that allows for some day to day consideration of strategy.

It is interesting to note that two investigators who have recently surveyed problems of mathematical models in psychology from a cultural standpoint somewhat different than that of the editors of our *Contemporary Developments* have arrived at a rather similar diagnosis and prescription:

> An analysis of the present situation shows that contemporary psychology and contemporary mathematical instruments are still not compatible enough with one another to allow mathematization to assume a central place in the development of psychological knowledge; the reason for this is not merely the low level of sophistication of the latter but also the lack of sufficiently sophisticated mathematical instruments that are especially adapted for use in psychology. What is required is a continual interaction between mathematics and psychology, an interaction that on the one hand would lead to a restructuring of psychological theories into forms more amenable to the proposed mathematical instruments and, on the other, to a revision of existing mathematical methods into forms more amenable to the proposed mathematized conceptual systems. (Leont'ev & Dzhafarov, 1974, p. 20).

REFERENCES

Allen, M. Graph theory, organization, and memory. Paper given at the meetings of the Eastern Psychological Association, New York, April, 1971.

Anderson, J. R., & Bower, G. H. *Human associative memory*. Washington, D.C.: V. H. Winston & Sons, 1973.

Atkinson, R. C. Optimizing the learning of a second-language vocabulary. *Journal of Experimental Psychology*, 1972, 96, 124–129.

Atkinson, R. C., Bower, G. H., & Crothers, E. J. *An introduction to mathematical learning theory*. New York: John Wiley & Sons, 1965.

Atkinson, R. C., & Crothers, E. J. A comparison of paired-associate learning models having different acquisition and retention axioms. *Journal of Mathematical Psychology*, 1964, 1, 285–315.

Atkinson, R. C., & Shiffrin, R. M. Human memory: A proposed system and its control processes. In K. W. Spence and J. T. Spence (Eds.), *The psychology of learning and motivation: Advances in research and theory*. Vol. 2. New York: Academic Press, 1968. Pp. 89–195.

Bernbach, H. A. A forgetting model for paired-associate learning. *Journal of Mathematical Psychology*, 1965, 2, 128–144.

Bjork, R. A. Learning and short-term retention of paired-associates in relation to specific sequences of interpresentation intervals. Technical Report #106, Institute for Mathematical Studies in the Social Sciences, Stanford University, 1966.

Bower, G. H. Application of a model to paired-associate learning. *Psychometrika*, 1961, 26, 255–280.

Bush, R. R., & Mosteller, F. A comparison of eight models. In R. R. Bush and W. K. Estes (Eds.), *Studies in mathematical learning theory*. Stanford, CA: Stanford University Press, 1959. Pp. 293–307.

Calfee, R. C. Interpresentation effects in paired-associate learning. *Journal of Verbal Learning and Verbal Behavior*, 1968, **7**, 1030-1036.

Chant, V. G., & Atkinson, R. C. Optimal allocation of instructional effort to interrelated learning strands. *Journal of Mathematical Psychology*, 1973, **10**, 1-25.

Collins, A. M., & Quillian, M. R. How to make a language user. In E. Tulving & W. Donaldson (Eds.), *Organization of memory*. New York: Academic Press, 1972. Pp. 309-351.

Coombs, C. H. *A theory of data*. New York: John Wiley & Sons, 1964.

Coombs, C. H., Dawes, R. M., & Tversky, A. *Mathematical psychology*. Englewood Cliffs, NJ: Prentice-Hall, Inc., 1970.

Dear, R. E., Silberman, H. F., Estavan, D. P., & Atkinson, R. C. An optimal strategy for the presentation of paired-associate items. *Behavioral Science*, 1967, **12**, 1-13.

Estes, W. K. New developments in statistical behavior theory: Differential tests of axioms for associative learning. *Psychometrika*, 1961, **26**, 73-84.

Estes, W. K. An associative basis for coding and organization in memory. In A. W. Melton and E. Martin (Eds.), *Coding processes in human memory*. Washington, D.C.: V. H. Winston & Sons, 1972. Pp. 161-190.

Estes, W. K., & DaPolito, F. Independent variation of information storage and retrieval processes in paired-associate learning. *Journal of Experimental Psychology*, 1967, **75**, 18-26.

Estes, W. K., & Taylor, H. A. A detection method and probabilistic models for assessing information processing from brief visual displays. *Proceedings of the National Academy of Sciences*, 1964, **52**, 446-454.

Feigenbaum, E. A. Simulation of verbal learning behavior. In E. A. Feigenbaum and J. Feldman (Eds.), *Computers and thought*. New York: McGraw-Hill, 1963. Pp. 297-309.

Gibson, E. J. A systematic application of the concepts of generalization and differentiation to verbal learning. *Psychological Review*, 1940, **47**, 196-229.

Glenberg, A. M. Retrieval factors and the lag effect. Ph.D. dissertation, University of Michigan, 1974.

Greeno, J. G. Paired-associate learning with short-term retention: Mathematical analysis and data regarding identification of parameters. *Journal of Mathematical Psychology*, 1967, **4**, 430-472.

Greeno, J. G. On the acquisition of a simple cognitive structure. In E. Tulving & W. Donaldson (Eds.), *Organization of memory*. New York: Academic Press, 1972. Pp. 352-377.

Hanna, J. F. Some information measures for testing stochastic models. *Journal of Mathematical Psychology*, 1969, **6**, 294-311.

Hintzman, D. L. Explorations with a discrimination net model for paired-associate learning. *Journal of Mathematical Psychology*, 1968, **5**, 123-162.

Hogan, R. M. Inter-item encoding and directed search. *Memory and Cognition*, 1975, **3**, 197-209.

Humphreys, M., & Greeno, J. G. Interpretation of the two-stage analysis of paired-associate memorizing. *Journal of Mathematical Psychology*, 1970, **7**, 275-292.

Kozielecki, J. (Ed.), *Problems of mathematical psychology*. Warsaw: PWN, 1971.

Krantz, D. H. A theory of magnitude estimation and cross-modality matching. *Journal of Mathematical Psychology*, 1972, **9**, 168–199.

Krantz, D. H., Atkinson, R. C., Luce, R. D., & Suppes, P. (Eds.), *Contemporary developments in mathematical psychology. Vol. 1. Learning, memory, and thinking*. San Francisco: W. H. Freeman, 1974.

Krantz, D. H., Luce, R. D., Suppes, P., & Tversky, A. *Foundations of measurement*. New York: Academic Press, 1971.

Laming, D. *Mathematical psychology*. New York: Academic Press, 1973.

Lee, W. *Decision theory and human behavior*. New York: John Wiley & Sons, 1971.

Leont'ev, A. N., & Dzhafarov, E. N. Mathematical modeling in psychology. *Soviet Psychology*, 1974, **122**, 3–22.

Luce, R. D. *Individual choice behavior*. New York: John Wiley & Sons, 1959.

Luce, R. D., Bush, R. R., & Galanter, E. (Eds.), *Handbook of mathematical psychology*. Vol. 1. New York: John Wiley & Sons, 1963.

Luce, R. D., & Suppes, P. Preference, utility, and subjective probability. In R. D. Luce, R. R. Bush, and E. Galanter (Eds.), *Handbook of mathematical psychology*. Vol. 3. New York: John Wiley & Sons, 1965. Pp. 249–410.

Mandler, G. Organization and recognition. In E. Tulving and W. Donaldson (Eds.), *Organization of memory*. New York: Academic Press, 1972. Pp. 139–166.

Murdock, B. B., Jr. *Human memory: theory and data*. New York: John Wiley & Sons, 1974.

Polson, M. C., Restle, F., & Polson, P. G. Association and discrimination in paired-associate learning. In E. D. Neimark & W. K. Estes (Eds.), *Stimulus sampling theory*. San Francisco, Holden-Day, 1967. Pp. 231–239.

Restle, F., & Greeno, J. G. *Introduction to mathematical psychology*. Reading, MA: Addison-Wesley, 1970.

Rumelhart, D. E. The effects of interpretation intervals on performance in a continuous paired-associate task. Technical Report #116, Institute for Mathematical Studies in the Social Sciences, Stanford University, 1967.

Rumelhart, D. E., Lindsay, P. H., & Norman, D. A. A process model for long-term memory. In E. Tulving & W. Donaldson (Eds.), *Organization of memory*. New York: Academic Press, 1972. Pp. 197–246.

Shiffrin, R. M. Memory search. In D. A. Norman (Ed.), *Models of human memory*. New York: Academic Press, 1970. Pp. 375–447.

Simon, H. A., & Feigenbaum, E. A. An information-processing theory of some effects of similarity, familiarity, and meaningfulness in verbal learning. *Journal of Verbal Learning and Verbal Behavior*, 1964, **3**, 385–396.

Sternberg, S. High-speed scanning in human memory. *Science*, 1966, **153**, 652–654.

Stevens, S. S. On the psychophysical law. *Psychological Review*, 1957, **64**, 153–181.

Swets, J. A. *Signal detection and recognition by human observers*. New York: John Wiley & Sons, 1964.

Tanner, W. P., & Swets, J. A. A decision-making theory of visual detection. *Psychological Review*, 1954, **61**, 401–409.

Townsend, J. T. Issues and models concerning the processing of a finite number of inputs. In B. H. Kantowitz (Ed.), *Human information processing: tutorials in performance and cognition*. Hillsdale, NJ: Erlbaum Associates, 1974. Pp. 133–185.

Tulving, E., & Donaldson, W. (Eds.), *Organization of memory*. New York: Academic Press, 1972.

Young, J. L. Reinforcement-test intervals in paired-associate learning. *Journal of Mathematical Psychology*, 1971, **8**, 58–81.

5

Issues in Method and Theory: Some Afterthoughts

REFLECTIONS ON ORIENTATION AND STRATEGY

The models and research developments represented in this book are linked theoretically at various levels in ways brought out in the introductions to Chapters 2, 3, and 4. A coherence also results, however, from the characteristic theoretical orientation and strategic preferences of a single investigator. These were described in Chapter 1, essentially as they appeared to me early in my scientific career. Now it may be of interest to comment on the way they have worked out in conjunction with research over several decades. I shall limit this discussion to three motifs that are related to controversies or debates currently live in the psychological literature: the general issue of continuity, reliance on laboratory experimentation as the principal basis for evaluating theories, and the role of formal models.

Continuity

In the context of theory construction, the notion of continuity appears in two senses. One has to do with a relation between older and newer theories or models for the same domain. In this sense, continuity refers to a relation whereby newer theories include predecessors as special cases. The other sense of continuity refers to relationships between models relating to phenomena at different ontogenetic or phylogenetic levels.

Continuity in the first sense has been recognized as an important attribute of models in many sciences, and its value would seem to come into question only to the extent that there is a trade-off between preserving continuity and taking advantage of the value of important, entirely new metaphors from other fields or undertaking theoretical revisions that depart radically from a prior framework (as in the paradigm shifts of Thomas Kuhn).

During the past twenty years or so in cognitive psychology, the values of discontinuity have been rather more conspicuous. The field has seemed to advance by discrete jumps on the importation of Piaget's conception of stages, information theory, Chomsky's approach to linguistics, and information-processing conceptions based on the computer metaphor. As I have indicated elsewhere (Estes, 1976a, 1978), I fully recognize the catalytic value of these interactions between cognitive psychology and other domains and the often sharp changes in theoretical outlook that have resulted from them. At the same time, a consequence of these discontinuities, perhaps inevitable, is a lack of cumulative theoretical progress that many investigators find unsatisfying.

In my own work, I think I have been stimulated as anyone by new metaphors and interactions with other disciplines, yet I have made a fairly consistent effort to make decisions on the side of continuity when possible in the course of developing new models and revising old ones. I can find little to say by way of evaluating this balanced approach, but the way it has been working out in practice will be apparent in subsequent sections on two specific research themes.

The issue of continuity in the other sense, pertaining to ontogenetic and phylogenetic levels, is most clearly exemplified in my long-term efforts to work toward a general interpretation of reinforcement in learning at both animal and human levels. Here, I am as impressed as anyone with the complex ways in which the predominantly verbal cognitive processes of adult human beings tend to override more primitive mechanisms involved in the control of behavior. At the same time, I remain convinced that we can hope to understand the processes that guide adult human behavior only within a rather broad framework in which they can be meaningfully related both to the more primitive or elementary processes from which they develop during the life of the individual and to those of lower organisms.

A human being is, first, an organism and thus a product of evolution. Typically, evolution works through endless variations on a limited repertory of themes. Similar mechanisms for accomplishing the same functions appear at many stages and levels of both phylogeny and ontogeny, and, as a consequence, clues to understanding complex processes of human cognition sometimes come from studying simpler forms. I find little enlightenment either in the pronounce- by some scientists that animal and human behavior are funda- mentally different or in debates concerning the extent to which we can extrapolate laws of conditioning and learning to the control of human behavior. Although there may be an element of subjectivity in the judgment, however, I think my researches on reinforcement and learning have yielded some rewards for continuing efforts to reformulate laws and principles arising from the animal laboratory in the light of facts of human behavior so as to generate more general principles that apply to both in special cases.

On Research Style, Artificiality, and Ecological Validity

Even within a fairly limited scientific area, such as experimental or cognitive psychology, one finds diverse styles of investigation. My own style, as one might induce from the samplings presented in this volume, has always depended heavily on the experimental investiga- tion of behavioral phenomena in the laboratory, together with closely related efforts to generalize and interpret the results by constructing models—first, models that are limited in scope and closely tied to particular kinds of experiments but then, over longer periods of time, models that are linked or generalized to form broader bodies of theory. At present in cognitive science, the re- search style most conspicuously different from mine is that of investigators who largely abjure experimental analysis of phenomena and construction of limited models, preferring instead to rely on construction of large-scale computer-simulation models and the test- ing of these against observations of behavior in everyday life settings (Schank, 1976).

Opinions on the relative merits of the differing approaches run so strong in some quarters that, for example, on may find in the statement of editorial policy of a major journal in the area of cogni- tive science that papers are considered inappropriate for publication in the journal unless the work involves the use of "computer simula- tion models of intelligent behavior."[1] In a less polemic context, a recent major review of research on human visual cognition (Seymour, 1979) presents and illustrates both viewpoints and suggests that, although the experimental approach has led to considerable progress in some respects, there are limits to what it can possibly accomplish with regard to interpreting cognitive processes.

How does one decide whether a scientific approach works—that is, contributes in the way one hopes for? The immediate answer, of course, is that it must result, over a reasonable period, in the accumulation of a coherent body of theory, which, in turn, plays a demonstrable role in the generation of new findings. The value of the theory and the findings both are then evaluated in terms of the degree to which they interest and influence investigators in the field. One might object that, to some extent, this criterion operates only within a closed system and that it is reasonable to expect the results of research to have implications for practical problems of importance outside the laboratory. The demand seems fair enough, but determining whether it is being satisfied is not so easy. Important practical applications are fine sources of evidence when they occur, but they are so sparsely distributed in the history of any science that it is not reasonable to look for them in any one discipline within a relatively short time span. A fairer demand, it seems to me, is that one should be able to see that individuals who know something about a given body of theory and research results are, on that account, better prepared to deal with some kinds of practical problems outside the laboratory. I am not going to try to assemble a box score that could be hoped to influence critics of my preferred style of research; however, for a rough evaluation of how the approach is working I find relevant the substantial number of former students and associates in this line of research who now are working in applied areas (health sciences, business, industry, education) and who seem to believe that what they have learned and are learning from the experimental-modeling approach to human cognition and learning is useful to them.

At the same time, I can see nothing good to be said for complacency. Currently, one sees a good deal of discussion in the literature concerning the importance of ecological validity of experimentation. This concept reflects the concern of many psychologists and others that research conducted in the laboratory may yield a closed body of theory that serves only to interpret and predict behavior in the laboratory. It certainly is true that most experimental methods and designs arise from previous research rather than from attempts to sample everyday life situations, and the concern that the standard approach might lead to a closed system needs to be addressed.

Why should one not be satisfied simply with the defense offered by some experimentalists—that the human being, or any organism, is the same organism and uses the same brain and nervous system in reacting to stimuli, learning, and solving problems inside the laboratory as it does outside, and hence that one may study the workings of the brain and therefore the mind as well in one context as the other? The principal answer to that defense is that organisms are complex, and their behavior nearly always reflects multiple sources of influence. Further, these sources of influence often interact in their effects, and one cannot hope to understand the complex system by studying interacting variables or processes singly, nor by studying only certain combinations and ignoring others, with the risk of missing important interactions that are implicated in the normal behavior of the system.

That argument is a bit abstract, but it can be made more concrete by illustration in terms of the specific notion of context dependence. Important aspects of behavior, ranging from changes in coloration of some animals' coats in relation to changing habitats or seasons to processes of human perception and memory, are known to depend importantly on the context in which the behavior occurs. Thus, there would seem to be no hope of understanding in any general way the capabilities or processes involved in an organism's learning or cognitive activities unless these are studied in relation to all the relevant kinds of contexts.

This issue has been pointed up in an important way by Atkinson and Shiffrin (1968) in their distinction between structural and control processes. *Structural* refers to abilities or processes that are, to an important degree, invariant over individuals within a normal population, and over time and particular variations in task demands on the part of any individual. *Control processes*, in contrast, are strongly dependent on the learning history of the individual and the task demands of the situation in which behavior is studied or tested. The control processes that will be operative when an individual is studied in a laboratory situation necessarily will depend on relations between that situation and others in which previous learning has occurred, hence the reinforcement of concerns about ecological validity. How to answer these concerns is another matter. For my own part, I can see no value in the commonly expressed idea that one should simply give up simplified laboratory experiments and construct experiments so that they resemble natural life situations as closely as possible. The difficulty with that idea is that, in everyday life situations, we do not know what factors are influencing an individual's behavior or how they are interacting, and hence we have no way of generalizing what is found from one situation to another.

What one can do is to enlarge one's perspective so that the relationship between a laboratory environment and situations of interest outside are brought into the research in a systematic way. That is, one can view an experiment not solely as a realization of certain theoretically significant requirements but also as a simulation of selected aspects of interesting nonlaboratory situations in the controlled laboratory environment. The degree to which these limited simulations actually do tap the relevant features of the non-laboratory situation can only be checked out by a continuing process of hypothesis and experiment, proceeding just as in any research but extending over a longer time span than single laboratory experiments do. The view I am expressing is by no means idiosyncratic. In fact, it is very well illustrated by substantial continuing efforts of many current investigators in the cognitive area, such as J. R. Anderson (1976), Atkinson (1975), Bjork (1978), Greeno (1980), and Kahneman and Tversky (1979). I do not claim to be a pacesetter in this regard, but instances of this motif can be seen clearly in a number of lines of my own research—for example, the study of discrimination learning in experimental situations contrived to simulate some aspects of medical diagnostic problems (Estes, 1972a), the nature of reinforcement in learning situations arranged to resemble the task of an aircraft controller (Estes, 1972b), or probability learning in situations designed to simulate some aspects of the way people learn from the results of opinion polls or preference surveys (Estes, 1976b).

Suggestions that there are inherent limitations on the approach to mental processes by way of experimentation and model construction are puzzling to me. I am unable to see how one could arrive at any informed opinion about the matter without knowing what the results will be of all the enlightenment that ultimately will be possible from all sources. I take the suggestions not as arguments open to any kind of objective evaluation but rather as expressions of impatience with the sometimes frustratingly slow progress that we are able to make on very difficult problems. A student of the history of older sciences may well find that similar expressions of dissatisfaction with the experimental method have often occurred, even in areas where the method has gone on to yield many new and at the time unsuspected findings. Looking at the other side of the coin, it is not clear to me on what grounds one should expect large-scale computer-simulation studies of cognitive activity to yield any insight into actual human cognitive and learning processes unless, in the course of time, the results of the simulation approach are brought into progressively sharper confrontations with fact under the discipline of the experimental approach.

The Role of Models

Although the hazards of premature quantification and excessive formalization of theories are often urged on psychologists, I have never found it interesting to engage in debates on such matters. Debates on methodology are unlikely to be fruitful in the absence of clear definitions. I suppose formalization is premature or excessive when it has not paid off, but then the issue is caught in a tautology. It would be another matter if one could know in advance what methods will pay off at a given time in a given area, but, if that were possible, science would not be as interesting or challenging as we know it to be. Perhaps the worry to some minds is that there may be a necessary trade-off between formalization and creativity. It is entirely possible that individuals who do not take to mathematical thinking may be more creative if they are not required to study mathematics. Individuals who do take to mathematical thinking, however, may be more creative by virtue of exploiting it. Although it is hard to be objective about such matters, I think my own research provides at least one case history supporting this diagnosis.

In my experience, both as an investigator and as an observer of other psychologists, the greatest bar to creativity is not rigidity arising from formalization but rather the illusion of understanding arising from vague and imprecise theorizing. The scientific problem-solving activities that, when we are fortunate, eventuate in creativity, are most surely instigated by occasions when we perceive clearly that we fail to understand a phenomenon. Time and again in my research, the occasion for a new insight has been the stubborn failure of a model incorporating what I know and think I understand about a phenomenon to predict correctly the result of some new variation in conditions. Among examples that come immediately to mind are findings on pattern coding in human discrimination learning (Estes & Hopkins, 1961; Estes, 1957, 1972a), the nature of the memory representation in human choice learning (the first paper reprinted in Chapter 3), and the multilevel representation of positional information in short-term memory for order of events (Lee & Estes, 1981). I have characterized the quality of models that makes these fruitful confrontations with data possible as *sharpness* in the more extended discussion given in the final paper in Chapter 4.

More generally, I have found that mathematical psychology, broadly defined, has a dual role in the research enterprise. One of its roles is to constitute a core specialty within which analytical researches may be carried out on formal methods and models (of the kind that characteristically appear in the *Journal of Mathematical Psychology*, for example) yet often seem too esoteric to be of interest to many researchers. The other role is to effect the diffusion of theoretical concepts and methods arising within the core specialty into research areas where they give rise to the wide variety of specific experimentally oriented models that are used ubiquitously in the formulation of research problems and the interpretation of results. My own activity has fluctuated continually between the two aspects.

REINFORCEMENT AND LEARNING

The dominant theme in my long-term efforts to help resolve issues regarding learning and reinforcement was set by a paradox that engaged the attention of investigators in this area at the time I entered the field and for many years thereafter. The question at issue was how to accommodate theoretically both the massive accumulation of detailed knowledge about the learning of animals in specific situations (T-mazes, Skinner boxes, runways) and one's intuitive characterization of the behavior of human beings and higher animals outside the laboratory. In laboratory investigations associated with what was generally termed *reinforcement theory*, animals received selective reward or punishment for specific responses in tightly controlled situations, with learning being measured by the relative frequencies or speeds of responses in the same situations (or perhaps in limited tests for generalization or transfer). Normally, of course, rewarded responses tended to increase in speed or frequency relative to nonrewarded ones, and statements of the contingencies responsible for these behavioral changes were given the status of laws or principles of learning.

The principles derived from very specific paradigms did not long remain confined to them, however. Rather, many adherents of reinforcement theory, perhaps most notably Skinner and his followers, took the view that these same principles in the same form would account for human and animal behavior in or out of the laboratory. Strict regard for parsimony seemed to dictate that one should accept the tenets of the reinforcement position until they were refuted by specific evidence—never an easy task to accomplish, given the ambiguous criteria for refuting very general propositions.

Set against the solid results of the reinforcement theorists were only a few specially contrived experiments dealing with "latent learning," and the like, and a mass of uncontrolled observation outside the laboratory, which seemed to convince many psychologists that the behavior of human beings and the higher animals rarely occurs in situations like those of the reinforcement studies. Rather, behavior outside the laboratory normally occurs in situations that do not recur in detail, and adjustment to changing environments generally seems to be accomplished by highly variable action patterns that are not tightly controlled by the immediate rewarding and non-rewarding consequences of each individual response.

Some theorists, perhaps the most influential being Tolman, did, indeed, attempt to formulate theories reflecting these latter considerations, but in doing so they dismissed reinforcement theories almost by fiat and failed to come to grips in any detailed way with the results on which those theories had been based. My own view, from my first introduction to this apparent impasse, was that it was necessary to work somehow toward theory that could accommodate both aspects. I think some progress has been made from the early 1940s to the present, but it has to be measured on a long road, whose end is not yet in sight.

A deterrent to theoretical progress for a considerable period was, I think, the rather self-contained character of much research on reinforcement and the concepts it gave rise to. New results on reward and punishment in animal learning that appeared during the 1940s and 1950s led to modifications of reinforcement theory, but only within the sharply delimited stimulus-response framework. New inputs from other disciplines were needed to instigate the deeper shifts of theoretical outlook that could begin to take account of the major role of organization in basic forms of learning, as well as in presumably higher processes of human memory.

Some of the most important of these inputs came from research on animal behavior outside the reinforcement tradition, particularly ethology and studies of the effects of hormones on behavior (for example, Hinde and Tinbergen, 1958, and Beach, 1948, respectively), which began to bring out the intricate and ubiquitous ways in which the learning and activities of the higher organisms are conditioned by the innate organization of the nervous system and behavioral dispositions. Clearly, the learning of animals, and to a lesser but still important degree even that of human beings, can no longer be considered in terms of formation or strengthening of arbitrary associations; rather, it must be conceived in terms of the modification and elaboration of already existing organizations of behavioral systems.

Some investigators, such as Seligman (1970), have taken the lesson of the numerous findings on species-specific behaviors to be that the search for general principles of learning should be given up as fruitless in principle. Leaning as much on analogies to better developed sciences as on our own data, I prefer the view that we need not, and in fact cannot, do without general principles if we ever are to have explanatory theories of learning and behavior. At the same time, we should not expect general laws or principles to take the forms of the simple formulas of the classical learning theories. General principles cannot be expected to take the form of descriptions of empirical regularities, such as the Law of Effect, but rather must refer to elements of a multilevel process, with the organized products of learning being related to behavior by way of species-specific systems in the lower animals and to a progressively higher extent by way of the formation of higher-order action routines and the feedback control of performance in higher organisms and human beings.

What can be said about the adequacy of present interpretations of reinforcement in learning? With regard to conditioning in animal learning, the situation still appears much as it did when I last thoroughly reviewed work at that level (Estes, 1969, 1973). Elementary learning seems to be primarily a matter of forming associations, or encoded representations, relating stimuli the organism has experienced, which may include those that would be called cues but also include aspects of background context and reinforcing events. These representations can be more complex than simple binary stimulus-response or even stimulus-stimulus connections. It seems fairly reinforcement may come to be related by way of multiple associations with control elements in such a way that reactivation of the representation of the reinforcing event may depend multiplicatively on combined input from cue and context (Estes, 1973).

With regard to contingencies between responses and rewards or punishments, I have found no reason to change materially the views expressed in my earliest theoretical articles to the effect that contingencies serve solely to control the specific conditions for associative learning, particularly the temporal and spatial contiguities of events or aspects of events that must be perceived in combination and enter into the memory representations needed to guide later performance.

The link between stored information and behavior now seems rather more complex than it did in the early theories, involving processes of memory search or vicarious trial and error and feedback control of responding. It appears that not only human beings but all the higher animals studied in learning experiments cope with choice situations by scanning stimulus arrays, initiating response sequences that have occurred in the same or similar situations, and recalling aspects of their previous consequences. The reactivated memory elements then lead, by way of amplifier mechanisms or the equivalent, to selective facilitation or inhibition of the partially excited responses.

Independent evidence has accumulated for all the separate elements of this account. In connection with the informational aspect of reinforcement, for example, studies on conditioned anticipation of rewarding and punishing events might be cited; regarding the memory search or vicarious trial-and-error process, the work of Bower (1959) might be examined; and with regard to feedback modulation of ongoing behavior, perhaps most important are the numerous studies of modification of performance by electrical stimulation of midbrain structures. The combination of these ingredients into an interpretation of trial-and-error learning in choice situations seems reasonable, although it should be recognized that much remains to be done by way of effective formalization of these ideas.

From some perspectives, human learning in relation to reinforcement seems basically similar to the animal case, but from others it is so different that the continuity becomes hard to discern. Similarities include the fundamental role of acquiring predictive information about reinforcing events, retrieval of the information in choice situations by way of memory-scanning processes, and its utilization in the feedback control of performance. Differences include the fact that, in the maturing human being, instrumental learning in choice behavior become less and less bound to species-specific systems and more strongly dependent on elaborate memory structures and retrieval processes. Conditions under which the necessary learning occurs, and the nature of the resulting mental representations, still present open questions, but extensive researches of the kinds sampled in Chapters 2 and 3 of this book have yielded some progress toward answers. On the other hand, working out the linkages between feedback processes at the cognitive level and physiological mechanisms implicated in facilitation and inhibition of actual behavioral routines is a task that has been hardly begun.

Perhaps the most profound differences between human and animal learning in relation to reinforcement have to do with the time dimension. In the reinforcement theories of animal learning, such as that of Hull (1943), it was an irreducible postulate that efficacy of reinforcement decreases with temporal delay between a response and its reinforcing outcome. During the period of Hull's major influence, there was a tendency to carry over the same principle by analogy to human learning. With the increasingly analytical quality of research on human learning, however, it became clear by the 1960s that the situation with regard to delay is much more complex for human learners (see, for example, Bourne, 1966; Kintsch & McCoy, 1964). Work of Atkinson and Wickens (1971) and Buchwald (1967), among others, made considerable progress in illuminating these complexities, showing that in the human case, at least, delay does not influence efficacy of reinforcement directly, but rather is a determinant of which particular combinations of events in a learning situation become encoded in memory in a form to influence later behavior.

Further, in normal human behavior, learning is by no means limited to situations that recur in such similar form that the learning can be considered analogous to multiple trials in a maze, successive reinforced responses in a Skinner box, or the like. Rather, much learning goes on in situations that never recur and is related to goals or incentives that have not been and may never be achieved. No one doubts that much human behavior is strongly related to events that are remote in the future—such as the possible receipt of a diploma, a marriage, or the purchase of a home—but we still have little theory bearing on the specific processes that mediate such dependencies. To be sure, theorists of the stimulus-response-reinforcement tradition have offered accounts in which such human behavior is hypothesized to be maintained by token rewards or secondary reinforcements, similarly to the way in which the bar-pressing behavior of a rat may be maintained by the sound of a food dispenser even during intervals when the dispenser is empty. In the human case, however, these secondary reinforcers are almost wholly hypothetical, and there is essentially no evidence that long-term organized behavioral routines are actually controlled by such events on a moment-to-moment or response-by-response basis.

An alternative view, as yet unrealized in any formal theory, is that individuals form mental representations of the possible time courses of events and get reinforcing feedback from the way their actions succeed or fail at producing events that intervene in the representations between their current situations and future goals. A conception of this kind can be seen as a rather direct extension of the body of theory reviewed in Chapter 2 of this volume, and the increasingly effective methods, both experimental and theoretical, that are becoming available in cognitive psychology for dealing with analog and symbolic memory representations give some reason to think that what is now just a hope may begin to be converted into actual theory. At any rate, this direction is where I personally look for the next major developments in the interpretation of reinforcement in human behavior.

DIRECTIONS IN THE STUDY OF HUMAN LEARNING

During fully the first half-century of active experimental research on learning, there was nearly exclusive concentration on the analysis of very simple learning situations. Animal learning research used the conditioning paradigm, the runway, and the bar-pressing situation; human learning research used paired associates, memorization of lists, simple concept identification, and binary-choice learning. During the same period, learning theory was naturally devoted largely to the interpretation and development of models for learning occurring in these same situations.

In relation to the broader goal of understanding animal and human learning in ordinary environments, what contributions can be anticipated from the analysis of artificially simplified situations and the associated theory? As was discussed in Chapter 1, a principal expectation, arising mainly from analogy to other sciences, has been that of finding elementary units or processes in learning and memory and the principles of their dynamics and interactions. Much of my work on learning from 1940 to 1970 fell on the main line of this effort, and it has been fairly well sampled in preceding chapters of this book.

What limits should we expect on potential contributions of this analytical approach to understanding normal human learning? Though not as impatient as some critics of the analytical approach (for example, J. R. Anderson, 1976), I share the belief of many investigators that, just as one cannot account for relationships between water, ice, and steam from the knowledge of the properties of hydrogen and oxygen atoms and molecules, one cannot expect to understand many forms of relatively complex learning solely on the basis of knowledge gained from the study of very elementary processes. It is most conspicuous that human learning occurs on many levels of complexity, and undoubtedly it must be necessary for the experimenter to cut into the stack at higher as well as lower levels.

I don't think this necessity escaped the attention of earlier experimental psychologists, but in earlier periods experimental and theoretical methods needed for fruitful attacks on complex forms of learning were not available. More recently, however, new resources have become available in both categories.

First, as indicated earlier, there has been substantial progress, aided by the flexibility of computer-assisted experimentation, in simulating under controlled laboratory conditions learning situations that occur outside the laboratory. Second, beginning in the early 1960s, the work of Feigenbaum (1963) and Hunt (1962), among others, led to the development of computer-implemented models capable of representing more complex forms of human learning than could be treated in terms of the formal methods of more classical learning theories. An extremely fruitful consequence of these methodological developments and the more recent confluence of ideas from learning theory and other themes in cognitive psychology has been the cultivation of theoretically significant work on such complex forms of human learning as the formation of natural categories and prototypes (Smith & Medin, 1981) and the acquisition of factual and propositional knowledge (J. R. Anderson, 1976, 1980; Smith, 1981).

There seems little doubt that in the near future we shall see a continuing shift of emphasis from the simpler forms of human learning of the paired-associate tradition to those on the level of categories and propositions. The only hazard I see in these developments is that, for a time at least, we seem likely to see almost as sharp a discontinuity between concepts and theories at the levels of complex and simple human learning as we did between human and animal learning. One reason for concern about this separation is that the important problems having to do with fundamental aspects of human learning—as, for example, the structure of the memory trace (Ross & Bower, 1981)—have not been solved but have been largely bypassed in the rush to complexity. A second concern is that, although one can expect the development of theories strictly at the level of complex learning to be of substantial heuristic value, progress toward theories that also offer explanatory power requires, in addition, theoretical connections between the more complex and the simpler levels (Estes, 1979). My work continuing beyond that represented in this book is concentrated largely on efforts toward integration in the sense of developing significant theoretical relationships between concepts of the descriptive theories of complex learning and those of more elementary units and constituent processes.

THE PROBLEM OF REPRESENTATION
IN MEMORY

The psychology of learning and memory around 1940 had scarcely begun to depart from the strong applied emphasis of functionalism and the methodological grip of operationism. Investigators were preoccupied with questions of the conditions of learning and conditions of retention, and questions of the form of internal representations of events and relations had yet even to be clearly posed. In the same field at present, in contrast, problems of the nature of mental representation are at the heart of what is termed *cognitive science*. It is hardly an exaggeration to say that current work in the field largely turns on efforts to deal with this question at various levels in analysis.

A résumé of my research and theoretical development over the same period has the appearance in retrospect of a microcosm of what has happened in the field at large, my thinking sometimes seeming to lead and sometimes to follow conceptual and methodological changes in the broad field of research on memory. I might be said to have led in trying to make a start on the problem of representation in some formal way in the context of learning, with a focus on the major role of categorical representations. However, in those early efforts, I did not yet perceive the magnitude of the problem, and I thought that the representation of effects of learning could be handled adequately by simple set-theoretical relationships. It will be apparent from the sequence of papers included in Chapter 3 of this book that I had begun to appreciate clearly the limitations of a simple statistical framework based on interchangeable abstract memory elements and to make use of concepts of multilevel representations even before weighty critiques of elementaristic stimulus-response models became fashionable (J. R. Anderson, 1976; Greeno, James, DaPolito, & Polson, 1978; Johnson, 1975). Currently, I have trouble keeping up with all the varieties of theories and models under active development—at levels of simple associations (Raiijmakers & Shiffrin, 1981), hierarchical associations (Estes, 1976c; McClelland & Rumelhart, 1981), linguistically labeled associations and production systems (J. R. Anderson, 1976), analog structures (Shepard & Podgorny, 1978), and propositional structures (J. R. Anderson, 1980)—much less claiming to be ahead of the field.

I don't doubt that the present broad-gauge approach to memory constitutes a salutory advance, but it is another matter to decide whether any substantial progress is being made toward a coherent body of theory. It is possible, for example, that the concepts and models at various levels do not correspond to any specific structures or processes in memory, but rather simply mirror the capability of the human being to respond selectively to varying degrees of patterning and organization of information inputs. Thus, for example, in some experiments subjects are able to recall or reconstitute information from previous sensory experiences that they would be expected to have if they were retrieving images having some of the properties of photographic or other analog representations. These results are intriguing, but nothing of explanatory value is added by hypothesizing that the individuals base their recall on images.

Some investigators (for example, Kosslyn, 1980, 1981) are keenly aware of this problem and are proceeding to answer critics (such as Pylyshyn, 1981) by painstakingly amassing evidence that the subjects' performance in these tasks does reflect memory structures that have imagelike properties. Regarding propositions, as well, it is a truism that whatever individuals prove able to remember from any experience can be stated in the form of propositions. It is quite another matter to justify the claim that propositions correspond one-to-one with memory structures that are implicated in the recall. Here again some investigators recognize the methodological problem well enough, and we are beginning to see some rather impressive demonstrations that propositions might indeed correspond in some way to units in organized memories (Kintsch, 1974; Ratcliff & McKoon, 1978). The general point I wish to make is simply that hypothesized entities at all levels—propositions, images, labeled associations, critical features, abstract memory elements—are on a par in that they all require a great deal of converging evidence before they can usefully be considered to correspond to significant units or components of individuals' internal representations of their experiences.

Another major set of questions about current work on representation has to do with the multiplicity of units and levels. With continuing theoretical progress, should we expect some of the currently recognized levels and units to disappear, with or without being replaced by others? Will the variety of units and levels continue to proliferate endlessly (like what were once thought to be elementary particles of physics)? I have no answers to offer, but I do feel that, just as posing the problem of representation was an important step in the transition from a rather barren functionalism to present-day cognitive science, posing and beginning to investigate these questions may be essential to continuing theoretical progress.

It seems to be possible for investigators, almost at will, to select a level of analysis of human intellectual performance, to hypothesize units of analysis and mental operations on the units, and to proceed to collect data that lend support to the hypotheses. I do not mean to make light of such activity, for these models can be expected to provide useful summaries of what is known about performance in cognitive tasks of various levels of complexity. I suspect, however, that the viability of the particular hypothesized mental entities and operations will be determined by the degree to which they can be knit into theoretical structures having vertical as well as horizontal organization. What has been dubbed the "psychological reality" of propositions cannot be determined by the inevitable accumulation of orderly data about recall performance scored in terms of propositions; rather, it must remain open until some progress is made toward deriving the properties of propositional memories from lower-level or more primitive concepts and properties of still more complex memories from models expressed in terms of propositions. This task of trying to find significant theoretical connections between the different levels of representation hypothesized in current models of memory has come to be perhaps my major theoretical interest in this area.

It is scarcely worth speculating on the form a more unified body of theory might take, but, until some better alternative comes to hand, I can see no better approach than to look for answers within the general framework of network models. Networks have some of the properties that seem necessary to offer any prospect of ultimate meshing of cognitive with neurophysiological theory, as witness the current efforts of J. A. Anderson (1973, 1977), Grossberg (1980), Sutton and Barto (1981). At almost the other extreme, network models are proving, in practice, to provide one of the most useful frameworks for cognitive approaches to complex learning (see, for example, Anderson, Kline, & Beasley, 1979) and for interpretations of the burgeoning literature on effects of priming on encoded representations in memory (Collins & Loftus, 1975; Posner, 1978; Ratcliff & McKoon, 1978). It has been argued that network and feature models are formally equivalent (Hollan, 1975). Although the claim may be justified in a sense, its relevance to theory construction is unclear, for in current models of memory only the most rudimentary aspects of network theory have yet found employment. A substantial body of formal theory of directed graphs and networks is available (see, for example, Roberts, 1976), and it will be interesting to see whether its more effective employment proves as fruitful as were the introduction of Markov models and computer-simulation models in the 1950s and 1960s. To recall a motif that has run through this book, the hazards of overformalization in cognitive psychology seem to me small compared to the hazards of failing to develop and use the formal methods that may be needed to cope with the forbiddingly difficult problems of understanding mental representation.

Current interests in the problem of representation go beyond a desire for models with heuristic value for the interpretation of reaction-time data. Is there reason to hope for cognitive models that might correspond to mental representations in any deeper sense? Opinions differ sharply, some (for example, J. R. Anderson, 1978) leaning toward the negative, others (Hayes-Roth, 1979; Pylyshyn, 1979) toward the affirmative. With no special sources of insight save the perspective lent by some varied experience in the field, I incline toward a qualified yes.

First, I will state the qualifications. A number of thoughtful discussions of the problem (Palmer, 1978; Shepard, 1978) leave effectively outmoded the once-popular ideas that memory structures correspond to sensory experiences or their external sources in the manner connoted by everyday usage of the term *representation.* In particular, there seem to be no grounds to think that properties of mental representations, as conceived in any known type of model, correspond to physical properties of the external world in the way that properties of an optical hologram do to a visual scene. Nor can any basis be found to expect cognitive models of memory representation to progress toward a status like that of atomic models in physics, with the physical reality of constituents of representations being established by converging operations in the manner of elementary particles.

On the other side, there seems no reason to doubt that we can hope to establish, with progressively increasing specificity, the properties, both dynamic and structural, that mental representations must have. It may be possible to develop models of representation and process that can serve cognitive psychology, as the double helix serves for genetics, for example. At a minimum, such models could summarize what we learn about the properties of representations in a form most useful to aid us in thinking about them. This much, some investigators will immediately note, could potentially be realized in the programs of computer-simulation models, although these programs do not seem to capture all the intuitive connotations of "representation."

There seems no assurance that we can go further, but the possibility is open. Sometimes models incorporate not only specific factual information but also the intuitions of scientists in a way that endows the models with predictive power (or surprising implications) that could not have been anticipated from knowledge of their ingredients. Instances of such successes in other sciences so far seem always to have been based on formalisms drawn from mathematics or physical analogies, so there is motivation for cognitive psychologists to try the same course (a strategy exemplified in my own approach, as exemplified in the preceding chapters of this book). However, there is no merit in clinging too tenaciously to the patterns of past successes, and I can see the values in exploring vigorously the possibility that comparable results may be achievable with models formulated in terms of sufficiently powerful programming languages.

One methodological implication of this discussion is that, although there may well be values in framing some of our research in terms of a long-range objective of achieving models of representation with deeper significance than computing devices, there is probably little value in devoting much energy at this stage to differential tests of alternative proposals. Less is likely to come from debates concerning analog versus propositional representations, for example, than from continuing efforts to narrow down the range of properties that must characterize both the representational and processing components of any adequate model.

What steps toward the desired objective can one discern in the long-term efforts on the problem of memory representation sampled in this volume? Without making exorbitant claims about progress, I might be able to lend the discussion more concreteness by bringing together in summary fashion a number of relevant concepts that have appeared in preceding chapters of the book.

One cluster of these concepts that was of major significance in the development of my statistical models for learning includes the notions of *redundancy, randomness,* and *fluctuation.* Memory for an event or relationship seems always to be supported by multiple representations, whether these be conceived as traces, associations, or encodings, only a sample of which is activated during any one learning or perceptual experience. Further, it seems that the availability or activity of these units must be assumed to fluctuate randomly over time. The consequence of these properties is a certain robustness of the memory system, in that retrieval of memories is possible despite wide variations in particular situational contexts and resistance to forgetting is built up for precisely the memories whose retrieval is most likely to be called for after long intervals (see the first paper reprinted in Chapter 2 and the first two papers in Chapter 3).

A second cluster of concepts has to do with the proclivity of the memory system to store varying degrees of partial information about events or relations and to do so in such a way that, when loss of information occurs during forgetting, the information most likely to be retained longest is that most important for the categorization of the event or relation on dimensions or attributes significant for intellectual function. Perhaps the most specific progress in working out these ideas has been accomplished relative to memories for temporal position or order of events, in the conception of *uncertainty gradients.* Information about the relative temporal position of events is subject to distortion or loss over time, but in the statistically orderly manner characterized by what has been termed a *perturbation process,* such that small errors in memory for chronology are more likely than larger errors (see the third paper in Chapter 3).

Finally, I will mention two concepts that have been important in my more recent work on organization in long-term memory. One of these is the concept of *control elements* in associative networks (see the second and fourth papers in Chapter 3). This notion differs from the one, more common in the literature, of nodes of a network that correspond directly to words or concepts in being more abstract and in having more the character of symbolizing relations among subsidiary representations. Control elements have the properties of logical AND gates in the associative network. They are important for representing the proclivity of the memory system to generate progressively higher order units as well as for important properties of context dependence.

The second of these general properties of long-term systems I have termed *recursiveness* (see the fourth paper in Chapter 3), referring to the way in which such cognitive operations as selective attending, comparison, or memory search may themselves be represented in the memory trace for an experience. A familiar specific instance of recursiveness is the way an individual's recognition of a semantic relation between words in a free-recall task may be incorporated in the memory of the experience of hearing the list and serve subsequently as the basis for an effective retrieval cue. A broader implication of recursiveness is that, in general, the memory system preserves a record not only of the objects and events the individual has encountered but also of the cognitive as well as overtly behavioral activities they gave rise to.

Naturally one must expect this or any such list of general concepts to be revised in makeup as well as extended in the course of time, but, to the extent that the strategy works, new formulations will preserve most of the essentials of older ones. Also, it is important to be clear that one should not regard any of these concepts or principles individually as empirically testable in the same sense as the innumerable particular models that arise from the interpretation of specific kinds of experiments. The idea, rather, is that, when the general concepts are well chosen, they prove to be ones that must be taken into account in any new theory for which some generality is claimed or else the theory, when tested as a whole, will be found empirically wanting. What I wish to propose is not that the set of concepts given here is optimal but only that continuing efforts to abstract general concepts and principles may be as essential to theoretical progress as formulating and testing specific models.

NOTE

1. *Cognitive Science,* 1977, *1,* 1-2. After a few years' experience, that policy was broadened to one that "welcomes high quality papers from the variety of perspectives that characterize the field" (*Cognitive Science,* 1981, *5,* iii.).

REFERENCES

Anderson, J. A. A theory for recognition of items from short memorized lists. *Psychological Review,* 1973, *80,* 417-438.

Anderson, J. A. Neural models with cognitive implications. In D. LaBerge & S. J. Samuels (Eds.), *Basic processes in reading: Perception and comprehension*, pp. 27–90. Hillsdale, N.J.: Lawrence Erlbaum Associates, 1977.

Anderson, J. R. *Language, memory, and thought*. Hillsdale, N.J.: Lawrence Erlbaum Associates, 1976.

Anderson, J. R. Arguments concerning representations for mental imagery. *Psychological Review*, 1978, *85*, 249–277.

Anderson, J. R. *Cognitive psychology*. San Francisco: W. H. Freeman, 1980.

Anderson, J. R., Kline, P. J., & Beasley, L. M. A general learning theory and its application to schema abstraction. In G. H. Bower (Ed.), *The psychology of learning and motivation: Advances in research and theory*. Vol. 13, pp. 277–318. New York: Academic Press, 1979.

Atkinson, R. C. Mnemotechnics in second-language learning. *American Psychologist*, 1975, *30*, 821–828.

Atkinson, R. C., & Shiffrin, R. M. Human memory: A proposed system and its control processes. In K. W. Spence & J. T. Spence (Eds.), *The psychology of learning and motivation: Advances in research and theory*, Vol. 2, pp. 89–195. New York: Academic Press, 1968.

Atkinson, R. C., & Wickens, T. D. Human memory and the concept of reinforcement. In R. Glaser (Ed.), *The nature of reinforcement*, pp. 66–120. New York: Academic Press, 1971.

Beach, F. A. *Hormones and behavior*. New York: Hoeber, 1948.

Bjork, R. A. The updating of human memory. In G. H. Bower (Ed.), *The psychology of learning and motivation: Advances in research and theory*, Vol. 12, pp. 235–259. New York: Academic Press, 1978.

Bourne, L. E. Information feedback. In E. A. Bilodeau (Ed.), *Acquisition of skill*, pp. 297–313. New York: Academic Press, 1966.

Bower, G. H. Choice-point behavior. In R. R. Bush & W. K. Estes (Eds.), *Studies in mathematical learning theory*. pp. 109–124. Stanford, Calif.: Stanford University Press, 1959.

Buchwald, A. M. Effects of immediate vs. delayed outcomes in associative learning. *Journal of Verbal Learning and Verbal Behavior*, 1967, *6*, 317–320.

Collins, A. M., & Loftus, E. F. A spreading activation theory of semantic processing. *Psychological Review*, 1975, *82*, 407–428.

Estes, W. K. Of models and men. *American Psychologist*, 1957, *12*, 609–617.

Estes, W. K. New perspectives on some old issues in association theory. In N. S. Mackintosh & W. K. Honig (Eds.), *Fundamental issues in associative learning*, pp. 162–189. Halifax: Dalhousie University Press, 1969.

Estes, W. K. Elements and patterns in diagnostic discrimination learning. *Annals of the New York Academy of Sciences*, 1972, *34*, 84–95. (a)

Estes, W. K. Reinforcement in human behavior. *American Scientist*, 1972, *60*, 723–729. (b)

Estes, W. K. Memory and conditioning. In F. J. McGuigan and D. B. Lumsden (Eds.), *Contemporary approaches to conditioning and learning*, pp. 265–286. Washington, D.C.: V. H. Winston, 1973.

Estes, W. K. Introduction. In W. K. Estes (Ed.), *Handbook of learning and cognitive processes*, Vol. 4, pp. 1–16. Hillsdale, N.J.: Lawrence Erlbaum Associates, 1976. (a)

Estes, W. K. The cognitive side of probability learning. *Psychological Review,* 1976, *83,* 37–64. (b)

Estes, W. K. Structural aspects of associative models for memory. In C. N. Cofer (Ed.), *The structure of human memory*, pp. 31–53. San Francisco: W. H. Freeman, 1976. (c)

Estes, W. K. On the organization and core concepts of learning theory and cognitive psychology. In W. K. Estes (Ed.), *Handbook of learning and cognitive processes*, Vol. 6, pp. 235–292. Hillsdale, N.J.: Lawrence Erlbaum Associates, 1978.

Estes, W. K. On the descriptive and explanatory functions of theories of memory. In L.-G. Nilsson (Ed.), *Perspectives on memory research*, pp. 35–60. Hillsdale, N.J.: Lawrence Erlbaum Associates, 1979.

Estes, W. K., & Hopkins, B. L. Acquisition and transfer in pattern-vs.-component discrimination learning. *Journal of Experimental Psychology,* 1961, *61,* 322–328.

Feigenbaum, E. A. Simulation of verbal learning behavior. In E. A. Feigenbaum & J. Feldman (Eds.), *Computers and thought*, pp. 297–309. New York: McGraw-Hill, 1963.

Greeno, J. G. Psychology of learning, 1960-1980. *American Psychologist,* 1980, *35,* 713–728.

Greeno, J. G., James, C. T., DaPolito, F., & Polson, P. G. *Associative learning: A cognitive analysis.* Englewood Cliffs, N.J.: Prentice-Hall, 1978.

Grossberg, S. How does a brain build a cognitive code? *Psychological Review,* 1980, *87,* 1–51.

Hayes-Roth, F. Distinguishing theories of representation. *Psychological Review,* 1979, *86,* 376–382.

Hinde, R. A., & Tinbergen, N. The comparative study of species-specific behavior. In A. Roe & G. G. Simpson (Eds.), *Behavior and evolution*, pp. 251–268. New Haven: Yale University Press, 1958.

Hollan, J. D. Features and semantic memory: Set-theoretic or network model? *Psychological Review,* 1975, *82,* 154–155.

Hull, C. L. *Principles of behavior.* New York: Appleton-Century-Crofts, 1943.

Hunt, E. *Concept learning: An information processing problem.* New York: Wiley, 1962.

Johnson, N. F. On the function of letters in word identification: Some data and a preliminary mode. *Journal of Verbal Learning and Verbal Behavior,* 1975, *14,* 17-29.

Kahneman, D., & Tversky, A. Prospect theory: An analysis of decision under risk. *Econometrica,* 1979, *47,* 263-291.

Kintsch, W. *The representation of meaning in memory.* New York: Wiley, 1974.

Kintsch, W., & McCoy, D. L. Delay of informative feedback in paired-associate learning. *Journal of Experimental Psychology,* 1964, *68,* 372-375.

Kosslyn, S. M. *Image and mind.* Cambridge, Mass.: Harvard University Press, 1980.

Kosslyn, S. M. The medium and the message in mental imagery. *Psychological Review*, 1981, *88*, 46–66.

Lee, C. L., & Estes, W. K. Item and order information in short-term memory: Evidence for multi-level perturbation processes. *Journal of Experimental Psychology: Human Learning and Memory*, 1981, 7, 149–169.

McClelland, J. L., & Rumelhart, D. E. An interactive activation model of context effects in letter perception: Part 1. An account of basic findings. *Psychological Review*, 1981, *88*, 375–407.

Palmer, S. E. Fundamental aspects of cognitive representation. In E. Rosch and B. B. Lloyd (Eds.), *Cognition and categorization*, pp. 259–303. Hillsdale, N.J.: Lawrence Erlbaum Associates, 1978.

Posner, M. I. *Chronometric explorations of mind*. Hillsdale, N.J.: Lawrence Erlbaum Associates, 1978.

Pylyshyn, Z. W. Validating computational models. *Psychological Review*, 1979, *86*, 383–394.

Pylyshyn, Z. W. The imagery debate: Analogue media versus tacit knowledge. *Psychological Review*, 1981, *88*, 16–45.

Raaijmakers, J. G., & Shiffrin, R. M. Search of associative memory. *Psychological Review*, 1981, *88*, 93–134.

Ratcliff, R., & McKoon, G. Priming in item recognition: Evidence for the propositional structure of sentences. *Journal of Verbal Learning and Verbal Behavior*, 1978, *17*, 403–417.

Roberts, F. S. *Discrete mathematical models*. Englewood Cliffs, N.J.: Prentice-Hall, 1976.

Ross, B. H., & Bower, G. H. Comparisons of models of associative recall. *Memory & Cognition*, 1981, *9*, 1–16.

Schank, R. C. The role of memory in language processing. In C. N. Cofer (Ed.), *The structure of human memory*, pp. 162–189. San Francisco: W. H. Freeman, 1976.

Seligman, M. E. P. On the generality of the laws of learning. *Psychological Review*, 1970, 77, 406–418.

Seymour, P. H. K. *Human visual cognition*. New York: St. Martins, 1979.

Shepard, R. N. The mental image. *American Psychologist*, 1978, *33*, 125–137.

Shepard, R. N., & Podgorny, P. Cognitive processes that resemble perceptual processes. In W. K. Estes (Ed.), *Handbook of learning and cognitive processes*, Vol. 5, pp. 189–237. Hillsdale, N.J.: Lawrence Erlbaum Associates, 1978.

Smith, E. E. Organization of factual knowledge. In J. H. Flowers (Ed.), *Nebraska symposium on motivation 1980: Cognitive processes*, pp. 161–209. Lincoln: Nebraska University Press, 1981.

Smith, E. E., & Medin, D. L. *Categories and concepts*. Cambridge, Mass.: Harvard University Press, 1981.

Sutton, R. S., & Barto, G. G. Toward a modern theory of adaptive networks: Expectation and prediction. *Psychological Review*, 1981, *88*, 135–170.

6

Autobiography

ACADEMIC ENVIRONMENTS

In brief outline, the settings for my academic activities have been as follows. My formal education in psychology was accomplished in two segments at the University of Minnesota—as an undergraduate from 1937 to 1940 and as a graduate student from 1940 to 1943. Following a gap in my academic career for military service, I entered my first teaching position, at Indiana University, in 1946. There I proceeded with satisfactory speed through all the ranks from instructor to professor, remaining until 1962. Brief digressions during that period included a summer of teaching at the University of Wisconsin in 1949, a year's leave at the Center for Advanced Study in the Behavioral Sciences in 1955-1956 (the first full year of operation of the Center), and a visiting appointment at Northwestern University in the spring of 1959. I moved to Stanford University as professor of psychology and member of the Institute for Mathematical Studies in the Social Sciences in 1962, remaining until 1968, then moved to Rockefeller University as professor and director of the Laboratory of Mathematical Psychology from 1968 to 1979. Since 1979 I have been professor of psychology at Harvard University.

I count myself fortunate in the experiences I have had at the institutions just listed. It is hard to see how I could have done better at finding a succession of universities providing such excellent support for the development of my scholarly and scientific capabilities.

When I was a student, the Department of Psychology at Minnesota did not include as many great names as some, but it provided sound training in all the basics, espoused a liberal attitude toward allowing students to follow academic interests outside their official specialties, and, in my experience at least, allowed almost unlimited freedom to follow one's research inclinations. The intellectual climate was highly stimulating, one manifestation being an unusual number of intellectually sharp undergraduates with strong theoretical interests.

In that climate, and continuing through graduate school, I enjoyed the activating effects of seeing a newly recruited and highly enterprising young instructor, B. F. Skinner, and a newly recruited and eminent philosopher of science, Herbert Feigl, running their own shows—to the discomfiture of some of the establishment in both psychology and philosophy.

However, Skinner's "experimental analysis of behavior" and Feigl's logical positivism weren't the only shows in town. During the same period, the department was providing, under Starke Hathaway's leadership, one of the breeding grounds for the newly emerging field of clinical psychology. As a graduate student, I served as the statistician among Hathaway's research assistants during the development of the ultimately famous Minnesota Multiphasic Personality Inventory, and, although clinical psychology was not to be my home, I have retained a continuing interest in the biological and experimental sides of that now sprawling specialty.

My research quickly settled in on learning theory and, in particular, the "experimental analysis of behavior," as Skinner termed his specialty. I was by no means alone in taking this direction, and I found myself for several years enjoying the congenial company and interactive learning environment provided by an enthusiastic band of Skinner's students—including Keller Breland, Norman Guttman (then an undergraduate in philosophy), Howard F. Hunt, Marian Kruse (Breland), and Katherine Walker. Research support was miniscule, but we were allowed to develop our own animal colony, starting with cast-off rats from breeding studies, and little more was needed. A year or so into graduate work, I formulated a plan for a Ph.D. dissertation based on analyses of interactions among motivational systems, and Skinner obtained a grant of some $300 from the University to pay for some necessary apparatus. Just then, however, the United States entered World War II, and Skinner decided the money was needed to support his efforts to train pigeons to guide steerable bombs. Time was of the essence for draft-eligible male students, so I quickly readjusted my plans and completed a study of punishment, already under way as a sideline, in time to meet Ph.D. requirements before I was called for military service (see Estes, 1944).

On entering the Army Air Force, I was first assigned to a psychological research unit[1] in Ft. Myers, Florida, where I became acquainted with a number of psychologists I was to know later as academic or professional colleagues—among them Nicholas Hobbs, Arthur Irion, Roger Russell, Moncrieff Smith, Larry Stolurow, and George Wischner. Despite a marked lack of aptitude for the military life, I was promoted through the ranks by some succession of accidents, and by one particular bit of good fortune I received a temporary duty assignment at the Radiation Laboratory in Cambridge, where I was permanently imprinted on the ambience of the area centered on M.I.T. and Harvard Square.

The next turn of events found me commissioned in the Adjutant General's Corps, ostensibly as a clinical psychologist, and shipped out to the Philippines with an army field hospital. There proved to be little scope for clinical psychology in that setting, however, and a series of administrative assignments ensued during the long period of preparation for the expected invasion of Japan. Those seemingly endless preparations were abruptly cut short not long after the August morning when the static of a portable shortwave receiver was penetrated by the announcement of the atomic blast at Hiroshima.

The war over, I arrived at Indiana University for my first teaching job, just at the beginning of the period of rapid expansion of psychology there from a small but sound department to a truly major one. I was brought to Indiana by its new chairman, my former teacher, B. F. Skinner, arriving late for the fall term in 1946 because of delays in getting back from my final overseas assignment. I had been offered only a temporary position, but the temporary aspect was quickly forgotten, and I remained for some fifteen years. Skinner, however, did prove to be temporary; before long he departed for Harvard, leaving behind him, among other legacies, the many able graduate students and junior staff he had attracted. I was the obvious heir in his specialty and enjoyed the challenge of shifting almost overnight from a teacher of multiple elementary laboratory sections to responsibility for a stable of high-achieving graduate students. I learned at least as much from them as they did from me, and, although I was no Skinner in either skill or zeal for promoting operant conditioning techniques and doctrine, I think the experience worked out well on both sides.

During the following decade and a half, the department prospered under the leadership of Douglas G. Ellson as chairman, with wise and supportive University President Herman B. Wells in the background. My scientific fortunes also prospered.

My move to Stanford in 1962 was occasioned partly by the prospects of implementing ideas developed in collaboration with Patrick Suppes for further development of the Institute for Mathematical Studies in the Social Sciences there and partly by the prospects of assembling a graduate program in mathematical psychology. The latter project, at least, worked out well. Suppes, Richard Atkinson, Gordon Bower, and I had the pleasant chore of working with a series of outstanding classes of students who were readily attracted to Stanford and seeing many of them become highly productive and influential scientists almost before they were out of our hands.

During this period I had, in my own thinking, slipped by almost imperceptible stages from the stimulus-response paradigm into the newly emerging one of information processing. I never lost contact with the older tradition, but in the setting of Stanford in the mid-1960s I quickly came to feel at home in the new one. My colleague Richard Atkinson had just begun to see the exciting potentialities of computer analogies for modeling human information processing (see, for example, Atkinson & Shiffrin, 1968), and for several years in Ventura Hall, (the home of the Institute for Mathematical Studies in the Social Sciences at Stanford) Dick and I, over the inevitable coffee, exchanged observations and thoughts on our experiences with this new motif in cognitive psychology.

However, there was no one official doctrine in Ventura Hall, and during much of the same period I was continuing collaborative work with Patrick Suppes on foundations of stimulus-response theories. My long and close association with both Atkinson and Suppes surely constitutes part of the reason that I am now one of the very few psychologists who see value in both the stimulus-response and the information-processing approaches to theory in psychology.

The period at Stanford was most rewarding, but, because my energies were so heavily concentrated in graduate training, the development of my own research was increasingly sidetracked, and, partly on that account, I was receptive to a proposal to move to Rockefeller University in 1968.

Rockefeller offered two major attractions. One was virtually unlimited freedom to develop my own research and to build a laboratory for mathematical and cognitive psychology in a new setting. The other was the grand vision of the president, Detlev Bronk, to expand the hitherto almost purely medical research orientation of the institution to include a major interdisciplinary program connected, on the one hand, to basic biological sciences and mathematics and extending, on the other, into potential applications to the human problems of the urban society in which the university was situated. Bronk had just made a most impressive start on his program by recruiting Carl Pfaffmann and Neal Miller to provide intellectual and scientific leadership, together with Floyd Ratliff and Donald Griffin, who had come as biologists before the first appearance of psychology on the campus.

A decade at Rockefeller with, during the early years at least, strong support from the institution, enabled me to move effectively from the earlier tradition of learning theory into the new mainstream of cognitive psychology and information processing. Significant influences on my thinking during this period came both from the generally activating intellectual environment provided by the behavioral science group, including some exceptional students, and from occasional collaboration and continuing interaction with my closest associates there, Michael Cole and Douglas Medin.

With the inauguration of a new president near the end of the 1970s, Rockefeller University abruptly dropped the role of cordial host to psychological sciences and began exhibiting instead something akin to the living body's immune reaction to foreign substances. Thus, an invitation to move to Harvard came at a time when even the costs of moving seemed manageable in proportion to the attractiveness of Harvard and Cambridge as a place to teach and do research in my specialties. It seems especially apt, at this juncture, to be preparing this volume in the same locale, indeed quite possibly in the same room,[2] where William James put the finishing touches to his *Principles of Psychology* some 90 years ago.

CIRCUMSTANCES OF MAJOR IDEAS ON RESEARCH AND THEORY

Although I have often found myself in the role of a rather solitary investigator for lengthy periods while working on specific problems, nearly all the major developments in my research career are associated in my mind with interactions with groups of people. This autobiographical sketch would be grievously incomplete if I failed to mention some of the social contexts that have strongly conditioned my thinking, but I do so with trepidation, for there will inevitably be a considerable element of randomness in the episodes that happen to come to mind at the time of writing. I will apologize once and for all, both for the inevitable omissions and to any people I mention who might not be happy with the way things learned from them have been transformed in my hands.

General Scientific Outlook

The key to my general orientation toward psychology is, perhaps, that I was devoted to science before being introduced to psychology. I think my father must be credited with the beginnings of my interest in science and a good deal of early scientific education, for I can't remember an age at which I didn't know that man had evolved from lower animals, that the earth was a planet, or that apparently solid substances are actually composed of little solar systems of invisible particles. High school science was a disappointment, being of what is now termed the Mickey Mouse variety, but mathematics was entirely to my liking; and other scientific interests could be kept alive by virtue of the invaluable resources of the Minneapolis Public Library. Any extinguishing effects of high school science were quickly disinhibited at the University of Minnesota, where I enrolled in premedicine because of family pressure, though with my heart secretly set on physics or astronomy—and destined for none of these.

My career decision came not as a consequence of rational decision making but rather as the outcome of a chance meeting, during the Christmas holidays of my sophomore year, with my elementary psychology instructor. I had not been overly exhilarated by the course, but on this occasion the instructor, B. F. Skinner, casually asked if I would care to come up and look at his laboratory. I soon found myself trailing Skinner through the laboratory while he delivered a rapid-fire lecture on the delicacies of probing for the causes of an animal's behavior, his hand wielding a soldering iron and his mind, as always, racing several problems ahead.

I was caught up by Skinner's infectious enthusiasm, or so I suppose I would have said. From another view, perhaps I was simply captured by the famous successive-approximations techniques of behavior modification. I felt that I simply had to have a hand in this fascinating enterprise, and, as an obvious prerequisite, I borrowed a library copy of *The Behavior of Organisms* and proceeded to read it through, at first with delight in the contrast between the rigor and power of the approach and the flaccid eclecticism of the official introductory psychology textbook, but then with growing anxiety as it began to appear that I had come on this field too late and that the interesting problems had all been worked out. On a second time through, however, I began to see a chink of daylight, in that emotion had never been properly fitted into the system. Given that emotion is not a response, a dictum that I could accept at least provisionally, then what is it? Meditating on the question led within a few months to the development of a research idea (the germ of the Estes & Skinner, 1941, "CER" study) that gained me access to the operant conditioning laboratory as an apprentice investigator.

Working with Skinner was an invaluable experience for a young scientist, and from him I learned a great deal about the spirit and skills of analyzing behavior in the laboratory. I found, however, that I could not rise entirely to the idea that controlling behavior should be the sole objective of psychology or the sole criterion of progress. Thus, at the same time that my hands were busy in the laboratory, I was greatly influenced by two members of the Minnesota faculty who were disinclined to experiments but strongly interested in the development of general theories in psychology and their connection with biology and natural sciences. One of these was the chairman of the department, Richard M. Elliott, famous in the field primarily as a recruiter of scientific talent (Skinner being one of his successes), who took a kindly and continuing interest in my intellectual development. The reasons were partly, I think, that he needed to recruit some graduate students to work with Skinner in order to help hold that increasingly visible young scientist on his staff, and partly because I was possibly an even more avid reader than he. Under Elliott's guidance I worked my way through shelves of the great classics of philosophy and biology (Child, Holmes, Holt, Jennings, Loeb, Northrop, Verworn, Whitehead, Woodger, and so on) that provided the ground from which he, and in due course I, felt that theory in psychology had to grow.

The other faculty member of somewhat similar orientation was William S. Carlson, a physicist temporarily turned psychologist, who made sure that I gained as thorough knowledge of other theoretical traditions in psychology—Gestalt and organismic psychology, psychophysics, the precursers of cognitive psychology—as I was doing voluntarily with the radical behaviorism in which for the moment I felt at home.

The influence of these individuals, resonating with the traces of my earlier imprinting on physics and biology, tended to counteract the narrow behavioral focus of the circle of behavior analyzers centered around Skinner and promoted a broad view of the theoretical traditions and problems of psychology. This view was subsequently reinforced by innumerable morning coffee-break discussions of such matters with Douglas G. Ellson at Indiana, continuations in the same vein with Patrick Suppes at Stanford, and, beginning with our sojourn at the Center for Advanced Study in the Behavioral Sciences, unfailingly catalyzing interactions with Frank Restle, whose quick wit and intuition kept me from any danger of lapsing into scientific smugness over the years, until his untimely death in 1980.

Origins of Statistical Learning Theory

So far as I can recall, the setting of my first serious attempt to formulate a quantitative model was the laboratory that Norman Guttman and I set in operation about the time of Skinner's departure from Indiana. We were particularly interested in the effects of magnitude of reward, defined experimentally in our apparatus in terms of the concentration of solutions of sucrose or saccharin given in small amounts as reinforcements for lever presses by rats. In the course of long periods of observation of our animals, I was increasingly impressed with a number of facts. One of these was that magnitude of reward seemed to exert no graded influence on the speed of acquisition of the bar-pressing response. Another was that the behavior typically occurred either at very low rates or at relatively high ones, with the transition in either direction being very abrupt. Another, and perhaps the most important, was that the cumulative number of rewards received by an animal was an exceedingly poor predictor of the point at which it would shift from near zero to a normal rate of responding, and, similarly, that the cumulative number of nonrewards during extinction was a poor predictor of the point at which the rate of responding would drop to near zero.

The intuitive impression was that the reinforcing events—rewards or nonrewards—were not directly strengthening or weakening anything but were simply providing repeated opportunities for some critical events to occur. Seeking a way of representing in a model what seemed to be going on in the animal, I began seeking physical processes that might have somewhat the same character, and I found one in molecular reactions. There, the course of a mass reaction gives rise to a smooth curve of observations versus time, but only as a consequence of averaging, for the underlying process is one of discrete association or dissociation of constituent particles. Further, sampling variability is inherent in the process, because, for example, ions in solution that must combine to form the molecular products of a reaction can do so only as they happen to come together. The analogy set me also to thinking about the special situation of molecules in living systems, where it is crucial not only what a molecule is but where it is located. The availability of molecules for particular processes depends on their crossing semipermeable membranes, which therefore serve in a sense as categorizers.

These ideas of the role of random sampling, fluctuations in the availability of constituent processes, discrete associations and dissociations of elementary units—drawn together by the view that learning might be basically a classificatory rather than a growth process—led directly to the mathematical models for learning presented in a series of *Psychological Review* papers (Estes, 1950, 1955a, b) and the initiation of an extended and varied program of experimental studies by me and my associates aimed at testing, refining, and extending the models. The fact that these models were so closely embedded in ongoing research was the key, I surmise, to their consequent appreciable influence in contrast to others (for example, Thurstone, 1930) that looked just as promising in the abstract but did not take root.

Although the original development of the statistical models was a rather solitary effort, the social setting was exceedingly important for the sequel. Most important, surely, were the graduate students working with me at Indiana, who began immediately, with a great deal of enthusiasm and ingenuity, to translate the theoretical ideas into experimental realizations. Among the first of these students were Solomon Weinstock, who conducted studies of heroic proportions bearing on the relationships between the animal's inferred state of learning and observable response latencies (Weinstock, 1954), and Max Schoeffler, who contrived a way to obtain elegant direct tests of the implications of the model for stimulus compounding and transfer (Schoeffler, 1954).

Nearly as important a role was played by some of my colleagues in the Psychology Department at Indiana, in some cases as catalyzers, in others as actual collaborators. Notable in the former category was William S. Verplanck (at that time a psychophysicist), who took a keen interest in my work and did a good deal to bring it to the attention of people outside the university, leading to some acquaintances that proved to be of considerable import. One of these was Clarence Graham, whom I looked up to as a very major senior figure in quantitative psychology at the time and whose kindly and supportive interest in my work was most reinforcing. Still more material consequences stemmed from Verplanck's interactions during a visit to Harvard with the statistician Frederick Mosteller and a postdoctoral associate, Robert R. Bush, who was just being "retooled" from physics to the emerging specialty of mathematical psychology. In the course of some work with drug dosages, these investigators had come up with a formalism virtually identical to the learning functions of my statistical model. Verplanck told them about my work, an incident that led immediately to correspondence between us, shortly thereafter to the beginnings of our personal acquaintance, and, most important, to the substantial interactions between Bush and me over the subsequent decade. Among the tangible outcomes of those interactions was the volume we edited on mathematical learning theory (Bush & Estes, 1959).

Two of my early collaborators at Indiana were C. J. Burke and Donald W. Lauer. Burke had just come from Iowa, where he had done his doctoral dissertation with Kenneth Spence and, I guess, he found himself in some conflict, with his strong loyalty to Spence set against his lively interest in my theoretical work. While identified only with the avowedly empirical Skinnerians, I could be, and was, ignored by Spence and his students. Once Burke had brought my work on models to Spence's attention, however, I finally qualified as a competing theorist. There ensued a friendly rivalry between the Indiana and Iowa departments; it was an excellent motivator on both sides and led more substantively to a series of visits back and forth for colloquia focused on our theoretical differences. Burke was a more proficient mathematician than I, and it was a great help to be sure that, once a memorandum or draft of a manuscript had been through his ferocious scrutiny, no later reader would find any holes in the mathematical arguments. He and I together obtained one of the earliest National Science Foundation grants in behavioral science—the first in psychology, I believe—for collaborative work on the extension of statistical learning theory to problems of discrimination and probabilistic discrimination learning.

Donald Lauer had come to Indiana from Michigan with a primary interest in developing a Pavlovian laboratory. However, the technical aspects of that project took time, and while waiting for various logistics to materialize, he embarked with me on an ambitious project to determine whether the basic parameters of the statistical learning model would hold up over a prolonged period. The experiment we conducted was in danger at times of breaking up both our families, for it continued through nearly an entire year, with one or the other of us running the animals every single night, including not only Sundays but Thanksgiving, Christmas, and New Year's Eve. The results were useful enough (Estes & Lauer, 1957) but scarcely commensurate with the effort, and neither of us was ever tempted to repeat the experience.

Although Indiana became famous as a home of stimulus-response learning theory following World War II, the department was infiltrated in the 1950s by two young psychologists from Stanford, Arnold Binder and David LaBerge, who tended to view theoretical issues from the standpoint of perception rather than association. A period of close collaboration with Binder on some problems of pattern recognition and much longer, continuing interactions with LaBerge on many themes were doubtless of no small import for my receptiveness to the new cognitive psychology that blossomed following the appearance of Neisser's (1967) integrative essay.

Probability Learning

As a graduate student, I had taken an interest in the early studies by Brunswik (1939) and Humphreys (1939) of the phenomenon later termed *probability learning*. In fact, with another graduate student, Katherine Walker, I carried out a pilot study with human subjects on much the same lines as the later major work of Grant, Hake, and Hornseth (1951). It seemed intriguing that, under some circumstances, both rats and people would tend to adjust their probabilities of making selective or predictive responses to match the observed probabilities of the corresponding reinforcing events. However, no theoretical interpretation came to mind during that earlier period, and the phenomenon was certainly not in my mind when I was embarking on the early work on statistical learning models at Indiana.

It was in the course of purely mathematical explorations of the properties of the early statistical learning model that I discovered the implication that just such a phenomenon should occur under some circumstances. Naturally, I remembered immediately the earlier suggestive results and proceeded to do much more extensive studies designed to test the implications of the model rigorously. The first of these studies was conducted together with a graduate assistant, James Straughan (Estes & Straughan, 1954); subsequent studies were done increasingly independently by a stream of able and enterprising Indiana graduate students (among them Richard C. Atkinson, Michael Cole, Morton P. Friedman, Marcia Johns, Richard B. Millward, and Edith D. Neimark).

The finding that the statistical model could predict the course of probability learning with surprising accuracy under some conditions led to a number of consequences. One was increased visibility for my theoretical efforts. Another effect, I think now, was some waste of energy, in that too many experimental efforts were directed to essentially unanswerable questions about the universality of probability matching. In compensation for that distraction, however, fruitful consequences ensued from presentations of the work at conferences that brought together investigators of decision theory from a variety of disciplines. One of these conferences was sponsored by the Ford Foundation and held at the Rand Corporation in 1952 (see Thrall, Coombs, & Davis, 1954), and another was convened by the Army Epidemiological Board in 1954 (see Dunlap and Associates,

1955). Discussions of my papers at these conferences (Estes, 1954, 1955c) acquainted me with investigators approaching decision theory from the standpoints of applied mathematics, game theory, statistics, and economics and led to long-term friendships and interactions with such individuals as Clyde Coombs and Jacob Marschak. The connections between statistical learning theory and decision theory have continued to be one of my major interests (see, for example, Estes, 1962, 1975, 1981).

Reinforcement Theory

I can scarcely remember a time when I was not deeply interested in questions having to do with the nature of reinforcement and whether reinforcement in any of its senses should be regarded as a necessary and sufficient condition for learning. At the time I first became acquainted with psychology, issues revolving around these questions were uppermost in the minds and discussions of investigators of learning and behavior. Under Skinner's tutelage, I naturally was imprinted very early on the power of the reinforcement concept and can remember defending that concept, as it had developed from Thorndike to Skinner, in conversations with Fred Sheffield, an enthusiastic follower of Guthrie, at my first APA meeting.

At the same time, I felt some dissatisfaction with the current concept of reinforcement, in that it seemed to provide rules only for changes in performance, and I was unable to accept the dictum of operant conditioning theory that equated learning with changes in performance tendencies. My first observations of animal learning in the laboratory seemed to confirm at an intuitive level my feeling that reinforcing events served as importantly to convey information as to exert any strengthening or weakening effects on actions. These impressions led directly to my work on conditioned anticipation, begun while I was a student at Minnesota and continued at Indiana after the war (Estes, 1943, 1948).

Some years later, when my interests had shifted from animal to human learning during the probability learning period, the same theme led to the other extensive researches on informational aspects of reinforcement in human behavior that have continued down to the present. Among specific incidents that were important to the conceptual developments along this path was my initial acquaintance with Gordon Bower and his ideas about vicarious trial-and-error models for relating learning to performance. This occurred, I believe, during a summer seminar at Stanford in 1957. Other influences were my more or less enforced acquaintance with the growing literature on electrical stimulation of the brain during my editorship of the *Journal of Comparative and Physiological Psychology,* and a series of conferences (one at Dalhousie and one at Princeton in 1969 and one at Pittsburgh in 1970) that caused me to bring a number of these trains of thought together into reformulations of the reinforcement concept for both animal and human behavior (Estes, 1969a, b, 1971, 1972a).

All-or-None versus Incremental Learning

In most of my early work on models for learning, I had been content to follow the tactic of formulating a model, deriving implications for behavior in familiar types of learning situations, and taking the results as supportive or not with regard to the model as a whole. There is nothing wrong with this time-tested strategy, but results obtained with it generally are not as intuitively compelling as more direct tests of specific theoretical assumptions. One reason such direct tests are not commonly found is that they are rarely possible within standard experimental paradigms. Rather, they tend to require new and ingenious departures from traditional designs and analyses. A provocative paper by Rock (1957) had the effect of shaking up my thinking and making me aware of the degree to which I had been following, perhaps too complacently, a single strategy of model testing. As an immediate consequence, I began thinking about ways of devising more direct tests of the basic conception of all-or-none association, or memory storage, in my own theory. Some interesting possibilities came to mind, and, again with the aid of some Indiana graduate students (in this instance, Edward J. Crothers and Billy Lee Hopkins), I soon succeeded in translating them into experiments of simple but novel design that yielded some fairly dramatic demonstrations of apparent all-or-none effects (Estes, 1960; Estes, Hopkins, & Crothers, 1960).

The findings and interpretations of Rock and myself proved controversial, to say the least, and they might well have been of some importance if they had had no other effect than to revive some interest in human learning outside the small core of investigators in the Ebbinghaus tradition. However, there were more specific consequences. On the one hand, investigators in the empirical verbal learning tradition who wished to dispute these findings found themselves taking a much more active interest in theoretical models than had been their custom in order to contest the distasteful findings that seemed to run counter to associationist ideas (for example, Postman, 1963). On the other side, several of the investigators interested in mathematical learning theory who gathered for informal conferences nearly every summer at Stanford immediately saw possibilities of building constructively on the all-or-none concept, and they generated a cascade of new theoretical and methodological results far out of proportion to the instigating stimuli of the original studies (Bower, 1961, 1962; Bower & Theios, 1964; Bower & Trabasso, 1963; Millward, 1964; Restle, 1965; Suppes & Ginsberg, 1962; Trabasso, 1963).

Models for Short-Term Memory

An important consequence of the all-or-none versus incremental work for my continuing theoretical effort was the observation that sharp demonstrations of all-or-none learning often seem to be associated with some kind of unitization—that is, an encoding or recoding of more elementary stimulus constituents or aspects into larger units (Estes & Hopkins, 1961). That train of thought was turned in the direction of research on human short-term memory, as distinguished from learning, almost by accident.

While looking for a suitable demonstration experiment on short-term memory for use in a graduate seminar at Rockefeller University, a research associate, Elizabeth Bjork, and I were impressed with the possibilities of the then recently reported study by Conrad (1967), which provided evidence of encoding of visually presented letters or digits in memory-span experiments in terms of auditory attributes. We thought it might be a good demonstration of methodology to show the students how simply expanding the quantitative power of the experiment by tracing the time course of appearance and disappearance of specific kinds of errors of recall over a retention interval would magnify the theoretical fruitfulness of the basic paradigm.

The results succeeded beyond our expectations. One member of the seminar was an exceptionally perceptive and highly motivated student, Alice Healy (then Alice Fenvessy), who quickly carried the work far beyond the dimensions of a class exercise and developed it into a series of studies that provided the empirical basis for much of my early theoretical work on order in short-term memory (Bjork & Healy, 1974; Healy, 1974, 1975).

More or less concurrently, I had been reading and meditating on the ideas of Konorski (1967) for neurophysiologically based interpretations of memory. One consequence was the recognition that a recycling process akin to the reverberatory loops of nerve impulses in Konorski's scheme might have just the properties needed to account for many aspects of the rapidly accumulating findings on short-term memory for order. The presentation of these ideas at a conference on coding and memory organized by Arthur W. Melton and Edwin Martin generated much useful feedback and led directly to the first of my papers on coding in short-term memory (Estes, 1972b) and, in the longer term, to a major new research interest that has continued to the present. Much of this work has been done in collaboration with Catherine Lee (Lee & Estes, 1977, 1981), and all of it has profited from the continuing friendly but incisive criticism provided by Richard Shiffrin.

Visual Information Processing

Though represented directly in this volume only in the paper "On the Interaction of Perception and Memory in Reading" in Chapter 3, one of my principal research efforts of the past decade and a half has had to do with the new paradigm of human information processing, especially in application to visual perception and pattern recognition. It is a little hard to knit this theme logically into the others represented in this book, for, once again, an extensive line of work got its start by accident rather than by design. It's not that design was lacking, but rather that the design proved to have little relation to the outcome.

Not long after arriving at Stanford, I carefully reviewed the work that I had been doing, with C. J. Burke and others, on human discrimination learning, and decided that further progress required more precise experimental techniques, especially with regard to the control of stimulus exposures. To that end, I secured the cooperation of Nicholas Pappas, a local engineer who was interested in designing psychological apparatus, and developed some suitable instrumentation, built around a modified tachistoscope. Then, in order to get an idea about suitable display characteristics for human subjects, I embarked on some pilot work, together with a graduate student, Henry ("Gus") Taylor, in which we simply obtained data on the ability of human subjects to report elements (letters or other simple stimuli) of brief visual displays.

The now famous monograph by Sperling (1960) happened to come to hand at just that time, and I was struck by the accuracy with which our data from the standard full report procedure replicated Sperling's functions. I was also much interested in Sperling's partial report technique, which seemed to begin to separate the roles of perception and memory by revealing a substantial disparity between the number of letters a subject could see in a brief display and the number that could be reported. I was stimulated by these results to seek a still more effective method for partialling out the role of memory in tachistoscopic perception, the result being the forced-choice detection method that has found rather wide application for the purpose (Estes & Taylor, 1964, 1966). As always, graduate students and postdoctoral associates (in this instance, Elizabeth Bjork, Gerald Gardner, Peter Shaw, James Townsend, David Wessell, and George Wolford) played a major part in translating the method into results of theoretical significance.

Some of the results of these first researches on tachistoscopic perception proved interpretable in terms of the stimulus-sampling model taken over directly from statistical learning theory. However, the model as it stood was not up to handling all the aspects of the data and seemed to need augmentation by an assumption to the effect that the basis for an observer's report of a display was a serial scan of a fading mental representation, or icon. The augmented model proved wrong in some details, perhaps most important being the locus of the scanning, but it nonetheless marked a step forward on a major path of theoretical development.

The next turn in my research on visual processing, one that brought it for the first time into contact with linguistic concepts, occurred after my move to Rockefeller—again without premeditation. While talking about some intriguing results reported by Reicher (1969), Elizabeth Bjork and I were struck by an apparent paradox. Reicher's data showed better recognition of a letter imbedded in a word than of the same letter presented alone, even though, in the former case, its perceptibility should have been impaired by lateral masking from adjacent letters. It happened that we had just programmed an experimental routine for some projected same-different studies and could adapt it with little effort to look at some variations on Reicher's techniques that we thought might help resolve the paradox. The results were fruitful out of proportion to the initiating problem, leading to the substantial experimental and theoretical effort on letter and word perception reviewed in the last paper in Chapter 3. As has been the case in other lines of research, a notable overall trend in this now lengthy series of studies has been from instigation of early experiments by particular unforeseen empirical twists to motivation and direction of later experiments by an accumulating body of theory.

ASSOCIATIONS AND CONTINUATIONS

It will be apparent from the preceding sketch that, at all four institutions where I have taught, my research has developed in the context of relatively close-knit groups of graduate students and postdoctoral associates. It is not feasible to trace the academic histories of the individuals involved, yet this account would be incomplete if I did not mention at least some of the major lines of continuing work now being pursued by former members of these groups as independent investigators. Other than a few exceptions, which will be noted, I will include in the following brief summary by areas only people who worked with me closely as graduate students, usually including my directing their doctoral research, or as postdoctoral associates early in their careers.

Learning

Perhaps because learning theory has declined in visibility with the rise of cognitive psychology, many students who did their graduate research in learning are no longer identified with the field. However, there are, happily, some substantial efforts to bridge the gap between research on animal learning and human cognitive psychology. Douglas Medin, my first postdoctoral fellow at Rockefeller, is a leader in this effort, along with Donald Robbins, also an early member of the laboratory there (although both have also developed substantial interests in human memory for categories and prototypes). From the early Indiana period, Norman Guttman, after achieving (with Harry Kalish) what may fairly be termed a breakthrough in the analysis of stimulus generalization, has returned to earlier concerns with the philosophy of our discipline, while Edith Neimark has pursued an independent course now centered on cognitive development. From the later period, Bruce Moore is contributing to a currently influential theme having to do with biological constraints on learning.

Memory and Cognition

In what might be termed the main line of the experimental psychology of long- and short-term memory, Robert Bjork from the Stanford group has become a most diversified and influential contributor; and Michael Humphreys and Chizuko Izawa are known for substantial continuing programs. From Rockefeller, several former graduate fellows, Mark Altom, Adam Drewnowski, and Alice Healy (with whom I enjoy a steadily continuing interaction) are already making their marks on the field; also, James Anderson was associated with my laboratory there during the period when he branched out from neurophysiology to the development of models for brain processes in memory. Catherine Lee, a valued associate of my research groups at both Rockefeller and Harvard, is extending her studies of short-term memory into a variety of linguistic contexts. In the broader field now known as cognitive science, Edward Crothers and Richard Millward from the Indiana group and David Rumelhart from Stanford are notable contributors to language comprehension, computer-simulation models, and complex learning.

Human Information Processing

Many significant developments with respect to random walk models for information processing, the parallel-serial processing issue, and the application of reaction time methods are associated with Stephen Link, James Townsend, and John Yellott of the Stanford Mathematical Psychology Program. Link and Townsend worked mainly with Richard Atkinson at Stanford, but they have been frequent visitors in my laboratory from their first postdoctoral years. Yellott began working with me on probability learning but left that area after one brilliant success for longer-persisting interests in choice models and visual perception. Another Stanford student, Ruth Day, an independent spirit from the start, has made distinctive contributions to research on selective attention, particularly in relation to dichotic listening. From the Rockefeller group, David Taylor is a continuing contributor to the interpretation of stage models of reaction time and other aspects of information processing, and David Noreen to the development of an integrated framework for detectability models. In the important subspecialty of visual information processing, George Wolford from the Stanford group has contributed to many aspects of tachistoscopic perception, perhaps most notably his model for transposition effects in letter displays; from the Rockefeller group, Elizabeth Bjork has continued with work on linguistic factors in tachistoscopic perception, and Yoshio Okada continues to work on basic visual processes.

Mental Development

Although I have had a lasting interest in furthering connections between general and developmental aspects of cognitive psychology (manifest, for example, in Estes, 1970), my picture of the scope and depth of the developmental side of the discipline has been shaped to an important extent through interactions with my former student and long-time colleague Michael Cole. After completing his doctoral research with me at Indiana, on a problem bordering on both probability learning and memory scanning, Cole next tried his hand at Pavlovian conditioning, under the influence of Alexander Luria. He then concluded that no specialty in psychology was quite right for him and proceeded to create his own—a blend that might be termed comparative-developmental cognition. After Cole joined my laboratory at Rockefeller in the early 1970s, the developmental subgroup flourished exuberantly, and some of the continuations by associates of that group—as represented, for example, in the work of Rachel Falmagne on reasoning and Sylvia Scribner on cross-cultural phenomena—quite outweigh the modest beginnings. As Michael Cole's research enterprises expanded (at times on a literally global scale), he went on to form his own research group, first at Rockefeller and subsequently at the University of California at San Diego.

Applications

Although my interests have always been primarily theoretical, brushes with theory have seemed to do no harm to students whose tastes have run more to applications of psychology. Among students from the Indiana period, Max Schoeffler and Burton Wolin early saw prospects in the rising field now known as human factors research and found their careers there, shading later into administration. Of those who went into some form of programmed learning, Lloyd Homme, at least, is still contributing; Judith Frankman and Morton Friedman shifted gradually from interests in the theoretical side of experimental psychology to its relevance to learning and communicative disabilities; Arnold Buss completed doctoral research with me on some aspects of reinforcement in human learning, but his heart, we fully understood, was in clinical psychology, where he has gone on to be a notable contributor.

I was associated with Richard Atkinson and Patrick Suppes in planning and securing support for the initial efforts on computer-assisted instruction at Stanford. Natural selection quickly made itself felt, however, and they went on to substantial achievements in that area while I remained wholly a laboratory experimental psychologist. We all believed, however, that it was important for the healthy growth of learning theory to provide convincing demonstrations of its relevance to education. In this vein, I should mention also Robert Glaser, whose leadership of the Learning Research and Development Center at the University of Pittsburgh has made it a model for the application of psychological research and theories to education. Although I helped educate Bob only by way of some graduate seminars at Indiana, there is credit enough to spare in his subsequent career. I suppose applications is as apt a category as any for Juliet Schaffer, first an assistant during my year at the Center and then a postdoctoral fellow at Indiana, who has found her niche more in statistics than psychology, and for Joseph Young from the Stanford group, who is now a program officer with the National Science Foundation.

Last but not Least

In this category I would like to mention a number of people who don't fit neatly elsewhere but have been part of a scientific and intellectual camaraderie whose contribution to my work and thought has undoubtedly been as important as it is hard to document specifically. Particularly salient in this respect is one group of people, including Roger Ratcliff, Richard Shiffrin, Edward E. Smith, and John Theios, who have been such frequent visitors to my research groups at Rockefeller and Harvard for periods of months to years as to be considered honorary members, and who deserve a good deal of credit for the intellectual liveliness in both these locales. This last comment is also very apt regarding Carol Krumhansl, a faculty associate of my laboratory for two years, bracketing my move from New York to Cambridge. Finally, I would not want to leave out of this résumé several scientists with whom I have brushed academic shoulders in many different settings and spent many agreeable and instructive hours in conversation on problems of theory, methods, and teaching in psychology—Alexander Buchwald, James Greeno, and Walter Kintsch. In this category also I would include Duncan Luce, with whom I have been engaged in a great many activities designed to advance the quantitative side of our discipline.

PROFESSIONAL ACTIVITIES

This section will be brief, for I have never set great store on professional and organizational activity outside the main line of research and teaching.

One useful function of scientific organizations is communication, and there, over a long period, I seem to have evinced some aptitude (or weakness) for editing. While still a young faculty member at Indiana I was pleased to be invited by Arthur Melton to join him and David Grant as an associate editor of the *Journal of Experimental Psychology,* and I learned a good deal about the journal business from those veterans. About the time of my move to Stanford, I succumbed to the urging of Harry Harlow and accepted the editorship of the *Journal of Comparative and Physiological Psychology*. That decision was a bit untimely in that my interests were shifting faster than I realized from animal learning and behavior to human learning and memory; on the other hand, six years as editor ensured my keeping in touch with the flow of new developments within the broadening sphere of the journal and probably reinforced my long-term efforts (mostly against the tide) to help keep some communication between the biological and cognitive sides of our discipline. Editing the *Psychological Review* (from 1977) has understandably been the most interesting assignment for an individual much inclined toward theory. During the late 1970s I also was engaged on the side in editing the *Handbook of Learning and Cognitive Processes*. That project was made manageable by the steady cooperation of the publisher, Larry Erlbaum, and the fact that, among the rather large number of psychologists who agreed to take part, the number who came through with valuable contributions was appreciably larger than the number who fell by the wayside. I think the *Handbook* has proved useful, but I also believe that the project was premature. It seems fairly clear to me now how the job could be done better, although I shall not be tempted to try.

I would say that the rewards of editing are rather indirect and intangible, except for the opportunity to gain closer acquaintance with the work of a larger number of investigators in one's field than would otherwise be likely. The more important motivation, I think, has something to do with social responsibility. The broad field of psychology, or behavioral science, can be viewed as a loose and informal confederation of clusters of people with similar ideas and interests. The system operates somewhat like representative government; individuals in the various clusters who achieve unusual visibility come to serve as journal editors, members of review panels, and the like, and thus are in a position to help see that members of their "constituencies" with similar ideas and interests get adequate representation in the perennial competition for publication outlets and research support. Once the novelty of editing and reviewing has worn off, I think an investigator's motivation for continuing is primarily just wishing to see that his own fields of interest continue to prosper.

As times change, so does the need for specialized scientific societies to meet particular communication needs. More societies are started than survive for long, but a few take hold and serve some useful purpose over a substantial period. I have received some satisfaction from being involved in the initiation of two that seem to fall in the latter category—the Psychonomic Society and the Society for Mathematical Psychology.

During the late 1950s, the increasing preoccupation of the American Psychological Association with professional and clinical affairs led many experimental psychologists to wish for an alternative association, similarly national in scope but devoted wholly to the furtherance of research and scientific communication. The idea was realized in the Psychonomic Society, beginning with a first informal meeting of a governing board at the University of Wisconsin on March 31, 1960 (Wilfred Brogden, Frank Geldard, Clarence Graham, Lloyd Humphreys, Clifford Morgan, Dewey Neff, Benton Underwood, William Verplanck, and I present, and Kenneth Spence and S. Smith Stevens in absentia). The society was incorporated the following day.

The original conception was for only a small group, perhaps not much larger than the Society of Experimental Psychologists. Evidently the ground was fertile, however, for the society grew steadily to its present membership of more than 2,000 and an annual meeting that can no longer be confined within two days of parallel sessions. I served two terms on the governing board and was chairman when the society's journal operation was initiated in 1972.

What is now the Society for Mathematical Psychology originated in lunch-table conversations during a summer gathering at Stanford, including, to the best of my recollection, Dick Atkinson, Bob Bush, Duncan Luce, Pat Suppes, and myself, and started with a wholly informal two-day session in August 1968. This modestly expanding interest group continued to meet annually, with no formal structure whatever, for the next ten years, responsibility for arranging meetings being passed on from one volunteer to another. The originators were also largely responsible for initiating the *Journal of Mathematical Psychology,* of which Atkinson was the first editor. The need for continuity in guiding the scientific operation of the journal, published by Academic Press, was one of the factors that led eventually to a decision to put up with the formalities of becoming an actual society, on which occasion I served as chairman of the organizing group.

It has been pleasant watching the growth of both societies. Beyond watching, I have not missed any of the fourteen consecutive Mathematical Psychology meetings and can say the same for the longer run of the Psychonomic Society, except for one lapse in 1979. I suppose the explanation of these attendance records is to be found in the concepts of reinforcement discussed at length elsewhere in this book.

Beyond these interest groups, I enjoy, though more irregularly, the sessions of the Society of Experimental Psychologists and the Psychology Section of the National Academy of Sciences; and I appreciate the many opportunities the academy has afforded for association and collaboration with scientists from other fields in projects relating to science and government. Also, I retain an attachment to the Midwestern Psychological Association, which I joined as a student and which provided a handful of tolerant listeners for my first paper presentation.

Finally, this section seems as appropriate as any in which to mention my long-term interest in developing communication and interactions with psychologists abroad. One of the first opportunities arose in 1961, when I was invited to give a series of lectures at University College, London (one of which is reproduced in essentials in the first paper in Chapter 2 of this book). A stimulating two weeks at University College led to continuing acquaintance with Robert Audley and Arthur Summerfield, among others, and many other visits to British universities. In 1962 I took part in a symposium on information processing in the nervous system at an international physiological congress in Leiden, The Netherlands; that occasion provided an unparalleled opportunity to exchange ideas with neurophysiologists whose work was relevant to the newly flourishing information-processing movement in psychology. In more recent years I have especially enjoyed visits to laboratories at the universities of Oslo, Uppsala, and Leuven. The last-named visit rounded out an exchange of visits with Gery d'Y dewalle and continued a long-term acquaintance with Josef Nuttin, both relating to our common interests in problems of reinforcement in human behavior.

My most sustained efforts toward international interchanges, however, have had to do with Eastern Europe, whose psychologists were effectively shut off from those in our country by the Iron Curtain during my early academic years. In the 1960s opportunities arose to visit academies of science in Prague and Warsaw. In neither did I find scientific interaction with psychologists that would motivate returns, but I have maintained a continuing acquaintance with Joseph Linhart, then head of the Psychology Section of the Czechoslovakian Academy, and I especially enjoyed interactions with Jerzy Konorski, of the Nencki Institute in Warsaw, on many occasions, both abroad and in this country. Among scientists I have known with major interests in problems of learning and conditioning theory on the border between psychology and physiology, I found Konorski's combination of acute perceptiveness and wide-ranging interests unequalled, except perhaps by those of my former colleague Neal Miller.

My most extended, and at some points arduous, attempts at interaction with Eastern European psychology had to do with the USSR, beginning with the International Congress in Moscow in

1966. With the help and encouragement of Michael Cole, who had previously spent a year in the Soviet Union, I was able to gain acquaintance with a number of Soviet psychologists, some of which have continued to the present. One person in this category is Boris Lomov, now head of the Institute of Psychology in Moscow, whom I have found friendly as an individual and earnest in his efforts toward developing communication between Soviet and American psychologists, though less easy to deal with in his role as an official. Ten years after the congress, I again visited Moscow, this time with a group of American psychologists engaged in trying to plan a series of binational seminars in experimental psychology. The series did get started, and in the early stages I served as chairman of an American delegation to a seminar on mathematical psychology in Tbilisi, USSR, in 1979. The turns in U.S.-Soviet political relations since then seem to make continuations unlikely, however. I don't mean to speak for the American delegation, but I think many members share some feeling of discouragement with the prospects of developing very effective scientific interchange with Soviet investigators. One reason is that experimental psychology above the physiological level is not yet very far developed in the Soviet Union by our standards. Perhaps a more important reason, however, is the difficulty in penetrating the official facade to get access to investigators who are actually doing research, as distinguished from those simply occupying official posts. Still, I think some may share my feeling that, nonetheless, efforts should continue if a change in climate again makes them feasible.

RESEARCH SUPPORT

If there are social values in the development of new scientific disciplines, cognitive and mathematical psychology as any other, they assuredly cannot be realized without material support. With all respect to the contributions of the universities where I worked, I must say that a great part of the research represented in this book could not possibly have been accomplished without substantial support from foundations and government agencies. Rather than adding a large number of footnotes throughout the text of the book, I would like to acknowledge here the support of my work over long periods by the National Science Foundation, the Office of Naval Research, and the National Institute of Mental Health. Support that has been for shorter terms but nonetheless extremely valuable on occasion has come from the Carnegie, Ford, and Kennedy Foundations, the National Institute of General Medical Sciences, and the Social Science Research Council. I would like to mention, also, the excellent cooperation I have had from program officers of these agencies, in several cases extending over many years. I think the contributions some of these individuals make to the development of the subdisciplines relating to their programs is rarely adequately acknowledged.

A PERSONAL NOTE

This brief scientific autobiography has stayed close to its assigned subject matter, but I don't believe science and life need be so sharply partitioned as to leave out mention of the individuals most important in my life during the period covered by this volume. I was married in 1942 to Katherine Walker. During the subsequent years, Kay has been sometimes a collaborator, always a valuable critic, and a source of support for my work in ways too numerous to mention. Our children, George and Gregory, were born in 1947 and 1949, respectively, and our grandson, Rhey (to George and his wife, Ellen) in 1977. George is now a software specialist with Western Electric Incorporated and Greg a chemist in government service. Rhey is cracking the code of English phonetics and syntax with cheerful abandon. The psychological research and ideas on which this book is based would seem rather sterile if they didn't fit very well with what George, Greg, and Rhey have shown me about the growth of the mind.

NOTES

1. Although the fact is not appreciated by the people currently engaged in ruthlessly cutting behavioral science research budgets in Washington, a large number of these units were engaged in the massive effort to select and train personnel for the highly specialized and demanding tasks of manning the unprecedentedly complex equipment pouring out of newly converted American factories for the about-to-be mechanized armed forces.
2. The room is the library at 95 Irving Street in Cambridge.

REFERENCES

Atkinson, R. C., & Shiffrin, R. M. Human memory: A proposed system and its control processes. In K. W. Spence & J. T. Spence (Eds.), *The psychology of learning and motivation: Advances in research and theory*, Vol. 2, pp. 89–195. New York: Academic Press, 1968.

Bjork, E. L., & Healy, A. F. Short-term order and item retention. *Journal of Verbal Learning and Verbal Behavior*, 1974, *13*, 80–97.

Bower, G. H. Application of a model to paired-associate learning. *Psychometrika*, 1961, *25*, 255–280.

Bower, G. H. An association model for response training variables in paired-associate learning. *Psychological Review*, 1962, *69*, 34–53.

Bower, G. H., & Theios, J. A learning model for discrete performance levels. In R. C. Atkinson (Ed.), *Studies in mathematical psychology*, pp. 1–31. Stanford, Calif.: Stanford University Press, 1964.

Bower, G. H., & Trabasso, T. Reversals prior to solution in concept identification. *Journal of Experimental Psychology*, 1963, *66*, 409–418.

Brunswik, E. Probability as a determiner of rat behavior. *Journal of Experimental Psychology*, 1939, *25*, 175–197.

Bush, R. R., & Estes, W. K. *Studies in mathematical learning theory*. Stanford, Calif.: Stanford University Press, 1959.

Conrad, R. Interference or decay over short retention intervals. *Journal of Verbal Learning and Verbal Behavior*, 1967, *6*, 49–54.

Dunlap, J. W., & Associates. *Mathematical models of human behavior. Proceedings of a symposium*. Stamford, Conn: Dunlap & Associates, 1955.

Estes, W. K. Discriminative conditioning. I. A discriminative property of conditioned anticipation. *Journal of Experimental Psychology*, 1943, *32*, 150–155.

Estes, W. K. An experimental study of punishment. *Psychological Monographs*, 1944, *57* (3, Whole No. 263).

Estes, W. K. Discriminative conditioning. II. Effects of a Pavlovian conditioned stimulus upon a subsequently established operant response. *Journal of Experimental Psychology*, 1948, *38*, 173–177.

Estes, W. K. Toward a statistical theory of learning. *Psychological Review*, 1950, *57*, 94–107.

Estes, W. K. Individual behavior in uncertain situations. In R. M. Thrall, C. H. Coombs, & R. L. Davis (Eds.), *Decision processes*, pp. 127–138. New York: Wiley, 1954.

Estes, W. K. Statistical theory of spontaneous recovery and regression. *Psychological Review*, 1955, *62*, 145–154. (a)

Estes, W. K. Statistical theory of distributional phenomena in learning. *Psychological Review*, 1955, *62*, 369–377. (b)

Estes, W. K. Theory of elementary predictive behavior: An exercise in the behavioral interpretation of a mathematical model. In J. W. Dunlap & Associates (Sponsors), *Mathematical models of human behavior. Proceedings of a symposium*, pp. 63–67. Stamford, Conn.: Dunlap & Associates, 1955. (c)

Estes, W. K. Learning theory and the new "mental chemistry." *Psychological Review*, 1960, *67*, 207–223.

Estes, W. K. Theoretical treatments of differential reward in multiple-choice learning and two-person interactions. In J. H. Criswell, H. Solomon, & P.

Suppes (Eds.), *Mathematical methods in small group processes*, pp. 133–149. Stanford, Calif.: Stanford University Press, 1962.

Estes, W. K. New perspectives on some old issues in association theory. In N.S. Mackintosh & W. K. Honig (Eds.), *Fundamental issues in associative learning*, pp. 162–189. Halifax: Dalhousie University Press, 1969. (a)

Estes, W. K. Outline of a theory of punishment. In B. A. Campbell & R. M. Church (Eds.), *Punishment and aversive behavior*, pp. 57–82. New York: Appleton-Century-Crofts, 1969. (b)

Estes, W. K. *Learning theory and mental development*. New York: Academic Press, 1970.

Estes, W. K. Reward in human learning. Theoretical issues and strategic choice points. In R. Glaser (Ed.), *The nature of reinforcement*, pp. 16–36. New York: Academic Press, 1971.

Estes, W. K. Reinforcement in human behavior. *American Scientist*, 1972, *60*, 723–729. (a)

Estes, W. K. An associative basis for coding and organization in memory. In A. W. Melton and E. Martin (Eds.), *Coding processes in human memory*, pp. 161–190. Washington, D.C.: V. H. Winston, 1972. (b)

Estes, W. K. Human behavior in mathematical perspective. *American Scientist*, 1975, *63*, 649–655.

Estes, W. K. Cognitive processes in reinforcement and choice. In G. d'Y dewalle & W. Lens (Eds.), *Cognition in human motivation and learning*, pp. 123–140. Leuven: Leuven University Press; and Hillsdale, N.J.: Lawrence Erlbaum Associates, 1981.

Estes, W. K., & Hopkins, B. L. Acquisition and transfer in pattern-vs.-component discrimination learning. *Journal of Experimental Psychology*, 1961, *61*, 322–328.

Estes, W. K., Hopkins, B. L., & Crothers, E. J. All-or-none and conservation effects in the learning and retention of paired associates. *Journal of Experimental Psychology*, 1960, *60*, 329–339.

Estes, W. K., & Lauer, D. W. Conditions of invariance and modifiability in simple reversal learning. *Journal of Comparative and Physiological Psychology*, 1957, *50*, 199–206.

Estes, W. K., & Skinner, B. F. Some quantitative properties of anxiety. *Journal of Experimental Psychology*, 1941, *29*, 390–400.

Estes, W. K. & Straughan, J. H. Analysis of a verbal conditioning situation in terms of statistical learning theory. *Journal of Experimental Psychology*, 1954, *47*, 225–234.

Estes, W. K., & Taylor, H. A. A detection method and probabilistic models for assessing information processing from brief visual displays. *Proceedings of the National Academy of Sciences*, 1964, *52*, 446–454.

Estes, W. K., & Taylor, H. A. Visual detection in relation to display size and redundancy of critical elements. *Perception & Psychophysics*, 1966, *1*, 9–16.

Grant, D. A., Hake, H. W., & Hornseth, J. P. Acquisition and extinction of a verbal conditioned response with differing percentages of reinforcement. *Journal of Experimental Psychology*, 1951, *42*, 1–5.

Healy, A. F. Separating item from order information in short-term memory. *Journal of Verbal Learning and Verbal Behavior*, 1974, *13*, 644–655.

Healy, A. F. Coding of temporal-spatial patterns in short-term memory. *Journal of Verbal Learning and Verbal Behavior*, 1975, *14*, 481–495.

Humphreys, L. G. Acquisition and extinction of verbal expectations in situations analogous to conditioning. *Journal of Experimental Psychology*, 1939, *25*, 294–301.

Konorski, J. *Integrative activity of the brain.* Chicago: University of Chicago Press, 1967.

Lee, C. L., & Estes, W. K. Order and position in primary memory for letter strings. *Journal of Verbal Learning and Verbal Behavior*, 1977, *16*, 395–418.

Lee, C. L., & Estes, W. K. Item and order information in short-term memory: Evidence for multi-level perturbation processes. *Journal of Experimental Psychology: Human Learning and Memory*, 1981, *7*, 149–169.

Millward, R. B. An all-or-none model for noncorrection routines with elimination of incorrect responses. *Journal of Mathematical Psychology*, 1964, *1*, 392–404.

Neisser, U. *Cognitive psychology.* New York: Appleton-Century-Crofts, 1967.

Postman, L. One trial learning. In C. N. Cofer & B. Musgrave (Eds.), *Verbal behavior and learning*, pp. 295–320. New York: McGraw Hill, 1963.

Reicher, G. M. Perceptual recognition as a function of meaningfulness of stimulus material. *Journal of Experimental Psychology*, 1969, *81*, 275–280.

Restle, F. Significance of all-or-none learning. *Psychological Bulletin*, 1965, *64*, 313–325.

Rock, I. The role of repetition in associative learning. *American Journal of Psychology*, 1957, *70*, 186–193.

Schoeffler, M. S. Probability of response to compounds of discriminated stimuli. *Journal of Experimental Psychology*, 1954, *48*, 323–329.

Sperling, G. The information available in brief visual presentations. *Psychological Monographs*, 1960, *74* (Whole No. 489), 1–29.

Suppes, P., & Ginsberg, R. Application of a stimulus sampling model to children's concept formation with and without overt correction responses. *Journal of Experimental Psychology*, 1962, *63*, 330–336.

Thrall, R. M., Coombs, C. H., & Davis, R. L. *Decision processes.* New York: Wiley, 1954.

Thurstone, L. L. The learning function. *Journal of General Psychology*, 1930, *3*, 469–493.

Trabasso, T. R. Stimulus emphasis and all-or-none learning in concept identification. *Journal of Experimental Psychology*, 1963, *65*, 398–406.

Weinstock, S. W. Resistance to extinction of a running response following partial reinforcement under widely spaced trials. *Journal of Comparative and Physiological Psychology*, 1954, *47*, 318–322.

Publications: A Comprehensive Bibliography

1940

A visual form of the verbal summator. *Psychological Record, 4,* 174–180.

1941

With B. F. Skinner. Some quantitative properties of anxiety. *Journal of Experimental Psychology, 29,* 390–400.

1942

Spontaneous recovery from extinction in maze-bright and maze-dull rats. *Journal of Comparative Psychology, 34,* 349–351.

1943

Discriminative conditioning. I. A discriminative property of conditioned anticipation. *Journal of Experimental Psychology, 32,* 150–155.

1944

1. An experimental study of punishment. *Psychological Monographs, 57* (3, Whole No. 263).
2. With K. W. Estes. A set of miniature scales for the measurement of attitudes related to morale. *Journal of Social Psychology, 20,* 265–276.

1948

Discriminative conditioning. II. Effects of a Pavlovian conditioned stimulus upon a subsequently established operant response. *Journal of Experimental Psychology, 38,* 173–177.

1949

1. Generalization of secondary reinforcement from the primary drive. *Journal of Comparative & Physiological Psychology, 42,* 286–295.
2. A study of motivating conditions necessary for secondary reinforcement. *Journal of Experimental Psychology, 39,* 306–310.
3. With N. Guttman. A modified apparatus for the study of operant behavior in the rat. *Journal of General Psychology, 41,* 297–301.

1950

1. Effects of competing reactions on the conditioning curve for bar pressing. *Journal of Experimental Psychology, 40,* 200–205.

2. Some reflections on the concept of secondary drive—a reply to Professor Mowrer. *Journal of Comparative & Physiological Psychology, 43*, 152–153.
3. Toward a statistical theory of learning. *Psychological Review, 57*, 94–107.

1952

Review of M. H. Marx, *Psychological theory. Psychological Bulletin, 49*, 355–357.

1953

With C. J. Burke. A theory of stimulus variability in learning. *Psychological Review, 60*, 276–286.

1954

1. Individual behavior in uncertain situations: An interpretation in terms of statistical association theory. In R. M. Thrall, C. H. Coombs, & R. L. Davis (Eds.), *Decision processes*, pp. 127–137. New York: Wiley.
2. Models for learning theory. In Committee on Human Resources, Research and Development Board, Department of Defense, *Symposium on psychology of learning basic to military training problems.* Washington, D.C., HR-HTD 201/1, pp. 21–38.
3. With C. J. Burke & S. Hellyer. Rate of verbal conditioning in relation to stimulus variability. *Journal of Experimental Psychology, 48*, 153–161.
4. With S. Koch, K. MacCorquodale, P. E. Meehl, C. G. Mueller, Jr., W. N. Schoenfeld, & W. S. Verplanck. *Modern learning theory.* New York: Appleton-Century-Crofts.
5. With J. H. Straughan. Analysis of a verbal conditioning situation in terms of statistical learning theory. *Journal of Experimental Psychology, 47*, 225–234.

1955

1. Statistical theory of spontaneous recovery and regression. *Psychological Review, 62*, 145–154.
2. Statistical theory of distributional phenomena in learning. *Psychological Review, 62*, 369–377.
3. Theory of elementary predictive behavior: An exercise in the behavioral interpretation of a mathematical model. In J. W. Dunlap & Associates (Sponsors), *Mathematical models of human behavior. Proceedings of a symposium,* pp. 63–67. Stamford, Conn.: Dunlap & Associates.
4. With C. J. Burke. Application of statistical model to simple discrimination learning in human subjects. *Journal of Experimental Psychology, 50*, 81–88.
5. With D. W. Lauer. Successive acquisitions and extinctions of a jumping habit in relation to schedule of reinforcement. *Journal of Comparative & Physiological Psychology, 48*, 8–13.
6. With M. S. Schoeffler. Analysis of variables influencing alternation after forced trials. *Journal of Comparative & Physiological Psychology, 48*, 357–362.

1956

1. Learning. *Annual Review of Psychology, 7,* 1–38.
2. The problem of inference from curves based on group data. *Psychological Bulletin, 53,* 134–140.
3. Review of R. R. Bush & F. Mosteller, *Stochastic models for learning. Comtemporary Psychology, 1,* 99–101.
4. Review of E. R. Hilgard, *Theories of learning. Contemporary Psychology, 1,* 307–308.

1957

1. Of models and men. *American Psychologist, 12,* 609–617.
2. Review of K. W. Spence, *Behavior theory and conditioning. Contemporary Psychology, 2,* 153–155.
3. Theory of learning with constant, variable, or contingent probabilities of reinforcement. *Psychometrika, 22,* 113–132.
4. With C. J. Burke. A component model for stimulus variables in discrimination learning. *Psychometrika, 22,* 133–145.
5. With C. J. Burke, R. C. Atkinson, & Judith P. Frankmann. Probabilistic discrimination learning. *Journal of Experimental Psychology, 54,* 233–239.
6. With D. W. Lauer. Conditions of invariance and modifiability in simple reversal learning. *Journal of Comparative & Physiological Psychology, 50,* 199–206.

1958

1. Stimulus-response theory of drive. In M. R. Jones (Ed.), *Nebraska symposium on motivation,* pp. 35–69. Lincoln: Nebraska University Press.
2. Review of C. B. Ferster & B. F. Skinner, *Schedules of reinforcement. Science, 127,* 477.
3. Review of K. W. Spence, *Behavior theory and conditioning. Human Biology, 30,* 99–101.
4. With M. D. Johns. Probability-learning with ambiguity in the reinforcing stimulus. *American Journal of Psychology, 71,* 219–228.

1959

1. Component and pattern models with Markovian interpretations. In R. R. Bush & W. K. Estes (Eds.), *Studies in mathematical learning theory,* pp. 9–52. Stanford, Calif.: Stanford University Press.
2. The statistical approach to learning theory. In S. Koch (Ed.), *Psychology: A study of a science,* Vol. 2, pp. 380–491. New York: McGraw-Hill.
3. With R. R. Bush (Ed.). *Studies in mathematical learning theory.* Stanford, Calif.: Stanford University Press.
4. With P. Suppes. Foundations of linear models. In R. R. Bush & W. K. Estes (Eds.), *Studies in mathematical learning theory,* pp. 137–179. Stanford, Calif.: Stanford University Press.

368 WILLIAM K. ESTES

5. With P. Suppes. Foundations of statistical learning theory. II. The stimulus sampling model. Tech. Rep. No. 26, Contract NR 171-034, Stanford University, 141 pp.

1960

1. Learning. In C. W. Harris (Ed.), *Encyclopedia of Educational Research*, pp. 752-770. New York: Macmillan.
2. Learning theory and the new "mental chemistry." *Psychological Review, 67*, 207-223.
3. A random-walk model for choice behavior. In K. J. Arrow, S. Karlin, & P. Suppes (Eds.), *Mathematical methods in the social sciences, 1959*, pp. 265-276. Stanford, Calif.: Stanford University Press.
4. Review of R. D. Luce, *Individual choice behavior. Contemporary Psychology, 5*, 113-116.
5. Statistical models for recall and recognition of stimulus patterns by human observers. In M. C. Yovits & S. Cameron (Eds.), *Self organizing systems*, pp. 51-62. Oxford: Pergamon Press.
6. With B. L. Hopkins & E. J. Crothers. All-or-none and conservation effects in the learning and retention of paired associates. *Journal of Experimental Psychology, 60*, 329-339.

1961

1. Apprendimento (Learning). In *Encyclopedia medica Italiana*, Vol. 1, pp. 312-317.
2. Growth and function of mathematical models for learning. In *Current trends in psychological theory*, pp. 134-151. Pittsburgh: University of Pittsburgh Press.
3. New developments in statistical behavior theory: Differential tests of axioms for associative learning. *Psychometrika, 26*, 73-84.
4. Review of P. Suppes and R. C. Atkinson, *Markov learning models for multiperson interactions. Naval Research Logistics Quarterly, 8*, 314-315.
5. Roland Clark Davis: 1902-1961. *American Journal of Psychology, 74*, 633-636.
6. With B. L. Hopkins. Acquisition and transfer in pattern-vs.-component discrimination learning. *Journal of Experimental Psychology, 61*, 322-328.

1962

1. A descriptive approach to the dynamics of choice behavior. In E. Nagel, P. Suppes, & A. Tarski (Eds.), *Logic, methodology, and philosophy of science: Proceedings of the 1960 International Congress*, pp. 424-433. Stanford, Calif.: Stanford University Press. (Also in *Behavioral Science*, 1961, *6*, 177-184.)
2. Learning theory. *Annual Review of Psychology, 13*, 107-144.
3. Theoretical treatments of differential reward in multiple-choice learning and two-person interactions. In J. H. Criswell, H. Solomon, & P. Suppes (Eds.),

Mathematical methods in small group processes, pp. 133–149. Stanford, Calif.: Stanford University Press.

1963

1. Editorial. *Journal of Comparative Physiological Psychology, 56,* 1.
2. With R. C. Atkinson. Stimulus sampling theory. In R. D. Luce, R. R. Bush, & E. Galanter (Eds.), *Handbook of mathematical psychology,* Vol. II, pp. 121–268. New York: Wiley.

1964

1. All-or-none processes in learning and retention. *American Psychologist, 19,* 16–25.
2. Editorial note. *Journal of Comparative Physiological Psychology, 57,* 1–2.
3. Information storage in behavior. In *Proceedings of the International Union of Physiological Science, Vol. III: Information processing in the nervous system,* pp. 280–287. Amsterdam: Excerpta Medica Foundation.
4. Probability learning. In A. W. Melton (Ed.), *Categories of human learning,* pp. 89–128. New York: Academic Press.
5. With M. P. Friedman, C. J. Burke, M. Cole, L. Keller, & R. B. Millward. Two-choice behavior under extended training with shifting probabilities of reinforcement. In R. C. Atkinson (Ed.), *Studies in mathematical psychology,* pp. 250–316. Stanford, Calif.: Stanford University Press.
6. With H. A. Taylor. A detection method and probabilistic models for assessing information processing from brief visual displays. *Proceedings of the National Academy of Sciences, 52,* 446–454.

1965

1. Information and behavioral approaches to foundations of scientific statements. In K. Adjukiewiez (Ed.), *The Foundations of Statements and Decisions,* pp. 343–350. Warsaw: PWN-Polish Scientific Publishers.
2. Review of S. Koch (Ed.), *Psychology: A study of a science II.* Vol. 5. *Contemporary Psychology, 5,* 196–199.
3. A technique for assessing variability of perceptual span. *Proceedings of the National Academy of Sciences, 54,* 403–407.
4. Transfer of verbal discriminations based on differential reward magnitudes. Tech. Rep. Contract No. Nonr. 225(73), Stanford University, Stanford, California. 15 pp.
5. With C. Izawa. Reinforcement-test sequences in paired-associate learning. Tech. Rep. No. 76, Contract No. Nonr. 225(73), Stanford University, Stanford, California.
6. With L. Keller, M. Cole, & C. J. Burke. Reward and information values of trial outcomes in paired-associate learning. *Psychological Monographs, 79* (12, Whole No. 605).

1966

1. Transfer of verbal discriminations based on differential reward magnitudes. *Journal of Experimental Psychology, 72,* 276–283.
2. With A. Binder. Transfer of response in visual recognition situations as a function of frequency variables. *Psychological Monographs, 80* (23, Whole No. 631).
3. With H. A. Taylor. Visual detection in relation to display size and redundancy of critical elements. *Perception & Psychophysics, 1,* 9–16.
4. With D. L. Wessel. Reaction time in relation to display size and correctness of response in forced choice visual signal detection. *Perception & Psychophysics, 1,* 369–373.

1967

1. With F. DaPolito. Independent variation of information storage and retrieval processes in paired-associate learning. *Journal of Experimental Psychology, 75,* 18–26.
2. With E. D. Neimark (Ed.). *Stimulus sampling theory.* San Francisco: Holden-Day.

1968

1. Review of K. W. Spence & J. T. Spence (Eds.), *The Psychology of learning and motivation: Advances in research and theory. Contemporary Psychology, 13,* 454–455.
2. With D. P. Horst. Latency as a function of number of response alternatives in paired-associate learning. Tech. Rep. No. 135, Institute for Mathematical Studies in the Social Sciences, Stanford University. 31 pp.
3. With M. S. Humphreys & G. A. Allen. Learning of two-choice, differential reward problems with informational constraints on payoff combinations. *Journal of Mathematical Psychology, 5,* 260–280.
4. With N. A. Stillings & G. A. Allen. Reaction time as a function of noncontingent reward magnitude. *Psychonomic Science, 10,* 337–338.
5. With G. L. Wolford & D. L. Wessel. Further evidence concerning scanning and sampling assumptions of visual detection models. *Perception & Psychophysics, 3,* 439–444.

1969

1. New perspectives on some old issues in association theory. In N. S. Mackintosh & W. K. Honig (Eds.), *Fundamental issues in associative learning,* pp. 162–189. Halifax: Dalhousie University Press.
2. Outline of a theory of punishment. In B. A. Campbell and R. M. Church (Eds.), *Punishment and aversive behavior,* pp. 57–82. New York: Appleton-Century-Crofts.
3. Reinforcement in human learning. In J. T. Tapp (Ed.), *Reinforcement and behavior,* pp. 63–94. New York: Academic Press.
4. Review of J. G. Greeno, *Elementary theoretical psychology. Contemporary Psychology, 14,* 590–593.

5. Transfer, Generalisation und Übung. In O. W. Haseloff (Ed.), *Lernen und Erziehung*, pp. 43–53. Berlin: Colloquium Verlag.
6. With G. A. Allen & W. A. Mahler. Effects of recall tests on long-term retention of paired-associates. *Journal of Verbal Learning and Verbal Behavior, 8,* 463–470.

1970

1. *Learning theory and mental development.* New York: Academic Press.
2. Lernen und Verhalten. In O. W. Haseloff (Ed.), *Struktur und Dynamik des menschlichen Verhaltens*, pp. 98–112. Stuttgart: Verlag W. Kohlhammer.
3. On the source of acoustic confusion in short-term memory for letter strings. In *Communications in mathematical psychology*, Mathematical Psychology Laboratory, Rockefeller University.
4. Theoretical trends and points of controversy. In J. Linhart (Ed.), *Proceedings of the International Conference on Psychology of Human Learning*, Vol. II, pp. 167–183. Prague: Czechoslovak Academy of Sciences.

1971

1. Learning and memory. In E. F. Beckenbach and C. B. Tompkins (Eds.), *Concepts of communication*, pp. 282–300. New York: Wiley.
2. Matemáticas y ciencias de la conducta. *Universitas enciclopedia temática*, XIV, fas. 201, 113–119.
3. On the role of signal-noise confusability in the determination of visual processing time. In *Communications in mathematical psychology*, Mathematical Psychology Laboratory, Rockefeller University.
4. Reward in human learning. Theoretical issues and strategic choice points. In R. Glaser (Ed.), *The nature of reinforcement*, pp. 16–36. New York: Academic Press.
5. With E. L. Bjork. Detection and placement of redundant signal elements in tachistoscopic displays of letters. *Perception & Psychophysics, 9,* 439–442.
6. With G. L. Wolford. Effects of spaces on report from tachistoscopically presented letter strings. *Psychonomic Science, 25,* 77–80.

1972

1. An associative basis for coding and organization in memory. In A. W. Melton & E. Martin (Eds.), *Coding processes in human memory*, pp. 161–190. Washington, D.C.: V. H. Winston.
2. Elements and patterns in diagnostic discrimination learning. *Annals of the New York Academy of Sciences, 34,* 84–95.
3. Interactions of signal and background variables in visual processing. *Perception & Psychophysics, 12,* 278–286.
4. Learning. In P. C. Dodwell (Ed.), *New horizons in psychology*, Vol. II, pp. 15–35. London: Penguin Books.
5. Reinforcement in human behavior. *American Scientist, 60,* 723–729.

6. Research and theory on the learning of probabilities. *Journal of the American Statistical Association, 67*, 81–102.
7. With G. A. Allen. Acquisition of correct choices and value judgments in binary choice learning with differential rewards. *Psychonomic Science, 27*, 68–72.

1973

1. Memory and conditioning. In F. J. McGuigan & D. B. Lumsden (Eds.), *Contemporary approaches to conditioning and learning*, pp. 265–286. Washington, D. C.: V. H. Winston.
2. Phonemic coding and rehearsal in short-term memory for letter strings. *Journal of Verbal Learning and Verbal Behavior, 12*, 360–372.
3. With E. L. Bjork. Letter identification in relation to linguistic context and masking conditions. *Memory & Cognition, 1*, 217–223.

1974

1. Learning theory and intelligence. *American Psychologist, 29*, 740–749.
2. Memory—east and west. A review of A. A. Smirnov, *Problems of the psychology of memory. Contemporary Psychology, 19*, 179–182.
3. Redundancy of noise elements and signals in visual detection of letters. *Perception & Psychophysics, 16*, 53–60.
4. With E. L. Bjork & E. Skaar. Detection of single letters and letters in words with changing vs. unchanging mask characters. *Bulletin of the Psychonomic Society, 3*, 201–203.
5. With P. Suppes. Foundations of stimulus sampling theory. In D. H. Krantz, R. C. Atkinson, R. D. Luce, & P. Suppes (Eds.), *Contemporary developments in mathematical psychology*, Vol. 1, pp. 163–183. San Francisco: W. H. Freeman.

1975

1. *Handbook of learning and cognitive processes* (Ed.), Vol. 1, 1975; Vols. 2–4, 1976; Vols. 5–6, 1978. Hillsdale, N.J.: Lawrence Erlbaum Associates.
2. Human behavior in mathematical perspective. *American Scientist, 63*, 649–655.
3. The locus of inferential and perceptual processes in letter identification. *Journal of Experimental Psychology: General, 104*, 122–145.
4. Memory, perception, and decision in letter identification. In R. L. Solso (Ed.), *Information processing and cognition: The Loyola Symposium*, pp. 3–30. Hillsdale, N.J.: Lawrence Erlbaum Associates.
5. Some targets for mathematical psychology. *Journal of Mathematical Psychology, 12*, 263–282.
6. The state of the field: General problems and issues of theory and meta-theory. In W. K. Estes (Ed.), *Handbook of learning and cognitive processes*, Vol. 1, pp. 1–24. Hillsdale, N.J.: Lawrence Erlbaum Associates.

1976

1. The cognitive side of probability learning. *Psychological Review, 83,* 37–64.
2. Intelligence and cognitive psychology. In L Resnick (Ed.), *The nature of intelligence,* pp. 295–305. Hillsdale, N.J.: Lawrence Erlbaum Associates.
3. Some functions of memory in probability learning and choice behavior. In G. H. Bower (Ed.), *Psychology of learning and motivation: Advances in research and theory,* Vol. 10, pp. 1–45. New York: Academic Press.
4. Structural aspects of associative models for memory. In C. N. Cofer (Ed.), *The structure of human memory,* pp. 31–53. San Francisco: W. H. Freeman.
5. With D. H. Allmeyer & S. M. Reder. Serial position functions for letter identification at brief and extended exposure durations. *Perception & Psychophysics, 19,* 1–15.

1977

1. On the interaction of perception and memory in reading. In D. LaBerge & S. J. Samuels (Eds.), *Basic processes in reading: Perception and comprehension,* pp. 1–25. Hillsdale, N.J.: Lawrence Erlbaum Associates.
2. The structure of human memory. In *Encyclopedia Britannica, Yearbook of Science and the Future* (1st printing, 1976). Chicago: Encyclopedia Britannica.
3. With C. L. Lee. Order and position in primary memory for letter strings. *Journal of Verbal Learning and Verbal Behavior, 16,* 395–418.

1978

1. The information-processing approach to cognition: A confluence of metaphors and methods. In W. K. Estes (Ed.), *Handbook of learning and cognitive processes,* Vol. 5, pp. 1–18. Hillsdale, N.J.: Lawrence Erlbaum Associates.
2. On the organization and core concepts of learning theory and cognitive psychology. In W. K. Estes (Ed.), *Handbook of learning and cognitive processes,* Vol. 6, pp. 235–292. Hillsdale, N.J.: Lawrence Erlbaum Associates.
3. Perceptual processing in letter recognition and reading. In E. C. Carterette & M. P. Friedman (Eds.), *Handbook of perception,* Vol. 9, pp. 163–220. New York: Academic Press.

1979

1. Cognitive processes in conditioning. In A. Dickinson & R. A. Boakes (Eds.), *Mechanisms of learning and motivation,* pp. 417–441. Hillsdale, N.J.: Lawrence Erlbaum Associates.
2. Experimental psychology: An overview. In E. Hearst (Ed.), *The first century of experimental psychology,* pp. 623–667. Hillsdale, N.J.: Lawrence Erlbaum Associates.
3. On the descriptive and explanatory functions of theories of memory. In L. -G. Nilsson (Ed.), *Perspectives on memory research,* pp. 35–60. Hillsdale, N.J.: Lawrence Erlbaum Associates.

4. Role of response availability in the effects of cued-recall tests on memory. *Journal of Experimental Psychology: Human Learning and Memory, 5,* 567–573.

5. With J. W. Whitlow. Judgments of relative frequency in relation to shifts of event frequencies: Evidence for a limited-capacity model. *Journal of Experimental Psychology: Human Learning and Memory, 5,* 395–408.

1980

1. Comments on directions and limitations of current efforts toward theories of decision making. In T. W. Wallsten (Ed.), *Cognitive processes in choice and decision behavior,* pp. 263–274. Hillsdale, N.J.: Lawrence Erlbaum Associates.

2. Is human memory obsolete? *American Scientist, 68,* 62–69.

1981

1. The Bible is out. (Retrospective review of R. S. Woodworth, *Experimental psychology.* New York: Holt, 1938). *Contemporary Psychology, 26,* 327–330.

2. Cognitive processes in reinforcement and choice. In G. d'Y dewalle & W. Lens (Eds.), *Cognition in human motivation and learning,* pp. 123–140. Leuven: Leuven University Press; and Hillsdale, N.J.: Lawrence Erlbaum Associates.

3. Intelligence and learning. In M. P. Friedman, J. P. Das, & N. O'Connor (Eds.), *Intelligence and learning,* pp. 3–23. New York: Plenum.

4. With C. L. Lee. Item and order information in short-term memory: Evidence for multi-level perturbation processes. *Journal of Experimental Psychology: Human Learning and Memory, 7,* 149–169.

In Press

1. Learning, memory, and intelligence. In R. J. Sternberg (Ed.), *Handbook of human intelligence.* New York: Cambridge University Press.

2. Multiple coding and processing stages: A review. (Presented at the XXII International Congress of Psychology, Leipzig, July 1980). In F. Klix, J. Hoffman, & E. van der Mer (Eds.), *Cognitve research in psychology.* Amsterdam: North-Holland.

3. Similarity-related channel interactions in visual processing. *Journal of Experimental Psychology: Human Perception and Performance, 8,* 353–381.

Name Index

Subject Index

Acoustic confusion errors, 147–150, 152, 159–160, 181–183; retention interval and, 147–149; transposition errors and, 148–150, 151; vowel phoneme and, 150

Acoustic feature(s), 149–150, 164–165, 183–185 (*see also* Critical feature)

Aircraft controllers, simulations of job of, 47–52, 318

All-or-none forgetting, 156, 185–186

All-or-none learning, 9–10, 29, 80–81, 92, 137, 249; boundary conditions and, 9–10; of "chunks," 156; of coding patterns, 95; of contextual cues, 95; direct test of, 349–350; incremental learning vs., 9–10, 349–350; individual vs. grouped data and, 9; of memory elements, 137; memory encoding and, 349–350; pattern model and, 95; perceptual development and, 10; statistical learning theory and, 10; unitization and, 349–350

Alternatives, 297; choice among, 57; irrelevant, 281–282; number of, 65, 80, 90–91, 303; order of scanning, 98–100

Analog structure, 327

Animal behavior: human research and, 61, 154, 257–258, 314; mental processes reflected in, 14

Anticipation, 18, 323, 348

A priori rational models (*see* Deductive models in psychology)

Association(s): automatic nature of, 197; availability of, 18, 108–111, 118; backward, 200; chain of, 200, 202–203; concept of, 6–7; directional, 200, 211–212; elements of, 25–26, 197; of ideas, 197; interitem, 112, 156–157; laws of, 23, 197; in measurement of intelligence, 108–109; network of, 8, 205; remote, 200; strength of, 8; stimulus-response, 4, 7, 80, 95–196

Association theory, 1, 14, 22, 109, 128, 129, 197–212; classical, 118, 129, 144, 156, 160, 161, 197–199, 202–203, 214; coding theory (models) and, 160–163, 205–212; interitem connections in, 127, 160; linguistic concepts in, 199; logical exclusive OR in, 198; logical form of, 198–199; memory and, 127, 213; monistic, 10; propositional representation and, 127; psycholinguistic, 203–205; re-

vised, 199–203; structure of memory in, 128, 197

Associative coding models, 92–93, 96–97, 203, 204, 205–212, 214–215 (*see also* Memory trace); control elements in, 160–163, 206–208, 210, 331–332; formalization of assumptions of, 210–211; hierarchical tree structure in, 207–208; motivation and, 162; pattern model and, 96; reading in, 207–208; recursiveness in, 207; relations in, 205–208

Associative memory, 94, 103

Associative networks, 203–205, 206; control elements in, 331–332; recall in, 205; recognition in, 205

Attention: to context, 94; to outcome, 98; selective, 354

Attentional processes, central, 10

Attributes (*see* Features)

Avoidance learning, 15

Axioms, 6

Axiomatic models, 249

Background cues, 8, 94–95, 96, 206; samples of, 97

Backward associations, 200, 211

Bayesian model, 81, 248

Behavior, 4–5, 17–18 (*see also* Human behavior); consequences of, 63; effect of hormones on, 321; learning and, 2–3; variability in, 13–14

Behavioral approach (to reinforcement), cognitive approach vs., 64

Behaviorism, 3, 7, 64; radical, 343

Behavior modification, 45, 60, 63, 343 (*see also* Conditioning, Operant conditioning)

Behavior theory, 17; issues in, 2

Belief, 312 (*see also* Probability learning); effect on behavior of, 273; modification of, 278–279, 282–283

Belongingness, 157

Beta model, 93

Blank trials, 95

Brain, 8, 116, 160–161; electrical stimulation of, 16, 55, 322–323, 348–349; mechanisms, 16; processes underlying learning, 16

British associationism, 197